LABOUR AT THE LAKEHEAD

Michel S. Beaulieu

LABOUR AT THE LAKEHEAD

Ethnicity, Socialism, and Politics, 1900-35

UBCPress · Vancouver · Toronto

21 20 19 18 17 16 15 14 13 12 11   5 4 3 2 1

Printed in Canada on FSC-certified ancient-forest-free paper (100% post-consumer recycled) that is processed chlorine- and acid-free.

Library and Archives Canada Cataloguing in Publication

Beaulieu, Michel S.
Labour at the Lakehead : ethnicity, socialism, and politics, 1900-35 / Michel S. Beaulieu

Includes bibliographical references and index.
ISBN 978-0-7748-2001-1 (bound); ISBN 978-0-7748-2002-8 (pbk.)

1. Labor movement – Ontario – Thunder Bay – History – 20th century. 2. Labor unions – Ontario – Thunder Bay – History – 20th century. 3. Thunder Bay (Ont.) – Ethnic relations. 4. Thunder Bay (Ont.) – Politics and government – 20th century. 5. Thunder Bay (Ont.) – Social conditions – 20th century. I. Title.

HD6529.T49B42 2011   331.8'097131209041   C2011-900898-X

e-book ISBNs: 978-0-7748-2003-5 (PDF); 978-0-7748-2004-2 (epub)

Canada

UBC Press gratefully acknowledges the financial support for our publishing program of the Government of Canada (through the Canada Book Fund), the Canada Council for the Arts, and the British Columbia Arts Council.

This book has been published with the help of a grant from the Canadian Federation for the Humanities and Social Sciences, through the Aid to Scholarly Publications Program, using funds provided by the Social Sciences and Humanities Research Council of Canada.

This book has been published with the help of the Lakehead University Senate Research Committee SSHRC Publication Assistance Grant.

UBC Press
The University of British Columbia
2029 West Mall
Vancouver, BC V6T 1Z2
www.ubcpress.ca

Contents

Illustrations / vii

Acknowledgments / ix

Abbreviations / xi

Introduction / 1

PART 1: THE ROOTS OF REVOLUTION?

1 Early Socialist Organizations at the Lakehead, 1900-14 / 15

2 Repression, Revitalization, and Revolutions, 1914-18 / 42

PART 2: FROM WINNIPEG TO THE WORKERS' UNITY LEAGUE

3 "The Hog Only Harms Himself if He Topples His Trough": The One Big Union, 1919-22 / 65

4 "Into the Masses!": The Communist Party of Canada at the Lakehead, 1922-25 / 90

5 Bolshevization and the Reorganization of the Lakehead Left, 1925-27 / 110

6 Turning to the Left, 1928-30 / 129

PART 3: THE GREAT DEPRESSION AND THE THIRD PERIOD

7 "Class against Class": Socialist Activities, 1930-32 / 153

8 Wobbly Relations: The Communist Party of Canada, the Industrial Workers of the World, and the Lakehead, 1932-35 / 179

Epilogue: 1935 / 202

Notes / 210

Bibliography / 271

Index / 285

Illustrations

1 Map of Lakehead district / 4

2 Labour Day gathering of Finnish people, 1907 / 21

3 1912 or 1914 Parade on Bay Street Port Arthur / 30

4 May Day Parade 1911 or 1912 / 32

5 Parade of people with sign "Women should vote," Port Arthur 1911 or 1912 / 35

6 CTKL Poster, "The Pyramid of Capitalist System" / 66

7 IWW Propoganda Meeting notice, 1927 / 122

8 Socialist Youth Conference, Young Workers League 1927 / 130

9 IWW pamphlet advertisement, ca. 1930 / 155

10 IWW Harvest Card for Agricultural Workers Industrial Union #710 / 192

Acknowledgments

The inspiration for this study came from pancakes – specifically, those pancakes served at the Hoito Restaurant located beneath the Finnish Labour Temple at 314 Bay Street in the present-day city of Thunder Bay (formerly Port Arthur). Opened in 1918 to serve hot meals at a fair price to workers, the Hoito has seen its fair share of debates and discussions and has served as the location of some of the key moments in the history of Canadian socialism. It was there in the fall of 1996, as I began my undergraduate degree, where I first heard of the Lakehead's early contribution to Canadian socialism. I would like to say that my experience in the mid-90s was a pivotal moment, or that it was at this time I felt some calling towards the present study. That is not the case.

My greatest intellectual and professional debts are to the teachers, scholars, and colleagues who have supported this project and me since its inception. My development as a historian of Canadian socialism would not have been possible without Ian McKay. A generation of historians owes a debt to his guidance, openness, encouragement, and insight. I am happy to have been one of them. Just as McKay's steady hand helped me to better articulate the experience of the left at the Lakehead as a doctoral project, Ronald Harpelle and the late Ernst Zimmermann exposed me, as an undergraduate student, graduate student, and later as a friend, to the accomplishments of rigorous historical thinking. Any work such as the one you are about to read also stands on the shoulders of all those historians who have come before. I am indebted to the Promethean efforts of Elinor Barr, Beth Boegh, Ernie Epp, Varpu Lindström, Jean Morrison, Peter Raffo, Kelly Saxberg, Thorold Tronrud, and Donald Wilson (to name but a few). They, and many others in Northwestern Ontario, have fought against the odds to have our history told. I would also like to thank my doctoral examination committee, Peter Campbell, Jane Errington, and Abigail Bakan, and my external reviewer, David Frank, for their suggestions, support, and advice.

The research phase of this project benefited from financial support from several institutions and agencies. A number of Ontario Graduate Scholarships, Queen's University scholarships, and a Social Sciences and Humanities Research Council of Canada Doctoral Fellowship supported me throughout the doctoral stage of this project. My research was also assisted by a host of archivists, librarians, and community historians throughout the country. I would like to especially thank the staff at the Queen's University Archives, Library and Archives Canada, the Northern Studies Resource Centre and University Archives at Lakehead University, the City of Thunder Bay Archives, and the staff at the Thunder Bay Historical Museum Society. In particular, the assistance and advice of Trudy Mauracher, Louise Wuorinen, Jeremy Mohr, and Thorold Tronrud were indispensable. I would also like to thank Heather McPherson, Tina Munroe, Laura Nigro, Samira Saramo, and Nicholas Sottilie for their work as research assistants.

I am deeply grateful to the two anonymous reviewers who provided comments, Jean Wilson who first believed in this book, and my editor Melissa Pitts whose dedication and encouragement has gone above and beyond. I would also like to thank Megan Brand and the UBC Press production team for their skills, dedication, and professionalism. A special thanks is owed to Jamie Paxton and David Ratz, who have been, and remain, a constant source of encouragement – their opinions and advice have made this a better work and have made me a better historian. I am proud to have them as friends and colleagues. Last but not least, Alyson Kailik has stuck with me all these years and loves me for reasons I cannot fathom but that I humbly and truly appreciate.

Finally, as I write these acknowledgments in the coffee shop that was once the Communist Hall at 316 Bay Street, I am still humbled and amazed by all those people who were young, gifted, and red, and who sought not just to not be viewed as "non-English-speaking crap" but had the vision to make better lives for us all. This is to their memory. Onwards and upwards!

Abbreviations

ACCL	All-Canadian Congress of Labour
AFL	American Federation of Labor
AIU	Agricultural Industrial Unit (Industrial Workers of the World)
AMW of NS	Amalgamated Mine Workers of Nova Scotia
CA	Canadian Administration (Industrial Workers of the World)
CBU	Canadian Bushmen's Union
CCF	Co-operative Commonwealth Federation
CDO	Canadian Defence Organization
CEB	Canadian Executive Branch (Industrial Workers of the World)
CEC	Central Executive Committee (Communist Party of Canada)
CIO	Congress of Industrial Organizations
CLC	Central Labour Council (One Big Union)
CLDL	Canadian Labour Defence League
CLP	Canadian Labour Party
CLU	Central Labour Union
CNR	Canadian Northern Railway
COD	Central Organization Department (Communist)
CPC	Communist Party of Canada
CPR	Canadian Pacific Railway
CRUA	Citizens' and Ratepayers' Unemployed Association
CSF	Canadian Socialist Federation
CSL	Canadian Socialist League
CTKL	*Canadan Teollisuusunionistinen Kannatus Liitto*
CUA	Citizens' Unemployed Association
FOC	Finnish Organization of Canada
FSOC	Finnish Socialist Organization of Canada
FUL	Farmers' Unity League
FWFF	Finnish Workers' and Farmers' Federation
GEB	General Executive Board (Industrial Workers of the World)

GRU	General Recruiting Union (Industrial Workers of the World)
ILP	Independent Labour Party
IWW	Industrial Workers of the World
LAWIU	Lumber and Agricultural Workers Industrial Union of Canada
Lib-Lab	Liberal-Labour
LWIU	Lumber Workers Industrial Union (IWW, 1913-19; OBU, 1919-24)
LWIUC	Lumber Workers Industrial Union of Canada (Communist)
NUWA	National Unemployed Workers' Association
OBU	One Big Union (Canada)
OPP	Ontario Provincial Police
OSL	Ontario Socialist League
OSP	Ontario Socialist Party
PAUA	Port Arthur Unemployment Association
RCMP	Royal Canadian Mounted Police
RCWU	Relief Camp Workers' Union (Communist)
RILU	Red International of Labour Unions
RNWMP	Royal North-West Mounted Police
SDPC	Social Democratic Party of Canada
SPC	Socialist Party of Canada
TLC	Trades and Labour Congress of Canada
TUEL	Trade Union Educational League
UATC	Unemployed Association of the Twin Cities
UBRE	United Brotherhood of Railway Employees
ULFTA	Ukrainian Labour-Farmer Temple Association
UAPA	Unemployed Association of Port Arthur
UWPA	Unemployed Workers' Protective Association
UYR	*Uusi Yrtys Raittiusseura*
WBA	Workers' Benevolent Association
WLL	Women's Labour League
WPC	Workers' Party of Canada
WUL	Workers' Unity League
YCL	Young Communist League

LABOUR AT THE LAKEHEAD

Introduction

In Petrozavodsk, Russia, there stands a thirty-foot-tall statue of Vladimir Il'ich Lenin built by Canadians. Towering over the central square, with an eternal flame burning in remembrance of the victims of the Second World War, it is a constant reminder to the people of this vibrant Russian city of their past.[1] In the early 1930s, it stood as a tribute to the ideals and spirit of the October Revolution and the socialist utopia that the Finnish Canadians who built it had come to establish in what was then Soviet Karelia. Disillusioned by their lives in Canada and tired of endless persecution by Canadian authorities, thousands of Finnish Canadians left that country in the late 1920s and early 1930s to take part in Russia's great experiment. To them, as to many other socialists in Canada, it seemed that capitalism had finally gone bankrupt.

As intriguing as the story of Karelia is, what follows is not an examination of the Stalinist purges of the 1930s and what other historians have described as a dark period in both Russian and Canadian socialist history.[2] Instead, what will unfold in this volume is the story of those socialists who remained in Canada. Many who contributed to the construction of Lenin's statue were from Port Arthur and Fort William, Ontario (present-day City of Thunder Bay), collectively known as the Lakehead.[3] The construction of the tribute to Lenin was possible because of the skills honed in the coal docks, railway yards, mines, and lumber camps of Northern Ontario. The same conviction and belief that went into the tribute to Lenin and the zealous attack on capitalism it represented had been used for over thirty years at the Lakehead to construct the many labour halls and temples that dotted the two cities and to agitate for the recognition of workers and their voice within society.

Although the statue of Lenin built by Canadians may surprise people today, in the 1920s and 1930s its existence would have confirmed what local and national authorities believed about socialists at the Lakehead. As Port Arthur Member of Parliament F.H. Keefer argued in 1919, certain areas of the country such as the Lakehead should be dealt with severely, as they were "breeding places of revolution."[4] The nature of the economic activity in the region – based on resource extraction – lent itself to widespread participation by the Lakehead labouring class in such movements as the Industrial Workers of the World, the One Big Union, and the Communist Party. In fact and legend, Lakehead workers were in the midst of a revolt from 1900 to 1935, one that has placed them at the very centre of Canadian working-class and left history.

Located at the geographic centre of Canada, bridging the eastern and western halves of the country, Northwestern Ontario is a region that has no official political definition. Indeed, it is a region whose boundaries have been shifted constantly over time. Yet although there is no official definition, it is very much a distinct region in the minds of most people who live there. Often, it is a key part of the identity of its inhabitants. For much of its past, it has been composed of the three districts of Thunder Bay, Rainy River, and Kenora. As such, it is the largest region of Ontario, covering 526,000 square kilometres. Its western boundary is Manitoba, while its northern boundary is Ontario's Hudson's Bay coastline and the James Bay coastline north of the mouth of the Albany River. Its southern boundary is composed of the American border and the north shore of Lake Superior west of the Pukuskwa River. The eastern border runs just east of the communities of Manitouwadge and Caramat. In area, it is a region that is bigger than most countries in the world.[5]

One might ask, why the Lakehead, and why look to the Lakehead for a study of socialism in Canada? There is certainly no shortage of scholarship examining the history of the left in Canada.[6] Few studies, however, have explored the relationship between ethnic groups, socialism, and the politics of labour in early twentieth-century Canada. Fewer still have focused their attention on the provincial norths.[7] This study reveals how the relationship between individuals and organizations in the region with their comrades and opponents elsewhere shaped the nature and characteristics of socialism both regionally and nationally. The twentieth-century Lakehead never lacked for a population of enthusiastic, energetic, and talented left-wingers, but throughout this period the movement never truly solidified and took hold. Socialist organizations, organizers, and organs came and went, leaving behind an enduring legacy, yet, paradoxically, the sum of their efforts came to less than the immense sacrifices and energies they had poured into them. During the first thirty-five years of the twentieth century, the region's working-class politics was shaped by the interaction of ideas drawn from the much larger North Atlantic socialist world with the particularities of Lakehead society and culture. International frameworks of analysis and activism were of necessity reshaped and revised in a local context in which ethnic divisions complicated and even undermined the class identities on which so many radical dreams and ambitions rested.

The Lakehead's economic opportunities (both real and anticipated) drew workers to the region during the first decades of the twentieth century. Located on the north shore of Lake Superior, it was believed by many to have the potential, like many regions of Canada at the turn of the twentieth century, for unlimited economic success. As the Port Arthur *Daily News* suggested in 1906: "The assets of Canada are stupendous, the country reeks with underdeveloped riches, agricultural soil, minerals, water power, navigable lakes and rivers, a healthy invigorating climate, in fact, everything that makes a country great, waiting only for capital and energy of a man to develop it."[8] From the heyday of Fort William as the inland headquarters of the North West Company to the brink of the Great Depression in 1929, the Lakehead was seen as a region of untapped and limitless resources, capable of fuelling continuous progress and development.[9] Jointly, the twin cities of Port Arthur and Fort William (both incorporated in 1907) acted as a metropole for a resource-rich hinterland. The dockyards, lumber mills, and railway yards of the two cities were also viewed as the hub of the Canadian nation, having become the central railway and shipping point for the transshipment of the west's staple products "in exchange for the manufacturing goods of the metropolitan centres" in the east.[10]

Thanks to the railway and the mining boom, the Lakehead was a prime destination for capital investment and for immigrants.[11] Both cities competed with each other for commerce and resources, and the working-class conflict was centred in different locations. In Port Arthur, the area around the Canadian Northern Railway (CNR) coal docks and freight sheds, as well as the Finnish quarter on Bay Street, were the focal points of socialist activities. In Fort William,

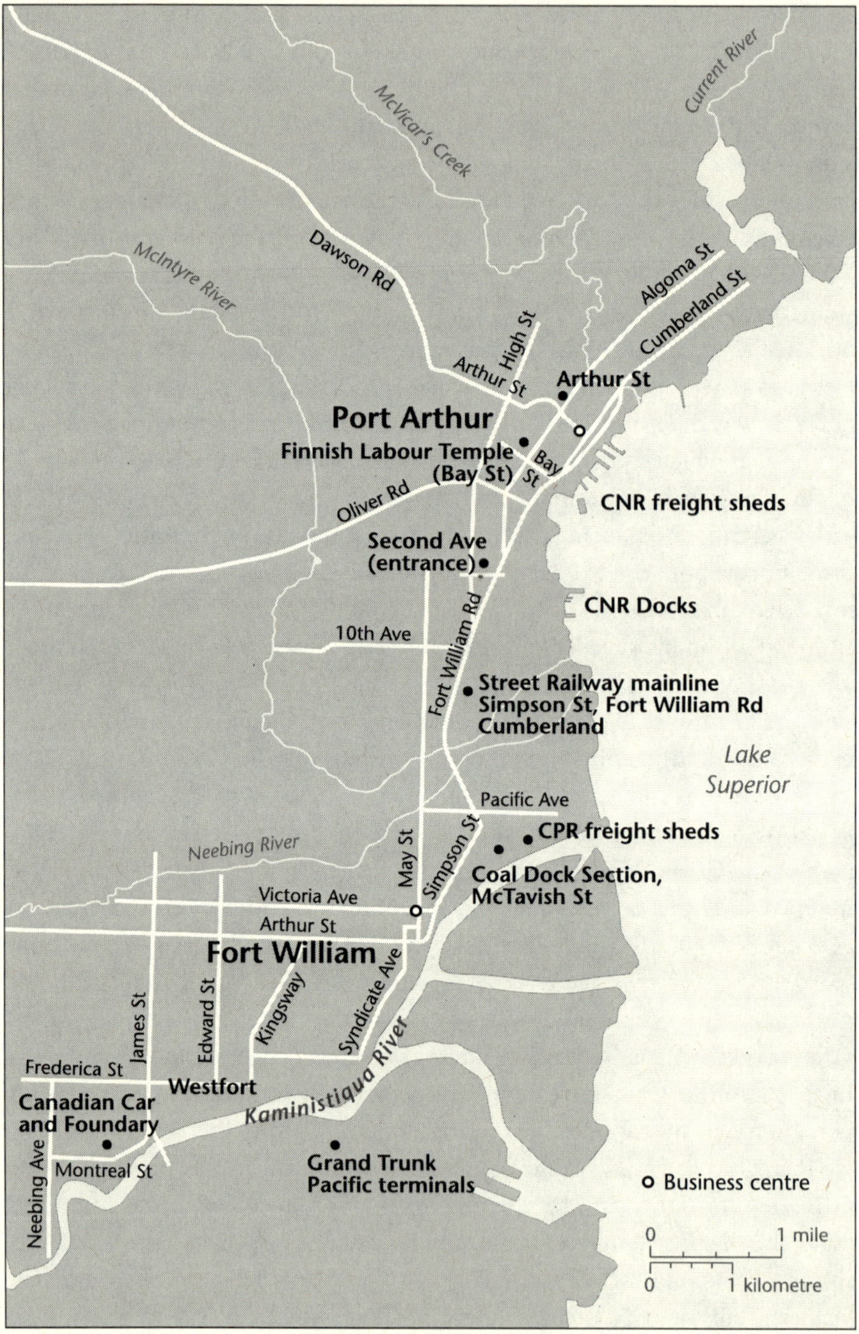

Figure 1 Map of Lakehead district.

the Canadian Pacific Railway (CPR) coal docks and freight sheds, and the area surrounding May Street, Miles Street, and Simpson Street were where much of the unrest of the period was expressed (see Figure 1). Much of the rivalry that has dominated the histories of the region was one produced, propagated, and used by the bourgeoisie of both cities, however.[12]

The two cities came to symbolize "the freedom, adventure, mystery and wealth of frontier America, the dime store novel Deadwood, Dodge or Carson City of Canada ... the village was described as the focal point of a mineral-rich region with unlimited potential."[13] Even following the collapse of the market for silver in the 1880s, with the CPR as the only significant object of development in the region, potential still existed. Besides assisting immigrants to settle in the western part of Canada, the CPR also acted as a conduit for "settlers" to transport their goods back to the eastern markets. The most prominent of these goods were wheat before 1913 and lumber after 1920. The Lakehead, as the central terminus for Canada, benefited immensely from the accompanying national expansion. Its fortunes increased with every bushel or cord transshipped.[14]

The wheat that flowed through the Lakehead was integral to the prosperity of the western world, the feeding of millions in Europe during the First World War, and the nourishment of the United Kingdom afterwards. Wood cut from the region helped build the cities of Central Canada during the industrial boom. The shipment of grain, wood, and other resources also led to the creation of a shipbuilding industry. Despite being over a thousand kilometres from the ocean, the Western Dry-dock in Fort William became the largest of its kind in Canada. Its existence epitomized the railway industry's influence and the optimism that it generated in those living in the region.[15] The emergence of the Lakehead as a major transshipment point in Canada and a demand for both skilled and unskilled labour in the region also led to its emergence as a destination for immigrant workers.[16]

As a central point in east-west communication, and combined with its ethnic diversity, the cities of Port Arthur and Fort William were storm centres in Canadian working-class history. In them, "eastern" and "western" socialists, trade unionists, and mainstream liberals fought, and frequently influenced, each other. The Lakehead thus interestingly complicates one of the major narratives of Canadian history – that of western exceptionalism – by raising the example of a region that was simultaneously *western* and *eastern*. Similarly, the Lakehead's political, economic, and historic linkages to Minnesota and the midwestern United States ensured that political and ideological fomentations to the south influenced many decisions to the north. In many respects, the Lakehead defies attempts to situate it within the canonical series of events that has been used to describe the progression of Canada from colony to nation, or, more appropriately, what has most recently been described as a process of liberal order.[17]

During the first three decades of the twentieth century, between 32 and 35 percent of the population in Port Arthur and Fort William were non-English-speaking immigrants.[18] Although few Europeans had settled in the region by 1871, the construction of the CPR had spurred rapid growth by 1911. In 1900, the population of Port Arthur was 3,214 and that of Fort William was 3,997. By 1911, the combined population of both cities exceeded 27,000,[19] and together they constituted Ontario's fifth-largest city.[20] The region accounted for barely 9 percent of Ontario's total population, however, and although the rest of Ontario was largely of British extraction by 1921, barely 50 percent of the population in Northern Ontario was.[21] Even in 1921, after some immigrants had left the region, the "British" still made up only 62.2 percent of the region's population. The number of "British" residents in the region had declined to 54.8 percent by 1931,[22] and this was reflected in the population of the twin cities, where close to 40 percent of the total population was of non-British origin by 1929. Although these populations were centred in neighbourhoods that were often treated like "ghettos" in the South end of Port Arthur and the East end and Westfort areas of Fort William, their influence on society extended well beyond such neighbourhoods.[23] For example, the city and region were home to the second-largest concentration of Finnish socialists outside of Finland, and they were not concentrated in just a few neighbourhoods.[24]

Divisions and exclusion were an inherent part of this ethnic and political mix, but they were also a dynamic force in the evolution of the twin cities and its hinterland.[25] Crusades to uphold Anglo-Saxon Protestant values and ideals led to a working class that was "neither a homogeneous or static mass, but rather represented a multiplicity of sub-groupings sometimes paralleling, sometimes overlapping one another."[26] Ordinary people lived and breathed the political and ethnic tension of the period. Lakehead and Canadian leftists were hardly unique in their many ideological shifts, however. Ideological transformation was a common occurrence among socialists throughout the world during the early twentieth century.

The work of Ian McKay has recently demonstrated that three distinct formations driven by specific ideological underpinnings drove socialists between

1900 and 1939.[27] As this book demonstrates, however, although members of various ethnic communities at the Lakehead often joined forces and fought for common goals, ideological and ethnic differences, whether perceived, invented, or real, ensure that pan-national generalizations about socialists and their organizations are problematic. None did so in "pure" form and each was significantly affected by the region's unique cultural and economic characteristics.[28] The presence of so many Finnish, Ukrainian, and Italian workers added an "ethnic" dimension to the ever-changing nature and characteristic of socialism at the Lakehead.[29] In many respects, beneath the class conflict of the early twentieth century was a more pronounced interclass turmoil whose distinguishing feature was ethnic difference rather than material interests.[30]

With such a wide variety of peoples from different parts of the world, many of whom were from different regions of the same nation-states, the experiences of the different groups at the Lakehead produced, defined, and gave language to the nature of their relationship with one another. In the twin cities, "ethnicity" was often tied to language usage, phenotypical appearance, and length of time in the country: the non-English-speaking, darker-looking, and more recently arrived "Finns" were considered to be radically different from, and in many ways inferior to, the English-speaking, fairer, and more settled "Anglo-Saxons."[31] Ethnicity arose from the interplay of such differences, arbitrary though they often were; and once a particular category was solidified – "the Finns," "the Galicians," "the Indians" – it was not easily questioned or replaced, even in the face of evidence that all such designated groups were internally differentiated, complexly demarcated, and fluid over time.[32]

Ethnicity both strengthened and weakened the left. It strengthened it by creating the cultural conditions under which left-wing ideas could be brought to groups culturally marginalized within the hegemonic cultural order, with such ideas serving as ways to understand and reshape the oppressive conditions of everyday life. It enabled radical ideas to go beyond their working-class bases into different socioeconomic strata. Yet it also weakened the left, because each ethnic group, in the relative "privacy" of its language, was likely to develop its own distinctive vocabulary of socialism. Moreover, those with superior positions in the game of ethnicity were almost inevitably bound to defend their relative privileges against those who were marked out as inferior, at the cost of a more fully fledged solidarity.

The Lakehead legacy was one in which socialist solidarity was always both intensified and qualified by ethnicity. A sense of ethnic identification and protests against ethnic discrimination fuelled many Lakehead leftists, particularly the region's many Finns and Ukrainians. Yet ethnic feelings also permeated the ranks of the Anglo-Saxon labour aristocracy, from which the Finns were largely excluded, and intensified its drive to circumvent radicalism with forms of conventional trade unionism or political centrism. As will become apparent, ethnicity both strengthened and weakened socialist organizations at the Lakehead. If working-class radicalism grew to almost unprecedented levels in the region – which became the epicentre of the Communist Party of Canada (CPC) – it also caused unrivalled levels of frustration. In this sense, the statue of Lenin in Petrozavodsk, marginal to this story in one sense, stands as one of its central symbols in another. Many of the Finns who built the statue did so out of their heightened sense of revolutionary activism, yet they built it thousands of miles away from Canada because they had come to believe that left politics in Canada itself was a hopeless endeavour. Stymied by factional infighting, labour-aristocratic opposition, and police repression, among other things, such activists as Aate Pitkänen, a well-known member of the Port Arthur District Young Communist League, would see in Soviet Karelia their only chance to play an active role in a socialist society.

Socialist movements necessarily combine social, cultural, and political work. Intrinsically committed to the fundamental restructuring of society, they recognize both the identities of individuals and those of the groups to which they belong. In a culturally heterogeneous terrain, a successful socialist movement will recognize the depth and tenacity of various forms of identity. It will struggle to articulate them to an overarching project, one that challenges the hierarchies and inequalities inherent in the capitalist system. In the early twentieth-century period covered in this book, the ideology of multiculturalism was unavailable as a way of thinking through such problems. In essence, the largely Anglo-Saxon-dominated labour movement, and even, paradoxically, a socialist movement made up disproportionately of recent immigrants, lacked the conceptual and political tools to address, let alone resolve, the problems raised by ethnic diversity and hierarchy. If at times this incapacity took the form of ethnic prejudice and exclusivism, at many others it simply assumed the unconscious, day-by-day repetition of the "commonsense" of the surrounding Canadian liberal order.[33] If any rigorous notion of "multiculturalism" requires (explicitly or implicitly) a "politics of recognition" – one that, philosopher Charles Taylor argues, must "*recognize* the equal value of different cultures" and not only allow them to survive "but acknowledge their *worth*" – the historian of Lakehead leftism often confronts the systemic *mis*recognition of the Other in the region.[34] During the first three decades of the twentieth century, socialist organizations in fact depended on the support of those ethnic groups that under the liberal order had been unable to achieve recognition.

Ethnicity, Socialism, and the Politics of Labour is organized into three sections, each chronicling a distinct phase in the early history of socialism at the Lakehead. Part 1, "The Roots of Revolution?" consists of the first two chapters and explores the period between the establishment of the first socialist organizations in the region in 1902 and the depression that hit the Lakehead shortly before the First World War. This section takes to heart the observation that the history of labour at the Lakehead "is largely a history of conflict, not only with business and management but also within labour's own ranks."[35]

Chapter 1 explores the period from the formation of the first known socialist party in the region to the internal split of the Socialist Party of Canada (SPC). It also discusses the establishment of the Social Democratic Party of Canada (SDPC) and its relationship with Independent Labour Party politics shortly before the First World War. Surprisingly, although many works mention and even briefly discuss the SDPC, no monograph on the party exists. This chapter provides the regional history of the organization and explains the internal turmoil that gripped it. Chapter 2 outlines the challenges and changes that socialists faced during the war years. It begins with the onset of the First World War and ends shortly after the Russian Revolution. The events in Russia, as Ian McKay claims, irrevocably altered the socialist landscape at the Lakehead. This chapter examines how socialists navigated the war years and how their journey, in turn, began to alter the nature and characteristics of socialism in the region.

Part 2, "From Winnipeg to the Workers' Unity League," consists of Chapters 3 to 6 and bridges the period between the Russian Revolution and the onset of the Great Depression in 1929. This period was marked by a profound change in the nature of socialism at the Lakehead. The evolutionary-based socialism that marked the period before the First World War was replaced by a more revolutionary brand inspired and, in many respects, dictated by the events in Russia following the October Revolution. As Ian McKay has suggested, however, when exploring this period "there is no point in looking for homogeneity."

Chapter 3 traces socialist activity from the end of the Winnipeg General Strike through the somewhat erratic existence of the One Big Union (OBU) and the Industrial Workers of the World (IWW) at the Lakehead. In particular, it explores the relationship of the two organizations with each other and with their memberships. The One Big Union, despite being a "flash in the pan," was the first "national" organization to embrace both revolutionary socialism and industrial unionism. Its rise and fall marked a turning point in the formation of the left at the Lakehead and in Canada.[36] Chapters 4 to 6 explore the establishment and eventual predominance (although not complete leftist hegemony) of the CPC at the Lakehead during the 1920s. Each of these chapters seeks to complicate the argument that immigrants, through their unwillingness to assimilate into the Canadian mainstream, prevented the CPC from flourishing. In many ways, the evidence suggests that Lakehead Communism flourished precisely because of the Finnish factor – with the Finns taking the lead not only in party building but also in participating in the many other fronts of Communist activity, from union building to cultural struggles. Yet it also suggests that, in part because of entrenched if unacknowledged Anglo-centrism, and in larger part because of the internal political dynamics of the international Communist movement, it was difficult to work such achievements into a more generalized, consistent, and persistent radical movement. In some respects, the Communists developed a massive base at the Lakehead, but lacked the theoretical or political tools with which to build on, or even to safeguard, it. As Chapter 6 reveals, they were also challenged within this base by other forms of revolutionary socialism, especially those associated with syndicalism, which severely tested the organizational capacities and ideological suppleness of the CPC.

The final part of this study, "The Great Depression and the Third Period," consists of Chapters 7 and 8 and examines the first five years of what is commonly referred to today as the Great Depression.[37] These chapters document the extreme difficulties engendered by the party's implementation of Stalin's "Bolshevization" plan. The CPC underwent another change, from favouring cooperation and a "united front" to organizing revolutionary unions of its own in keeping with the Communist International's declaration that capitalism had entered the Third Period and revolutionary change was imminent. These chapters demonstrate that despite massive demonstrations and the outward appearance of growing solidarity, the Communist movement became fractured along ethnic lines, and tensions between organizations, particularly between the CPC and IWW, hampered the organization and mobilization of workers.[38]

This book concludes with a brief overview of the events of 1935. The election of 1935 was a pivotal moment in the history of Canada, the Lakehead, and the Canadian left. Internationally, the Communist International adopted that year a strategy known as the Popular Front. By doing so, it decided to "drop its harsh critique of social democrats" and instead "build alliances with them (and other parties)" in an attempt to stem the spread of fascism.[39] Nationally, the election swept into power William Lyon Mackenzie King's Liberals and ushered in a new era in federal politics. While the Liberals swept both the ridings encompassing Port Arthur and Fort William, the Co-operative Commonwealth Federation (CCF), in its first federal election, drew support away from candidates supporting the CPC. From this point forward, none of the socialist organizations in the region would again threaten the CCF on the left for political prominence.[40] The year 1935 was also a turning point because of the establishment of the Congress of Industrial Organizations (CIO) and the end of the Workers' Unity League (WUL).[41] The formation of the Lumber and Sawmill Workers Union to replace the Lumber Workers Industrial Union of Canada (LWIUC) and the near collapse of the IWW Lumber Workers Industrial Union (LWIU) ended the existence of powerful revolutionary unions in the region.

The primary focus of this book is on institutions, especially parties and unions, with close attention to the ideas and principles championed by these organizations and the ways in which they challenged or confirmed underlying social and cultural patterns. Many fascinating cultural topics and personal biographies lie outside its scope. This somewhat traditional focus can be justified with particular force in the case of the Lakehead, because no other study has sought to bring this institutional history together, and also because only on the basis of such a solid framework can more wide-ranging theoretical and ideological analyses be successfully undertaken. Much more work still needs to be done in the years to come, but, just as the work of Ian McKay and Suzanne Morton on the labour revolt in the Maritimes between 1919 and 1920 attempts to bring it back into the collective memory of that region, so this study of socialist organization at the Lakehead between 1900 and 1935 aims to remember its contested and complicated legacy for the benefit of a new generation of activists and scholars.[42]

PART 1
THE ROOTS OF REVOLUTION?

1

Early Socialist Organizations at the Lakehead
1900-14

At the turn of the twentieth century, many middle-class men and women in Port Arthur and Fort William imagined their communities to be forward-looking towns, perhaps even the future metropoles of a booming North.[1] Their impressions were understandable. The twin cities were growing. They were at the centre of the transshipment of goods in and out of the North. The export of the rapidly expanding wheat harvest depended on them, and their industries and businesses were expanding. In addition, with this economic growth came a social transformation, as thousands of immigrants came to the Lakehead. The twin cities acquired all the accoutrements of North American modernity – a growing culture of consumption, an urban cityscape, up-to-date utilities. One might also have predicted the emergence of a strong and unified labour movement. Here, however, there were regional peculiarities that told against any such development.

Some have seen the roots of the division that existed within the Lakehead labour movement as a conflict between traditional craft unions and a growing socialist element more at home among the unskilled workers and immigrants – one, that is, of "Labourism vs. Socialism."[2] The former first participated in politics either as part of the Liberal Party's "left wing" or within "a semi-independent Liberal-Labour, or 'Lib-Lab,' position." The latter generated new movements and parties that sought to rally workers against such class alliances, and led to a flourishing of a "multiplicity of radical sects competing for the labour vote and official endorsement of organized labour."[3] Any examination of the relationship between labourites and socialists at the Lakehead between 1900 and 1914 demonstrates, however, that added to this classic tension between skilled trades and other workers was the unavoidable question of ethnic differences. The Finns in particular challenged the contours of the Lakehead left. As one Finnish socialist observed about the socialist organizations in his community, "the name and direction was changed several times, always according to advancements made in the labour movement. An attempt was made, as is often said, to stay abreast of the times."[4] As in the rest of Canada, many organizations claiming to be socialist in nature appeared and disappeared. Each of these organizations claimed to understand Marx better than their competition, and each had a platform from which its members proselytized to any who would listen. Those that lasted longer than a few months, the typical lifespan for most organizations, even had notions of pan-national grandeur.

Although the twin cities of Port Arthur and Fort William may have been undergoing an economic expansion, when American Federation of Labor (AFL) organizer Harry Bryan arrived at the Lakehead in 1902, he found a region practically devoid of labour and socialist organizations. True, the employees of the Canadian Northern Railway (CNR) and the Canadian Pacific Railway (CPR) had branches of their national bodies in Port Arthur and Fort William and local Finnish carpenters had established a union, but these largely looked after their own and concerned themselves little with the larger social questions. As a result, "industrial unionism remained an ideal for progressive-minded labour leaders, as did the goal of organizing the unskilled."[5]

Bryan exemplified an era that would see the creation of a vibrant and diverse socialist culture in the region.[6] Enamoured by the philosophy behind the Knights of Labor, he acted as an organizer for them during the late 1870s and 1880s in St. Thomas, Ontario.[7] Bryan's activities with the Knights of Labor ultimately anticipated what would be called the Social Gospel Movement, in harmony with his strong Methodist upbringing and radical ideology. It was these characteristics that put Bryan considerably to the left of mainstream Canadian society and Canadian Methodism. He left for the United States in the early 1880s and soon befriended Samuel Gompers and Eugene Debs. By the turn of the twentieth century, he had been a successful organizer for the AFL in the US.[8] Bryan's position as a union leader and his role in a number of prominent strikes in Cleveland eventually led to his being blacklisted by most employers, and he and his family had no choice but to leave. With no other prospects, he was convinced by the AFL leadership to return to Canada to organize workers at the Lakehead.

Bryan was drawn by the region's extraordinary growth rates at the turn of the century. Its location at the head of Lake Superior, combined with nearby natural resources and the phenomenal expansion of the Canadian wheat economy, made Lakehead a magnet for immigrants. Within the cities, the railway yards, coal docks, grain elevators, and shipbuilding yards that hugged the shore of Lake Superior provided the bulk of the employment for labourers (both skilled and unskilled) and were the driving force of the regional economy until the 1920s, when pulp and paper mills would join the mix.[9] When Bryan arrived, the vast majority of workers in these occupations belonged to no union.

Bryan's declaration to the editor of the Fort William *Daily Times-Journal* in 1903 that he was going to organize all the trades and workers into the AFL was more than bluster. The region presented him with the type of challenge he craved.[10] "The year 1903," according to Jean Morrison, "would herald many other firsts for labour: the first strikes organized and settled locally, a publicly acclaimed first Labour Day parade, and the first labour council, a Central Labour Union, affiliated to the American Federation of Labor."[11] Utilizing all the skills acquired in working for the American labour movement, in a few short years Bryan established perhaps as many as twenty-two unions in Port Arthur and Fort William.[12]

Bryan's dedication to the political movement was as important as the unions he helped establish. Ideologically, he did not blame capitalists for the plight of workers. He believed the system needed to be changed and warned local workers that the capitalists were as much victims as workers. For this reason, he argued, as long as capitalists were willing to change, they should be given a chance to cooperate.[13] This manifested itself in a belief in municipal ownership of public services and utilities, a battle that manifested itself in a referendum during the 1902 civic election that pitted municipal control against Bell Telephone.[14] The extent of municipal ownership in Port Arthur was virtually unequalled (with perhaps the exception of Fort William) in North America.[15] Municipally controlled telephone systems carried the day, but Bryan was blacklisted and forced to leave the city after he publicly humiliated Bell by exposing its collusion with local businesses and politicians to undermine the referendum.[16]

The success of the 1902 referendum on municipally controlled telephone systems did not reflect a working-class victory, however.[17] Conservative Dr. T.S.T. Smellie's electoral success, for instance, demonstrated that the citizens of Fort William and Port Arthur were willing to vote in favour of public ownership of the telephone system but had not embraced the working-class candidates.[18] Within the twin cities, residents, while constantly extracting what they could from the metropolis, had adopted "the tactic of voting, in the main, for the party in power at both the federal and provincial levels." G.R. Weller points out that this was in stark contrast to the "conventional wisdom about the reaction of voters in many provincial and supraprovincial hinterland regions, who are normally regarded as likely to vote for opposition or third parties as a means of remedying their lot."[19]

Harry Bryan's treatment incensed many of those in Port Arthur and Fort William who, already dissatisfied with how politicians and local labour leaders in the twin cities had handled the telephone scandal, had begun to search for an alternative. Under the guidance of E.C. Jordan, a branch of the Canadian Socialist League (CSL) was formed in Port Arthur shortly before the provincial election was called in 1904. While scholars differ in their opinion about the nature of the CSL, it combined middle-of-the-road liberals and Christian socialists with up-and-coming Marxists. The Socialist Party of Canada (SPC) grew out of the CSL, as many Marxist militants could already be found within the latter's ranks.[20]

In Ontario, the CSL became the Ontario Socialist League (OSL) in 1902 and then the Ontario Socialist Party (OSP) in 1903, to better reflect the group's intention of contesting elections.[21] Its 1903 convention drew delegates from across the province, with Jordan representing socialists in both Port Arthur and Fort William. As Martin Robin notes, those in attendance decided on a platform accepting, as "democratic" and therefore "socialist," "the reform measures of direct legislation, proportional representation, and public ownership of public utilities but recognized the fact that 'when administered by a capitalist government they cannot be but palliatives.'"[22]

The OSP found a sympathetic audience in the region. The October convention itself called for delegates to be "rigidly against any fusion or alliance with any independent or so-called reform party advocating any or all these or other demands that does not include the aims and purposes" of the OSP.[23] This automatically put them in conflict with those candidates in Port Arthur and Fort William who were running under the Independent Labour Party (ILP) banner and who were supported publicly by Bryan and the newly established Central Labour Union (CLU).

In fact, organized labour had sought to cultivate an alliance with the business community during the federal election of 1904. With backing from the CLU, railway unions, and Bryan, local Liberal Louis Peltier was selected as the ILP candidate for the riding of Thunder Bay and Rainy River, an area covering half of Northwestern Ontario.[24] Peltier advocated "labour's entry into electoral politics on its own behalf, a policy endorsed by the Trades and Labour Congress of Canada but denounced by the American Federation of Labor."[25] The key plank of his ten-point platform remained municipal ownership and the protection and preservation of the right of workers to organize.[26] Although not elected, he did receive 14 percent of the final vote, representing organized labour's entry into direct politics.[27]

The loose coalition of unions backing Peltier and organized by Bryan under the CLU for the federal election was at best unstable.[28] Despite ties to local labour and the vote of confidence he received from Bryan, Peltier's close association with the Liberal Party did not endear him to all. His close relationship with Sir Wilfrid Laurier, Clifford Sifton, and railway magnates Lord Shaughnessy and James Stephenson, in particular, concerned the more radical elements in Port Arthur and Fort William. His candidacy did not elicit support from all unions in the riding and, of the nineteen listed in his manifesto, "all were from the railways with the exception of the Fort William Central Labour Union, the Teamsters, the Bartenders, and the Iron Workers." Many opposed to Peltier reasoned that his participation in the election merely meant that two Liberal candidates were in the running. Perhaps because of this, Bryan's name was noticeably absent from the ILP platform despite his being a prominent figure at Peltier's nomination.[29]

By this point, others in the region had also begun to think like Jordan, who, speaking to the CLU in June 1904, argued that "the worker must capture political power [directly]."[30] Despite fielding no candidate, the OSP attacked Peltier and the ILP during the federal election of 1904 for what it perceived as an unholy "class alliance."[31] The public condemnation by the OSP did have an effect on Bryan, as, shortly after the election, he and many other likeminded workers became active members. Considering his past experiences in the US, his growing disputes with many in the ILP over AFL policy, his admiration for the thoughts and ideas of Eugene Debs, and his past involvement with the Socialist Party of America, Bryan's break with the ILP is not surprising.[32]

The OSP's positions on issues such as wages, working conditions, and class would have appealed to him. The OSP also appeared to espouse another tenet of Marxism that, in practice, was not reflected in the organizations found in Port Arthur and Fort William. Unlike the craft unions and the Anglo-oriented ILP, the OSP sought to more fully unite and integrate all socialists in the region, regardless of ethnic background. Bryan had previously convinced the fledgling Finnish carpenters' union to join with the AFL Brotherhood of Carpenters and Joiners branch in 1902. In approaching the Finnish Workingmen's Association of Port Arthur, established in 1903 and the largest workers' organization in Northwestern Ontario, Bryan brought together with the Finns other ethnic workers to discuss the issues facing all workers in the region.[33]

While Greek, Italian, Ukrainian, and Finnish workers all participated in the labour unrest and organization of unions in Fort William and Port Arthur, only the Finns had initially sought to establish workingmen's organizations of their own. True, all ethnic groups at the Lakehead formed some type of community organization, but, aside from the Italians, none was large enough or inclined to go beyond its ethnic boundary. Finnish immigrants were also much more steeped in the socialist thought spreading across Europe during the late nineteenth and early twentieth century. Industrialization, Russification campaigns, and the commercialization of agriculture had led to a surging popularity of social democratic movements in Finland.[34]

According to the available statistics, Finns who came to the Lakehead preferred Port Arthur to Fort William; the population of the latter city remained stable at approximately 3.2 to 3.7 percent of the total population, although hundreds more could be found in the surrounding countryside.[35] Finns in Port Arthur could be found living in a number of "ethnic" neighbourhoods, but the primary areas were those streets in the immediate area surrounding Bay Street, where, in 1910, the Finnish Labour Temple would be constructed.[36] The Finnish community generally consisted of Church Finns, Lutheran in denomination, and socialist Finns. These categories were hardly exclusive, as both groups shared similar positions on many issues, temperance being one during the first years of the twentieth century.[37]

On their arrival in Canada, most Finnish workers did not have common cause with the existing Anglo-dominated trade unions organized under the American Federation of Labor and later the Trades and Labour Congress of Canada. The TLC in fact advertised itself locally as the only organization in the region capable of protecting workers from "cheap, foreign-born labour."[38]

Figure 2 Labour Day gathering of Finnish people, 1907. *Courtesy of Lakehead University Library Archives*

As a result, Finns formed their own workers' associations, based on the same principles that had guided the Finnish cooperative movement in the late nineteenth century. The Port Arthur Finnish Workingmen's Association, *Imatra #9* (formed in 1903), was one such organization.[39]

An affiliate of the Brooklyn-based *Amerikan Suomalainen Työväenliito Imatra* (the Finnish-American Workers' League), it drew its membership from those Finns dissatisfied with the social and political discussions in the local churches and temperance associations.[40] The expressed goal of the *Amerikan Suomalainen Työväenliito Imatra* was to disseminate socialism by taking an active role in cultural, educational, and political activities.[41] The Finnish socialists thus sought to compete with the *Pohjankukka,* the Fort William Temperance Society, by building an all-encompassing organization for the Finns in both cities.[42]

The *Amerikan Suomalainen Työväenliito Imatra* also embodied one of the defining characteristics of Finnish Canadian socialism in the early twentieth century – its borderless nature. Consisting of thirty-two workingmen's associations in both the United States and Canada, from its establishment *Imatra #9* was involved in supporting Finnish workers' efforts throughout the US. Internationally, *Imatra #9* helped raise funds for the Finnish franchise movement and various strikes held by workers in various Finnish cities and towns against Russian oppression. Within its first year of existence, the association established its own hall and claimed a membership of over 130, of whom thirty were women. By 1906, this number had increased to 164.[43] Although discussions over the construction of a joint hall were held with the much larger temperance society, *Uusi Yrtys Raittiusseura* (UYR), throughout 1905, nothing materialized.[44]

A similar course of events unfolded in Fort William, but with some differences. By 1905, Finns in that city had also established their own reading room. As the population of the community continued to grow and the influence of the *Pohjankukka* decreased, Finnish socialists in Fort William began to explore establishing their own organization. In 1907, they separated and formed their own branch of it with the blessing of *Imatra #9*. Nothing exists to indicate the relationship between the two organizations and, because most of the branch's membership also belonged to the *Pohjankukka,* it was "comparatively ineffectual in the community" as socialists did not have their own home, meetings were sporadic, and membership fees (which decreased as membership dwindled) formed the only source of funds.[45] As in Port Arthur, with the collapse of the local temperance society in 1908, the Fort William *Imatra* merged with the remaining members of the temperance organization and took control of their hall, which they had been using since its establishment.

Recognizing the growing strength of Finnish socialists in the region, local union organizers in both cities began in 1904 to approach *Imatra #9* for its support during strikes. In 1905, the recently returned Harry Bryan, along with the OSP's representative, E.C. Jordan, actively promoted the party to Finnish socialists in both cities and in the outlying region. It appears that Bryan and Jordan went so far as to propose the creation of a joint Finnish-English socialist newspaper at the Lakehead – an enterprise evidently doomed by the small number of Anglo socialists.[46] Although no paper came into being, the *Imatra #9* executive decided to allow non-Finnish socialists to attend meetings and, in 1906, accepted Jordan "as a member even though he was not a Finn."[47] It appears that the membership of *Imatra #9* had discussed the possibility of joining the newly formed Socialist Party of Canada in October 1904.[48]

These positions placed Finnish socialists at odds with many in their community and with their American parent organization. As reconstructed by such historians as Varpu Lindström and Donald Wilson, the Finnish experience of emigration to Canada combined relatively small numbers (only about 21,494 in 1921, according to the Census of Canada) with high levels of politicization. Finland gained its independence from Russia as late as 6 December 1917. Before that, and for most of the previous century, the Finns were part of the autonomous Grand Duchy of Russia. In essence, Finns were fighting a national liberation struggle against Russia in the early twentieth century – a struggle that split the country into Reds and Whites and eventually plunged it into a civil war whose repercussions, as we shall see in later chapters, were felt strongly at the Lakehead.[49] The introduction of universal suffrage in 1906 – with Finnish women becoming the first in Europe to win the vote – created a massive base for the Social Democrats, which became the strongest social democratic party in Europe, paradoxically still under the tutelage of the Tsar, the "Grand Duke" of Finland. Finnish leftists at the Lakehead, a beleaguered minority in some senses, could also legitimately feel themselves to be emissaries from a land in which the socialist movement was far more developed than in Canada. From early in the twentieth century, in the temperance societies, then in the socialist halls, and then in the halls attached to the Finnish Socialist Organization of Canada (FSOC), Finnish Canadian socialism was unusually influenced by social and cultural activities centred on the halls. No matter what the state of play among rival parties and groups on the left was, this "hall socialism" remained a powerful force.[50]

Dissatisfied, however, with the lack of political action undertaken by the parent organization, Finnish socialists in Port Arthur and Fort William began actively pushing it to play a greater role in politics and unions where Finnish populations existed. *Imatra #9* even publicly criticized the parent organization's newspaper, *Pohjantahi,* after it attacked the Finnish American socialist paper *Työmies.*[51] Whether by coincidence or in part because of Bryan's and Jordan's persuasiveness, *Imatra #9* broke from the *Amerikan Suomalainen Työväenliito Imatra* in 1905 and acted as an independent organization for the next two years.

These changes within the Finnish socialist community occurred just as the Port Arthur branch of the OSP was established due to the formation of the Socialist Party of Canada resulting from the merger of the CSL with the Socialist Party of British Columbia, the Revolutionary Socialist Party of British Columbia, and other smaller organizations in 1904.[52] In reality, the joining of these organizations meant little to members of the OSP. Unlike its counterpart in British Columbia, the OSP had been ineffectual politically and unable to garner support from the Independent Labour Party. It remains unclear how many locals joined the SPC automatically, but neither Port Arthur nor Fort William was initially among them.[53] The official SPC position – one that was contradicted by many an SPC trade union leader – was that trade unionism at best offered palliatives to wage slavery. And SPCers were also identified with the "single-plank" platform, which precluded their cooperation or sharing of platforms with members of other political parties, even those claiming labour and left credentials.[54]

Inspired by the creation of the SPC, Harry Bryan invited Leo T. English, one of the Socialist Party's leading theoreticians, to the region to speak.[55] English, a well-known opponent of organizations structured along the lines of the British Labour Party, found a receptive audience.[56] Although attempts to integrate with the Finns failed, English, Bryan, and another worker named John McKiernan nonetheless were able to establish an English-language branch of the SPC in April 1906. They joined the three other Ontario English-language locals operating in Hamilton, Toronto, and Berlin. It appears, though, that this first branch of the SPC was short-lived, as the *Western Clarion* would later report, in September 1908, the creation of Port Arthur's only English-language branch.[57]

Long blocked from political involvement and frustrated by the English orientation of trade unions, local Finnish workers also established a branch of the SPC in Port Arthur in 1906.[58] The SPC provided a natural home for those Finnish Canadian socialists who had left the *Imatra* league and who were looking to take a more active political role within Canada.[59] As with the OSP, however, Jordan and Bryan convinced Finnish socialists in the region to join by November 1907 and create the Port Arthur Finnish Socialist Local #6 *(Suomalainen Sosialisti Osasto)*.[60] A newly established Fort William Workingmen's Association, in the midst of consolidating its membership, followed suit a year later and formed the Fort William Socialist Local #25 with seventy members, a significant number compared with other well-established locals in the country.[61]

Like the Toronto locals, the decision to join appeared to rest on the idea that Finnish socialists could revolutionize Canadian society only by engaging in mainstream Canadian socialist activities.[62] The decision to directly affiliate with a non-Finnish Canadian party also resulted from a lack of widespread linkages between the existing Finnish Canadian associations. The decision to join the SPC resulted from a desire on the part of Finnish Canadian socialists to be part of the Canadian working-class and labour movement. By 1909, the Finnish members constituted the largest ethnic group in the SPC after the English and Ukrainians. According to Varpu Lindström, Finnish socialists accounted for up to two-thirds of the local membership.[63] She has also argued that historians such as A. Ross McCormack, who have suggested that the SPC resulted in Anglo-Saxon radicals' organizing of "European immigrants," are not correct. "The SPC did not 'organize' the Finns," Lindström observes; "rather, it was the Finns who 'organized' a significant section of the Socialist Party of Canada."[64] Nowhere was this truer than at the Lakehead.

By 1906, the ILP no longer existed, the trade unions Bryan had established had become pawns of Lib-Labs, and new tensions had appeared within the working class at the Lakehead. Part of the explanation lay in the experiences of the unorganized workers. These workers were largely Italian, Greek, Finnish, and Ukrainian in origin and could be found employed as freight handlers for the CPR in Fort William and the CNR in Port Arthur. Many also lived in the coal dock sections of the two cities, a region located in the southern portion of Fort William hugging the outskirts of the industrial area, and notorious for substandard living conditions and overcrowding. The work was hard, heavy, and sporadic, and paid lower than the national average for unskilled labour. Not surprisingly, this area was also the centre of most of the labour unrest between 1906 and 1914. For example, a full-fledged gunfight erupted when authorities imported four train cars full of strikebreakers to break a Fort William freight handlers' strike in 1906.[65]

Local newspapers, disregarding the Anglo-Saxon identities of the strike's leaders, focused relentlessly on the theme of "British citizens" struggling with "foreigners." For the Port Arthur *Daily News,* the very eruption of the strike had constituted an insult to the community, which it defined in very nativist terms: "For a community of British citizens to have to submit to the insult and armed defiance from a disorganized horde of ignorant and low-down mongrel swash bucklers and peanut vendors is making a demand upon national pride which has no excuse."[66] Likewise, when the CPR refused to hire Greek or Italian workers on account of their role in the previous year's strikes, British and Northern European workers, two groups deemed to have been moderate during the strikes, were hired as they were thought to be "more than a match for [the] Greeks" should trouble arise.[67] It was into this strife-ridden situation that the SPC was relaunched in 1908.

At the same time, while the more radical English-language socialists were organizing themselves, Frederick Urry formed the Port Arthur Trades and Labour Council in April 1908.[68] Much like Bryan in his first days in the region, Urry was an admirer of the British labour movement. Before his arrival in

Canada, he had been a member of the British Independent Labour Party.[69] Between his arrival and his death in October 1927, Urry would play a prominent role in all aspects of the labour movement, continually working, one biography argues, "for a community of interests between Christians, socialists and trade unionists."[70] Conscious of the relationship needed between trade unionists, the social gospel, socialism, and local politics, Urry launched himself more directly than previous socialists into the ideological debate facing the left in the first two decades of the twentieth century. In 1908 he became the regional representative to the Presbyterian Church of Canada's Board of Social and Moral Reform and later its representative to Canadian labour. Urry was also one of three from Port Arthur who attended the founding of the SPC's Ontario section as official delegates, and who attended the TLC's annual meeting in Halifax on behalf of the Port Arthur Trades and Labour Council. As Morrison justifiably suggests, "his participation in these conferences symbolizes his attempt to use and unite trade unionism, socialism and the social gospel" to further his vision of a "co-operative commonwealth based on social and class harmony."[71]

Urry's position met with hostility from some in the region. No incident better illustrates this than the founding meeting of the Port Arthur Trades and Labour Council in 1908. Invited by Urry to the event was the national chairman of the Board of Social and Moral Reform, the Reverend J.G. Shearer; Mayor J.J. Carrick, perennial Conservative candidate; the Reverend Dr. S.C. Murray of St. Paul's Presbyterian Church; and F.B. Allen, publisher of the Port Arthur *News-Chronicle* and a prominent member of the Liberal Party.[72] Representing the Fort William Trades and Labour Council was a member of the International Typographical Union, Leo T. English. Speaking on behalf of the SPC, English expressed his disgust, remarking: "I have come to the meeting hoping to hear a workingman's story, but instead I have heard a couple of politicians and a couple of ministers."[73] He attacked Shearer, declaring to all those present that "human advancement is not made by making laws. It is made by breaking laws."[74]

With the strike of 1906 and the law's failure to protect workers still fresh in the minds of workers, many shared this sentiment. Urry's response was quick and just as provocative. In his capacity as president and secretary of the labour council, he declared that English's tactics would "bring discredit to the Labor movement." The Port Arthur *Daily News*, backed by Conservative J.J. Carrick, declared English to be a student of "the anarchistic school being propagated in Canada by 'the Appeal to Reason,' which does all but openly advocate murder."[75]

The newspaper also linked English to F.B. Allen, the Liberal candidate and editor of the *Chronicle*. It was a brazen attempt, as Jean Morrison argues, "to break the seemingly close relationship between organized labour and the Liberals."[76]

Local Liberals and Conservatives, already conscious of the growing strength of organized labour and the SPC, further assisted in widening the growing gap between moderate and radical socialists in the region. Despite the *Daily News'* gleeful denunciation of English and the SPC for the incident at the first meeting of the Port Arthur Trades and Labour Council, the paper reversed its position during the provincial election campaign of June 1908. Fearing a Conservative victory due to a split in the labour vote, the Liberals withdrew their candidates in favour of "independent" ones. At a nomination meeting organized by the recently resigned Liberal candidate, F.B. Allen, George Mooring was chosen as the Independent Labour candidate. For even the most reform-minded SPC supporters in the region, Mooring's candidacy would have been unacceptable, as he was a well-known timber contractor.

Not surprisingly, the SPC in the region was the first to speak out against Mooring and what it perceived as an emergent class alliance.[77] The day after Mooring's nomination, the Port Arthur Trades and Labour Council voted in a new permanent council with Frederick Urry as secretary and James Brooker as president. With support from John T. Mortimer, former president of the Trades and Labour Congress of Manitoba, the council's first action was to withdraw its support from Mooring and place it behind the SPC's candidate, English.[78] This support was mixed, however.

Unsure about the local SPC and cautious about its Anglo-Saxon and trade-union-dominated executive, many Finns opted to run their own candidates in the municipal election of 1908. Despite the community's relatively small size and its candidates' remote chances of winning, many in Port Arthur and Fort William became alarmed and viewed the situation as a "serious danger" to the region.[79] Both Conservatives and Liberals increasingly characterized the Finns, and all those associated with publications such as *Appeal to Reason,* as "socialistic" and "anarchistic."[80]

The salience of this journal in the region suggested some of its underlying patterns of leftism. Although isolated and marginalized in one sense, the Lakehead was tightly integrated into North American patterns of Finnish and Ukrainian settlement and wide open to currents of radicalism south of the border. Thus, although the English-language branch of the SPC may have become inactive shortly after its creation, those drawn to socialism were not left without sources of information and inspiration. The Kansas-based *Appeal to Reason* became the focus of the ire of those against socialism. Local authorities were so concerned that they banned the paper, along with the satirical Finnish socialist paper *Väkäleuka,* in April 1908.[81] Although the move appealed to some Finns who worried that Finnish radicalism threatened the community's image of respectability, it was so draconian that even mainstream local newspapers found it excessive.[82]

At the Ontario convention of the SPC that year, delegates from the Lakehead joined the fifteen locals and 500 to 600 members. Despite impressive election results in Toronto, however, Ontario locals saw their numbers gradually decrease because of internal divisions rooted in regional peculiarities, incompatible personalities, and disagreements over the SPC's role in municipal politics.[83] For SPC supporters at the Lakehead such as Bryan and English, the various elections and the collusion of labour politicians against workers was proof that class alliances benefited only the master class.[84]

The SPC and the Port Arthur and Fort William Trades and Labour Councils did unite during the 1908 federal election to endorse Frederick Urry's nomination for the riding of Thunder Bay–Rainy River. Despite the growing divisions between labourites and socialists, Urry appears to have been the only jointly sponsored SPC and organized-labour candidate in the country.[85] What his joint candidacy reveals is still open to speculation. Clearly, the position of SPCers was much more heterogeneous than the previous literature on the SPC has suggested. Urry's willingness to represent a community of interest both helped and dampened his appeal. Although the labour and SPC candidate, he had only "mixed support" from the Port Arthur Trades and Labour Council because of his connections to socialists.[86] Urry's experiment in bridging the socialist/labourite division was, unsurprisingly, short-lived – it did not even outlive the election itself.

It certainly did not help that the local newspapers (which publicly supported either the Liberal or the Conservative candidate) denigrated both him and his candidacy for associating with Finnish socialists who allegedly practised "free love."[87] Perhaps local newspapers made these claims in the hope that voters would draw comparisons to the recent attention given to the activities in Canada of Emma Goldman and the Industrial Workers of the World.[88] They were also responding to actual instances of Finnish socialists defying convention and forming conjugal partnerships without benefit of clergy, as a manifestation of their critique of religion and, at least for some, patriarchal conventions.[89]

Despite receiving a respectable 752 votes out of a total of 4,562, the SPC denounced Urry following the election for his support of a pension scheme based on "'sane' principles, and equal wage for women and men when engaged in the same work, and a fair day's wage for a fair day's work."[90] The *Western Clarion,* an SPC organ, described his position as "sickly sentimental reforms" and, despite his significant showing in the election, labelled Urry a "half-baked socialist" and "another example of a distorted and disordered imagination suggestive [of] Keir Hardie Labor-Socialism – a concoction noted for its inspired nothings."[91] Not surprisingly, Urry resigned from the SPC soon after, chastised local socialists for their "delight in abusing the workers," and declared that the SPC could not be the Socialist Party of Canada until it abandoned such tactics and focused instead on enlisting workers.[92]

The growing rift between labourites and socialists by 1909 was nowhere more apparent than in the Fort William freight handlers' strike at the docks and encompassing the southern part of the city that began on 12 August 1909.[93] The strike was over wages and working conditions, and the *Industrial Banner* would later argue that "the poor, exploited foreigners had good cause for revolt."[94] *Cotton's Weekly* categorized the strikers as "martyrs since, through them and their deeds, the conditions of wage slavery of their comrades have been discovered."[95] Negotiations brokered by the mayor of Fort William, Louis Peltier, were proceeding until, under the cover of night, the CPR brought in enough constables, the railway's chief security agent told local newspapers, "to compete with a company of soldiers, let alone foreigners."[96] Tensions continued to mount the next day when Peltier, only recently elected on the labour ticket, "succumbed to pressure," read the Riot Act to strikers, mobilized the local militia, and asked that the Royal Canadian Mounted Police be brought in from Winnipeg.[97] In Peltier's view, the decision to subdue the strikers was justified as he had "done everything possible to bring about a peaceable settlement." As he declared in the local newspapers: "I am through. The men who have brought on this trouble must take consequences. The law of the land must be protected."[98] For their part, the local police, militia, and legendary Mountie Sam Steele viewed force as necessary "owing to the very great number of foreigners in the two cities."[99]

Both the strikers and workers sympathetic to their cause rioted after attempts by railway police to forcefully remove those impeding strikebreakers. The armed confrontation resulted in a running gunfight that left eight strikers dead and four police officers, two bystanders, and thirty strikers wounded. The *Industrial Banner* described the incident as "probably the bloodiest labor riot

Figure 3 1912 or 1914 Parade on Bay Street Port Arthur. *Courtesy of Lakehead University Library Archives*

ever in Canada."[100] The incident ended only when Peltier convinced the strikers to submit their case to a conciliation board.[101] For his part, Urry struggled to mobilize public opinion against official violence. He rallied the Port Arthur Trades and Labour Council "to denounce the use of the local militia." He also sought to resolve the conflict through the mediation of the federal Department of Labour.[102] With respect to the Anglo-Saxon workers and mainstream opinion in the twin cities, the damage to the immigrants' image was difficult to repair, even for so capable and determined a fence mender. The Fort William *Daily Times-Journal* compared the recent events to the Haymarket Riot in the United States, which, it pointed out, had concluded with the hanging of foreign anarchists. A composite image of the "dangerous foreigner" was taking hold.[103]

Understandably, the events of 1909 created a certain amount of animosity within the remaining socialist organizations. Peltier's stance alienated the strikers. His position as a local union leader and ILP activist also drove another wedge between non-Anglo socialists, trade unions, and the local establishment.

It meant little that after the incident the Deputy Minister of Labour wrote that the CPR bore much of the blame and "that a less prominent display of force would have been dictated by prudence and might have helped to avert the calamity that followed."[104]

The events surrounding the elections of 1908 and the unrest of 1909 reveal that a division did indeed exist between foreigner/non-foreigner, radical/moderate, and socialist/non-socialist elements within the Lakehead's workforce. Thus, the decision to hold the 1910 annual meeting of the TLC at the newly constructed Finnish Labour Temple on Bay Street, in the heart of Port Arthur's Finnish community, was not coincidental.[105] By lobbying for it as the main site of the convention, Urry attempted to bridge the growing socialist/labourite divide at the Lakehead. It was also an attempt to reach out to those, mostly Finnish workers, who had become dissatisfied with the status quo. Ultimately, however, he was unsuccessful.

One of the main issues discussed at the convention was how to deal with unorganized workers. Some, such as Secretary-Treasurer P.M. Draper, urged their inclusion, whereas the majority felt that it was the duty of the TLC to protect its membership from the growing number of immigrant workers. Significantly, these workers happened to comprise the majority of those that the TLC considered unorganized. There were socialist activists among the ranks of TLC unionists – most famously James Simpson – but at the Lakehead most trade unionists were not socialists, and most socialists were not trade unionists. Among the numerous Finnish socialists of the Lakehead, ethnic and fraternal organizations, but not trade unions, were the important foci of working-class activism before 1918. The same might be said for Italians and Ukrainians. Many did not belong to TLC-affiliated craft unions. They tended to look to their own cultural associations and mutual-aid groups. As one local newspaper cautioned: "The aristocracy of Labor cannot afford to neglect the grave and pressing questions in which its weaker brother is deeply interested, but which he has no voice to proclaim. It is only by enrolling under its banner the interests of this silent army that the present Labor party of Canada can become a great power."[106]

By 1910, such stark divisions had taken a toll on the Socialist Party of Canada in the region. As throughout Ontario, members, much more linked to the trade union movement, began to express a desire for changes in the party's position on industrial disputes. In addition, they sought an end to what they perceived as the "autocratic control of the Vancouver leadership."[107] Perhaps most damaging was the position taken by non-Anglo locals that systemic ethnic

Figure 4 May Day Parade 1911 or 1912. *Courtesy of Lakehead University Library Archives*

prejudice existed within the SPC. Despite being numerous enough to have elected members to the executive, language locals were almost unrepresented. The *Western Clarion* itself blamed this on a conscious attempt by English-language locals to hold on to power. One common tactic, it suggested, was the withholding of membership dues stamps at election times so that foreign members could not vote.[108]

Anglo-Canadian labour leaders exacerbated this divisive situation. They refused to concede to the demands of ethnic minorities within the SPC, typified by the Finns of Toronto and the Lakehead.[109] Since they first joined the SPC, Finnish members had been proponents of a form of socialism that owed its ideas and theories more to European than North American theoreticians.[110] Many Finnish members continued to argue for the SPC's affiliation with the Second International, a position many branches rejected in 1909 because of the International's admission of non-socialist bodies such as the British Labour Party.[111] Regardless, Finnish branches such as the one in Port Arthur held out hope that they could influence the SPC to adopt some of the reforms and tactics then in use in Europe.[112] This put them increasingly at odds with the more doctrinaire theoreticians of the party such as Leo T. English.[113]

Predictably, Finnish SPC members at the Lakehead became progressively more disillusioned with the party.[114] The election of essentially Lib-Lab labour candidates supported by the English-language branches and the arbitrary actions of local labour councils were seen as instances of the failure of the Anglo labour movement, and even of the Socialist Party of Canada itself. This internal conflict came to a head when the Toronto Finnish local passed a resolution calling for affiliation with the Second International in 1909. This resolution – which was enough to earn the local its expulsion from the party – had repercussions at the Lakehead, where the Finnish-influenced Port Arthur and Fort William locals made common cause with the Toronto dissidents.

Although differences in ideology and opinions about where the party should go played a part in the rift, another possible, and more sinister, reason lay behind the expulsions. A.W. Rasporich, for instance, has argued that "the expulsion of the Finnish socialists from the Socialist Party of Canada in 1910 was the direct result of English-speaking members' suspicion of the Finnish socialists."[115] J.W. Ahlqvist, a leading member of the Toronto local, recalled that behind the rift was a growing resentment of immigrant workers on the part of English-speaking members.[116] This explosive combination of fear of job competition and cultural misunderstanding meant that the expulsion of the Finnish locals in Ontario sent shockwaves throughout the entire SPC.

The actions of the Vancouver-based leadership were seen by many Finnish and non-Finnish members to have been maladroit. Many other locals left the SPC to protest them. Some of the Ontario branches banded together and met in Berlin, Ontario, in May 1910. Another group, consisting of branches and members from Ontario, the Maritimes, and British Columbia, and the Finnish branches at the Lakehead, formed the Canadian Socialist Federation (CSF). In British Columbia and Manitoba, dissatisfied SPCers formed provincial Social Democratic parties. Many Ukrainians chose to form their own Ukrainian Social Democratic Party.[117]

The formation of these separate groups only served to weaken the ability of socialists to contest elections and to mobilize workers on a national and regional scale. Desiring to provide socialists with a new national alternative, the former Port Arthur Finnish SPC local called for a dominion convention to unite the various dissatisfied factions. Its proposal met with enthusiastic support from the dissidents and was actively promoted by the socialist paper *Cotton's Weekly*, which, after the convention was over, became the SPC's official English-language organ. A preliminary meeting was held in Toronto in April 1911, with

Bryan leading the 4 delegates from Northwestern Ontario among 32 delegates representing 1,196 "socialists."[118] Representatives met again at the Lakehead on 30 and 31 December 1911 to formally discuss unity.

The location was symbolic. With its foot firmly in both the eastern and western Canadian socialist movements, the Lakehead was seen as a bridge to what many in attendance hoped was the beginning of a pan-national party. What initially began as a merger of the Manitoba Social Democratic Party and the eastern-based CSF soon included representatives from Berlin, Ontario, once delegates agreed that any Provincial Executive Committee for Ontario would be established in that city.[119] The goal of the newly formed Social Democratic Party of Canada (SDPC) was "to educate the workers of Canada to consciousness of their class position in society, their economic servitude to the owners of capital, and to organize them into a political party to seize the reins of government and transform all capitalist property into the collective property of the working class."[120] In enunciating these goals, the SDPC was declaring that it shared many of the SPC's ideas. Its more federal structure, however, distinguished it sharply from the older party, as did its decision to join the Second International.[121]

To ensure a level of independence and to avoid the problems that had led to the SPC's implosion, Finnish members, following a plan first suggested by Port Arthur Finns in September 1911, also decided to form a separate but affiliated organization, headquartered in Toronto. By October, the Finnish Socialist Organization of Canada (FSOC) had been formed and John W. Ahlqvist had been chosen as its first chairman to lead the way in the creation of "a new society." Initially, 19 locals affiliated with the FSOC, for a combined membership of 1,205. By 1914, this number had increased to 3,000 members in over 64 locals throughout the country,[122] including branches in Port Arthur, Fort William, and communities throughout the Northwest such as Nolalu and Nipigon. Operating under the same charter as the Port Arthur branch was a chapter in the rural Finnish community of Kivikoski, a small farming village sixteen kilometres away. Port Arthur and Fort William alone accounted for over 31.9 percent of all FSOC members in Canada.[123] The Port Arthur branch, in particular, was instrumental in the later formation of branches in Intola, Ostola, and many other smaller communities in Northwestern Ontario.[124]

It would be wrong to assume that all SPCers joined the SDPC. As in much of Canada, the English-speaking nuclei in many Ontario SPC locals continued to operate and most of the locals in British Columbia remained intact.[125] The

Figure 5 Parade of people with sign "Women should vote," Port Arthur 1911 or 1912.
Courtesy of Lakehead University Library Archives

withdrawal of Finnish socialists, however, did leave the English-language branches in Port Arthur and Fort William impotent. The situation was exacerbated when Leo T. English left for British Columbia, and the "British element" opted to join the Independent Labour Party (ILP) of New Ontario in 1911.[126] The platform of the ILP of New Ontario was essentially that of a British-style labour party. It called for "the transformation of all private monopolies into the collective property of the people" and "the establishment of production for use and not for profit." Frederick Urry, one of the forces behind the ILP's creation, "equated labour's message with that of Christianity to the oppressed."[127] Formed as a distinct political party for workers and socialists in Northern Ontario, one of its first activities was the establishment of its own newspaper, the *Wage Earner*. Edited by Urry, it declared its dedication to the socialist cause and its focus on "all aspects of the working populace rather than with any specific trade or line of endeavour."[128]

The formation of the SDPC led to increased tensions at the Lakehead. For example, both the SDPC and the ILP used the Labour Day parade of 1911 as an occasion to try to convince workers of their individual platforms. Speaking on behalf of the ILP, Urry discussed the internationalism of the labour movement and argued that success could be achieved only if workers stood together. As Morrison explains, he also "made a special appeal to the immigrant workers, warning that if they were 'led astray by politicians' those conditions they had fled would prevail in Canada."[129] These calls for class solidarity had little impact. Much of the working class in Port Arthur, for instance, swung during the election from the Labour-Liberal alliance and supported the Conservative candidate, J.J. Carrick. There was more concern over the issue of reciprocity with the United States, which Carrick opposed, than over local labour disputes.[130]

Animosity between the ILP and the SDPC continued during the provincial election of 1911. Urry, with support from the Port Arthur Trades and Labour Council, was nominated as the ILP candidate. Fearing his candidacy, the Liberals withdrew and actively supported the Conservative candidate to ensure his victory despite the fact that Urry polled an outstanding 27.4 percent of the total vote.[131] In Fort William, the Liberals did not withdraw their candidate but the working-class vote was split between the Liberals and ILP, ensuring a Conservative victory. Interestingly, in both cities, the Finnish locals of the SDPC refused to support the ILP candidates and the ILP candidates, in turn, refused to support the Finnish ones.[132]

In Port Arthur, this divisiveness also spilled over into the municipal elections. Finnish socialists ran candidates in direct opposition to the ILP of New Ontario. All candidates, however, targeted the Finnish vote. For example, the Port Arthur City Council wanted a number of referendum questions passed and admitted that without the Finnish vote it stood a good chance of failing. At a meeting held at the Finnish Labour Temple, the Mayor of Port Arthur courted its votes by proposing that if the Finns's supported specific bylaws, a tax exemption for the Labour Temple would be placed on the ballot as well. An active campaign ensued in which civic officials portrayed the Finns, the Labour Temple, and the Finns' supposed willingness to assimilate as positive and desirable. Politicians suggested to the residents of Port Arthur that a vote in favour of the tax exemption would be "a demonstration in Port Arthur of the contempt for and protest against Russian atrocities" and would move many Finns away from the socialist movement.[133]

Although the ILP in Fort William managed to elect one of its candidates to the municipal council, both ILP and Finnish Socialist candidates fared poorly in Port Arthur due to vote splitting. The proposed tax exemption was also defeated.[134] These defeats did not lessen the perceived impact of socialists in the region, however. In Port Arthur, for example, Mayor S.C. Young blamed "the Labor and Socialistic Element" for the defeat of several questions put to the electorate dealing with bonusing.[135]

The SDPC at the Lakehead appears not to have been content merely to contest elections. In 1912, having recently formed a union, the mostly immigrant workers of the Canadian Northern Coal and Ore Dock Company went on strike for better wages, hours, and working conditions. Bloodshed resulted when company officials, using local police and the militia, tried to suppress the striking coal handlers. The chief of police, two constables, and two Italian strikers were wounded.[136] Fearing a general strike, the CNR quickly acquiesced to the demands of the coal handlers.

There was much in this incident that recalled earlier labour strife at the Lakehead. A new element, however, was the growing influence of radical socialists, who were thought to have sway over the coal handlers and to have been instrumental in their inclusion in the trade union movement.[137] Prominent among the activists were "members of the Social Democratic Party of Canada," including the party's organizers for Port Arthur and Fort William, the cobalt miners' union leader James P. McGuire and the Reverend William Madison Hicks, as well as Herbert Barker, a volunteer organizer for the AFL.[138] In April 1912, the three men led a number of English-speaking socialists in Fort William in establishing Ontario Local 51 of the SDPC. Initial members also included W.J. Carter; an architect named Richard Lockhead; Sid Wilson, a member of the British-based Amalgamated Carpenters; and Fred Moore, owner of the printing press that printed Urry's the *Wage Earner.* Significantly, most of the members appear to have been Finnish or Ukrainian.[139]

Before the strike, members of the Fort William SDPC had spoken at meetings of the coal handlers and, in the case of Hicks, played an active role by leading a parade of workers in confronting Port Arthur mayor S.W. Ray on his way to read the Riot Act to the strikers.[140] The meeting between the two men and the violence that ensued were coincidental, according to Morrison, as "the Social Democratic party posed no real or imagined menace to the citizens of Port Arthur ... what alarmed the English-speaking community was the newly won influence of the socialists with the immigrant workers."[141] Supporters of the ILP of New Ontario such as Urry found themselves "at odds with radical socialism" as "not only had the socialists played a prominent part in the strike, though not the riot, but they were also attempting to organize Thunder Bay's entire waterfront."[142]

Urry viewed use of the strike as a last resort when all other avenues of conciliation had failed. He found the SDPC, and Hicks in particular, too radical for the Lakehead. Writing as one socialist "in the great movement of the democracy" to another, he rejected Hicks's submission to the *Wage Earner,* "Girls and Wages in Fort William – A Problem for Society," in May 1912. Explaining that he would "like to stand shoulder to shoulder" with Hicks, he added that he would do so only "with clean methods and reasonable criticism."[143] While the content of Hicks's article remains unknown, its ultra-radical tone may be surmised from Urry's critique of it: "If the article in question is a fair sample of the language you are using from the platform, then allow me to say, as a Socialist that your efforts in these cities will have no abiding effect for good." Urry concluded with the following advice: "If Fort William and Port Arthur are to become socialistic it will have to be done by the men and women of these cities who will dare to stand by each other and be prepared to bear burdens and sacrifice. Ten men and women of this caliber will do more than a thousand excited to applause by inflammatory oratory."[144] Even though newspapers declared that only Italians had taken up arms during the strike, Hicks and the SDPC bore much of the blame because of their calls for a general strike of all workers on the waterfront to win similar concessions for the dockworkers.

Calls for Hicks's arrest began to appear in newspapers in both cities and the surrounding countryside. On 1 August 1912, officials arrested him for his role in a "tumultuous assembly ... likely to promote a breach of the public peace."[145] Shortly after Hicks's arrest and conviction (although he received a suspended sentence), SDPC organizers began an active campaign to take control, or at the very least undermine, the ILP-led Trades and Labour Councils. Following the strike, they sought to stage a general strike on the waterfront and, ideally, spread it throughout both Port Arthur and Fort William. As Jean Morrison writes, however, this was "a move disparaged by the British labour men for its disregard of the law which required negotiations and conciliation preceding strikes by transportation workers."[146] The attempt failed and widened the rift formed during the municipal, provincial, and federal elections of 1908 and 1911 and the labour unrest earlier in 1912.

The SDPC was also not left untouched. In preparation for the 1913 Fort William civic election, Urry and Hicks jointly developed in opposition to the SDPC a manifesto describing the class struggle in general and the issues facing the region's workers in particular.[147] At the same time, Hicks appears to have entered into collusion with the ILP; the Dominion Executive of the SDPC shocked the Fort William local by notifying it that SDPC branches in Northeastern Ontario had levelled complaints of fraud against him. On the recommendation of the Elk Lake, Porcupine, and Cobalt locals that Hicks be expelled, the matter was referred to the Fort William membership. Despite facing the possibility that its charter would be revoked, Local 51 refused to expel Hicks and launched a vigorous defence on his behalf. The convincing agitator had a coterie of true believers, who "defended him to the last ditch refusing to believe that Hicks would do anything wrong."[148] He also had his critics, evidently including the 400-strong Fort William branch, which, it appears, sided with the Dominion Executive and expelled Hicks.[149]

After Hicks's expulsion, the remaining SDPC branches in Port Arthur refused to support Urry's candidacy for the Joint Board of the Port Arthur and Fort William Street Railway. They declared non-confidence in ILP candidates in both cities for their unwillingness to "recognize the class struggle and the necessity for abolishing capitalism."[150] Although the ILP controlled the labour councils in both cities (consisting of twenty-two unions), had successfully elected members to both city councils, and possessed its own paper, its prospects of electoral success relied on the support of the SDPC, with its mass base among the Ukrainians and Finns.[151]

By 1913, the SDPC locals in Port Arthur and Fort William were among the fifty-eight reportedly active in Ontario. There were calls to reunite with the SPC to create a strong national party.[152] During the municipal election of 1913, the SDPC in Port Arthur, backed numerically by Finns, opted to field candidates of its own in direct opposition to the ILP. Whereas the ILP drew its candidates from among the Anglo-Canadian labour leaders, the Port Arthur branch of the SDPC differentiated itself by running candidates better representing the ethnic composition of the working class in the region.[153] In Fort William, with a much larger base, the ILP fared better, electing A.H. Dennis to the municipal council and Louis Peltier as mayor once again. In perhaps one of the SDPC's first electoral successes in Canada, however, K.E. Gröndahl, manager of the Fort William Finnish cooperative, managed to get elected to council. Peltier's success was also in large part due to the decision of the SDPC branches in Fort William and of the local Italian community to support his candidacy.[154] This support was criticized by many, including William Madison Hicks, who, on behalf of the newly formed Workingmen's Club – which he claimed boasted a membership of over ten nationalities – refused to endorse Peltier or his opponent. Incidentally, Hicks left the Lakehead shortly afterwards, but not before defrauding local residents of an estimated $2,250.[155]

With him departed one highly personalized version of a response to the ambiguous legacy of Lakehead socialism. Both the ILP and the SDPC grew rapidly during 1913. The labour councils in the twin cities began to discuss unity, in the form of construction of a joint Central Labour Temple. The Finnish branch of the SDPC in Port Arthur also called out for working-class and socialist unity. Moreover, as a more tangible indication of potential unification of the socialist and labour movements, SDPC organizer Herbert Barker was elected president of the Port Arthur Trades and Labour Council in April 1913.[156]

As so often proved to be the case, however, such incipient unity was challenged by the region's sheer class volatility. The strike by street railway workers in May 1913 was a volcanic moment. As David Bercuson writes: "The walk-out provided a focal point for much of the hatred and bitterness that had developed between labour and its enemies in the twin cities for several years."[157] Rioting and violence were sparked by the CPR's attempts to use strikebreakers. When strikers overturned a streetcar operated by strikebreakers, police arrested one of the participants and, when a crowd tried to get him out of jail, fired into the crowd, killing a bystander.[158] Local newspapers tried to pin the violence on the socialists, who were allegedly responsible for agitating the crowd.[159]

The railway workers belonged to the Trades and Labour Councils in both cities and, in a show of solidarity, both councils called for a general sympathy strike. These calls went unheeded and most workers returned to work after four days of protest.[160] In response, Urry, James Booker, McGuire, Bryan, and many members of the SDPC met at the Finnish Labour Temple. They criticized the local trades and labour councils "for not being radical enough to resist the ruling of an unscrupulous upper class." They hoped the councils would become "more radical." Not surprisingly, the obviously inflamed right-wing media in the twin cities characterized the meeting as one of "sedition, anarchy, socialism, violence and most everything else calculated to worry orderly society and responsible government."[161]

It was not a critique of the Lakehead workers reserved for the mainstream press. Mayor John Oliver of Port Arthur summed up the situation well when he argued that the continued unrest in Port Arthur and Fort William was not wholly due to working conditions. Making specific mention of the strikes of 1909, 1912, and 1913, he suggested that the unrest had been the result of socialist agitators. "There is hardly a night in the week," Oliver wrote, "that inflammatory speeches have not been made by several agitators ... something will have to be done to either remove them or check their actions." Interestingly, Frederick Urry and J.P. McGuire were specifically named for their alleged advocacy of a general strike. McGuire was further singled out for his reputed suggestion that it would be an easy thing to cut telephone, telegraph, and electric lines.[162]

Some saw signs of growing unity within the working class. In his 1913 social survey of Port Arthur, Bryce Stewart attributed to the ILP a drive to achieve the "solidarity of the working classes." Yet, his pioneering work of sociological research also introduced many empirical details that showed how difficult such unity would be to achieve. The population of the two cities was understood to be separated into "three distinct grades of society." These included the well-to-do, an artisan class composed primarily of English-speaking residents, and the "ever increasing horde of unskilled workers."[163] The suppression of the 1912 strike of dockworkers in Fort William and the differing opinions during the protests of 1913 only reinforced the underlying interclass and intra-ethnic conflict that characterizes this period.

By 1914, the notion that socialists and violence were synonymous had been planted in the minds of many in the community. So too had the role of immigrants within socialist organizations and their role in radicalizing local union activities. The limitations and strengths of socialism at the Lakehead revolved around the issues of both ethnicity and ideology. Coming to grips with these two factors had enabled Harry Bryan and others to successfully mobilize workers to protest their conditions, and had resulted at times in real electoral successes. The events that took place between 1900 and 1913 demonstrate that, despite the existence of significant division, the bonds of solidarity could prevail. As one local newspaper, ironically and for other reasons, aptly observed: "For the time being the labor and socialist parties, which have recently been drifting apart, merged their interests. The hatchet was buried, a love feast was held." Yet, it went on, "this alliance was accompanied by strident rhetoric in which the movement's enemies were denounced as 'traitors,' 'unscrupulous capitalists,' and 'pig headed mutts,' to say nothing of other terms of derision."[164] Deep-seated patterns that had taken hold would make the working-class unity so feared by the newspaper a distant menace for its mainstream readers, and a much sought-for objective for labour and the left at the Lakehead.

2

Repression, Revitalization, and Revolutions
1914-18

The First World War irrevocably changed the nature and characteristics of the left in Canada. The four years of the war saw Canada undergo one of the most remarkable periods of economic and social change in its history.[1] At the same time that Canada was supposedly coming of age as a nation, the working class experienced one of its most harrowing periods.[2] Persecution turned to unrest, and led to an increasing radicalization of the Canadian workforce.[3] The Lakehead left was no different and was caught up in these dramatic changes. The period between 1900 and 1914 had been challenging for socialists in the region. Friction between employers, civic officials, and workers had often led to violent conflicts. It was also a period of growth, with the formation of dozens of unions and the establishment for the first time of socialist organizations composed of workers from all ethnic backgrounds.

Although the participation of Finns in particular had resulted in substantial success, ethnic prejudice within the general society and among the Anglo-Saxon trade union aristocracy led to divisions and weakened solidarity. For workers at the Lakehead, the war merely proved to be a further "embittering experience," much as it was for their brothers and sisters across the country.[4] Its conclusion, coupled with the events in Russia in October 1917, led to a "sense of grievance" among many that provided an opening for a more radical form of social and political protest that would successfully challenge the power of the Trades and Labour Congress of Canada (TLC).[5]

The end of the war transformed the world of Lakehead leftism. Recent immigrants, with the apparent exception of the Italians, turned en masse to more radical organizations. Despite the Canadian government's eagerness to persecute all members of the working class regardless of ethnic background, Anglo-dominated unions and organizations were more than willing to differentiate themselves from Finnish, Ukrainian, and any other "foreign" workers.[6] Second, by 1914 class conflict at the Lakehead often had more to do with issues of ethnicity than with class. During the war, anti-war sentiments galvanized socialists and labourites, syndicalists and social democrats, yet ethnic prejudices further complicated these relationships.[7] Ethnically based conflict, often accompanied by bouts of violence, polarized Fort William and Port Arthur into "foreigners" and "non-foreigners." Despite all this, however, the First World War also brought the left together in new and surprising ways. The Russian Revolution, in addition to being a new force in western agitation, also sparked renewed enthusiasm for socialism at the Lakehead.[8]

Even before the outbreak of war, the situation facing workers at both the Lakehead and across Canada looked grim. The prewar depression that began in 1912 and dragged through the first years of the war decimated union ranks and left "an army of unemployed that furnished the first huge wave of recruits for the Canadian Expeditionary Force in August 1914."[9] At the Lakehead, the end of the wheat boom paralyzed the local economy, throwing thousands of workers out of their jobs; those lucky enough to still have work suffered drastic wage cuts.[10] By 1915, many of the region's largest employers had shut their doors, leading to an abrupt decline in the region's population.[11] In the first three years of the war, Fort William alone saw its population decrease from 27,000 in 1914 to 21,000 in 1915 and 19,000 by 1916.[12] Business depression accompanied population decline. A sizeable portion of those now unemployed and those who had left the region were members of the various branches of the Social Democratic Party of Canada (SDPC), the only socialist organization still operating in the region. Socialists, however, continued to voice concerns and, despite ever-increasing marginalization, began to subtly alter the political and social landscape in preparation for the postwar period. After 1916, socialist activism and class polarization increased together.[13]

The outbreak of war only made a bad situation worse. Socialists at the Lakehead soon found themselves the objects of suspicion. In the case of the many Finns and Ukrainians in the region, oppression and suspicion hardened into repression. As the work of Franca Iacovetta has demonstrated, "the First World War provided the pretext for the Canadian state to deal with foreign-born labour radicals through disenfranchisement and deportation of even naturalized citizens."[14] In many respects, the war provided both traditional trade unionists and government officials with an opportunity to deal with radical socialists. The war also served to reveal the deep mistrust of "foreigners" that still existed in the region. The belief in the foreigner-violence connection did not lessen despite the dramatic decrease in labour unrest in the region in late 1913 and early 1914.

Replacing the labour unrest, however, were growing tensions between local labour and socialist organizations.[15] For example, during the provincial election of 1914, Fort William socialists nominated a candidate to run in direct opposition to candidates supported by the local trade unions. This was typical of the lack of cooperation between "possibilists," "impossibilists," and Independent Labour Party (ILP) supporters throughout the province.[16] Although the ILP under Frederick Urry and the local branches of the SDPC had been adamant in their opposition to militarism and imperialism in late 1913, they quickly threw their support behind calls for the defence of Belgium and France.[17] The municipal election had resulted in a number of labour and socialist-supported candidates winning both council and school board seats, but it appears that many followed the lead of SDPCer Sid Wilson and backed resolutions supporting Canada's involvement in the war.[18] Once again, in the particular political climate of the Lakehead, a national pattern was transformed in its regional manifestation.

SDPCers such as Harry Bryan took a lead role during the 1914 provincial election campaign in Port Arthur and in the nomination of the SDPC local's secretary, S.F.H. Sangster.[19] Sangster polled a respectable 838 votes, the second-largest number in the province and 13 percent of the SDPC's provincial total.[20] Local socialists believed that the total would have been much higher if not for the "abolish the bar issue." SDPCers in particular were apt to blame the successes of Liberals and Conservatives on these parties' focus on the liquor trade as the cause of many ills, including poor economic conditions.[21]

Although he had succumbed to pressure from government officials and the Canadian Pacific Railway (CPR) in 1909 and took a position against the strikers during the Fort William freight handlers' strike. Louis Peltier's endorsement of socialism in 1914 reveals that a level of fluidity still existed in the region. Speaking to the Fort William Trades and Labour Council in July 1914, he argued that "being a socialist is no less [than being] a man. The socialist party and the labor party are the only two parties which stand clearly for labor, and when they remain divided as they were at the present time it only pleased the third party, or the so-called capitalist class. Every effort on the part of trades unionism to better the lot of mankind is socialism."[22] As Martin Robin suggests, however, "little was accomplished by the campaign of 1914 except to drive a wedge between independent labor and socialist groups. The 1914 vote for socialist and labor candidates was much smaller than in the minor campaign run three years earlier."[23] Once again, the Lakehead pattern does not precisely bear out the pattern seen in the country as a whole; in this region, the total vote in fact increased from 243 in 1911 to 838 in 1914.[24]

By the time of the 1915 civic elections, few in the region openly opposed the war. Such a position led to a moderate level of success for socialist and labour candidates, who gained seats on city councils, school boards, and public commissions in both cities.[25] Their success came at a cost. Although many voters believed in "the sincerity of labour's claims and the men who were their candidates," they still feared labour's ulterior goals of taking control of the city council. "Surely the labour element are not endeavoring to obtain control of the Council," as one concerned citizen wrote to the editor of the Port Arthur *Daily News*.[26] The views of "concerned citizens" aside, however, substantive gains had been made.

Unfortunately, at the same time, another, more ominous threat began to influence non-English socialists at the Lakehead. The general anti-war position of the SDPC before the war and its role in radicalizing local union activities during the strike of 1913 made socialists and non-English workers the subject of rumours and speculation regarding plots of espionage and sabotage.[27] As in many communities throughout Canada, this belief was rooted in two things that demonstrate how many residents of the twin cities imagined their communities' roles within both Canada and the world.[28] The editor of the Port Arthur *Daily News* best summarized what many in the region felt in an editorial published on 25 June 1915. He charged that Port Arthur, as a port of strategic national importance, needed to become more vigilant against impending threats to the community.[29] This position was strengthened by the apparent sabotage of a government wireless station in Port Arthur.[30]

The stationing of men from the local militia and police departments at those industries and services deemed critical only served to heighten tensions. Incidents between workers and soldiers increased during the first years of the war at the coal docks and grain elevators of both cities, including gun battles and fistfights. Although labourers from every ethnic group participated in the taunting and fighting, however, the local press targeted only "aliens" and known socialists in its condemnation.[31] As the work of Gerald Ross has revealed, "in spite of the perceived notion that the threat of sabotage came largely from the unemployed and impoverished workers, there was also strong sentiment among Anglo-Canadians and immigrant workers from all allied powers that the enemy aliens should be released from their jobs."[32] This resulted not only in the dismissal of thousands of workers across Canada but also in the establishment of work camps throughout Northwestern Ontario under the War Measures Act.[33]

Internment plainly often had more to do with relieving governments of the burden of maintaining the unemployed than with questions of national security. It was of a piece with a growing climate of hostility against "foreigners," one from which members of the left were by no means exempt. Moreover, it fit comfortably into a long-standing state interest in repressing labour. Workers participating in strikes were considered by local authorities to be unemployed and they, along with "any suspicious individuals," could be arrested and interned.[34] For many, internment meant both being sent to work camps located in the Canadian hinterland and confiscation of property. Far from doing nothing, internees were required to build additional camps and their labour was used for road building, land clearing, woodcutting, and railway construction.[35]

By November 1914, the Dominion government had established registration offices in both Port Arthur and Fort William.[36] Of the estimated 5,441 non-prisoners-of-war interned in Canada during the war, roughly 5,000 were of Ukrainian origin and an additional 80,000 were registered as "enemy aliens."[37] In Fort William, 2,270 (or 9 percent of the total population of 24,071) were designated as enemy aliens.[38] Although changing economic conditions and a growing labour shortage led to the release of many of the internees, by 1916 the number had risen to over 3,450 (15 percent of the population).[39] The city of Port Arthur reported similar numbers. By December 1914, 223 men, 111 children, and 62 women had been registered as enemy aliens out of a total population, based on the most recent census, of 590 Austrians, 535 Galicians, 104 Germans, and 189 Poles who fell under the enemy alien category.[40]

The Lakehead held one of the largest prewar Ukrainian communities in the country, and although little is known about them, they comprised a significant portion of the working class. This included a purported Ukrainian-language branch of the SDPC.[41] The nature of the Ukrainian workforce in Fort William was similar to those in Edmonton and Montreal. Ukrainians in Fort William predominantly worked for the CPR as freight and coal handlers, and in the local iron foundries in the eastern part of the city. The work was hard, heavy, dirty, and often some of the most dangerous in the region. These areas of employment were also ones in which labour unrest had been rampant before 1914, and thus were targeted by officials.[42]

Italians living in Fort William and Port Arthur were also treated with suspicion despite the significant role Italian troops were playing in the fight against Germany. This had more to do, however, with their involvement in past labour unrest than with any real concern felt by employers over the loyalty of their employees, a situation highlighted by the fact that preference continued to be given to Austrian and German workers in both cities. So acute had the situation become by June 1915 that the Italian consular agent, E. Marino, publicly criticized local hiring practices. He chided employers for ignoring the fact that, unlike many in the region, these men were "offering themselves for service in defense of the principles [for] which Britishers were fighting in France against Germany."[43]

Those most targeted for their "socialistic tendencies," however, were members of the Finnish community. In large part, such attention was due to the leading role many Finns in Port Arthur and Fort William had played in the establishment of the Finnish Socialist Organization of Canada (FSOC) in early 1914. That March, the Port Arthur Finnish Labour Temple had in fact been the site of the first convention, which had been attended by delegates representing 3,062 Finns from Finnish socialist societies across Canada.[44] From Northwestern Ontario, locals from Port Arthur (359 members), Fort William (235 members), Nolalu (16 members), Nipigon (42 members), Kivikoski (39 members), Fort Frances (27 members), Intola (37 members), and Wolf Siding (37 members) were present.[45] Those in attendance included a young Sanna Kannasto, who was given the task of organizing both men and women in Northern Ontario.[46]

Prompted by the FSOC's apparent interest in radicalizing Lakehead workers and the salience of socialists in its leadership, the RCMP began an intensive campaign of harassment. As future Industrial Workers of the World (IWW) and Communist organizer Amos Tobias (A.T.) Hill later recalled, more than once the RCMP would "march to the [Finnish] hall during just an ordinary dance, or during the middle of a play, and stop everything, then [demand] naturalization papers or other forms of identification to prove that they were 'loyal Canadians.'" It was not uncommon for a dozen people attending a dance to be arrested and imprisoned in the local jail for a couple of days.[47]

Considering the ethnic factionalism that defined the experience of the working class at the Lakehead before the war, it should come as no surprise that the predominantly Anglo-controlled labour organizations remained relatively quiet about this issue. Even as hundreds of local workers were interned, the local trades and labour councils supported government officials. Only when federal or municipal officials intended to let employers use "alien labourers" did they protest.[48] Workers, who had stood shoulder to shoulder in strikes before the war, were divided further between those labelled "enemy aliens" and those who were not.[49] For all those deemed to be a menace, real or imagined, the threat of deportation was an ever-present danger. This included any who spoke out against municipal, provincial, and federal authorities or against the war in general.[50]

Although many in the twin cities were concerned over the activities of the ILP and the TLC, the rise of the SDPC and the accompanying increase in Finnish radicalism received the bulk of local attention. For example, even before the war, Mayor John Oliver of Port Arthur had singled out Finnish socialists for their allegedly anti-British and anti-Canadian position.[51] He pleaded on more than one occasion for the Minister of Justice to "help in keeping this condition from spreading to other places, as you are no doubt aware this City has a very large foreign population, of which the greater number are Finnish, and it is possible that three-quarters of these are socialists."[52]

By 1915, union membership in both Port Arthur and Fort William had declined dramatically, membership in the English-language branches of the SDPC in both cities had dwindled to the point that the Port Arthur SDPC branches barely operated, and the SDPC-controlled newspaper the *Wage-Earner* had gone bankrupt.[53] Nationally, Finnish-language branches of the SDPC experienced significant losses as their membership dropped from 3,062 in 1914 to 1,867 by the end of 1915.[54] In contrast, the newly established Fort William Socialist Local 25 had grown to 235 members. When combined with the Port Arthur local, this gave the region the two largest and most active Finnish socialist locals in Canada.[55] Although membership in the local Finnish-language branches of the SDPC remained relatively stable during the war, they still experienced crushing financial constraints as the war progressed.[56]

The continued complacency of the local trades and labour councils and the growing hostility towards unions and non-British workers did not sit well with many socialists in the region. With his belief in the ineffectiveness of the existing organizations confirmed, and desiring a more robust ideological atmosphere, local printer Fred E. Moore spearheaded in May 1915 a movement to re-establish some form of socialist party. Unsure of the SDPC's stance on key issues, he contacted the Dominion Executive in Berlin, Ontario, to inquire about this and the fate of the branch established by William Hicks in 1912.

The head of the Ontario section, an enigmatic figure named W. Manthus, granted Moore permission to form a new English-language branch of the SDPC in Fort William as long as the disgraced Hicks was in no way associated with it. Moore quickly began the process of establishing the new branch.[57] He appears to have also contemplated the creation of an associated paper, but decided against it after his father counselled against such a move and urged him to be wary of the working class.[58] The position of the local labour councils did not help the situation either. Speaking to local unionists on 19 June 1915, J.C. Watters, president of the TLC, argued that the congress, not socialist organizations such as the SDPC, were responsible for the improvement in wages, conditions, and the standard of living conditions throughout Canada.[59] Shortly after, the Port Arthur *Daily News* openly attacked the Trades and Labour Council's backing of a strike by regional plumbers. Declaring the strike "more than unpatriotic," the view of the *Daily News* was that any British workman involved cared little for the needs of the nation and that these fights over "union rules" were both shortsighted and selfish. Workers throughout the region were put on notice that for "hampering the defensive measures of the government ... they are inviting their ruin."[60]

For local authorities, the most alarming change was the formation, mostly by immigrants, of a branch of the Industrial Workers of the World (IWW, or Wobblies) in Port Arthur and Fort William. Well known for its participation in labour action throughout the United States, "the early sweep of IWW industrial unionism," according to early IWW organizer and future Communist stalwart A.T. Hill, "was presented as a working class organization across the continent."[61] Established in reaction to the American Federation of Labor (AFL) decision not to support the organization of industrial workers, the IWW was formed in 1905 to give the working classes in industrial settings an opportunity to organize and mobilize.[62] During this period, it also emphasized industrial unionism, rather than direct political action, as the key to social change. Under the guidance of William Haywood, and largely through the activities of the Western Federation of Miners, the IWW quickly distinguished itself as one of the most active socialist organizations of the period before the First World War.

Upset with the activities of the local AFL unions and the general apathy towards lumber workers on the part of both the Trades and Labour Congress and local labour councils, Hill and Harry Bryan (who, after establishing a branch of the SDPC in Dorion in 1913, appears to have organized on behalf of the Wobblies for a brief period), established an IWW presence sometime in 1916. The IWW carried out its activities through Lumber Workers Industrial Union (LWIU) support circles located in the largely Finnish lumber camps that dotted the countryside around the twin cities.[63] The IWW first entered Northwestern Ontario through the Mesabi Iron Range in Minnesota.[64] After establishing a foothold within both the mining and lumber unions in that state, it worked through seasonal Finnish workers such as Hill to infiltrate mining and lumber camps in both Northeastern and Northwestern Ontario.[65]

Although the IWW appealed to many English-speaking workers, the backbone of the IWW during this period was the FSOC. The previous FSOC branches found in those communities that were dependent on the lumber industry began to favour the IWW. The change had a lot to do with the conversion of leading organizers to the Wobbly cause. Hill, for example, was such an individual.[66] In the particular milieu of the Lakehead left, seemingly hard-and-fast ideological and tactical lines separating organizations of different types frequently proved far less formidable on the ground than they appeared in theory.

Hill's story before arriving in Northwestern Ontario is typical of those of many Finns. On arriving in North America, he worked as a seasonal worker for a number of years in both the United States and Canada, alternating between jobs in North Dakota, Montana, Minnesota, and Northwestern Ontario. Like most Finnish migrants during this period, he belonged to a socialist family that had fled a turbulent and often hostile political climate in Finland. In the United States, this socialist background found expression through the IWW and his participation in strikes such as the Copper Country Strike of 1913.[67] His involvement in Eugene Debs's 1912 election campaign and time spent at the Marxist Work People's College *(Työväen Opisto)* reinforced his desire to participate in radical labour action.[68]

Unlike most existing organizations in Canada, the IWW provided immigrant workers with the opportunity to become involved in the actual workings of the union, and had low membership fees compared with those charged by AFL and TLC affiliates. Its membership cards were transferable from union to union. Most important, however, was the IWW's ability to remain consistent and relatively focused in purpose and actions. As Donald Avery has stated, the IWW was not preoccupied "with sterile ideological controversy: despite their syndicalist underpinnings their attention was focused on specific grievances."[69] In late 1915, Hill began organizing and agitating in the small lumber town of Fort Frances, Ontario, to establish an IWW presence in the region. With the help of the Fort Frances Finnish section of the SDPC, he organized workers under the IWW banner at the Shevlin Clark Sawmill and other company camps.[70] In keeping with the IWW's general philosophy, the goal of the Lumber Workers Industrial Union Local 120 was the overthrow of capitalism by industrial, not political, action.[71]

Lumber work presented unique challenges for socialist organizers, however. Unlike in mining, where sites were often organized around a central location, the lumber industry was decentralized and composed of a series of "camps" with no central location aside from the company's head office, which was often located hundreds of kilometres away.[72] Despite these obstacles, the LWIU succeeded in organizing workers in the northwestern United States and Canada before and during the early years of the First World War. Predictably, local, provincial, and federal authorities greeted the IWW's re-entry into Canada with hostility. The American IWW leadership's prewar adoption of sabotage as a means of protest only heightened the concern of officials already worried about such tactics being employed by enemy aliens.[73] Although the Canadian leadership attempted to distance itself from this position and emphasize the IWW's nonviolent nature, its position as a revolutionary organization, and the perception by many that revolution equalled violence, only increased the tension at the Lakehead. As a result, officials began to attack local Finnish socialists, regardless of affiliation, in an attempt to root out socialist tendencies. The IWW's general lack of support from Anglo-Canadian workers further isolated it and its non-Anglo supporters.[74]

The threat of unrest increasingly concerned employers in Fort William and Port Arthur as labour became scarce in the twin cities. Many of the workers who left may well have been prompted by rumours of an impending policy of conscription.[75] Many workers involved in the strikes were no doubt among those who left for the United States over concerns that it would not be long before legislation mandating conscription would be passed by the federal government.[76] The Western Dry Dock and Shipbuilding Company of Fort William, for instance, reported that it was losing men daily, and that it was becoming increasingly difficult to meet demands. Many of the company's projects were war related. Mayor Donald Cowan even went so far as to petition the Militia Department to determine whether shipbuilding was an essential industry.[77] It was a gesture, echoing the region's violent history, that suggested the depth of official concern.

Tensions came to a head when the federal government announced that it was contemplating conscription. For reasons unknown, both unions and the Trades and Labour Councils in both Port Arthur and Fort William reversed their previous position and joined local socialists in condemning the idea.[78] The subsequent qualified decision of the TLC to approve the government's conscription policy exacerbated the growing divide within the region. Predictably, local newspapers began to attack all those who opposed both the idea of conscription and the signing of national service cards. In turn, socialists became more vocal in their denunciation of the local press. Most meetings occurred in the Port Arthur Finnish Labour Temple, which was still under the control of the local Finnish branch of the SDPC.

In January 1917, 700 men in Port Arthur rallied to the banner of the SDPC at a meeting about the National Service Bureau and its plans for a manpower survey, accurately interpreted as a first step towards a conscription policy. "The government ignored us then and has done so since," Bryan declared, "except when they wanted to use us for their purposes." He also proclaimed to the largely "foreign-born" audience that "they [the government] will never force me to sign this card, but they may put me where it is unnecessary to do so. If they made a practice of this, they will have a large board bill to pay. How many of you are willing not to sign the cards and go behind the bars if necessary? To be behind them would not be much more a form of slavery than that we are now in." To those who stood up and began to cheer, Bryan said: "This was the kind of spirit that will make them [the government] sit up and take notice."[79]

The Port Arthur gathering was one of many that would sweep the Lakehead and the west, culminating in the famous Walker Theatre meeting in Winnipeg, whose ringing declarations against the war and for the Russian Revolution were to resound later in the trials following the Winnipeg General Strike.[80] A growing spirit of revolt was in the air. Yet there was, in Port Arthur, an equally powerful spirit of dissension. Bryan went so far as to attack the "Anglos" who were reluctant to make their private anti-war feelings public. About half the audience at the Port Arthur meeting refused to declare themselves in favour of his motion.[81]

The Russian Revolution also appears to have led to a revitalization of activity on the part of both labour and socialist organizations at the Lakehead. As William Rodney has suggested: "The news that the Tsar of Russia had been deposed, coinciding more or less as it did with the conscription issue, did much to break down the inhibitions against organization and expression within the labour and radical groups caused by the war effort and, more particularly, by the War Measures Act."[82] Debates immediately erupted as to what the events in Russia meant for the war effort. Initially, the media covered favoured articles syndicated from Toronto and Ottawa on the concern over the new Russian government's continued participation in the war effort. As one member of Port Arthur's Russian community stated to the editor of the Port Arthur *News-Chronicle*: "As a result of the changed conditions in Russia I think the chief feature will be a more vigorous presectuion [sic] of the war. The nation will have but one enemy to fight, the Germans at the front."[83] After reports that this would be the case, local media tended to cover Russian military successes in much the same fashion as Italian and other allied offensives.

By March, the exact situation in Russia had become unclear. Rumours began to circulate that a counter-revolution was now a possibility. As one newspaper report exclaimed: "The work of agitators whose efforts are designed to hinder the successful accomplishment of the revolution is becoming apparent with the subsidence of activity on the part of the military, which forced the supporters of the old regime to keep in hiding during the early days of the upheaval."[84] As the spring of 1917 turned to summer, the tone of local newspaper articles increasingly began to suggest that something was wrong in Russia. Lenin was often blamed. Suddenly Canadian socialists were front and centre in the public eye, as both their supporters and their critics drew direct and tenuous connections between their propaganda and the Russian situation.

Lenin's willingness to talk peace with the Germans led to sweeping criticism and mounting concerns. His determination to take Russia out of the war intensified Western anxiety about socialism and gave new strength to the forces of repression.[85] Sensational headlines such as "Lenine [sic] Would Release Million Hun Prisoners" became the norm.[86] Corporate interests watched the situation with concern. The Mutual Elevator Company of Fort William, for example, asked the city council for increased protection.[87] It was the IWW and the Finns that initially took the lead in supporting the Russian Revolution, which had profoundly influenced political developments in Finland.[88] The overthrow of the Tsar, in particular, was very popular among local Finns. For many, Russia was seen as the Finns's ancient adversary. Finland had often been caught in the middle of Russian conflicts with Sweden and, in 1809, had fallen completely under the domination of the Russian Empire. Tsar Alexander I's process of Russification of the now Grand Duchy of Finland irked many. Tensions only mounted when Tsar Nicolas II, on assumption of the throne in 1894, intensified the process.[89] For nationalist Finns, the revolution provided an opportunity to seize independence.[90] A Finnish parliament was established and, on 6 December 1917, it declared independence from Soviet Russia. The resulting civil war, fought between nationalist "Finnish White Guards" (who received military support from Germany) and the "Finnish Red Guards," the largely working-class supporters of the Soviet system, lasted until 1918.[91] The victorious White Guards began a campaign terrorizing those who had been members of the Social Democratic Party or who had merely sympathized with the Red cause.[92] Many of these "Reds" migrated, eventually making their way into the bush camps of Northern Ontario.[93] Throughout North America, this new influx of Finns brought with them their dedication to socialism and breathed new life into the Finnish and non-Finnish socialist organizations that predated their arrival.[94]

According to A.T. Hill, local Wobblies "hailed the Russian Bolshevic [sic] revolution as something that had followed the IWW economic blueprint."[95] Mass meetings to protest the continued involvement of Canadian armed forces in Russia were organized.[96] A "Friends of Russia" committee, composed of workers representing a number of organizations and trade unions in Port Arthur and Fort William, was also established. And, as Hill remembered, within the columns of the newly created *Vapaus* newspaper, members of the Finnish community could engage with recent events in Russia and forge closer bonds with fellow Finns working in other lumber camps.[97]

Many Wobblies viewed the Russian Revolution in much the same way as other socialist organizations in North America. Its success was seen as an indication that the end of capitalism was at hand and that workers in North America should take heart from the events in Russia.[98] Despite becoming largely inactive in the region during the second half of the First World War, the IWW remained vigorous across the border in Minnesota and Wisconsin. Most notably, the Superior District Lumber Workers Industrial Union No. 500 continued to agitate and to lead strikes.[99] It was among the lumber workers in Wisconsin and Minnesota and in classes taken at the Work People's College in Duluth, Minnesota, that Hill spent much of the war.

Drawn to the growing unrest at the Lakehead, Hill moved to Port Arthur in 1917 and dedicated himself to the activities of local Finnish socialists. On behalf of the IWW LWIU, Hill and those he recruited toured much of Northwestern Ontario in an attempt to organize workers and drum up subscriptions for *Vapaus*. Much of the IWW's attention was focused on the Russell and Newaygo Timber Company and its operations within the district of Thunder Bay. Despite high hopes, in the end Hill was fired (both for his agitation and for conflicts with Lutheran Finnish workers). There now existed within the camps a rift between non-socialists and socialists, and debates over the various interpretations of Marxism.

The IWW appealed greatly to immigrant workers in Northwestern Ontario. As Holmer Borg, a Swedish lumber worker and IWW organizer, recalled in 1972: "The IWW organized through its members. Every member was expected to organize, not necessarily by having well organized meetings, [but] simply by talking among workers."[100] The IWW also tended to focus on the immediate issues that faced workers where they organized.[101] In addition, many recent immigrants were drawn to unions whose organizers actually spoke their language.[102] Most of the other established trade unions tended to send English-speaking organizers who had little or no actual experience in the regions they were visiting or with the workers they were trying to organize.

Largely because of the revitalization of the SDPC and the formation of the IWW, the police spent much of the First World War watching socialist organizations at the Lakehead very closely, the Finns in particular.[103] Although many Finnish socialists, such as Martin Hendrickson, F.J. Syrjälä, and Sanna Kallio-Kannasto, toured Canada at the start of the First World War speaking against the conflict and selling literature, this surveillance often had as much to do with domestic concerns as with international events.[104] One report by the Dominion Police referred to the Finns in Port Arthur as "anarchists pure and simple."[105] As increasingly became the case in the months following the first Russian Revolution in February 1917, the ethnicity of the strikers became the main point of discussion in local newspapers and in negotiations with government officials. A strike by pulp mill workers and freight handlers in Fort William in April, for instance, immediately led to concerns over a general strike and a focus on the fact that many "non-naturalized immigrants" were on the strike committee.[106]

A more radical opposition to conscription accompanied the renewed strike activity. Since 1914, SDPC locals at the Lakehead had increasingly aligned themselves with the party's anti-war position. For example, over 850 men and women, mostly from the Finnish and Greek communities of both cities, attended a meeting chaired by Bryan in the Port Arthur Finnish Labour Temple on 3 June and passed a resolution condemning conscription.[107] Although the 1916 anti-registration rallies featured a number of moderate socialists, it is telling that the leadership of this particular struggle was composed of those who, in a few short years, would form the core of the local Communist movement.[108] The meeting featured an open discussion by those in favour and those against conscription.[109] Both Herbert Barker and A.E. Kettridge, members of the Port Arthur SDPC English-branch executive, pointed out to those in attendance that "twenty-three men owning ninety out of 101 industries control ninety per cent of the capital of the country." They went on to argue that a "selective draft" would mean "that the government can pick but the Liberals and labor men and keep the power of the country in their hands indefinitely." Many applauded William Welsh when he told the government officials present, "I'll fight for my country when you show me where my country is." Bryan, quoting from a speech made by German socialists to the Reichstag, told those present that "it is the duty of workers to fight the tyranny of government in their own country. Because a man is born on a piece of land which he never owns is no reason for his having to fight for it." Supporting conscription, he argued, "means that we favor putting a debt on the heads of our children. They will have to pay the national debt when we are dead."[110]

Tensions came to a head in late July, when Fort William police uncovered the existence of an anti-conscription league operating in the twin cities. Headquartered in Port Arthur, the league's membership drew heavily from members of the SDPC. Its executive consisted of Kettridge (president), Barker (treasurer), and J. Brown (secretary).[111] Despite attempts by local officials assisted by the militia, meetings occurred in secret and, as one newspaper reported in September, "all is quiet and [unclear] along Bay street, especially in the neighborhood of the [Finnish Labour Temple] which is generally supposed to be the headquarters of the socialistic and anti-conscription element."[112]

In early October 1917, about 1,100 elevator employees in both Port Arthur and Fort William went on strike over wages, hours, and working conditions. All activity in both cities ground to a halt as the ports could no longer take incoming ships and the CPR became congested when grain coming from the west could no longer be unloaded. Much of the discussion in both cities regarding the strike focused on conflicting reports over how many "aliens" were involved. The Grain Elevator Workers' Union Local 934, in particular, took issue with claims by employers and some officials that workers of certain (i.e., non-English) "nationalities" on strike had been discriminating against returned soldiers. The unions involved claimed that only 40 percent of the militants were "aliens," whereas the employers reported to local newspapers that such people made up over 80 percent of the strikers. The ethnicity of the strikers was clearly a paramount issue in public discussions of the strike.[113] By the fifth day, the workers were being ordered back to work, on pain of being arrested. They refused. Only after the personal intervention of Prime Minister Robert Borden – who assured strikers that arbitration proceedings would be instituted and that the government would assume control of the elevators – did they return to work after two more days.[114]

The spectre of socialism and the involvement of aliens in the growing labour unrest in the region also figured prominently during the run-up to the federal election of 1917, the election that, according to Desmond Morton and Terry Copp, "gave Canadian labour its first real opportunity to test its strength at the ballot box."[115] Socialists at the Lakehead united behind labour candidates throughout Northwestern Ontario.[116] The local ILP, operating under the banner of the Ontario Labour Party created in Hamilton, nominated former alderman and recently wounded soldier Sid Wilson.[117] Wilson declined, however, and James Dunbar took his place. Dunbar's campaign centred on the slogan "It is a struggle between democracy and autocracy." Specifically attacking the Borden government, he described the Conservatives as "organized hypocrisy" and declared that "Borden was either a traitor to the principles of conservatism or a traitor to democracy."[118] Dunbar disturbed the local establishment press because he seemed capable of uniting pro- and anti-labour elements in his opposition to conscription. "This little group of men have suddenly buried their own name," the editor of the newspaper Port Arthur *Daily News* commented, "which, by their conduct and advocacy they had utterly discredited and now bob up as independent labor men. Life has its ironies, but the leopard cannot change its skin and the autocrats of the Socialist party will, without a doubt, seek to be the autocrats of the new Independent Labour Party."[119]

Dunbar and Albert Hugh Dennis, a candidate in the riding of Fort William-Kenora, received the endorsement of English and non-English-speaking socialists. Their platforms focused on the unequal treatment meted out to various groups of workers, and generally condemned capitalism. Both men, speaking at the Port Arthur Finnish Labour Temple in early December, argued that within three months Germany would experience what had happened in Russia. Canada, they suggested, would soon follow suit. "For my part," one speaker finished to thunderous applause, "I hope to see it."[120]

Despite his ostensible enthusiasm for radical change, however, the centrist Dunbar distanced himself from socialist organizations in Port Arthur as the campaign progressed. He declared that he was not "a representative of the Socialist party in Port Arthur or any other association and that he was nominated as a straight Independent candidate by the Trade Unions in Port Arthur." In fact, his attitude revealed the rift that continued to exist within the region. In his very short speech to those gathered at the Port Arthur Finnish Labour Temple, he declared that "if the working class stood together they could win" and denied being a socialist in any sense of the word. Rumours even circulated in the city that he had gone so far as to send a letter to the local Liberal Association endorsing Laurier's candidacy.[121]

Such gestures were not enough to win Dunbar and Dennis the support of the mainstream media. Its attacks on them were doubtless sharper because they were seemingly uniting, in an original manner, the region's disparate socialist and labour elements. "Genuine Labor Union Men," the Unionist candidate for the riding of Port Arthur–Rainy River, F.H. Keefer, advised the local newspapers "are like Samuel Gompers – their President fighting and working to win the war."[122] Despite the very vocal and public support given to the war effort by labour councillors such as Sid Wilson, union and socialist organizers were increasingly targeted because of their position on conscription and their support for the events in Russia. The advertisements on behalf of both Robert Manion, the Fort William-Kenora Unionist candidate and future Conservative Party leader, and E.H. Keefer stooped to unprecedented levels of viciousness. Daily, banners could be found in local newspapers suggesting that "Between Keefer and Dunbar, the Kaiser Would Vote for Dunbar!" and "Shall we go on with the war in which we started three and a half years ago, or shall we quit as the Russians have done?"[123]

The ILP candidates in both ridings were viewed as "merely obstructionists." The party had been subverted by "socialist elements," declared the Liberal-supporting Port Arthur *News-Chronicle*.[124] Although the spectre of socialism and the appeal to prejudice against enemy aliens by Manion and Keefer carried the day, Dennis and Dunbar did receive over 2,000 votes each in their respective ridings.[125] These results and the formation of a new branch of the SDPC in Fort William and the election of Bryan as its secretary shortly afterwards certainly did not calm the fears of right-wing opinion,[126] which turned increasingly to the vilification of the Finns.

The increasing focus on the Finns in Port Arthur doubtless resulted in part from the shift in the focus of IWW agitation in Ontario to the Finnish Labour Temple in 1917. Throughout the winter of 1917-18, Hill and other Wobbly organizers set out from the city and successfully organized lumber workers throughout Northwestern Ontario under the IWW banner. Their success was limited to those regions not dominated by the railroad and AFL-affiliated unions, to lumber camps where Finnish workers were predominant, but in Fort William and Port Arthur, a series of strikes involving hundreds of workers between April and July were perceived to have been motivated by the Wobblies. Such a belief was strengthened by reports in April 1918 that "enemy aliens" intended to organize a massive strike in both cities to protest the war and internment. The agitators turned out to be non-enemy foreign socialists led by the Finns.[127]

Growing unrest and a series of barely averted strikes in May led the mayors of Port Arthur and Fort William to petition the provincial and federal governments for remedial action.[128] In June 1918, the federal government appointed C.H. Cahan, a wealthy Montreal lawyer and notorious alarmist throughout the war years, to examine the activities of the organization in the region.[129] Cahan's report was based on the testimony of local police officials and, most interestingly, "respectable labour leaders."[130] His findings supported the government's belief that a "Bolshevick [sic] conspiracy" was developing in those areas where Russian, Finnish, and Ukrainian workers could be found in large numbers. His report also concluded that the growing disturbances at the Lakehead and throughout the country had more to do with the activities of the Bolsheviks in Russia than with the war. As a result, Cahan's final report in September recommended that Ukrainian, Finnish, and Russian workers and their organizations be added to the list of "enemy aliens."[131] The Dominion government accepted his recommendations, and on 25 September 1918 passed an Order-in-Council declaring that, under the War Measures Act, "all socialist, syndicalist, anarchist and other subversive organizations" were illegal. Over fifteen socialist organizations were mentioned by name in this ban, including the IWW, SDPC, and FSOC, but, interestingly, not the Socialist Party of Canada (SPC).[132] In addition, most domestic and imported socialist publications were also declared illegal, including *Työmes* and *Industrialisti*.[133]

By 1918, the growing unrest among workers began to manifest itself in the pages of non-English-language newspapers across the country. Demonstrations and strikes became common. In response, officials at the Lakehead, fearing the worst, began to call for the suppression of all workers' organizations in the region. The earliest such calls were made by patriotic organizations such as the Great War Veterans' Association. They demanded that all "enemy alien" newspapers be suppressed, called for "compulsory badges for 'foreigners,'" and championed "forced labour for 'Austrians' and German men in Canada."[134] In Port Arthur and Fort William, this intensified nativism influenced the newly formed branches of the IWW, SDPC, and FSOC. It also affected the Finnish and Ukrainian communities. Both languages were declared "enemy languages."[135] Cahan, for example, suggested that the registration of aliens should include Russians, Ukrainians, and Finns, as they "are now being thoroughly saturated with the Socialistic doctrines which have been proclaimed by the Bolsheviki [sic] faction of Russia." This was also extended to the IWW for its radical actions before the war in the United States and western Canada, and the SDPC, as many of the leaders in Russia and in the Finnish Red Guards had been prominent in these two organizations.[136] The government also targeted the SDPC because its membership was largely composed of recent immigrants.[137]

The FSOC appealed its inclusion. In doing so, however, it drove a wedge between its membership and the socialist community at large. Although the organization needed to distinguish itself from other groups in order to become exempt, its leaders were not unlike other trade unionists and independent labourites who saved their organizations at the expense of class solidarity. For example, in his attempt to have both *Vapaus* and the FSOC reinstated by federal authorities, J.W. Ahlqvist, former secretary of the FSOC, attacked other organizations instead of discussing the merits of the workers they represented.[138] By December, the organization had succeeded and received permission to reorganize as the FSOC on the condition that it not be involved in any workers' party.

The suppression of the IWW, the SDPC, and other working-class organizations in 1918 did little to dampen the desire of workers in the region to organize and fight for immediate changes in working conditions and for the eventual restructuring of society. Although hampered in its ability to organize workers and play an active role in labour disputes, a makeshift apparatus of the IWW continued to operate and agitate under the guidance of Hill in small underground groups supported by the Finnish Federation of the SDPC.[139] In addition, Finnish and Ukrainian workers' organizations continued to operate, though in a much more limited capacity. Unorganized workers also continued to fight for recognition despite the threat of violence, incarceration, and impressments into military service. Lakehead organizers had many grounds on which they could organize local leftists.[140] For Finnish socialists at the Lakehead, the period, according to Nick Viita, was "fateful."[141]

Many of the workers' and cooperative restaurants in Port Arthur and Fort William closed. Even the Port Arthur Finnish Labour Temple, for example, was closed by the Canada Permanent Mortgage Company after the Finnish Building Company defaulted on its loan. Another result of the First World War was the movement of the Italian community in both Fort William and Port Arthur away from labour action. They had been key to the vibrant protests of the prewar period. Many had fought the Germans, serving in both the Canadian and Italian forces. Now they were persecuted by the Canadian state. Many chose silence, while others abandoned leftism for participation in mainstream political parties.[142] As Penny Petrone would later remember: "'Communist' [was] a word we whispered because it was supposed to be 'bad' although we did not know why."[143]

In his speech to the 1917 TLC convention, longtime labourite Louis Peltier captured the feeling of socialists at the Lakehead during the final years of the war: "Every wreath of smoke from the battlefields of Europe is weaving a rope that will hang every vestige of capitalism."[144] Such socialists felt themselves to be living in a time of drastic, even apocalyptic change. Moreover, many believed that they should respond to such a time with new kinds of organizations fighting for a more rigorous kind of socialism. The structure of socialist organizations operating at the Lakehead would shortly undergo a dramatic change. The February and October revolutions in Russia brought with them both new inspiration for local socialists and a focal point for attacks by anti-socialists. Government officials firmly believed that strikes, if left unchecked, would lead to a socialist uprising in Canada.[145] Subsequent government repression created a legacy of resistance.

Many of those interned later felt that the very internment camps intended to stem the influence of "agitators" galvanized and reinvigorated the movement. Internees, despite doing the same work under worse conditions, were paid far less than the actual value of their labour. As Lubomyr Luciuk has stated: "While passive resistance was common, some internees were more vigorous in protesting against the conditions in which they found themselves."[146] As a result, the end of the war did not bring about ethnic or class harmony. Socialists at the Lakehead, then, would appear to have been given the necessary catalyst for the construction of a renewed sense of purpose.

By the end of the First World War, a multitude of socialist organizations had made an appearance at the Lakehead. All shared the same goal: the transformation of society into one that was more equitable for the working masses. Such organizations inherited a complex Lakehead legacy, one that combined moments of divisiveness and ethnic tension with subtler bonds of unity and solidarity. Although the largely Anglo-Saxon leaders may have appeared to be the prime movers, they were subject to the concerns and desires of the "ethnic" majority, led by the Finns, which provided much of the rank-and-file strength. The participation of the Finns and their organizations at the Lakehead was clearly a prerequisite for the success of regional and, as Part 2 will establish, even national organizations.

PART 2

FROM WINNIPEG TO THE WORKERS' UNITY LEAGUE

3

"The Hog Only Harms Himself if He Topples His Trough"

The One Big Union, 1919-22

The end of the First World War was accompanied by a sense of resentment on the part of many workers. The year 1919, in particular, has assumed a mythical role in the struggle of labouring peoples from coast to coast. The Winnipeg General Strike and the creation of the One Big Union (OBU) has long been a watershed event. In fact, most works on the history of the left in Canada consider the strike to be the significant moment in the left's response to the intensified capitalist exploitation of workers following the First World War. Although the history of the strike and its aftermath remains a matter of debate among academics, it deeply influenced the nature of socialist organizations in Canada and ushered in a new era.[1] It also profoundly changed how the Canadian government viewed socialism in general.[2]

For these and other reasons, the period between 1919 and 1922 was also a pivotal one for socialists at the Lakehead. The Finnish proverb "The hog only harms himself if he topples his trough" perhaps best encapsulates this period.[3] Factionalism, ethnic tensions, and the growing differences between socialists about the nature, form, and substance of working-class activity defined this period at the Lakehead.

The OBU was toppled from power in the region more because of its own internal wrangling than because its enemies defeated it. The Lakehead – the

Figure 6 CTKL Poster, "The Pyramid of Capitalist System." *Courtesy of Lakehead University Library Archives*

major centre of the Lumber Workers Industrial Union (LWIU), which comprised a substantial proportion of the OBU's membership in 1920 – was the decisive battleground where the OBU's marginalization within Canadian labour was settled.[4] Many of the movement's difficulties – lack of ideological clarity, unresolved regional tensions, the enduring legacy of ethnic rivalries and chauvinism – were showcased here as nowhere else. As the 1920 convention held in Port Arthur reveals, not only did the predominantly Finnish LWIU branch at the Lakehead become the "unopposed master of the lumber camps" but in the end it also determined the fate of the OBU.[5] Harry Bryan, as in the years before the war, also played an important role in ushering in the changes at the Lakehead during this period. According to William Holder, a former OBU organizer, Bryan was "a guiding light" for many as he attempted to bridge the growing divide.[6]

Signs of division within the Lakehead left became increasingly apparent during the Winnipeg General Strike. Although historians have long made the jump in logic that Port Arthur and Fort William, known throughout the prewar period as two of the most unsettled regions of the country, would undoubtedly support the Winnipeg strikers, no such unrest occurred.[7] Simply, the absence of dramatic Lakehead support in the form of strike action in 1919 stemmed from the region's distinctive class chemistry in the prewar years, with past ethnically tinged violence and socialist/trade unionist tensions continuing to be influential and, in a sense, functioning as cautionary tales.[8] If prewar conflicts were any guide, few informed local people would have been oblivious to the risk of a substantial loss of life. Second, what today can be labelled the centre-left, embodied in a solid local Liberal-Labour (Lib-Lab) element, managed to mobilize much more effectively and appeal to a wider base of support.

At the Lakehead, the issue appears to have been one largely framed around the question of supporting the Winnipeg strikers, as 1919 was a period of relative labour harmony in the region. Although meetings led by Harry Bryan and attended by hundreds of unorganized Finns and Ukrainians attempted to place the item on the agendas of the Trades and Labour Councils of both cities, the establishment of a Citizens' Committee in Port Arthur and a Citizens' League in Fort William by a variety of trade unionists and Lib-Lab supporters, backed by both city councils, successfully defused the very real threat of strike action. Many socialists and trade unionists at the Lakehead believed wholeheartedly in what their Winnipeg comrades were ostensibly fighting to achieve, but although many of the barriers separating various workers began to break down in 1919, pre-existing divisions within the labour movement could not be overcome – a situation that recent scholarship has established was replicated throughout the country.[9]

Initially, the beneficiaries of the Lakehead's subdued "labour revolt" of 1919 were the labour centrists – the craft unionists, Lib-Lab supporters, and city councillors distrustful of both the Unionist government and the Winnipeg radicals. As one such centrist proclaimed, Lakehead workers had shown "more common sense" than the "ultra-radicals" of Winnipeg. Such labour centrists were generally Anglos who often disparaged political intransigence as the vice of foreigners. Although the Winnipeg General Strike may have in fact occurred after a referendum by the local trades council, it served the purpose of those who dominated the labour councils at the Lakehead in 1919 to exacerbate a public, government-fuelled perception that radicals had somehow become ascendant in Winnipeg, a situation to be feared in Port Arthur and Fort William. The following years, however, would reveal that these centrists, although powerful in their own circles, could not contain the more polarized class politics that emerged in the wake of Winnipeg.[10]

In the months following the Winnipeg General Strike, growing unrest at the Lakehead manifested itself not only against the various levels of government in Canada but also against the Trades and Labour Congress (TLC). The position of the congress towards the war and conscription had led to the creation of a secessionist movement rooted in western Canada. The defeat of the western-based James Watters by the craft-oriented Tom Moore in the race for the TLC presidency, and the subsequent rejection of a proposal to reorganize the TLC along industrial lines at its 1918 conference in Quebec City, resulted in the fracturing of the congress, partly along geographical lines.[11] One direct consequence was the formation of the OBU at the Western Labour Conference held in Calgary in March 1919. Like the Industrial Workers of the World (IWW), the OBU was organized along industrial rather than geographical lines, but unlike the IWW, the OBU never renounced participation in politics. In essence, the OBU, as described by Larry Gambone, was both a "child of impossibilism" and the offspring of syndicalism.[12] The Socialist Party of Canada (SPC) saw it as the means of both uniting the working class and educating the workers. This stance was reflected in the prominent role that many SPC leaders took in organizing, and later leading, the organization.[13]

The OBU played a distinctive unifying role by filling the vacuum created by the Canadian government's ban on the Social Democratic Party of Canada (SDPC), the IWW, and other socialist organizations. It also provided an outlet for workers in the region upset with the stance taken by the existing trade unions during the Winnipeg General Strike. The local OBU cadres, for example, were made up of former SPCers, SDPCers, Wobblies, and leading supporters of the Winnipeg strike such as Harry Bryan. Members of the Finnish Organization of Canada (FOC) had also begun to search for a new left-wing party to affiliate with after the SPC, SDPC, and Independent Labour Party (ILP) proved unsuitable.[14] The Russian Revolution was seen as a symbol of solidarity, the antithesis of the class collaboration and Lib-Lab centrism so evident in some Lakehead responses to the Winnipeg strike in 1919. The OBU provided a natural, if temporary, home for many of these radicals.

The OBU has been extensively studied from various perspectives,[15] but it has not as often been studied intensively in specific regions.[16] This examination of the Lakehead evidence suggests the need for some changes in the accepted interpretation of the OBU. In essence, it argues that although many radicals were drawn into the OBU, and although it did capture some of the spirit of the Russian Revolution and the Winnipeg General Strike, the new organization did not articulate a coherent alternative to labour centrism. Tensions between radicals and moderates within the OBU were not resolved. Many of the OBU's early supporters were "sold" on the pragmatic arguments for a new form of unionism, but were not persuaded by the case for impossibilist socialism. Between 1919 and 1922, as traditional trade unionists and apostles of the OBU fought each other for influence within the working-class movement, many of the OBU's weaknesses came to the fore. It proved especially vulnerable to more clearly developed and prestigious radical alternatives, especially those identified with a re-emergent IWW and with a strengthening Communist Party.

Without seeking to separate the OBU from the legacy of Winnipeg, it is important to remember that the events culminating in the OBU preceded the Winnipeg General Strike.[17] Although the post-strike trials were carried out with the obvious intention of linking the OBU with Winnipeg, much of the movement's history and trajectory were not directly derived from the strike itself.[18] Rather, they were influenced by long-standing critiques of the narrowness of craft unionism and the huge gap, blatantly obvious at the Lakehead, between the interests and achievements of the urban craft unionists and the often-desperate plight of the unorganized and stigmatized resource workers in the bush. Had the OBU not existed, there would have been other attempts to organize the unorganized workers of the woods, as the IWW, the OBU's nemesis and successor, demonstrated so clearly.

It is perhaps telling that of those who met in Calgary to discuss the formation of a new industrial organization with the goal of freeing western Canadian workers from the eastern-based Trades and Labour Congress, the only representatives to attend from east of Winnipeg were two workers from the

Lakehead.[19] As early as late December 1918, the Fort William Trades and Labour Council and its secretary, Fred Moore, had been interested in attending the "Western inter-provincial Convention" in Vancouver and Calgary.[20] In fact, it was decided that the referendum question on severing "affiliation with the international organizations as a first step to form an industrial organization of all the workers" would not include Port Arthur, "as the dividing line between East and West."[21]

The presence of representatives from the Lakehead, and the subsequent affiliation of many regional unions in the month following, reveal the commitment of many at the Lakehead to industrial unionism and social advocacy. In Port Arthur, over 1,380 workers and almost all the unions affiliated with that city's Trades and Labour Council joined the OBU under the leadership of William Checkley and J.P. Harris.[22] The appeal does not appear to have united workers in both cities, however. While sympathetic, workers and unions affiliated with the Fort William Trades and Labour Council appear to have been much more cautious in their support, just as they had been during the Winnipeg General Strike.

The popularity of the OBU in Port Arthur no doubt had to do also with its adoption of many of the IWW's principles. As a result, it appealed to the large number of Wobblies in the region who, due to government restrictions, could not operate in the open. The OBU's decision to adopt, in contrast to the IWW, a political policy also brought former Wobblies together with former members of the SDPC and SPC in the twin cities and the surrounding region. Especially appealing to the many Finnish socialists in the region were the conference's support for the "aims and purposes of the Russian Bolshevik and German Spartacist revolutions" and its demand that Canadian and allied troops withdraw from Russian territory.[23] The perception that the Winnipeg General Strike had been "perpetuated by the Bolshevik radicals behind the One Big Union," combined with the local ILP's and trade unionists' lack of support for action in both Port Arthur and Fort William, also prompted radicals in both cities to seek another vehicle for their politics.[24]

With the IWW now operating underground and the OBU attaining great stature due to its supposed connection with the Winnipeg General Strike, former Wobblies at the Lakehead elected to join the new organization en masse in order to have at least some vehicle for their activism. As A.T. Hill later recalled, the decision by the FOC to affiliate managed to solidify "the Finnish socialists and the IWW supporters" initially.[25] Most important, however, what the former members of the IWW in Northwestern Ontario brought with them to the OBU were the LWIU support circles established by Hill before the war and, combined with those members in British Columbia who had already joined, a membership that totalled over 12,000 by early 1920.[26] Issues to be resolved included what was to be done about those who had initially supported the OBU but who had since "retreated," and those workers who supported its goals but still belonged to the Internationals and paid dues to "those who are co-operating with the enemy, the master-class through the government."[27] One commentator suggested that the first lot were obsessed with respectability, while the second were unable to move without a leader and "are waiting for Moses to give them the lead."[28] The OBU viewed industrial unionism as the successor to the trade unions.[29] Inspiration was found in the early days of the Russian Revolution and the establishment of the Soviet state.[30]

Unlike most of their brothers and sisters in eastern Canada, socialists in both Port Arthur and Fort William wholeheartedly embraced the creation of the OBU. By October 1919, all 160 starch workers, all the bakers, and 18 general workers in Fort William united with the members of the IWW's LWIU in Port Arthur and joined.[31] The FOC's decision to declare itself a propaganda organization of the OBU created an auxiliary in Port Arthur that gained control of the Finnish Labour Temple by assuming its debt.[32]

In the midst of the election campaign of October 1919, local newspapers reported that the OBU had established branches in the region and that an OBU-affiliated Central Labour Council (CLC) had been established in Fort William.[33] The council adopted the structure, constitution, and bylaws of the Winnipeg council. Well attended by workers of all nationalities and by a variety of unions, the council heard predictions that the local trades and labour councils would disappear within the next few months.[34] The newly formed executive board of the CLC reported that both the coal handlers of Fort William, who had been responsible for a number of the strikes before the First World War, and the pulp and paper mill workers were engaged in discussions that would see them joining the OBU within the next few weeks. The Brotherhood of Carpenters local, consisting of 250 members, had already gone over to the OBU. The General Workers' Unit reported 60 new members in the last week alone.[35]

The OBU thus appealed to a variety of strata within the working class and, in principle and up to a point in reality, transcended the region's deep-seated ethnic divisions. Finnish workers, however, made up by far the largest ethnic group within its ranks. Well aware of this fact, and in order to discourage their further radicalization, police in both cities began a campaign of repression and harassment that, not incidentally, coincided with the 1919 election. Soon after the establishment of the first OBU branches in Port Arthur, for example, a series of raids shook that city's "Finnish quarter" (the area immediately around the Finnish Labour Temple on Bay Street). Both local and Royal North-West Mounted Police (RNWMP) admitted to having searched, on 9 October, seven homes described as "propaganda depots," confiscating a large amount of "Bolshevik" literature and arresting seven "Finlanders." These arrests were followed the next day by the search and seizure of "red" material at the Fort William bookstore of Edward Ollikkala, including a large amount of IWW literature.[36] The RNWMP was quick to point out that "of the three centers of foreign population," the Fort William coal dock section remained quiet and those arrested were not "enemy aliens," merely "aliens."[37]

The presence of the OBU at the Lakehead worried the TLC so much that it sent William Varley, an American Federation of Labor (AFL) organizer from Toronto, to the region in late October to address the local Trades and Labour Councils and the General Workers' Unit of the OBU in Fort William.[38] Varley devoted much of his time to demonizing the Winnipeg General Strike and the "hopelessness of this form of action." He contended that the AFL "had done much for the workers and was the only form of organization." Not surprisingly, his comments were met with ridicule, contempt, and often laughter.[39] Rather than promoting a discussion about bridging the growing division among the region's more radical unions, the ILP, and TLC members, the meeting intensified the general hostility towards the distant labour centre. ILP alderman A.H. Dennis, for example, contended that the TLC and it alone was to blame for the division that existed both locally and nationally among workers. As he suggestively remarked, "Labour had shown by the elections in Fort William, what they could do when it got together." The TLC, he suggested, "was out of harmony altogether with the workers," and it no longer represented "the workers any more than the Government did the people." The OBU, the majority present agreed, was a necessity because of the past actions of the TLC and the AFL. It appears that at this point both leftists and centrists at the Lakehead supported the OBU and identified it as the defender of regional interests against the aloof bureaucrats of the TLC. As one delegate, tired of the double-speak and manipulation demonstrated by Varley, declared: "Well, if that's what you want, let's hand in our charter."[40]

The Fort William Trades and Labour Council never did hand in its charter, but a motion put forward by Fred Moore to reaffirm the independence of the council and its resentment of the meddling on the part of the Trades and Labour Congress of Canada passed unanimously. Likewise, predictions that the council would disappear within months proved premature. In the aftermath of the meeting, the Fort William council, although adamant in its rejection of TLC meddling, also opted to distance itself from the OBU and the more "radical" socialists, as it had during the Winnipeg conflict. It appears that the more centrist element backed by the trade unionists and led by Moore once again reasserted itself, since a resolution to "completely and forever purge the council" of OBU business occurred shortly after.[41]

Fort William now had two labour councils. The OBU-affiliated CLC had the support of the longshoremen, coal handlers, and carpenters. In addition, over 100 members were also affiliated through the General Workers' Unit. Through his adamant campaign on behalf of the TLC, Varley had essentially undermined its support in the region. As one correspondent of the *One Big Union Bulletin* remarked: "If Varley will only stay here for about three months, we won't have many Internationals by that time."[42] Labourites in the twin cities, however, used their column in the Fort William *Daily Times-Journal* to quell increasing reports that a "split" had occurred in the labour movement at the Lakehead. "Nothing could be further from the truth," wrote the weekly columnist "Liberator." "Almost perfect harmony and universal satisfaction prevails." The Trades and Labour Councils in both Port Arthur and Fort William were described as having "up until recently cared for the business of the [OBU]." Despite the withdrawal of a number of OBU units from the labour councils following the establishment of the CLC, harmony existed, as they did not "function industrially." The recent election of Harry Mills, described as "by no means a satisfactory candidate," was nonetheless used as such an example of the solidarity present at the Lakehead.[43]

The early support for the OBU in Fort William was mirrored in Port Arthur. In addition to the Finnish lumber workers who had joined en masse, by mid-November the Port Arthur railroad workers had organized a unit and formed an executive made up of longtime agitators. This new unit of the CLC began to organize the Fort William railroad workers, who historically had had a much closer connection to the labour councils, as evidenced by the continued prominent role of one of their own, former mayor Louis Peltier, at the national level.

The civic employees in both cities also began holding meetings to discuss the formation of a joint unit, and by December A.E. Kettridge, former member of the local SDPC branch, reported that they, along with the workers in four barbershops, were ready to join.[44]

Unlike the labour councils and the ILP during the war, the OBU described the Finns of both cities as "good citizens" who, although because of custom "arbitrate their personal differences in their own way," had a "love for their land and wished to see it well governed." Their native radicalism was seen as a natural response to tsarist oppression, and its manifestation in Canada was a result of the similar authoritarianism of the Canadian government – a regime, the *Bulletin* argued in October 1919, that "does not understand these people, has turned an ignorant constabulary to harry them under the theory that this radicalism is revolutionary activity tending to subvert the Canadian institutions ... [if the Finns had] been left undisturbed by the minions of the law they would have believed that Canada was a land of good government. Now they are sure, in their own way of thinking, that Czarism is duplicated in Canada."[45]

The twin cities of Port Arthur and Fort William acted as a central meeting place for the thousands of workers participating in the resource-based activities that dominated much of the regional economy. Although not the location of organizing efforts or striking picketers, the two cities, particularly the Bay Street corridor in Port Arthur and the May Street area in Fort William, were home to the offices of many unions and socialist organizations and often became the centre of public displays of solidarity or protest over issues raging throughout the district of Thunder Bay. The Finnish Labour Temple on Bay Street in Port Arthur became the focal point for many Finnish socialists throughout Northwestern Ontario.

The industry in which Finns were most involved was the lumber industry. In the study of Canadian labour history, the woodsmen of Northwestern Ontario have received close attention. Ian Radforth has demonstrated that the OBU's success in the region can clearly be understood as a function of its ability to organize and absorb the previously IWW-controlled Finnish lumber unions, as indicated by the turnover of control over the Finnish Labour Temple from the IWW to the OBU in late 1919.[46] By mid-1920, however, the LWIU had "become the unopposed master of the lumber camps" in Northwestern Ontario.[47] Finns in British Columbia and Northwestern Ontario joined the LWIU because they believed it would incorporate "revolutionary socialism and militant unionism."[48] In fact, the FOC had begun incorporating the policies of the Third

International into its own program shortly after its formation in March 1919. By January 1921, it had proclaimed "its support for 'class Unionism' before 'industrial unionism.'" Its leadership criticized the OBU program as "one-sided" and declared "that it was not possible to build direct action industrial unions to replace the old existing trade (craft) unions."[49] As a result, the FOC did not join the OBU directly in 1920, opting instead to declare itself a propaganda organization.[50]

Numbering in the thousands, the Finnish lumber workers of Northwestern Ontario were of special interest to the OBU. Because of their strong past connections to the IWW, workers in the region – who had experienced much worse conditions and tyranny than their British Columbia comrades – were seen as sympathetic to the OBU's type of radicalism.[51] As one worker wrote in the *Bulletin:* "Lumber camps in BC are not anything to write home about, but they are a palace when compared to the 'Hog Pens' of Ontario." Drawn by promises to improve conditions, 500 new members signed OBU cards in the month of November alone.[52] By mid-December, this number had reached almost a thousand. This early success was not limited to the lumber camps. Memberships also grew in related industries. Pulp-mill employees, for example, enlisted so many of their numbers in the General Workers' Unit that the CLC considered allowing them their own unit.[53] By the end of 1919, the OBU had come to dominate Port Arthur to such an extent that the Trades and Labour Council ceased to function as a separate entity and the local AFL affiliates joined the OBU en masse.[54] In Fort William, however, where support for the TLC and ILP remained strong and Finnish socialists were less numerous, the OBU had lost its support. Some trade unionists, led by Fred Moore and A.H. Dennis, now refused to have anything to do with it.[55]

For the Finns, part of the allure of the OBU stemmed from its similarities with the IWW, which had long attracted militant bushworkers on both sides of the border. Although the OBU and the IWW shared a common interest in the general strike as a tactic that would leave workers in control of production, the two movements were in fact not identical.[56] The IWW did not agree with the OBU's continuing interest in the socialist political movement, and it believed itself to be the more authentic voice of working-class emancipation. By the fall of 1919, IWW organizers began touring the lumber camps and harvest fields of Northwestern Ontario, speaking against the leaders of the OBU and signing up members. Specifically targeted were those areas that had previously been strongholds of the LWIU.

To some alarmed authorities, the situation recalled the stark class polarization of 1912 and 1913. In response to the OBU's growing presence in the region, authorities renewed raids on the homes, businesses, and meeting places of workers in both Port Arthur and Fort William. In keeping with the growing resentment nationally towards non-Anglo-Saxon immigrants, local authorities specifically targeted the "foreign" workers they considered to be at the root of the growing radicalism.[57] By October, membership in the newly established General Workers' Unit (established by the OBU for those workers in no established union) numbered in the hundreds, and the street railway workers were reported to be reporting for work all sporting OBU buttons. The civic employees and shipbuilders had yet to join, but organizers believed their recruitment to be only a matter of time.[58]

In response, the RCMP and Ontario Provincial Police (OPP) flooded the region with undercover officers in an attempt to infiltrate the movement and stem the flow of information and individuals coming from the United States. Establishing themselves in Port Arthur and using the city as their base of operations, the IWW organizers began moving through the lumber camps in the district, speaking to workers and advocating better wages and working conditions.[59] By September 1919, the IWW had established a headquarters in Port Arthur and had begun sending organizers throughout the region. Stationed in Port Arthur, the OPP monitored the IWW in both Fort William and Port Arthur. A branch of the IWW's LWIU had been established and a man named Pelto was receiving $25 a week from the IWW to act as an organizer.[60] Finns in Northwestern Ontario were drawn to the IWW for reasons similar to those that made many of them sympathetic to it before the First World War. The revitalization of the organization within Canada, however, can also be attributed to the general dissatisfaction felt by many workers over the decision by most trade unions to support the war effort. The IWW, like the SPC and many members of the SDPC, had remained firm in its anti-war stance even in the face of persecution.[61]

The IWW's efforts met with success as its members soon came to dominate the OBU's LWIU and its leadership.[62] As the vast majority of lumber workers and IWW agitators were Finnish, it is not surprising that they became the focus of the OBU's ire. Both the RCMP and the OBU believed that the Finns "were trying to obtain control of the OBU for furtherance of IWW or Socialistic schemes of such a Radical complexion as to conflict with the policy laid down for OBU." As one informant in the Sudbury region commented: "The Finns are the most dangerous part of the OBU in this district, they have associations within themselves of a revolutionary nature and are only using the OBU for their own purposes."[63] Rumours also persisted that the Finns were in "close touch with European Bolshevists" and that "a good deal goes on among the Finns that is closely associated with European politics."[64] In the eyes of authorities, the boundaries separating the socialist organizations at the Lakehead, all now suffused with a shared Finnish radicalism, appeared to be alarmingly fluid.

Because Finns predominated on the far left of the labour movement, their shared cultural and political ties could mitigate the antagonisms between rival organizations and leaders. The relationship between the OBU and the IWW was not always antagonistic largely because the Finns predominated in both organizations. The IWW's General Executive Board (GEB) kept track of the spread of organizations referring to themselves as the "One Big Union" throughout the world and reported their success in the various Wobbly papers. Space was also set aside in the IWW organ, the *One Big Union Monthly,* to list "the most important resolutions [of the meetings in Calgary], as a matter of record, and to allow of comparison with our own movement and similar movements in other countries." It was suggested that the resolutions, in their entirety, would meet with a good response in the United States and provide an example of the success that industrial unionism could have.[65]

Still, the GEB also advanced some criticisms of the OBU. The program of the Canadian One Big Union, it argued, was "sufficiently like the IWW program to make us forget the small differences." A core principle of the IWW remained its resistance to political action. The Canadian (and Australian) adoption of political activism was seen as a characteristic of their newborn status. The GEB believed that over time this political focus would be abandoned, as it had been in the United States, "to save [their] life as an industrial organization." Until that day, the OBU in Canada and Australia, having "both declared for industrial unions by means of which to take over the means of production and distribution," could be regarded as allies.[66]

Wobblies viewed Bolshevism as a great popular uprising against the upper class of the Old World. They looked to the continuing fight in Russia, as well as events in Germany and Eastern Europe, as inspirations for the fight in North America. They argued, however, that the Bolshevik revolution was still a political revolution and the culmination of political socialism. The method by which power had been obtained in Russia – the capture of the government and the replacement of tsarist officials with socialists – still fell within "the institutions we call 'the state.'" The GEB argued that although the Bolsheviks and the IWW used the same expressions – "the abolition of classes," "the abolition of capitalism," "the socialization of the means of production," "the establishment of the socialist republic" – they did not actually use them to mean the same things.[67] Even the Soviets, the central pillars of the new system in Russia, were viewed as "hasty" and, as a result, unable to properly take over the means of production. The growing tendency of the ruling party to resort to cooperative movements and direct state control was, the IWW argued, the root of the problems in Russia. "In short," the GEB argued, "the Bolshevik revolution in Russia has not resulted in Industrial Democracy, but in a makeshift or temporary arrangement without stability, without any pretense of a final solution."[68]

The Bolshevik revolution did serve as an opportunity for the IWW to argue that "economic reconstruction of society cannot be accomplished by a government trying to order things with a high hand through laws and regulations, but has to be an organic outgrowth from the bottom, through the industrial organization of the workers at the place of work." "Bolshevism," it contended, "is the fire that clears off the old vegetation, 'the brush.' To plow, sow, reap among the charred stumps will be the immense task they will bequeath to us, the industrial organizers, the builders of the One Big Union."[69] Understandably, supporters of the Bolsheviks in the United States viewed the IWW as essentially revolutionary, yet "starting at the wrong end." Their position was that the "revolutionary proletariat must first seize the power of the state." The IWW countered by arguing that it would rather see "a gradual transition than a 'revolutionary' shock." The IWW evidently believed that "as industrial evolution progresses the parliamentary state will become more and more inadequate for handling the problems of society." The apparatus established by the IWW would assume control of these functions.[70] Other left organizations in the United States, oriented more to the achievement of the dictatorship of the proletariat, advanced very different analyses.

Contradicting its prewar policy, most postwar intellectuals of the IWW viewed the "shocks of revolution" as "undesirable, because they cause bloodshed and suffering. On the other hand, we do not consider it advisable to destroy social organs, before we have the new organ ready which is to take its place. We think it is about time that men disabuse their minds of the idea that violence is absolutely necessary or desirable for social change." Public consent, these Wobblies argued, would be the necessary precondition of radical change – and not vanguard-orchestrated mass action "à la Bolshevik." Socialists and workers, it was argued, need only look to Canada and Australia and to the fifteen unions the IWW had organized "over the last 12 years" to see success. In addition, where were the revolutionists to come from? Did any plans exist concerning how the revolution would progress and what the next step would be for power to be obtained? "Social changes are not made," the GEB argued, "in the wink of an eye, like changing your shirt."[71]

Initial support for the OBU had much to do with the IWW's positive reaction to the Winnipeg General Strike. For Wobblies in the United States and Canada, the strike was seen as an inspirational event that socialists in North America could take heart from and even emulate. "It was plain from the start that the affair," the *One Big Union Monthly* stated in July 1919, "was something more than a common scrap over small differences between workers and their employers. Everybody feels and knows that it is a general muster of the two opposing world forces today preparatory to the final battle."[72]

Following the strike, reputed strikers toured the United States and spoke of both the strike and the One Big Union movement in Canada. Exactly which OBU was discussed at these presentations remains unclear, but the message was the same: "Canadian workers stand shoulder to shoulder with the labour prisoners of Winnipeg. But we want the united support of all American workers, regardless of which side of the boundary line they live on. This is not a Canadian matter only, but concerns the working class of all America. If the employers are successful in crucifying the militant workers of Canada it will encourage the employers of the United States."[73]

By April 1920, the IWW reported that a Canadian local existed with nearly a thousand members.[74] Although these numbers cannot be substantiated (and are no doubt an exaggeration), the activities of both the OBU and the IWW in the Lakehead region did lead to increased surveillance by federal, provincial, and municipal authorities. The existence of the *Monthly* and other publications in the declassified files of American and Canadian archives indicates that authorities in both countries watched both organizations carefully. The RCMP and OPP were keenly aware that IWWism was indifferent to borders. Minnesota was an IWW stronghold in the United States. The Lakehead Finns, especially, were suspected of being influenced by cross-border radicalism. Suspected agitators were often arrested on both sides of the border. Worried about a possible repeat of Winnipeg in Northwestern Ontario, authorities identified the Lakehead as the centre of any potential problems and began to clamp down on the activities of all groups. Anything and anyone even remotely suspected of being revolutionary fell under surveillance. Suspected agitators were often arrested.[75]

The OPP in Northwestern Ontario worked closely with its American and RCMP counterparts in investigations involving the OBU and IWW. The proposed strike of January 1920, for example, saw RCMP, regional OPP, and District Intelligence Officers from St. Paul, Minneapolis, and Duluth all working together. Officials shared intelligence and coordinated their activities in an attempt to disrupt these organizations and arrest workers. The OPP concluded that the OBU and IWW were the same (even if they were in fact two separate bodies). They noted that most of the OBU organizers in the region had come from British Columbia and Minnesota. According to a plan adopted on both sides of the Minnesota-Ontario border, if a strike did occur, lumber companies would shut down and "try, and starve the strikers out."[76] Canadian and American authorities also worked together to stem the flow of socialist material between the two countries and to deport to Europe suspected Wobblies.

Following a tip from American authorities, the RCMP, for example, arrested William Salo of Fort William for possessing "socialist" literature. His Winnipeg lawyer, E.J. McMurray, described Salo's actions as merely "stepping outside of the iron band that the government proposed to put around his mind, and desired to find out what was being done in the outside world, which the government endeavours to keep hidden from the eyes of the people of this country." For McMurray, this was an issue of liberty and freedom from the growing intolerance of the Canadian government, which he compared to pre-revolutionary Russia. The case against Salo, he argued, was "a case of brainless police court jurisdiction, a performance by an immature mind on the magisterial bench that has made the justice of this land in many cases an object of contempt and enmity rather than a respected institution."[77]

McMurray was also involved in the deportation case involving Sava W. Zura, a leading member of the Ukrainian League formed in April 1919. A resident of the Lakehead for over seven years, Zura's bakeshop had been searched in late September and, after being apprehended by police at the border, he had been arrested and convicted for possessing "Bolsheviki" and IWW literature. Police in Fort William considered him the "main promoter" of "prohibited literature among the foreign element."[78] Workers in both cities rallied behind Zura, with Harry Bryan being the most notable voice.[79] Despite the absence of prior transgressions and the testimony by many local residents as to his good character,

Zura was sentenced to two years in Stony Mountain Penitentiary in Manitoba. Mrs. Zura was later apprehended by Immigration Department agents in Winnipeg, and was also interrogated concerning the evidence.[80]

Although the Chicago-based IWW viewed the establishment of the Canadian One Big Union with enthusiasm, the OBU worked quickly to distinguish itself from the older organization. Even shortly after its formation, the OBU's leadership began to argue that the industrial unionism of the OBU was not synonymous with "IWWism, but the direct opposite."[81] "The OBU of Canada differs from the IWW in that it endorses political action in theory," proclaimed the *One Big Union Monthly.* Advocates of the OBU further argued that the two organizations differed in terms of their respective structures. The OBU, instead of allowing separate affiliated organizations to develop separate treasuries, proposed to pool all the members' funds in one common pot, thus enhancing the unity among its units.[82]

These differences, and the prior existence of the Wobblies in Northwestern Ontario, laid the foundation for factionalism. Further, unlike the OBU, the IWW during the period immediately following the First World War sought inspiration from the activities of its fellow syndicalists in Finland, Germany, and Scandinavia, who actively fought against both Social Democratic and Bolshevik forces.[83] At the Lakehead, this international syndicalist vision both attracted and repelled workers. For the Finnish workers, who comprised the largest single group in the OBU's LWIU, Social Democratic tendencies ran high for some, while recent immigrants had become disillusioned with events in Finland. Moreover, the Bolshevik Revolution, as we have seen, had inspired many. Hence, lines that clearly separated syndicalists from revolutionary socialists in the eyes of IWW advocates were not as clearly or neatly drawn among Canadian proponents of the OBU.

In early 1920, the Port Arthur local of the FOC turned over its majority shares in the Finnish Building Company (which controlled the Labour Temple) to the OBU and, in keeping with the decision of the FOC's national executive, declared itself a propaganda agency of the OBU. The decision to join the OBU was not much of a leap for Finnish socialists already inclined towards industrial unionism. In fact, most of the newly formed locals throughout Ontario had previously been support circles for the Industrial Workers of the World. The decision was not without controversy, however. Evert Maki of Sudbury, for example, in his June 1920 report of district secretaries, suggested that the Finnish Socialist Party of Canada "was a great hinderance [sic] to the activities of the OBU that is if some quick changes do not take place in said organization."[84] As speeches by leading Finnish socialists such as J. Ahlqvist revealed, much of the concern was over the amount of control the OBU executive would have over Finnish affiliates, their cultural and educational activities, and the newspaper *Vapaus*. Further, Henry Puro (also known as John Wiita), editor of *Vapaus*, contended that Maki's real reason for being dissatisfied with both the paper and the Finnish Socialist Federation was that "we *[Vapaus]* do not agree with him that the IWW and its methods are the only means which lead the workers to freedom."[85]

Although differences of opinions may have been aired, the Port Arthur district convention of the LWIU of the OBU, Bryan reported, had been amicable. All those who attended had placed the best interests of the OBU before their own personal concerns.[86] Growing support for the dismantling of the lumber workers' union and the reorganization of the OBU along geographical versus industrial lines led to a number of disputes at the district level, however.[87] Divisions, pitting the eastern membership against the western, over the very nature and structure of the organization were surfacing. Thus, the selection of Port Arthur as the location for the OBU's second national convention in 1920 was clearly not arbitrary.

One of the main purposes of the convention was to impress on workers the inefficiencies present in the system advocated by the AFL. Speakers included Beckie Buhay, of the general workers' committee of Montreal, who spoke on the inefficiencies of the AFL and argued that the "salvation" of workers lay with the OBU.[88] Many delegates saw the convention as an opportunity to bridge the growing rift between the rank and file and the leadership as well as the eastern-based trade unions that, so far, had failed to join the movement.[89] The growing conflict between the lumber workers in British Columbia and Northwestern Ontario and the Winnipeg leadership came to a head at the convention, however.[90]

Much of the underlying tension resulted from a number of interrelated internal squabbles. One that had been simmering in the background for quite some time was the personal conflict between E.E. Winch, head of the LWIU, and OBU leader Victor Midgley.[91] Each man thought the other was trying to oust him from the leadership. Midgley viewed Winch's attempts to extend the LWIU as a direct threat to the power of the central offices and a way to deprive them of much-needed financial resources. Winch, on the other hand, viewed Midgley's desire to move the LWIU headquarters to Winnipeg in order to extend its reach eastward as a mere pretext to weaken the union and centralize power.[92] Despite the large number of lumber workers in the region, Winch "tried unsuccessfully to have the meeting moved to a more westerly point" than Port Arthur because he wanted to send as many western delegates as possible.[93] One reason for this bitter personal rivalry may have been the inherent differences that had developed between the BC lumber workers and those in Northwestern Ontario. Although an IWW stronghold before the First World War, the lumber camps of British Columbia had not flocked back to the IWW in the same numbers as their Northwestern Ontario comrades.[94] Another element in this dispute was an underlying difference in organizational perspective: Should the OBU be a geographically based or an industry-based organization?[95]

Those who advocated an industry-based organization (such as the one in place in 1920) favoured a model similar to that used by the IWW. Delegates to conventions represented workers belonging to a specific industrial union. The total number of delegates a union could send was determined by membership strength. In contrast, the geographically based model called for delegates to represent predetermined regions, and the number of delegates allowed to sit at conventions was dictated by the total number of members (regardless of union affiliation) found in the region. Many western-based lumber workers as well as non-Anglo members opposed such a geographical strategy, as it would only weaken the power of the LWIU, the union to which most non-Anglo workers belonged. Finnish members in particular, with their long ties to the IWW and the industrial union movement, were the most vocal in opposition. Finnish and non-Finnish lumber workers were also aware that the only chance to implement a move from industrial to geographic lines would involve undercutting the power of the lumber workers. The OBU leadership appears to have also come to the convention unprepared to relinquish power to the representatives of the LWIU because of its strong ties to the IWW of the Finnish radicals.[96]

An attempt was first made to hamper the participation of the Finnish majority by holding all meetings in English (not coincidentally the language spoken by the majority of the leadership).[97] Second, the LWIU and its local representatives were denied proportional representation, in direct violation of the OBU constitution.[98] LWIU delegates, including Winch, were denied representation on the basis that their per capita dues payments were in arrears (this delinquency was hardly unique, as an examination by the Credentials Committee had discovered that almost all units had failed to pay the August tax and many had been inconsistent in their payments since the last convention in January).[99]

Not surprisingly, the LWIU "demanded their full representation by the payment of their arrears in per capita." They noted that "failure upon the part of the Convention to concede to them this request would involve serious consequences."[100] The Credentials Committee's report was accepted and the LWIU was refused credentials. In protest, all LWIU delegates but one joined those who had been refused standing, and left the hall. The movement was irrevocably split.

The exit of the LWIU undermined the OBU's power and the legitimacy of the resolutions under discussion.[101] It was not lost on many present that the Credentials Committee's decision to seat delegates by district rather than by union was de facto (even though this core issue had not been debated or resolved) a move towards geographical as opposed to industrial representation. Winch and other LWIU representatives advised the committee, and through it the wider OBU, that they were violating the OBU's own charter and engaging in blatant discrimination. The withdrawal of the LWIU called into question the legitimacy of the movement's new leadership and fatally injured the OBU in general. Some units, such as that of Port Arthur, were allowed to sit at the convention, even though they were far behind in their dues. Through such devices, a region that represented a huge proportion of OBU members was marginalized, alienating most OBU supporters in the region and damaging the chances of an alliance with the IWW.

The split at the convention had an immediate impact on organizing efforts across Northwestern Ontario. For example, the organization of lumber workers in the Thunder Bay District "ground to a halt" during the winter of 1920-21.[102] The CLC's stance against the bulk of its membership and affiliates contributed to the OBU's anemic state. In the following months, members questioned the leadership and openly pondered leaving the union. Local members of the Finnish Organization of Canada also supported their national executive's decision to discontinue support for the OBU, although this appears to have been partly a result of the ongoing debates between Finnish socialists over the nature and characteristics of socialism.

Despite the growing regional turmoil, the CLC continued, seemingly undaunted, with the task of organizing workers in the region. Under Harry Bryan's leadership, a "Council of Action" consisting of three delegates elected from the CLC was formed. These men were charged with acting in case of an emergency and commanded "to devise ways and means for more energetic propaganda: to arrange public propaganda meetings of all members in the district." Although the Council of Action was intended to be "subject at all times to the approval of the Central Labour Council," in practice it placed the remaining elements of the OBU in the region in the hands of a relatively few individuals.[103] As Bryan explained, these changes were designed to counteract the efforts of "police and stool pigeons."[104]

Because many of the local lumber workers refused to participate in the OBU, the two largest unions in the CLC were now the starch workers' (connected to the pulp and paper mills and starch plants) and railway unions. The CLC reported that workers were "suffering from a severe attack of fear" as "the masters here [at the Lakehead] have a fine organization and are supporting each other in a thoroughly class-conscious manner. Special police, watchmen, and stool pigeons are the order of the day."[105] Increasing unemployment in the region also hampered organizing efforts. For example, much of the CLC's membership was soon unemployed.[106] Although meetings in Port Arthur remained relatively well attended, those in Fort William declined to such a point that joint meetings with the Port Arthur membership became necessary.[107]

The regional leadership of the OBU also began a campaign to dissipate any controversy. An open letter written by Joe Naylor, a member of the new national executive, perhaps best demonstrates the failure of the OBU's leaders to truly grasp the plight of the union. While declaring that he "did not like giving our internal squabbles away to our enemies, the master class," he attacked the leadership of the LWIU, and Winch in particular, as being "sick, sick with a drunken orgy after power, and the squandering of money like capitalist politicians, while your black-listed delegates were roaming the country for a job."[108] Not to be outdone, the LWIU engaged in a vigorous campaign to undermine the position taken by its Credentials Committee at the convention and the new General Executive Board.[109] At the Lakehead, the LWIU continued to operate, but it is unclear how many of the Finnish lumber workers were still closely connected with it. The decision to establish the headquarters of the CLC away from the Finnish Labour Temple on Bay Street, the former heart of OBU support in the region, is highly suggestive.

By November, the OBU wave was receding at the Lakehead almost as fast as it had arisen. The CLC, for example, faced continual difficulties organizing and retaining its members. An attempt to organize the women telephone operators foundered amid bitter charges of backsliding.[110] An attempt to organize a women's auxiliary generated little support.[111] A protest against the Fort William council's concessions to a local pulp and paper company was ignored.[112] Finnish and Ukrainian members were increasingly isolated from their ethnic compatriots. Even the Nipigon Finnish Dramatic Club's production of a "working-class" play dealing with "the gun and spy methods of the master class" played to a largely English audience. Bryan had to explain the plot before the curtain went up.[113]

The meetings held during November and December 1920 did little to address either the internal problems facing the local units or the immediate regional issues facing workers. With little in the way of an actual plan of action, all the CLC could tell fellow OBU units was that it would "enforce our demands when we are thoroughly organized and not before. The master class are making the conditions, let us explain them."[114] These presentations had little to do with actual experience, however. As in the case of Bryan's "Labor Laws of Soviet Russia, in Contrast with Labor Laws of Canada," the content of the presentations came from OBU propaganda, an assortment of IWW publications, and reactions to local news coverage.[115] From the evidence available, socializing and the presentation of dramatic productions began to outweigh any interest in addressing the growing unemployment in the region.[116]

These problems no doubt contributed to Bryan's loss to Richard Lockhead (or Loughead) for the position of secretary-treasurer at the December 1920 lumber workers' district convention in Port Arthur. Lockhead's win concerned many in the CLC, as he was seen as an IWW sympathizer.[117] As a concerned member of the OBU wrote to E.E. Winch: "It seems that Lockhead, or Doughhead, or whatever thay [sic] call that 'Mush-Eating Fakir' they appointed in PA is neither able or willing to do the work ... Probably some of those guys on the Coast who are in the habit of throwing secretaries down stairs, might make a start on this boob ... He must be a genuine 'Wobbly.'"[118]

Despite the change in leadership, Bryan continued to be the glue that kept the OBU together in the region. He travelled extensively during this period, used every connection to the labour movement at his disposal to keep workers engaged, and personally arranged for speakers such as Joe Knight to come to the area. While many Finnish lumber workers had become dissatisfied with the OBU, Bryan persuaded many others to remain, and encouraged members of the Fort William Ukrainian community, such as Eric Holm, to fill vacant positions on the district executive. Bryan also arranged for individuals to speak on issues relating to Soviet Russia, and facilitated collections in both Port Arthur and Fort William for relief initiatives such as the Soviet Russia and Ukraine

Medical Relief. He himself frequently spoke on issues dealing with Soviet Russia and its comparison to Canada.[119]

So acute had problems become by the end of December 1920 that reports of the growing strife within the OBU had reached the General Executive Board of the IWW in the United States. The growing internal divide was viewed by Wobblies as one between those advocating a militant form of the organization and others who were for "a geographical (district) beans and soup association" – one separating militant lumber workers from the "city 'home' guard element." In contrast to those who belonged to trade unions in the towns and cities, the migratory nature of the lumber workers, the GEB argued, had exposed them to the "bitter school of actual life," which had informed their knowledge and assisted in their development of a class consciousness. "City slaves," on the other hand, "got their training from the A.F. of L. and in other yellow institutions that serve to build up the capitalist system and now function to brace and patch it up."[120] Clearly, from this perspective, a growing difference in how city-dwelling unionists and bushworkers viewed the struggle had developed.

These growing differences did not stop the CLC, after not supporting the local LWIU during the convention, from extending an olive branch by exempting each local unit from paying the per capita tax to "assist them in financing their organization."[121] Bryan also toured the lumber camps in the region, reported on the prevailing conditions, and shored up support for the union.[122] He frequently attended other regional LWIU conventions as the Port Arthur District fraternal delegate.[123] It appears, however, that by January 1921, the Central Labour Council had come to realize just how important the LWIU was to the continued operation of the OBU in the district. Unfortunately, it was too late. At a conference held in Vancouver that same month, the vast majority of the LWIU locals voted in favour of secession from the OBU. In the following weeks, a series of meetings were held in branches throughout Ontario and western Canada at which workers discussed rejoining the OBU, joining the IWW, or creating an entirely new organization.[124] Others in the region followed A.T. Hill and joined the newly formed Communist Party of Canada. Many of the lumber workers who had been refused seating at the Port Arthur convention, for example, joined Hill in forming the Communist Lumber Workers Industrial Union of Canada (LWIUC).[125] The FOC in Port Arthur became heavily involved in organizing on behalf of the American Communist Trade Union Educational League (TUEL).[126]

Although Midgley dismissed the loss of the lumber workers, stating that they had been only loosely attached to the OBU, the actions taken against them during the previous year ultimately sealed the OBU's fate.[127] The loss of most of the lumber workers constituted an estimated one-quarter decline in total membership. The loss of Northwestern Ontario was of special concern as the eastward progress of the union effectively stalled without the connections of regional unions and the support of the Finnish- and Ukrainian-language organizations. The OBU did retain a small presence in Northwestern Ontario, where lumber workers in Fort Frances and Kenora rejoined the OBU's LWIU shortly after leaving it for the IWW.[128] Generally, however, "throughout the winter of 1920-1," as Ian Radforth writes, "the OBU and Lumber Workers in Ontario and the west watched members abandon ship in droves." Those lumber workers who had remained in the months following the convention were supported financially from "the thriving social clubs in Port Arthur, Nipigon, the Sault, Timmins, and Sudbury," but remained relatively weak, ineffectual, and subject to successful undermining by the IWW.[129]

The problems stemming from the split in 1920 and the exodus of the lumber workers in 1921 were only exacerbated by the general decline in the resource sectors of the economy. The inability of the OBU to consolidate its position after the Winnipeg General Strike, coupled with the economic downturn, resulted in the sinking of the working class "back into passivity."[130] Although the events of 1919 were inspirational, the actions of socialists between 1920 and 1922 signalled to some that "none in Canada are worthy considering from a revolutionary political standpoint. If there is need of one, then it must be started outside of the OBU."[131] The FOC's support for the OBU was just as fleeting. According to J.W. Ahlqvist and A.T. Hill, "the Finns lost their enthusiasm for the OBU as quickly as the rest." By the end of 1921, the FOC ceased to be a supporting organization of the labour central.[132]

The LWIU's decision in January 1921 to withdraw from the One Big Union was a pivotal moment in the history of socialism in the region. For all its obvious limitations, the OBU had been a movement with a vast potential to unite workers from many cultures, living in both the twin cities and their hinterlands, even across ideological barriers. It had seemed to foreshadow a much more cohesive and effective regional working-class and socialist movement. Yet, its success was short-lived and its promise never achieved. Nationally, the OBU's membership dwindled from 41,000 to 5,300 in three short years.[133] Regionally, the movement was a spent force by 1922. Even its most ardent organizers, including

Bryan, were by then looking for alternatives.[134] Despite some limited participation in a few strikes during the 1920s, the OBU both nationally and locally had become little more than "a weak protest movement, a symbol of a revolutionary threat, and after 1929 something even less."[135]

The decline and fall of the OBU in the region brought to the fore the underlying issues of Lakehead socialism. Ethnic differences, especially those pitting Finns against Anglos, were substantial. If centrist labourism had lost much of its appeal, and the mainstream trade unions had proven unable to reach much beyond their craft citadels in the cities, the OBU's stormy years also suggested how hard it would be to organize effective alternatives. Two buildings in Port Arthur suggested the distinct possibilities open to those who wanted to persevere in building Lakehead leftism. One, the Finnish Labour Temple at 314 Bay Street, once more became a focal point of IWW agitation – for, to an extent that was highly unusual in all of interwar North America, the Wobblies were able to capitalize on the collapse of the OBU to mount a series of powerful labour struggles. The other, at 316 Bay Street, was the headquarters of the newly formed Communist Party of Canada, which had bought and renovated the former *Työkansa* building in 1922. From 1922 to 1935, Lakehead socialism would be shaped and reshaped by the overlapping and often rival strategies fashioned at these two centres.

4

"Into the Masses!"
The Communist Party of Canada at the Lakehead, 1922-25

The years following the Winnipeg General Strike and the heyday of the One Big Union (OBU) – from 1922 to 1925 – were much more critical than any other period to the changing nature and characteristics of socialism at the Lakehead. From the frustration of radicals thwarted in their efforts to demonstrate their solidarity with their Winnipeg brethren, to those disillusioned with the OBU and the internal divisions that had torn it asunder, a search began for an alternative that would bring about the desired change. The establishment of the Third International in Moscow provided the impetus for Canadian socialism to undergo another profound and dramatic change.[1]

The period between 1921 and 1925 has been described as the "classic period of the united front."[2] Socialists in Canada were greatly influenced by Lenin's *Left-Wing Communism: An Infantile Disorder*,[3] in which he argued that "Communists in western countries must participate actively in parliaments and trade unions, and not shrink from the compromises inherent in such participation."[4] Communism, at least the variant that grew out of the Third World Congress in 1921, advocated the United Front as one of its core principles. This ethos of cooperation advocated through the United Front also appealed to the syndicalist and social democratic threads found in the Canadian Finnish socialist movement.[5] The Communist International (Comintern) supported the development of language organizations in recognition of the specific cultural characteristics of the Communist movement in North America.[6] Finns and Ukrainians were attracted to the CPC because of their familiarity with, and continuing links to, European left movements.[7] Communism also appealed to both groups because the Russian Revolution, in ending tsarism in Russia, had eliminated a force that had been oppressive to both nationalities. Communism provided opportunities for Finns to improve not only their working conditions but also their political situation at home and abroad.[8]

The central contradiction of Leninist trade union policy becomes apparent, however, when it is studied in the context of the Lakehead.[9] In contrast to many other areas, such as coalfields and urban centres, the most important workers in the region did not have a stable union. Those unions that did develop in the 1920s were not conservative craft unions but experimental industrial unions, such as the Lumber Workers Industrial Union (LWIU), linked first to the One Big Union and later to the Industrial Workers of the World (IWW). The Lakehead had the paradoxical result of encouraging Communists to enter into alliances (both short-term and even longer-term) with their enemies the syndicalists. In other settings, such as in France, Communists and syndicalists have never been in bed with each other, or entered into temporary, single-issue alliances that were short-lived.[10] In large part, this resulted from the fact that at the Lakehead the IWW and OBU were the largest established labour bodies. The strict application of the strategy recommended in *Left-Wing Communism* required that Communists work alongside them, even though in other contexts they were sworn enemies.

Two competing organizations dominated the activities of socialists at the Lakehead during the first half of the 1920s. The first was composed of remnants of the OBU and a revitalized IWW (whose members were often referred to as Wobblies). The second, composed of disillusioned socialists from a host of organizations, would eventually become the Communist Party of Canada (CPC). With the virtual collapse of the OBU in the region at the end of 1922, the IWW and the newly established CPC "all made bids for the former members."[11] This chapter and the two that follow build on Rodney's classic analysis of the CPC and its relationship with the Comintern during the 1920s but improve on it by addressing the CPC's relationship, at least at the Lakehead, with other socialist elements.

The story of the CPC's formation is a thing of lore more than of fact in the annals of Canadian labour history. Contradictory and often exaggerated recollections have appeared since the fateful day in May 1921 when a host of individuals representing a number of socialist organizations met in a barn in Guelph, Ontario, to discuss the formation of Canada's newest revolutionary socialist party. This meeting resulted from a gradual shift in the nature and characteristics of socialist thought in Canada. In the years following the Winnipeg General Strike, many had become disillusioned with organizations that had failed to affiliate with the Comintern or the Communist Red International of Labour Unions (RILU). In particular, the leadership of the IWW and the OBU had alienated many.[12]

The activities of A.T. Hill during these years provide an example of how many socialists at the Lakehead reacted to the changing circumstances in Canada.[13] Like many, Hill had re-evaluated his ideological position following the end of the Winnipeg General Strike and during the tumultuous years when the OBU and IWW had fought for hegemony in the region. By early 1920, he no longer believed that either the syndicalism offered by the IWW or the variation espoused by the OBU would result in the social change he desired. Travelling to Superior, Wisconsin, where he had worked in the past as a harvester and lumber worker, he enrolled in the American Finnish Socialist Federation's school. There he and fellow future prominent Finnish Canadian Communists fell under the influence of Emeli Parras, editor of *Työmies* and secretary of a local unit of the American Communist Party. Parras's courses spurred Hill to join William Z. Foster and Charles Ruthenberg's United Communist Party. Shortly after, he became one of its many members who flooded the Canadian borderlands speaking to workers about Leninism and the Communist movement.

At first, Communist efforts focused on former IWW strongholds and those towns and regions where growing dissatisfaction with the OBU was greatest. Hill began agitating in Fort Frances, Ontario. Gradually, building on his earlier reputation as an organizer throughout the Lakehead area, he became a leading radical throughout the region.[14] Often pitting himself against William Arnberg, a former organizer for the OBU and now a Wobbly agitator, he argued that the Soviet state, as constructed by Lenin and the Bolsheviks, was a necessary precondition for the transformation of capitalism into socialism.[15] Social Democratic Party of Canada (SDPC) activists such as Richard Loughead (also referred to as Lockhead), William Checkley, and Harry Bryan followed Hill in seeing the Communist Party as a way to preserve and develop the radicalism they had developed before 1918.

At the clandestine meeting of socialists in Guelph, the alternative many were seeking was born. Largely pre-arranged through the Comintern representatives, the meeting agreed on a plan to form a single Communist party in Canada and formally petition the Comintern for entry into the Third International. On the Comintern's unanimous decision to grant the CPC membership in the Third International in December 1921, the SDPC, OBU, and various ethnic organizations, such as the Finnish Organization of Canada (FOC), were invited to plan a unity convention.[16] Due to the restrictions against socialist organizations still in place under the 1918 invocation of the War Measures Act, the CPC created a legal party, the Workers' Party of Canada (WPC), as its public face and operated an illegal underground section.[17] The five-point program adopted by the WPC/CPC differentiated it from its predecessors such as the OBU and SDPC, and its adoption of a policy of political action distinguished it from the IWW.[18]

Communists were influenced by Lenin's writings, particularly *Left-Wing Communism.*[19] For them, "the essence of the united front line in industry," contends historian John Manley, "was the struggle for immediate working class demands and a clean break from both anarcho-syndicalism and 'ultra-left' abstentionism – the view that partial demands were on principle reformist and had to be shunned."[20] The CPC's belief in the imminence of "the overthrow of capitalism and capitalist dictatorship by the establishment of the working class dictatorship and the workers' republic" and its emphasis on the decisive role of a vanguard party made its socialism significantly different from previous versions espoused in Canada.[21] What had been created, essentially, was intended to be a "highly centralized organization composed of a disciplined proletarian vanguard whose mission was to destroy the bourgeois state machinery, to establish the dictatorship of the proletariat, and to replace the capitalist system with a communist society."[22]

The WPC consisted of groups of five to ten members, which, on reaching ten, formed a branch. Two or more branches formed a local that belonged to a subdistrict within a larger geographically designated district. Theoretically, each group possessed an elected "Organizer," and these in turn formed the "Branch Executive Committee." This committee elected a "Branch Organizer," who in turn led the formation of a "Local Executive Committee." The committee's representative, a "Local Organizer," joined with others to form a Sub-District Committee that, along with any "Language Section District Committees," acted on the District Committee that sent a representative to the Central Executive Committee of the party.[23]

Unfortunately, this structure rarely worked as planned. The highly centralized structure envisaged by Communists came up against the deeply rooted realities of ethnic and regional politics. Adequate organizers were often difficult to find and the more successful ones tended to be moved to those regions deemed most important. Factionalism also emerged almost immediately. Rooted in the differences that had existed among the organizations before the founding convention, it would form a consistent thread through the 1920s and early 1930s,[24] often manifesting itself in the ethnic differences that existed within the new party. These tensions were not the creation of the WPC/CPC. They were merely new variations on the old problems that had first divided the Socialist Party of Canada (SPC) in 1910 and later the SDPC and the OBU.[25]

The first few years of the legal and illegal groups' existence were spent attempting to meet the Comintern Executive Committee's instructions to be diligent in working with the labour movement, agitating but also working towards the CPC's theoretical and practical goals.[26] In fact, the Anglo-American Secretariat considered the CPC's activities to be of passing interest only. Records reveal that the secretariat was much more concerned with issues dealing with the party in the United States, Britain, and even Egypt.[27] During these early years, the Anglo-American Secretariat also treated the Canadian party as a mere extension of the American one.[28]

The CPC leadership focused on consolidating its position within the Canadian left and establishing party unity. This was no small task, considering the disparate elements brought together under its umbrella.[29] By 1922, most of the SPC's membership had joined the new Workers' Party of Canada.[30] Disillusioned members of the OBU, the SDPC, and the IWW joined from all parts of the country.[31] Very early on, the various ethnically based language organizations that had once been associated with the SDPC and the OBU became the backbone of the WPC. Owing to their strength, language sections with a certain level of autonomy were established to stave off the divisions that had plagued the SPC and the OBU in earlier times.[32] One of the earliest language sections to be formed, and the one with the greatest influence at the Lakehead, was Finnish.

Hill's election to the nine-person provisional executive in December assured both the legal and illegal parties of affiliation with the FOC. He figured prominently in the formation of the first Finnish Socialist Section of the WPC, was integral to the FOC's decision to affiliate directly with the WPC in 1922, and assisted in its reorganization on a club basis.[33] In the months following the formation of the WPC, Hill and other well-known socialists, such as Alf Hautamäki, began making periodic trips to Northwestern Ontario, extolling the virtues of the Comintern and scouting locations for potential branches.

Hautamäki is an intriguing character who, in many respects, is symptomatic of the Finnish socialist experience. Nothing is known of his life before he appeared in Ontario lumber camps in the early 1920s as an organizer for the fledgling Lumber Workers Industrial Union of the One Big Union. Like many Finns, he appears to have migrated from Finland in search of work, but with a strong belief in socialism, particularly the version emanating from revolutionary Russia. Following the OBU split in 1920 and the formation of the CPC in 1921, Hautamäki joined as an organizer. He quickly rose to prominence as a leading member of the FOC and editor of the Toronto-based Finnish Communist newspaper *Metsätyöläinen (the Lumber Worker)*. He became head of the CPC's powerful lumber workers' union, and the leading Communist figure at the Lakehead. Within the twin cities and in the surrounding countryside, he was just as well known for his worker-poetry and plays that focused on topics such as lumber camp life, love, strikes, and alcoholism. His plays were frequently performed in Finnish halls from Sudbury to the Manitoba border. Hautamäki's story ended just as mysteriously as it began. He disappeared from the record in the mid-1930s, like so many migrant Finnish workers during the period.[34]

In keeping with his personality, the meetings that Hautamäki organized with Finnish socialists at the Lakehead in the early 1920s were open and frank. They included members from the Finnish Support Circle of the OBU, with which many of the Communists had joint memberships. In February 1921, through a morphing of the Finnish Support Circle and the Finnish Association, a branch of the FOC was formally re-established and immediately affiliated with the WPC. Although the FOC would join "in its entirety as the Workers' Party Finnish Section in February 1922,"[35] many Finns preferred in 1921 to affiliate only with the Trade Union Educational League, a "non-partisan trade union auxiliary, interested only in the 'renovation' of a declining trade union movement."[36]

The Ukrainian Labour-Farmer Temple Association (ULFTA) also eventually affiliated with the WPC, and constituted the second-largest ethnic section, after the Finns.[37] Formed in late 1917 by Matthew Popovich and other Ukrainian socialists as the Ukrainian Social Democratic Party, by 1919 the Winnipeg-based organization had established a number of branches in Northern Ontario and western Canada. Its strength remained, however, in the Rocky Mountain mining region and in the cities of Winnipeg and Edmonton. The spread of the ULFTA had been hampered during the final years of the First World War when the Canadian government declared it an "illegal Bolshevik Organization."[38] When it re-emerged in the early 1920s, it did so slowly and cautiously, often choosing to infiltrate existing organizations.

Such was the case at the Lakehead. During the late 1910s and early 1920s, Ukrainian socialists chose to work through the Winnipeg-based Workers' Benevolent Association (WBA). Just months after the establishment of the WBA in Winnipeg, a branch appeared in West Fort William. A second branch followed in April 1923 and a third, in Port Arthur, by April 1926.[39] As indicated by Popovich's role as its president, a connection between the WBA and the ULFTA existed from the start. Not surprisingly, shortly after the ULFTA's affiliation with the WPC, the WPC used the WBA as a beachhead within the Ukrainian community.[40] Ukrainians associated with the ULFTA at the Lakehead would reflect the national composition of the CPC and form the second-largest regional group, after the Finns.

Ian Angus has argued that the WPC "gathered into its ranks a clear majority of the organized left."[41] The validity of this claim largely depends on what is meant by the "organized left." It is true that the WPC, and through it the Communists, became the largest single political party on the Canadian left in the 1920s. The SDPC disappeared, and the SPC shrank in numbers. Various labour parties, organized federally or provincially, were often not "left" in a very rigorous sense, and the Communists would eventually penetrate many in any event.[42] The adherence to the Workers' Party by the ULFTA and FOC gave the Communists the prospect of a mass base. At the same time, the Lakehead evidence suggests the continuing power of alternative forms of leftism, such as those associated with the IWW.[43] Overall, the "organized left" as a movement declined rapidly in the 1920s, in the face of economic crisis and right-wing reaction.

The delicate situation among the organizations was well known to Harry Bryan. He had been at the centre of the conflict within the OBU at the convention in 1920. Even before he broke his ties with the OBU, the events and ideology originating in Russia and the failure of past organizations to make a lasting impact on the working class had caused him to reconsider what he believed. Bryan had been integral in the establishment of a short-lived lumber workers' union in Sudbury in 1920.[44] Although this union disappeared during the winter, Bryan, along with Hill, met other likeminded workers the following spring in Sault Ste. Marie, and formed, under the aegis of the newly established WPC, the Lumber Workers Industrial Union of Canada (LWIUC).[45] Bryan was appointed its first secretary-organizer. A period of inactivity followed, then longtime Eastern Ontario lumber worker Ed Kuusela replaced Bryan for yet undetermined reasons.[46] Kuusela's efforts focused mostly on the Sudbury region, and there was little organizing in Northwestern Ontario.[47]

Communist activities at the Lakehead received a boost when Bryan moved back shortly after being relieved of his duties in Sudbury. During the spring and summer of 1921, much of the organizing at the Lakehead had been done by travelling organizers who spent one or two days in the twin cities and visited selected lumber camps before returning south or moving on to larger centres in Manitoba and Saskatchewan.[48] With Bryan now in the region more or less permanently, it was hoped that much more substantial gains would be made.

It remains unclear when the WPC officially established a branch at the Lakehead. Arnold Beck, a leading member of the Finnish Building Company (the entity that controlled the Finnish Labour Temple in Port Arthur), recalled in the late 1970s that the party's first regional committee was multi-ethnic in composition. Beck himself claims to have been the first regional secretary. Einar Nordstrom describes the committee as having been composed of Anglo-Saxon workers Doug Boom, Angus McLeod, and Finley McLeod; Finns Beck and Arne Skarra; a Ukrainian named Boiko; and a number of unnamed Italians.[49] Bryan, no doubt, was also a member, as he appears to have played a lead role in speaking out against both the OBU and the IWW.

Considering his position as former head of the OBU-dominated Central Labour Council and a well-known, if not always well liked, member of the working class at the Lakehead, Bryan's conversion was a coup for the WPC in the area. His speeches provide an indication of what attracted regional workers to the CPC. Typically, they attacked syndicalism and the IWW's refusal to become politically active. The demands of workers, he often argued, could not be realized solely through concessions wrung from employers. Political participation was necessary for lasting changes in Canadian society. One of his favourite means of getting the central issue across was a simple example, traceable to his early involvement with notable early American socialist Daniel De Leon, which he shared with hundreds throughout Northwestern Ontario. Bryan told the story of a man going down a street with his hands behind his back. The man meets a police officer who, because the man is a labourer, wants to club him or arrest him. The man would have no chance in this encounter, in the same way that the working class would have no chance if it relied only on its industrial arm and neglected its political arm.[50]

A number of factors continued to complicate attempts by Bryan and others to organize workers at the Lakehead during this period. First, a decision by the CPC executive resulted in the bisection of the area, with Port Arthur placed in District 2 and Fort William in District 3.[51] Most likely, this reflected the geographic provincial and federal political division of the region. Second, the region possessed neither an organizer nor, after the apparent collapse of the first one, a branch until 1923. As a result, despite the best efforts of Bryan and Hill, recruiting efforts were largely unsuccessful by February 1922. Although hundreds of workers in the twin cities and surrounding countryside belonged to the FOC and the ULFTA, total direct membership in the WPC amounted to only six in Port Arthur (all Finnish) and a mere nineteen in Fort William (ten Ukrainian and nine Finnish).[52] This would seem to indicate that many socialists in the region remained hesitant about the WPC and possibly about Communism in general, preferring to work solely through their language organizations.

Decisions made by the WPC Central Executive Committee in March would not have helped the situation. The appointment of Tim Buck as the organizer for District 3 (Ontario, from Port Arthur to Quebec but excluding Ottawa) and H.M. Bartholomew for District 4 (Saskatchewan, Manitoba, and Ontario up to Port Arthur) ensured that organizing activities would be centred only in the major metropolitan areas. As a result, organizational efforts in the region were sporadic at best over the next year.[53]

Many in the language federations were reluctant to throw themselves into the activities of the WPC. For example, Ukrainians from the Lakehead attended as delegates to the Third Convention of the ULFTA held in February to decide whether the association would participate in the formation of the WPC and send its delegates to the party's convention. "All the delegates, with the exception of two, were instructed by their organizations to support participation in the formation of the WPC and send delegates to the convention of that party."[54] Support, though, was conditional on "a revolutionary platform and programme and an open declaration for the Third (Communist) International and a guarantee in the party constitution of democratic centralism in the party while allowing the sections the possibility of conducting their work without unnecessary hindrance or constraint."[55] As a result, despite participating in the formation of a Ukrainian section of the WPC, the ULFTA did not immediately affiliate directly as the FOC had.[56]

Like many Ukrainian socialists at the Lakehead, Mike Cosmishin postponed joining the CPC until the late 1920s, content for the time being with local Ukrainian organizations that, while not necessarily socialist in nature, provided a linguistic, ethnic, and cultural oasis. Born in 1911 to a Ukrainian agricultural worker, Cosmishin immigrated to Canada with his family in 1922 and joined the youth section of the ULFTA shortly after. According to him, he joined because of the association's "progressive" nature and its dedication to culture, language, and the immediate problems and issues facing workers. Coming from a "foreign country," he also saw the association as a necessary means of "get[ting] acquainted with life and conditions in Canada." Although appealing, the WPC was ill-equipped to help him in these areas.[57]

The lack of a district branch at the Lakehead apparently did not stop the CPC executive from including Communists in the region when it chastised members and branches for their lack of support for the *Worker.* The party's organ, they suggested, was the vehicle through which the battle against capitalism must advance. The criticisms were addressed especially to the non-English members, who were encouraged to subscribe "irrespective [of] his language. If the member cannot read English, he can pass it on to someone who does."[58] The WPC appears not to have attempted to publish information in the *Worker* in any other language than English. Instead, it preferred to leave such things up to the language sections and the affiliated organizations.

In fact, the WPC and the underground group appear to have increasingly taken the membership of non-English workers for granted. For example, the Organizing Committee of the Administrative Council led by J. MacDonald and William Moriarty issued instructions to branch officers and executive committees that "great care must be exercised in advertising and organizing mass meetings," and that "English-speaking districts must receive preference on all occasions."[59] Recommendations such as these typically ended with a declaration that "no matter what the difference that may be developed in party discussion on question of policy, once a decision is made, it shall be considered binding upon all members."[60]

By August 1922, both the WPC and the underground section reported that they were still fraught with internal difficulties stemming from the existence of two identifiable fractions. One group consisted of those who had been the more radical elements in the SPC and SDPC. The other group comprised those who had belonged to the language organizations that had been declared illegal in 1918. Factional disputes across the border also affected the Canadian party's operations.[61] As Moriarty concluded in his August report to the Anglo-American Secretariat:

> We do not consider that the Party is as yet a well developed Party of record. However, we do believe that we have made a good start in the right direction. We also recognize clearly that, because of our youth, the Party is lacking in comrades who possess the necessary ability for organization and executive work. But experience is fast teaching the leading elements of the Party and we are anxious to make progress. We appeal to you, therefore, to advise and assist us in every way possible, so that we might become real factors in the revolutionary struggle.[62]

In Port Arthur and Fort William, hundreds of workers flocked to May Day celebrations in 1922, yet few were recruited into the Party. One possible explanation lies in the unpopularity of the organizers sent to address non-English-speaking workers. The issue of unsuitable or unpopular organizers among the Finns became a real concern, as approximately 2,000 of the CPC's 6,000 affiliated members were now Finnish.[63] By 1923, although overall party numbers had decreased, Finnish representation had increased to 2,028 of 4,808 members. As a result, they contributed, according to William Rodney, two-thirds of total revenue.[64]

The party's ideology may also explain some of its early mixed results. Despite advocating United Front action with other organizations (something favoured by the Finns), the WPC also stressed that its platform was in no way reformist, even if other groups appeared to share its goals. "A reformist platform," the WPC executive secretary argued, "is one based on the theory that the establishment of same will secure for the capitalist class a definite degree of equilibrium, for its form of society."[65] Essentially, the WPC held the position that reformists were under the delusion that stable conditions would lead to better security for the working class. "Marxists," it contended, "reject such theories as being unsound, and will recognize that our program will not succeed in minimizing the class struggle, but will intensify it." The "justness" of workers' claims, and the intrinsic inability of capitalists to grant them, would lead to "the fight which inevitably must arise."[66]

Socialists at the Lakehead appeared unsure how to respond to the WPC's position. Finnish workers were wary of a complete rejection of the past. So too were many Anglo-Saxon workers, who had a long, and often successful, tradition of independent labour politics in the region. Fearing the worst, Communist organizers were sent into the area in late November 1922 in an attempt to avert a split such as that with the SDPC in 1910 and with the OBU in 1920. The "secessionalists" in the region, the *Worker* reported, received a "trouncing" that apparently "acted as a tonic."[67] In the aftermath of this struggle, the Finnish section in particular made substantial gains, in no small part through the efforts of Hill and Hautamäki. Both men had spent much of the winter lumber season speaking on behalf of the Finnish section, the WPC, and the LWIUC. In Northwestern Ontario, the Finnish section had also been highly active in the cultural aspects of the Port Arthur community, especially among the children and youth. An indication of their success is seen in the number of theatrical plays, sporting events, subscriptions to Finnish newspapers, and overall new membership. For example, by early spring of 1923, the Finnish section consisted of eighty-nine branches with a total membership of more than 2,000.[68] Stability at the Lakehead continued to be challenged by the "the old traditions of syndicalism," however, particularly in the lumber camps.[69]

The situation at the Lakehead was not necessarily the fault of organizers. The WPC had inherited many of the problems that had faced both the SDPC and the OBU during the previous decade. The IWW posed by far the greatest problem. Sensing the growing threat represented by the CPC, the IWW moved quickly to re-establish itself in Northwestern Ontario and elsewhere in Canada when wartime restrictions were repealed in 1923. Much of its renewed strength resulted from the decision by many former members of the OBU's LWIU to affiliate in early 1923. This included the former Northwestern Ontario strongholds of Fort Frances, Fort William, Nipigon, Port Arthur, and Sioux Lookout.[70]

The problems facing the WPC continued despite the best efforts of members such as Bryan, who toured the region attempting to recruit members without receiving pay or compensation. By the time of the WPC's second annual convention in late February 1923, neither Port Arthur nor Fort William still possessed an official branch.[71] Part of the blame rested with the local Ukrainian and Finnish socialists, who still refused to become fully involved in the party. The Finns in particular were singled out, as their reluctance to respond to the call for union activity was blamed on the prevalence of syndicalism among them. This was problematic, as over half of the WPC's 4,808 members were now Finnish (2,028) and Ukrainian (880) in nationality but did not belong to any of the WPC's mass organizations.[72] Nationally, the party was little better either financially or organizationally, with only District 2 and District 3 reporting solvency and a stable party apparatus.[73]

In response, Maurice Spector spent much of April and May touring western Canada discussing the Comintern, the United Front policy, and the Canadian Labour Party in an attempt to win over workers. He targeted those regions where the OBU, the IWW, and various other socialist parties had been previously, or continued to be, most active.[74] For example, he used his April presentation in Port Arthur to condemn "the capitalistic system and urged the workers to form a united front against their enemies." Such a strategy, he argued, "was necessary not only in taking power into the hands of the workers, but it was absolutely necessary in securing temporary improvements in the conditions in which the workers were living."[75] Despite his being sponsored by the local branch of the FOC, however, only twenty people attended the presentation. Nearly all were Finns, along with the obligatory government spy.[76]

Given this mediocre record of accomplishment among the Finns, the Communists could take some heart from their activities among the English-speakers of Port Arthur. Two labour activists named Alex Gibson and Long, who had recently resolved to fight both the OBU and the IWW in their campaigns to organize the region, founded the largely English-speaking local there.[77] Both worked through the still-functioning Thunder Bay District Central Labour Council and the Port Arthur Trades and Labour Council.[78] The *Worker* was encouraged and the CPC's Executive Committee resolved to bestow special attention on the "new local." By June, Port Arthur and Fort William had become regular stops on the tours of Communist leaders through the country, and Hill often arranged for such visitors to venture out to address area lumber workers. Evidence of growing Communist popularity could also be found in the emergence of an Italian section in Port Arthur.[79]

There were also setbacks, however. Organizers did not stay put. Harry Bryan's candidacy in the provincial election – the first openly Communist candidate to run in the area – netted only 200 votes (the moderate candidate backed by the railway union polled over 1,600).[80] Communists, though, remained undaunted and redoubled their efforts during the summer. They were rewarded with the establishment of a WPC branch in Port Arthur and increasing regional membership, including a substantial number of Finns. As delegates to the Enlarged Session of the Central Executive Committee of the Workers' Party of Canada held in Edmonton were informed, "Port Arthur and Fort William had shown a better appreciation of the Party Program of late and we had progressed in the Twin Cities." Specific mention was also made of the Finnish section, which "in particular was making steady progress in the region much like in the rest of the province." "After a long fight in Port Arthur," one delegate declared, "they had been successful in getting a firm footing."[81]

Some of this success had to do with the decision to reorganize the FOC with the support of the Finnish section of the WPC. Like most former FSOC locals, the Port Arthur *Suomalainen Osasto* had turned over its property and assets to the FOC when it was formed after the easing of War Measures Act restrictions in 1921.[82] Although concerned primarily with cultural and educational work among Finnish socialists and with remaining a distinct and separate entity, it shared a common membership with the Finnish section of the WPC.[83] Another factor, and perhaps the immediate concern for many, was to ensure that control over its property and activities remained in the hands of its membership and not the non-Finnish CPC leadership. This autonomy, paralleled by similar developments south of the border, would eventually be the cause of much consternation within the North American parties and the Comintern in the second half of the 1920s.[84]

The situation within the Ukrainian community of Fort William was even more contentious. By the spring of 1923, it had become clear that many Ukrainians, both socialists and nationalists, were concerned over the increasing role played by Communists in their organizations. For example, a small group within the WBA had voiced their opposition to greater integration with the ULFTA. Members of the nationalist Fort William East End Provista Society went so far as to take legal action against the ULFTA in April for what it perceived as the latter's attempts to illegally transform itself into a "Revolutionary, Communistic, and Bolshevik Society in affiliation with the Third International of Moscow."[85] The Provista Society argued that socialists were seeking to undermine it by "boring from within" and sought "to wrest its purpose from that of culture into the promulgation of the doctrines of Sovietism and Communism and to make a branch of the International Organization."[86]

Not surprisingly, the local press framed the fight as one of "pioneering conservatives" versus "bolsheviki." Both the Manitoba *Free Press* and the *Worker* commented on the court case and used the incident as an example of the presence of a strong Communist movement among the Ukrainian population at the Lakehead.[87] In the end, the Provista Society won and succeeded in blocking the ULFTA from gaining control of the hall. The negative press and now substantiated fears made it difficult for the ULFTA to rent suitable space for meetings and activities until it built its own temples in Fort William in 1925 and Port Arthur and Current River in 1928.[88] Organizing efforts were curtailed as its 200 members (circa 1925) were forced to rely on the WBA for support.[89]

Despite taking a much more active role in the region and increasing its membership, the WPC was far from flourishing by the end of 1923. Most of the party's non-Finnish and non-Ukrainian apparatus had ceased to operate. Even the children's clubs established by the Young Communist League (YCL) in 1921 remained viable only through the efforts of the Finnish membership.[90] Disheartened and at times frustrated, members of the WPC fought on. Despite reports that the Port Arthur branch had become defunct, its former members, under the direction of district organizer William Checkley, mounted a successful celebration of Liebknecht Day on 20 January 1924.[91]

Lenin's death in January 1924 also sparked renewed dedication to the party's activities. Hundreds of workers representing the Ukrainian, Finnish, English, and Italian sections of the WPC in the region attended the memorial held in Fort William. The gathering opened with a rendition of the *Internationale* by the Finnish section's choir. Members of the Ukrainian, Finnish, and English branches made speeches. Bryan, in particular, "rose to a lofty height of eloquence as he feelingly spoke of our departed comrade and leader." His speech was punctuated by a declaration that brought "many strong men and women" to tears: "When we gaze upon this black drapery we are painfully aware that Lenin is dead; but when we lift the red we know that Lenin lives with us forever."[92]

The CPC registered some significant gains the following year. For example, Checkley reported in March that thirty-eight young workers had attended a meeting organized by the Finnish WPC members on the goals and principles of the YCL. So persuasive had the presentation been that these workers formed a branch at the conclusion of the meeting, electing officers and appointing a secretary-treasurer and a five-member executive committee. They also decided to organize a production of a play based on the Winnipeg General Strike as part of their recruiting drive.[93]

Responding to the growing needs of bushworkers for inexpensive food, the International Co-operative was also established in early 1924. By the end of its second year of operation, nine branch stores had opened in Port Arthur, Fort William, Westfort, Lappe, Intola, Kaministiqua, Schreiber, and Kivikoski.[94] The cooperative movement was especially important for Finnish members of the CPC. It was a way to challenge the institutions and the nature of social relations within the capitalist system, and it provided members in rural communities with a means to better connect with the party centre in Port Arthur and Fort William.[95] The cooperatives would play a significant role both in supplying goods during strikes over the next decade and in the later conflict between the CPC and the IWW.

The WPC convention in April 1924 registered significant gains at the Lakehead, as in all of District 3. At the same time, the party's Central Executive Committee was unsettled by the decline in the English-speaking membership of District 3 that counterbalanced, in its estimation, the district's success in recruiting Finns. The district was even criticized for not organizing effectively, even though the District Executive Committee had lost three secretaries in the past year.[96]

The activities of the IWW were also of growing concern. The WPC's policy towards independent unions (to build and strengthen the most powerful body in a locality) had in fact led it to support Wobbly-controlled unions. Representatives from the Lakehead argued that this substantially weakened the party, as the IWW would "use Party members for their own purposes, if they can, and when they have no further use for them they will stab them in the back." As the district report contended: "They [the IWW] are more Jesuitical than any adherent of the Jesuit Order."[97] By April 1924, the IWW had also wrested complete control of the Finnish Labour Temple from the remaining Finnish OBU members. Following the split with those who joined the CPC in 1924, the Finns who remained formed a relationship with the IWW. After a period of coexistence, they were absorbed into the IWW *Canadan Teollisuusunionistinen Kannatus Liitto* (the Support League of Canadian Industrial Unionists, or CTKL). Although the OBU faithful reported that only a few members in Port Arthur had gone over and that propaganda had been working in their favour, this was a pipe dream.[98] With those who rejoined the IWW also went the controlling shares of the Finnish Building Company, which owned the Finnish Labour Temple and the Hoito restaurant.

James Dixon, head of the Central Labour Council, had continually requested organizers and support from the Winnipeg executive, to no avail. All finances were completely locally raised and used, but the Coal Handlers' Unit in Port Arthur and the Building Unit, the strength of the CLC after the departure of the lumber workers in 1922, had stopped paying dues. Although R.B. Russell and other figures did visit the region periodically, there was no full-time organizer in either Port Arthur or Fort William.[99] By the end of 1926, the OBU in the region had become so moribund that a new organizer, a member of the

Barbers' Unit in Fort William named W. Howard, requested assistance to re-establish it. So pessimistic was his report that the Winnipeg Central Labour Council actually advocated censoring him for "making such a request, as he pointed out that it was a waste of money to send an organizer down there, when such conditions existed."[100]

As with the OBU and the CPC, the IWW's continued success relied heavily on its ability to embrace recently arrived immigrants who had been involved in socialist activities or had been Wobblies in western Canada or overseas.[101] Most were migrant workers in the lumber industry who, through fellow workers, were put in touch with the local organizers and cultural associations. Swedish worker L. Friberg, for example, had been a syndicalist before coming to Port Arthur in 1923. On his arrival, he searched for the closest thing and joined the IWW after a friend brought him to a meeting. What struck Friberg was that the IWW consisted of many nationalities, although most of them, he later recalled, were English- and Finnish-speaking. While this made meetings difficult to follow, he admired their attempt to involve all workers regardless of ethnic background.[102]

Similarly, Holmer Borg had been a member of the Social Democratic Party in Sweden and later of a syndicalist group before immigrating to Canada in 1923. Becoming acquainted with the IWW while working as a harvester in Saskatchewan, Borg admired the Wobblies for their solidarity in the field, their commitment to direct action when necessary, and their ability to win the grudging admiration of many farmers. Borg moved to Fort Frances and organized for the IWW, eventually settling in Port Arthur. He describes the activities of the OBU during this period as more concerned with "selling tickets" and "running a lottery." The CPC, while present in name, did little organizing until sometime after 1925, according to Borg.[103]

Even the RCMP was impressed by the impact of the IWW in Northwestern Ontario in the mid-1920s. The Wobblies' presence was, the police noted, having a "good effect" because it confused the workers to the point of immobilizing them.[104] For the CPC, the IWW was a constant irritant. William Checkley's submission to the Third National Convention of the WPC in 1924 reveals that, although many of the Finnish members may have been willing to entertain the idea of possible union, the English members in the region viewed the IWW as ideologically incompatible. "They have proved to themselves to be the possessors of a great ability to tear down," the district executive informed the convention, "but completely lacking in ability to build." Further, "when trouble is on

[Wobblies] flock to that point, fight until the battle is over, and then leave the vicinity to repeat the performance elsewhere."[105] While the United Front continued to be applied, the complexities of uniting with other organizations such as the IWW had not been thought out. "There is a very strong tendency," Checkley argued, "to make this united front into a love-feast; a unity on the other fellow's terms, and where Party members have not even the right to criticize." This, above all else, was a major issue for workers at the Lakehead and in the west, where the IWW was a force to be reckoned with.[106]

The 1924 national convention also resulted in the reorganization of the CPC from six to nine districts. Ontario was split into three new administrative districts; Fort William and Port Arthur formed the centre of the new District 6.[107] As Ivan Avakumovic points out, "the geographical distribution of party organizations shows that between one-half and two-thirds of them were in Ontario. Thunder Bay and the Sudbury region each had as many as Southern Ontario."[108] The convention also resulted in the dissolution of the WPC and the decision that an underground party was no longer required, resulting in the open existence of the Communist Party of Canada. Both decisions were in keeping with decisions reached by the Communist International at its Fourth Congress in 1922. Many in the party did not embrace the decision enthusiastically.[109] William Moriarty and Trevor Maguire, backed by the Ukrainian and Finnish section representatives Michael Boychuk and A.T. Hill, respectively, led the opposition. These men believed that the open association with the Comintern would lead to increased police surveillance and persecution. For the Finnish and Ukrainian affiliates, the memory of their persecution during the First World War made them much more sensitive than their English-speaking counterparts to what Canadian authorities could do to them.[110]

Although the concerns of the Finns and Ukrainians could not be entirely ignored, as they comprised the bulk of the party's estimated 4,000 members, the delegates were more interested in the growth of branches and membership elsewhere, which was attributed to the "building up of the Canadian Labour Party and the crystallization of the left wing in the Trade Union movement." In addition, as Jack MacDonald reported to the convention delegates, "prevailing objective conditions in Canada have militated against the numerical increase in the party membership."[111] Increases in immigration and the belief that the CPC would find "much good material amongst the new comers" were being offset by the loss of many of the party's "active and experienced members" to the United States due to the poor economic conditions in Canada. The dramatic increase in Finnish members was attributed to better conditions within the lumber, mining, and farming industries. In addition, as with the Ukrainians, the Finns's national societies were viewed as "rallying centres" through which the CPC could more easily approach the bulk of the workers.[112]

The May Day celebrations of 1924 demonstrated that deep schisms still existed within the left at the Lakehead. The Fort William and Port Arthur branches of the WPC were forced to hold separate meetings to celebrate the day, as no other unions or labour organizations had answered calls to plan for mass parades in each city. Remnants of the OBU and Wobblies issued the most vocal rejection, and each issued their own calls in response. Predictably, Communists at the Lakehead argued that this was merely another example of their "[un]willingness to co-operate in the struggle against capitalism."[113]

The small Communist-led demonstration in Port Arthur displayed the party's strengths – a new hall, an impressive turnout from the Ukrainians and Finns, and the singing and plays (including *The Strike,* put on by the Young Communist League) that contributed to a sense of an emergent counterculture.[114] Leslie Morris spoke of the imminent destruction of the capitalist system and the organizational strength of the new party. There were further speeches in Ukrainian, Finnish, Italian, and English. By June, the city's Communists had helped form an unemployed association, whose demands for work, food, and clothing for the unemployed precipitated the arrest of three militants, who were, doubtless to the chagrin of party loyalists, condemned as Wobblies in the courtroom and media.[115]

The reorganization of the Communist Party also resulted in the appointment of Jack MacDonald and Maurice Spector – two high-ranking English-speaking members – as executive members on the Finnish and Ukrainian committees. Efforts by the CPC executive to play down the extent of their Finnish membership caused concern among some Finns about their representation on the executive, however. Although Finns now made up approximately 2,620, or 60 percent, of the party's 4,000 members in 1925, only Hill and J.W. Ahlqvist held executive positions.[116] In addition, despite the fact that the overwhelming majority of the party's membership resided in Northwestern Ontario, no one from the region could be found in the party's upper echelons. Despite repeated calls for more organizers and better instructions from the party leadership, the Central Executive Committee appeared more interested in criticizing failure than in facilitating success.[117] It was this attitude that led the IWW to claim 3,000 members in Ontario by 1924, most of them in Northwestern

Ontario.[118] The vast majority of these came from the ranks of the former OBU members in Northwestern Ontario and those workers who had joined the CPC only to find it less palatable than the available alternatives.

As this chapter has shown, at the end of 1925 socialists at the Lakehead were continuing their move towards more radical organizations and were introduced to another alternative in the form of the CPC. As one military observer reported to the Department of National Defence:

> The OBU is practically dead in Port Arthur and the union will take any steps to try to get into strength again. At present the dominant party in Port Arthur is the Workers Party or Communist Party in Canada ... the strongest aggregation are the Finns who the police at present classify as practically a separate unit – they joined the OBU ... [which] proved too pacifist for the Finns who believe that the best way to change the political status of the country is by war.[119]

As the presentations in Port Arthur by district organizer William Checkley and Malcolm Bruce in late November revealed, no one organization completely controlled workers in the region. One worker reportedly asked Bruce whether he took his orders from Moscow." Bruce replied, "Yes," to which the "questioner, a 'profound Marxian' of the district, sat down saying, 'that's all I want.'"[120] The CPC was succeeding, both nationally and at the Lakehead, in drawing many immigrant workers to its banner. Yet it also confronted, especially at the Lakehead, an unusually dogged revolutionary opposition in the form of the IWW, as well as perennial problems in recruiting topnotch organizers and in the form of barely subdued ethnic tensions. These patterns would persist well into the late 1920s.

5

Bolshevization and the Reorganization of the Lakehead Left 1925-27

Lenin's death in January 1924 ushered in significant changes within the Communist International that profoundly influenced the shape of not only the Communist Party of Canada (CPC) but also world socialism. Originally conceived as a global forum for Communist parties and not intended as a propaganda machine for the Community Party of Russia, the Communist International (Comintern) under Joseph Stalin became exactly the latter.[1] It also underwent an ideological shift, moving away from promoting world revolution towards Stalin's much narrower "socialism in one country" – a policy favouring the policies of the USSR above all else.[2] More specifically, the previous policy of forming coalitions and generating mass appeal was now deemed undesirable as Marxism-Leninism became interpreted as the only acceptable form of socialist doctrine.[3] Just as important for the Lakehead was the reorganization of the Comintern and the international party structure through a policy known as "Bolshevization," which, although a Communist platform, significantly impacted all socialists in Canada and at the Lakehead.[4]

By early 1926, the CPC had embarked on the implementation of this policy, and although units could still possess language factions, this new direction sought to eliminate their autonomy within the party.[5] The Comintern hoped that this reorganization would reinvigorate the revolutionary fervour of the national parties through their reorganization along factory and industrial lines rather than geographic and ethnic ones. The decision to reorganize was not an abrupt one; rather, it was the result of a series of discussions that began at the Fifth Congress of the Third International in 1924, where the Executive Committee of the Comintern adopted the proposal in principle.[6] The subsequent decision of the CPC to support the decision was not made lightly. In fact, the CPC leadership initially resisted the idea, paying it only lip service at the Third Convention in April 1924.[7] Prominent Communists advanced various reasons for their skepticism. Tim Buck opposed the proposal because of the lack of large-scale heavy industry or factory work in many parts of the country. Others, such as A.T. Hill and Matthew Popovich, opposed the measure because about 80 percent of the party was made up of non-English-speaking members. The possibility of alienating the majority of the party's membership was their prime concern.[8] The Comintern cared little for the Canadian situation, however, and, with the formal adoption of the policy, directed the CPC to prepare for the change.[9] The party was also told to focus specifically on English-speaking workers in the industrial regions of the country. The little opposition within Canada quickly disappeared and its leadership, Buck most of all, became unswerving in their desire to see the policy instituted.

While recognizing the importance played by Finns in the Communist movement in North America, historians have viewed the policy of Bolshevization, although both "lasting and pervasive," as "hardly [meriting] all the fanfare" it has received.[10] Not only is this view problematic for its inherent focus on the Anglo leadership of the party, but it also downplays the divisiveness of the issue among the mostly non-English rank and file in the United States.[11] As demonstrated in Chapter 4, language organizations within the CPC played an important role. Ironically, however, they were clearly the cause of the Comintern's belief in the chaotic nature of the Communist movement in North America.[12] The chief "culprit" was the continuing social democratic tradition among many European immigrants to North America, who comprised the vast majority of the membership in the language organizations.[13]

Yet, although the majority of party members were not native English-speakers, the leaders were. Perhaps some held prejudices similar to those earlier evident in radical organizations. Yet one should also recognize that, from a Leninist standpoint, a party divided into a variety of quasi-autonomous language-based groups, with but vestigial links between the periphery and the centre, posed very real theoretical and political dangers. In a world revolutionary organization that conceptualized each particular party as one component in a world army of revolution, a party divided into "subparties," each with its own identity and interests, was an affront to the principles of democratic centralism. As Beckie Buhay noted, a "centralized party leadership" was impossible without a thoroughgoing Bolshevization – that is, the rooting out of ethnic and linguistic particularisms in the interests of party discipline.[14]

Unsurprisingly, from the standpoint of the language federations themselves, such policies could be viewed as outright assaults on the rights and privileges of their members, many of whom might justifiably claim to constitute the Communists' strongest financial and political backers.[15] Without the Finns in the United States and Canada, much of the Communist Party would have been little more than a rumour in many parts of both countries. Although acceptance of multiculturalism might seem to a contemporary eye to be a logical acknowledgment of cultural and social realities, it was not necessarily seen that way at the time, in either Toronto or Moscow.

The period between 1925 and 1927 was one in which socialists at the Lakehead were not merely spectators. Further, although by 1926 the CPC had displaced both the Industrial Workers of the World (IWW) and the One Big Union (OBU) as the prime concern of the Royal Canadian Mounted Police, it failed to dominate socialists in the region because of its continued inability to adequately deal with its inherently multicultural nature.[16] One of the ironic results of the CPC's difficulties with regard to ethnic diversity was a new lease on life for the interwar IWW.

By 1925, the ongoing turmoil within working-class organizations at the Lakehead had begun to take its toll. Socialists of all stripes became increasingly worried over the situation in Port Arthur and Fort William. As the *Worker* reported in February: "The apathy amongst the workers here is beginning to worry those who are interested in Unionism as well as in independent political action on the part of the working class." In response, both socialists and trade unionists began to bring in well-known speakers to mobilize the local working class. Receiving the most attention was a visit by Malcolm Bruce. On behalf of the CPC, he spoke against the effort of the "reactionary officialdom to change the unions into mere fraternal, class-collaborationist organizations instead of making them mass instruments of class struggle." He also urged the unions to pay more attention to the unemployed.[17]

Whereas Bruce attempted to shore up support within the twin cities, Harry Bryan was active in the surrounding countryside. Spending much of February speaking to branches throughout the district, he paid particular attention to establishing branches of the Young Communist League (YCL). Relying heavily on "the generosity of our Finnish comrades," he took part in a number of cultural and social events. As was often the case with Bryan, he found himself with a splendid opportunity to use his own significant skills to stand on the podium speaking of the Communist platform and "backing up God's efforts to get the worker to go into action on his own behalf."[18]

Another well-received speaker during the early months of 1925 was A.E. Smith. His presentations as head of the Ontario section of the Canadian Labour Party (CLP) at the Wobbly-controlled Port Arthur Labour Temple, the Orpheum theatre in Fort William, and the Fort William Auditorium focused on unemployment associations and the progress made "in forming educational classes in the East." They were well attended. Once again, Fred Moore chaired the Fort William meetings.[19] He used them to convince those in attendance that "the radical labour movements were converging towards 'the day' when a social revolution would bring about a complete change in system." The main duty of a labour representative in Parliament, he contended, "should be to weaken, hamper and embarrass the bourgeois parliament." The process of social revolution, described as a "grim business," was but a "natural evolution."[20]

Although the predominance of Finnish women in the CPC's membership at the Lakehead and their allegiance to the women's auxiliary of the Finnish Organization of Canada (FOC) had thwarted early attempts to establish a branch of the Women's Labour League (WLL), one was formed in Fort William in May, under the guidance of Fred Moore's wife.[21] It soon became quite active in its attempts to mobilize Anglo-Saxon women and Finnish domestic servants.[22] The Fort William WLL also convinced the league's executive to send a number of speakers to the region throughout 1925. One of the earliest speakers was Annie Buller, who, to standing-room-only audiences in both the Port Arthur and Fort William halls, spoke at some length on the conditions of the workers in Nova Scotia and across Canada.[23]

The Lumber Workers Industrial Union of Canada (LWIUC) likewise undertook to reorganize itself during the spring of 1925 to better deal with the issues facing its membership. According to Ahti Tolvanen, however, reorganization "removed the centre of activity from the district office, which was closed most of the time, as delegate-organizers such as Alf Hautamäki and Kalle Salo toured the committees throughout the province."[24] In effect, the region was left susceptible to other influences.

While Salo and Hautamäki were travelling elsewhere in Ontario, the IWW sent Sam Scarlett to the region. He spent much of the summer of 1925 heaping plaudits on the Wobblies, condemning the CPC, and performing what the *Industrial Pioneer* described as "missionary work in the Canadian wheat fields."[25] Scarlett's preaching to the harvesters profoundly influenced the IWW's fortunes at the Lakehead. Migratory by nature, many of the men working in the fields went east to secure jobs in the lumber camps during the winter. The most active in the area over the next few years, such as Holmer Borg, first became members of the IWW in Saskatchewan during an early tour by Scarlett, and continued to agitate on behalf of the men in the lumber camps once the lumber season began in Northwestern Ontario.[26]

The activities of organizers from both the IWW and the CPC caught the attention of regional politicians and traditional labour leaders, who began to voice their opposition to immigration and the flood of radical workers into the country.[27] Not all of the attention was negative. The recent success of the Communists, for example, caught the attention of Peter Heenan, the Kenora Labour member of the provincial parliament (MPP) who had been elected in 1919 and again in 1923. Sensing a shift in provincial politics, he sought to tap into the CPC's growing support despite having recently accepted nomination from the Liberal party. He was refused a meeting.[28]

Sensing an opportunity of its own, the CPC parachuted party stalwart A.E. Smith into Port Arthur to run in the riding of Port Arthur-Thunder Bay during the 1925 federal election.[29] Smith and the CPC's Central Executive Committee (CEC) chose the riding because both felt that the support from the Finnish lumber workers might well carry the day.[30] His candidacy also received the support of the local Canadian Labour Party (no surprise, as Smith was president of the Ontario section) and from Alex Gibson and the Port Arthur Trades and Labour Council. Once more, Smith's candidacy would reveal the mileage that the Lakehead left could get by attempting to occupy at least some of the political space normally occupied by the centrists.

Much of Smith's platform reiterated the speeches he had given in the region earlier in the year. Local newspapers described him as eloquent, with even normally skeptical journalists suggesting that "oratory like his had not flown from the tongue of any speaker on the platform in Port Arthur." Moreover, his politics were clearly enunciated. At the Port Arthur Armoury, for example, he addressed the crowd of 2,000 directly as a "deliberative assembly, a parliament of the people, who are the first factor ... in political power."[31] Smith did well, garnering 1,363 of a total 9,068 votes in perhaps the best showing of any federal Communist candidate in the 1920s.[32] Even the Port Arthur *News-Chronicle* described the election as the "Most Vigorously Contested in the History of Port Arthur."

The CPC considered Smith's showing a clear indication of its growing stature in the region.[33] As Anthony Rasporich's work reveals, "near majorities were in fact recorded over the Conservative, Liberal, and independent candidates in the south end polls dominated by the Slavs and Finns, and in radical rural pockets of Finns to the north and west of Port Arthur."[34] It is revealing, however, that he won only three rural polls by narrow margins, and that the Finnish vote was split almost equally among all candidates.[35]

Clearly, the year 1925 may have begun slowly for the CPC in the region but it ended with a number of tangible successes. Building on this, the LWIUC sent a number of organizers into the camps in Northwestern Ontario in order to recruit workers and establish camp committees. It estimated that at least 2,000 Finns, 600 Swedes, and 300 workers of various ethnic backgrounds could be organized.[36] How many of these new unionists became Communists is unclear, but the party was showing such new vigour that, according to Donald Avery, it had displaced the IWW as the main worry of Dominion, provincial, and local officials.[37]

Communists were also achieving success organizing workers and their children during this period. The *Young Worker* proudly reported in April 1925 that the efforts of organizers had resulted in the establishment of half a dozen branches of the YCL in Port Arthur and in Finnish communities in the surrounding countryside.[38] By February 1926, membership in Port Arthur had increased so much that educational classes for workers were offered on a regular basis.[39] Visiting the region in February, Malcolm Bruce reported optimistically that inroads would continue to be made in the coming months.[40] It appears that he spoke too soon, however.

Although a successful women's conference was held in April and the May Day celebrations organized by the CPC were some of the best attended ever, most functions continued to be overwhelmingly composed of Finnish and Ukrainian workers.[41] Whereas hundreds of Finnish and Ukrainian members turned out to the events, only a "sprinkling" of English-speaking workers showed up. In fact, Italian and Scandinavian Communists, numerically the smallest in the region, had almost as many participants as their Anglo-Saxon comrades.[42] Even a somewhat patriotically based focus in Fort William on the recent general strike of miners and transport workers in Great Britain, coupled with the oft-repeated mantra that local workers should "Look to England," garnered few results.[43] As a local correspondent to the *Worker* commented: "It seems as if the English-speaking workers like to bow the knee to the boss, and are satisfied with the Labour Day handed out to them on the first Monday in September."[44] It is interesting to note that even so orthodox a voice of Communist opinion could avoid attributing causal efficacy to cultural divisions.

At the Fifth Convention of the CPC in 1926, the Politburo fell in line with the Comintern's decision to centralize power and counter the growing influence and dominance of the various language federations. Its policy of Bolshevization amounted to an attempt to overcome the dominance of the Ukrainian and Finnish language federations.[45] Bolshevization also affected the nature of the relationship between the CPC and the existing trade union movement. The CPC's policy during the 1920s had been to infiltrate and eventually control the existing unions. This was thought to be necessary because the vast majority of workers likely to be supportive of the Communist cause had previously been organized by either the American Federation of Labor (AFL) or the Trades and Labour Congress of Canada (TLC). Tim Buck later recalled that the opposite occurred, and the CPC's involvement in the AFL and TLC unions led to a theoretical lowering of the party's ideological work and to the debasement of the fundamental principle of the revolution.[46]

Although compliance with the Comintern directive was not complete until 1929, Hill reported to the CEC as early as September 1926 that "Port Arthur and Fort William had shown a better appreciation of the Party program of late and we had progressed in the Twin Cities. More than half of the members of the Section were in the farming centres, while those in the industrial areas still showed traces of their antipathy to the older unions. The work among the women and youth had seen productive results." The reality of the situation at the Lakehead, though, was that continuing participation by Finnish socialists was a necessity. As Hill also pointed out, all of the recent progress was due to the activities of the Finnish section of the party in the region.[47]

On returning from his tour of Northwestern Ontario in late September, William Moriarty painted a sobering picture of the activities in the region. He argued that the region was in dire need of more attention. Although many workers were sympathetic to the Communist platform, the lack of an organizer left them largely without a connection to the party's centre. For example, Moriarty told the CEC that the work in Port Arthur was "not all it could be," and even the work among the Finnish membership had become "very unsatisfactory." The same situation could be found in other regional towns, such as Nipigon, where his meeting had been attended by almost no one. Much of the reason for these shortcomings, Moriarty explained, rested with the failure of the District 6 Executive Committee to function properly. Moriarty did report, however, that "there were hopes," as "he was sure that the English membership couls [sic] be increased."[48]

No doubt it was this belief that drove delegates to the August convention of the Port Arthur branch of the Canadian Labour Party to unanimously nominate A.E. Smith as their candidate for the federal election in the riding of Port Arthur-Thunder Bay, and local union organizer William Nasau Welsh for Fort William.[49] The CLP, according to Ian Angus, was "a loose federation of provincial ILP's formed initially in 1917 in reaction to the Trades and Labour Congress attempt to divert anti-conscription sentiment into electoral victory." After the formation of the Workers' Party of Canada (WPC), the CLP had become the mechanism by which the CPC usually contested federal elections.[50] The CLP's program typically called for "demands for proportional representation, the abolition of the BNA Act, the nationalization of public utilities, and social legislation to improve the lot of workers."[51] Ultimately, the WPC had only limited success throughout the period, managing to accumulate only 9,000 members by 1926 as a result of its affiliation with the Ontario section of the CLP. Its low numbers never enabled it to become the Farmer-Labour Party envisioned by the Comintern.[52] As Angus suggests, "the Canadian Labour Party, with its very tenuous, limited roots in the unions and its lack of popular support, was not even a pale reflection of the British Labor Party, let alone the Bolshevik Party!"[53]

Could the Communists make an electoral breakthrough at the Lakehead in 1926? The CLP leadership was drawn exclusively from Southern Ontario, but within the Lakehead region the party had such high-profile supporters as Bryan.[54] It was also thought to be attractive to many Finns.[55] In the days leading up to the election, however, the simmering unrest in the lumber camps in Northwestern Ontario erupted in a series of strikes.[56] According to Ian Radforth, "preparation had begun in the summer, when joint meetings of Wobbly and LWIUC camp delegates met to decide on wage demands." Following the rejection of the workers' demands by a number of companies, a "test of strength ensued."[57] From newspaper interviews and reports, Hautamäki and Bryan appear to have been the strike leaders, representing a joint LWIUC and IWW committee.[58] When the strikes finally ended eight weeks later, over thirty companies and 3,000 men across Northwestern Ontario had been embroiled in the conflict.[59] In the Thunder Bay District, roughly 2,500 workers had been involved, with protests occurring both in the twin cities and in the camps.[60]

While the sheer number of participants makes the strike stand out, it was also a pivotal moment for the nature of socialism in the region. Described as "almost unique in the history of Canadian unionism," the sheer number of participants in the strike (over 3,000) was felt to be a "splendid illustration that where the rank and file has the will, a united front of two union organizations can be satisfactorily made." The *Worker* suggested that the strike in the Port Arthur District provided the clearest example yet of what could be accomplished by "the unorganized mass of workers," if only they would unite.[61]

The participation of the LWIUC, in what appears to have been its first industry-wide strike, demonstrated its continued willingness to form a united front with the IWW in the district.[62] Initially, the CPC viewed the cooperation between the two organizations as an example of the strength and success that solidarity could achieve following the Comintern's policy. During the first few weeks, for example, the mass organization committee had unprecedented success in persuading strikebreakers to join the strike.[63] The fact that Wobblies held the most important positions on the joint strike committee, however, concerned the CPC leadership as they entered into the arrangement on equal footing and often took the lead. The growing influence of the IWW at the Lakehead was evident in a petition by LWIUC members to the CPC Organization Committee, asking to be allowed to hold joint membership in the syndicalist-oriented Lumber Workers Industrial Union (LWIU) linked to the IWW.[64]

Not surprisingly, the petition was rejected and, sensing the danger posed by the IWW, the CPC began a campaign to undermine the role of the IWW despite the fact that during the strike its "claim to leadership was not disputed by the Communist Party's paper the *Worker*."[65] During the final days of the strike, the CPC leaders were convinced that their party had become the preferred voice of socialists in the region.[66] Certainly, the CPC had made gains. At the same time, as William Moriarty's reception at the Lakehead would confirm, many lumber workers were not averse to subjecting CPC policies to skeptical examination. Many seemed convinced that they benefited when the CPC and IWW cooperated and lost when the two organizations struggled with each other for political supremacy.[67]

Such dreams of left unity proved evanescent. The inherent contradictions within the organizations and the desire of the LWIUC to control the camps led to increasing bickering on both the picket lines and in the joint strike committee meetings. Tensions between the two organizations even spilled onto the streets when one drunken Finnish Wobbly reportedly stabbed a Finnish Communist in the face over ideological differences.[68] On 28 October, the joint committee abruptly ended when the IWW moved that the strike take on a more active fight "in the IWW tradition," but lost "the vote to those supporting [CPC] affiliation." Under the leadership of Communist organizer Alf Hautamäki, those remaining decided to enter into negotiations, resulting in an end to the strike shortly afterwards.[69] The thirty-six-day strike did result, however, in improved conditions and increases in pay for both monthly wages and piecework.[70] Despite the inter-left squabble during its final days, "in the years following the 1926 breakthrough," Radforth has observed, "no other strike involved as many pulp cutters or brought the unions such favourable results."[71]

While Smith's federal election campaign had also attempted to capitalize on the LWIUC's prominent role in the strike, it also featured a number of progressive initiatives meant to appeal to working-class voters. His platform was essentially a commitment to fight for unemployment insurance, minimum wages for men and women, education for all children, safety standards, old-age pensions, and free medical aid for workers. To support him, the CPC mobilized a number of its key organizers to work in the region. Smith's campaign stressed that, as the recent strike had demonstrated, it was the CPC that "represents the true interests of the workers."[72] His campaign posters, however, although highlighting his connections to the CPC and his role as general secretary of the Canadian Labour Defence League (CLDL), focused more on his "British" roots.[73]

As in the 1925 election, to counter criticisms and deflect attention away from the party's "ethnic" bases, Smith most often campaigned on his personal virtues, stressing his being "born in Canada [as] the son of a British soldier." It certainly did not hurt that leading newspapers were describing him as a moderate. "What manner of man is the Rev. A.E. Smith, at once Methodist minister and red, who has been chosen as head of the Ontario Section of the Labour Party?" asked the *Toronto Star*. "Surely no man milder in appearance and manner was ever classed as a Bolshevik."[74] His nomination had been opposed by many labour unions in the region,[75] but he was able, to some extent, to present an image attractive to the mainstream Lakehead voter.

Sensing a division within the working class, the Liberals in Port Arthur approached both the loosely defined progressive camp and the Independent Labour Party (ILP) about running a "Lib-Pro-Lab" candidate. Although the CPC had dismissed the ILP as "a few fossilized old timers, who years ago were on the Trades Council," they could ill afford to lose even a handful of votes to them.[76] For example, James Southern, a member of the Brotherhood of Locomotive Firemen and Engineers and an ILP supporter, spoke out against the CLP, describing it as a Toronto-centred party. The assessment was entirely accurate when one considers that Smith had been parachuted into the riding following his defeat in the Toronto civic election.[77] The irony of a candidate with no local connection criticizing his opponents as opportunistic was not lost on many voters in the riding.

In stark contrast to the previous year, Smith lost by over 1,746 votes to the Conservative candidate. Although he managed a very respectable 1,382 votes, the "victory" was marred by his inability to win a single urban or rural poll in the riding.[78] In Fort William, William Welsh's campaign for the CLP used pretty much the same message as Smith, but what Welsh lacked in Smith's national profile he gained in being part of the local working class.[79] The potential success of Welsh and the CPC spurred the Lib-Lab candidate to pull out to ensure a Communist defeat. Although he finished a distant second to the incumbent, Robert Manion, he managed a respectable 2,400 votes.[80]

The end of the strike and Smith's defeat did not mean an end to the increased activity of the CPC at the Lakehead. The CPC flooded the region with speakers to capitalize on its self-promoted role in the strike and the "success" of Smith and Welsh. Beckie Buhay's weeklong visit, in particular, succeeded in bringing together hundreds of Finnish, Ukrainian, and English men and women to hear her speak on Russia and the Communist movement. Her presentations to workers in both Fort William and Port Arthur led to invitations to meet with the membership of the local branch of the Ukrainian Labour-Farmer Temple Association (ULFTA) and to give an additional speech to workers at the Lyceum Theatre. Harry Bryan, Alex Gibson, and a full orchestra frequently accompanied her presentations.[81] A year later, in March 1927, the CPC would claim that 50 percent of the workers involved in the strike had joined the LWIUC due to organizing in the following months.[82]

Subsequent events held at the Port Arthur Workers' Hall at 316 Bay Street and in Fort William to celebrate the ninth anniversary of the Russian Revolution drew equally large crowds. The Port Arthur event was so large that hundreds had to be turned away for lack of room. Those lucky enough to stay were treated to a multilingual event filled with fiery speeches by Hautamäki and Bryan, music by the local Finnish and Ukrainian orchestras, the Ukrainian Boys' Band, and English musicians.[83] As Buhay reported in the *Worker,* "the splendid co-operation of all comrades, particularly of the Ukrainians and the Finnish women comrades, and the English, helped to make this week a success."[84]

By this point, it had become clear to local and national CPC officials that the October 1926 strike had reinvigorated the IWW in the region. Because of the IWW's appeal to the Finnish lumber workers, the largest element in the CPC's LWIUC, this worried many. The CPC faced a paradox. If it cooperated with the IWW, it would win points with workers for effectively helping them to organize, but it would also provide its rival with the means to make substantial gains. For their part, the Wobblies viewed their role in the strike as a success. Prompted by a strike-induced growth in membership, the LWIU moved its headquarters from Sudbury to Port Arthur and a local organizer, Nick Viita, became its general secretary. The offices of the Canadian news bureau for the weekly American-based Finnish newspaper *Industrialisti* also made the move.[85]

The IWW's lack of a rigid hierarchy and commitment to rank-and-file democracy appealed to many non-English-speaking socialists at the Lakehead.[86] Although the CPC's work within unions often entailed practices that were no less democratic and open, its general image was that of a highly disciplined, top-down party. Like many, Holmer Berg, a Swedish immigrant who had been an organizer for the IWW in Saskatchewan and Port Arthur during the strike, supported the IWW because, unlike the Communists, they organized through their membership and expected everyone to participate, whether they were part of the leadership or a member of the rank and file.[87] The IWW also appealed to many in the mid-1920s, Donald Avery argues, because it was not preoccupied with "sterile ideological controversy: despite their syndicalist underpinnings their attention was focused on specific grievances."[88]

Although the *Worker* described the strike as illustrating "the fine spirit of solidarity," the CPC did not wait long to try to turn the tangible gains into partisan ones. A joint committee consisting of representatives from the two unions was responsible for seeing that the agreement was honoured by the signatories, but the LWIUC immediately began a campaign to undercut the IWW's contribution, by using the strike as an opportunity to strengthen itself. In fact, a bigger deal was made of the opportunity for gain and the CPC's efforts than the actual outcome of the strike itself. Rather than continue the fight in

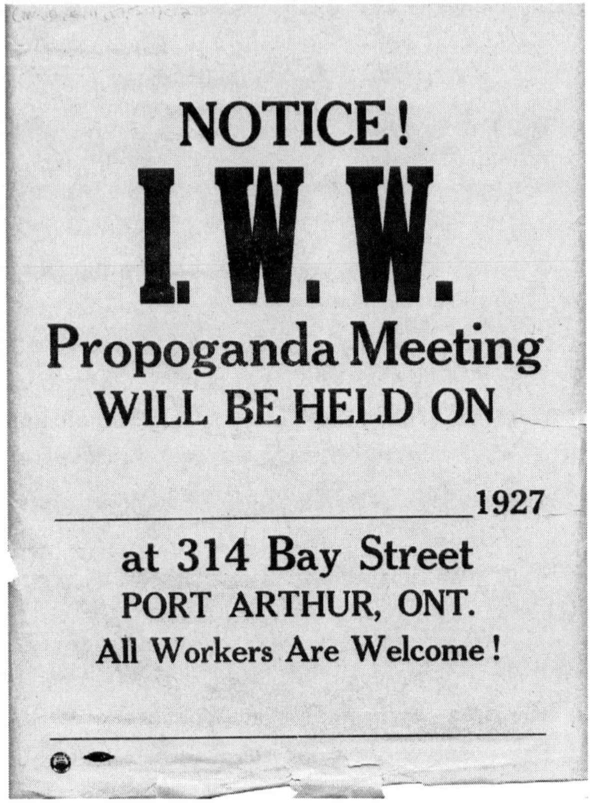

Figure 7 IWW Propoganda Meeting notice, 1927.
Courtesy of Lakehead University Library Archives

other camps or other industries, the CPC turned its attention to "a big organization campaign" among the workers who had just gone back to work.[89]

The IWW was in reality no different. During the strike, it had sent out appeals to various Wobbly branches and to both *Industrial Solidarity* and *Industrial Worker,* asking for donations. Readers were informed by a Canadian organizer named J.A. MacDonald that the funds would not only ensure a victory for the strikers in Northwestern Ontario but also the organization of the lumber industry into the IWW.[90] Shortly after the strike, the Port Arthur branch issued a bulletin both praising the cooperation among itself, the LWIUC, and the unorganized workers and arguing that only organizations that followed the same principles that it did would ensure the continued recognition of what had been won.[91]

The Wobblies were not the only ones to criticize the Communists. Workers in Cochrane, Ontario, for example, complained to the Department of Labour that they had been forced to provide funds during the strike or stop working. If they had refused, their names would have been "published in the Finnish paper 'Vapaus' as strikebreakers." Such threats were not something to be taken lightly, as the Communist-sponsored *Vapaus* was one of the most widely read Finnish newspapers in North America, and such a public indictment would have resulted in those listed being barred from employment and ostracized in the Finnish community.[92]

Interestingly, neither union sought recognition during the strike. Speaking to reporters early on, joint strike committee spokesman Harry Bryan adamantly denied rumours that the LWIUC and LWIU were seeking recognition as part of the strikers' demands. This reflected not only an attempt to allay the concerns of many citizens in the region but also the reality that the vast majority of workers did not belong to either union and continued to express a desire to remain independent. As Bryan himself commented: "All [the] men want is the granting of their wage demands and with an agreement made with the contractors along those terms the men are willing to go to work at once."[93]

There can be no doubt that the LWIUC needed the IWW during the strike of 1926. Compared with the Communists' network in the region, the IWW's Finnish support circle was both better organized and more financially stable. Its halls were the natural gathering points for the lumber workers, the majority of whom were Finnish. In fact, due to the IWW's size and the large number of Wobblies involved in the joint strike committee, most strike meetings were held in the much larger IWW Labour Temple at 314 Bay Street. The decision to appoint LWIU member Thomas Hill as the treasurer of the joint strike committee also reflected the greater resources that the Wobbly Finnish auxiliary could mobilize. The differences are apparent, for example, in fundraising efforts. While both unions appealed for funds through national and international organs, local entertainments were put on, with all proceeds being donated to the strike committee. Typical were the events held on the evening of 27 September at both 314 and 316 Bay Street. Whereas the Communists took in $28, the Finnish auxiliary raised over $188.[94] So successful had the IWW become that four Wobbly-supported schools were operating in Northwestern Ontario, with one in Fort William run by a man named David Aho and another in Port Arthur, serving 200 children, run by William Arnberg. Two other schools operated close by, in Intola and Nipigon.[95]

The CPC's situation was no less rosy, according to Tim Buck in his January 1927 report to the Comintern's National Secretary of America and Canada. He described a party on the brink of massive expansion, even though membership had actually decreased between 1924 and November 1926, from 4,500 to 3,150.[96] This decline, in Buck's interpretation, did not "reflect so much a loss of influence by the Party" as the difficulties experienced following the decision by the Comintern to reorganize in 1925.[97] The CPC leadership claimed to have abolished the language sections, established national language agitprops, and reorganized "the Central Executive Committee into a Political Bureau and department for Agitprop, Trade Union work, Organization, Women's Work, Youth and Press."[98]

The party remained approximately 85 percent non-English-speaking. In part, the CPC leadership claimed, this was due to the large number of immigrants, most notably from Finland. In response to questions from the National Secretary of America and Canada, they also explained that the pattern could be attributed to the loss of over 300 English-speaking members through emigration to the United States during the last three or four years. "Whole branches are dissolved," Buck stated, "because of this emigration ... We have been able to increase our foreign born membership because they are easier to organize and also for the fact that they cannot emigrate to the United States as easily as the English speaking people."[99]

Tim Buck's report also outlined a list of successes in the development of a united front. Figuring prominently were the activities of the CLP's approximately 54,000 affiliated members and its electoral results, including Smith's performance at the Lakehead. The CPC took credit for eighteen of the twenty labour/farmer candidates, who ran in the 1925 federal election with support from the CLP, and for the success in the recent civic elections of the forty-six labour candidates, only a few of them Communists, who had won. The CLDL, under the direction of Smith, claimed to possess forty-six branches throughout the country, while the WLL had eighteen locals operating under party direction and had established an official organ, the *Woman Worker*. In the realm of trade union work, it was reported that it "has been particularly successful in the basic industries: coal mining, lumbering, and on the railways."[100]

In reality, the CPC continued to have problems in recruiting district organizers throughout 1927. At the time of its annual report, the party informed the Comintern that there were only two district organizers in the nine districts. While acknowledging that the CEC needed to give more attention to this issue, it placed much of the blame on the shoulders of the district committees. "Instead of functioning as political organs," the report states, "district committees merely act as administrative bodies. Too much of the work of the [district committee] in a political sense, is undertaken by the CEC." The CEC also argued that its general weakness during 1926 and the first half of 1927 reflected the "general apathy in the trade union movement and the necessity of properly establishing and organizing Communist trade union factions."[101]

Despite such limitations, the growing prominence of Communists in Port Arthur became clearer and clearer through the course of 1927. When members of the Eastern section of the LWIUC met in Port Arthur in early March, it boasted 1,500 members with branches throughout Northern Ontario. Members from the Lakehead dominated the executive, with Alf Hautamäki as secretary and Harry Bryan as president.[102] The union's organizers won the respect and admiration of the workers. "It was tough," comments Edwin Suski, an LWIUC militant between 1926 and 1927. "There's not much friendliness. You have to walk from the railroad 28 to 30 miles through the bush, and when you get there you get a very cold reception from the camp foreman if he happened to be there."[103]

As in the rest of the country, good organizers, especially English-speaking ones, remained difficult to find at the Lakehead. This became more and more problematic as the CPC almost obsessively began focusing on increasing the total number of English-speaking members. The apathy towards the CPC on the part of most Anglo labour leaders in the region and their tendency to favour traditional trade unionism and British-style labour politics contributed to the party's reaching into the past to find a populist type of organizer with pre-existing ties to the community. To that end, Beckie Buhay wrote to Harry Bryan in April, wondering whether he would be willing to become more active.

Although Bryan had been involved with the CPC during its first few years, he had not taken a direct role apart from the 1926 strike. A longtime friend of Buhay, he had recently hosted her at his home, where she had taken the opportunity to see whether he was willing to become the literary agent for the district. Buhay soon after encouraged Bryan to become more involved, admitting that the leaders of the CPC "were very anxious" to have him do the work. Buhay also attempted to appeal to Bryan's wallet by suggesting he would be able to "make it go financially as well." In the end, he agreed, but his instructions from the leadership went beyond merely assisting with organizational efforts in the region. The party also charged him with keeping an eye on the lumber workers, particularly Hautamäki.[104]

Bryan would figure prominently in the Port Arthur and Fort William celebrations of the Paris Commune and the anniversary of the CPC. On a number of occasions, the Workers' Hall in Port Arthur and the Robertson Street Finnish Hall in Fort William were filled to capacity to hear him speak of the party's past struggles and of the difficulties it currently faced.[105] Bryan also involved himself in the early cooperative moment begun by Finnish farmers in the rural areas surrounding the Lakehead in 1927.[106]

Bryan's efforts and an increase in CPC propaganda in the region led to a resurgence of the party. In particular, this was apparent in the renewal of a branch of the WLL in Port Arthur. An outgrowth of the Finnish Women's Federation section established by Sanna Kannasto during the previous year, it held a successful conference in April at the Worker's Hall, with branches from Alpila, Intola, North Branch, Finland, Nipigon, Nolalu, Fort William, and Port Arthur in attendance.[107] The WLL had also been integral to the organizational efforts of the Young Pioneers and YCL in the twin cities and the surrounding region. The Young Pioneers in particular reported significant gains in membership and the creation of educational courses at the Lakehead. In Fort William alone, over forty new Pioneers were reported to have joined in the final months of 1927.[108] Following the departure of Kannasto, the branch became an extension of the LWIUC. A reflection of the links between the union and the youth organization can be found in the election of Ailiane Hautamäki, the wife of Alf Hautamäki, as secretary of the YCL branch.[109]

The Ukrainian community of Fort William appears to have become much more active within the CPC during this same period. It would not be too much of a stretch to link this growth to Bryan's renewed involvement. As his efforts before the First World War reveal, Bryan had previously been successful in bridging the ethnic divides between worker organizations at the Lakehead. In addition, it was well known that his role in the 1920s split had to do with ideological rather than ethnic differences. Led by a labourer named Michael Biniowsky, an acquaintance of Bryan's, the Ukrainian Agitprop became the most active after the Finns.[110]

Bryan's talents were also used to tackle the growing problem of the IWW. Despite claims by the CPC that its rival was on the road to extinction, the April issue of the Wobblies' Port Arthur branch newsletter reveals an organization undergoing revival.[111] Since the transfer of the LWIU's headquarters from Sudbury to Port Arthur in July 1926, the LWIU had improved both financially and in membership. Wobbly agitation committees and several of its auxiliaries had "swamped northern and western Ontario with leaflets, papers and pamphlets." The LWIUC's own annual report for 1926-27 acknowledged the presence of the IWW in the lumber camps and warned CPC leaders that nothing could be accomplished in the region as long as two unions existed.[112] The CPC blamed the LWIUC's inexperience for the general lack of progress at the Lakehead, but no excuses for the IWW's growing influence in other aspects of the region's economy were forthcoming. By April, the IWW appears to have expanded beyond the lumber industry, as members of the Marine and Transport Union were actively agitating when the shipping season began.

Increased activity was not without its problems. IWW attempts to establish a Construction Workers' Unit faced significant hurdles, as "few real live ... delegates who properly understand this industry and the problems of its workers" could be found.[113] Unlike Vancouver, which benefited from its close proximity to the Seattle branch during this period, the Lakehead was left without a direct connection to other branches due to a police crackdown at the Minnesota-Ontario border. The only correspondence received typically contained reminders to remit dues and invoices for cards, buttons, and stamps.[114] As a result, by 1927 the Port Arthur branch operated largely independently of the General Executive Board in Chicago, taking the initiative on a number of matters and consulting headquarters only after changes had been made.[115]

One such initiative involved the repeated attempts by the Port Arthur branch of the LWIU to convince the Work People's College in Minnesota to establish a branch in Canada. It was felt that such a move was necessary due to the increasing number of problems that workers were experiencing in trying to cross the border to attend the school. Such a move was also necessary to meet the demand in Northwestern Ontario, as the proposed Port Arthur location would easily have an annual attendance larger than that in Duluth. Ultimately, the Work People's College did not establish a school in Port Arthur but agreed to arrange for courses to be taught in the city when instructors were available.[116]

Despite the difficulties experienced between 1925 and 1929, it is clear that the Lakehead had two very active socialist organizations. Both the IWW and the CPC sought the allegiance of the mostly Finnish lumber workers in the region, while at the same time fighting for better wages and conditions for the working class more generally. Although the Wobblies had made substantial inroads over the past few years, by the end of 1927 the District 6 Executive Committee of the CPC reported that its membership included representatives from subcommittees located in Port Arthur, Nipigon, Intola, Fort William, and

Nolalu. Financially, the District Executive Committee was also much more stable.[117] Robust Finnish and Ukrainian agitprops could also be found in Port Arthur, Fort William, and the outlying communities.[118] Although the CPC's membership continued to be primarily non-Anglo-Saxon in origin, a source of persistent tensions within the party, modest gains in English membership and the establishment by Fred Moore of an English branch of the CLDL provided some hope for the party's leadership.[119] Communists could also be found among the reported twenty-eight branches of trade unions in Fort William and the twenty-seven branches in Port Arthur. [120] The Communists' fortunes were clearly on the rise.

6

Turning to the Left
1928-30

When Communists from around the world gathered in Moscow in the spring of 1925 for the Fifth Plenum of the Communist International (Comintern), few knew that their national parties and the International itself were about to embark on a new path. The accession of Joseph Stalin would lead to a gradual change in the nature and characteristics of the Comintern. Policies of Bolshevization that had preceded Stalin, which had remained largely a dead letter in Canada, would be given new emphasis. Between 1928 and 1929, a new Canadian leadership came to terms with the "New Line."[1] The infamous "Third Period" in the world Communist movement was now underway.

At the ninth Executive Committee of the Communist International Plenum held in February 1928, a new line was adopted to reflect the prevailing belief that "capitalism was now moving back into crisis" and that the movement had entered the Third Period.[2] The central thesis of Third Period political theory was that the Communists' rivals on the left were social fascists. Other socialist parties, such as social democrats throughout much of the west, were predestined to act as the "'last reserve' of the old order," and it "was the duty of the Communists to unmask the role being played in the labour movement by socialist leaders, including left-wingers, and to win over the socialist rank-and-file."

Figure 8 Socialist Youth Conference, Young Workers League 1927. *Courtesy of Lakehead University Library Archives*

According to the Comintern, the slogan "class against class" now characterized "the struggle throughout the world."[3]

Historians have described the Third Period as the abandonment of the United Front with other socialists and a turn to the left.[4] Within the Comintern and in the Russian party, this pitted Stalin against Bukharin and Trotsky. In Canada, the pattern manifested itself in an internal fight between Tim Buck and Stewart Smith that climaxed in July 1929. Tim Buck's accession "was no simple change of personnel, but a total change in the policies and program of the Canadian Communist movement." In keeping with decisions reached in Moscow, the Communist movement in Canada became "subordinate to the foreign policy goals of the Stalinist leadership."[5] The Communist Party of Canada (CPC) held out against these changes, but once it adopted Stalin's policies, the new line exerted a profound influence over its strategy and tactics.[6] Its efforts to enact the directives of the Comintern (particularly Bolshevization) had unexpected consequences, however.

At the Lakehead, as throughout much of Canada, the CPC's adoption of a "class against class policy" not only resulted in a loss of almost half its membership between 1925 and 1929 but also led to a reconfiguration of socialist organizations and activities.[7] The predominance of the lumber workers in the region and the large number of Finns and Ukrainians resulted in the majority of the district leadership's becoming non-Anglo in origin, a situation exacerbated by the overall decline (mostly of Anglos) in membership.[8] Nationally, 80 percent of the party's members did not speak English and 60 percent continued to be Finnish.[9] Much as in other regions with high proportions of non-Anglo members during this period, tensions began to mount at the Lakehead because of the growing disconnect between the policies of the leadership and the concerns of socialists. The most significant consequence of Moscow's insistence on Bolshevization by 1930 was the growth in influence of the Industrial Workers of the World (IWW) at the Lakehead, despite the Wobblies's insignificance elsewhere in interwar Canada.

In the summer of 1928, the Sixth Congress of the Communist International declared that national organizations should prepare for the onset of a worldwide revolution, but the CPC was too embroiled in its own internal struggles to respond effectively to the call. At the Fourth Congress of the Red International of Labour Unions (RILU, also known as the Profintern) in March and April, calls were made for the Trade Union Educational League "to become the nucleus of a new organization for the workers in organized industries, while at the same time remaining the focal point for the left-wing members of the 'reformist unions.'" By the time of the Comintern's Sixth Congress in July and August, a policy of dual unionism and a shift to "a class against class policy" had been adopted.[10]

The Anglo-American Secretariat appears to have also become increasingly concerned over the CPC's slow progress in popularizing the decisions reached at the Ninth Plenum. As one of the last parties in the world to be fully "Stalinized," and given the continued leadership role of the pro-Trotsky Maurice Spector and the equivocal Jack MacDonald until 1928 and 1929, respectively, the CPC was rebuked for lagging behind the world Communist movement. It was argued that the CPC needed to "bring out in a more clear and sharp form the identity of the Party as the revolutionary party of the Canadian working class."[11] Addressing this issue was of utmost importance, the Anglo-American Secretariat contended, as the economic and political situation in Canada placed the country "definitely in the midst of the 'third period' outlined in the thesis of the VI Congress of the Communist International. The stabilization, rationalization and increased development of Canadian capitalism is fraught with contradictions that will embroil the country in the coming imperialist war."[12]

Central to tackling the problem were the trade unions. The CPC leadership believed that only by "winning the masses of workers" in the All-Canadian Congress of Labour (ACCL) and the Trades and Labour Congress of Canada (TLC) (the two national trade union organizations) could the party be in a position to take advantage of the turmoil that would inevitably grip the country. The Anglo-American Secretariat criticized the CPC for its past efforts, however, and rebuked the Central Executive Committee (CEC) for its past work. The Canadian party had "too often been directed from the 'top' instead of from the rank-and-file, as is evidenced by the slogan 'Amalgamation of the two Congresses.'" Similarly, in attempting to organize the unorganized, the CPC was cautioned to "clarify its present unclear industrial policy, educate activise [sic] its members, and take the initiative in building new revolutionary unions and creating a broad Left Wing opposition movement."[13] Perhaps the greatest obstacle in implementing a successful recruiting campaign was the lack of a significant number of Anglo-Saxon organizers. There was also the continued conflict between the CEC and non-English-speaking members. "The membership of the Party still remains," the Comintern remarked, "of an unsatisfactory quality. Greater efforts must be made by the Party to recruit Anglo-Saxon workers from the best elements of the progressives in the trade unions."[14]

For example, the recent split within the CPC over the question of the Ukrainian-language organizations was viewed as "an example of the unhealthy state of the Party apparatus." The "liquadory tendencies," underestimations of party work, failure to extend propaganda, and so on "must be overcome by centrally directed agit-prop work that will organize and control fractional activity within the language organizations. In no sense must the language agit-props supplant Party fractions as tends to be the case now."[15] Finally, the Anglo-American Secretariat attempted to defuse internal wrangling within the Canadian party by establishing the political line of Tim Buck as the one the CPC should follow.[16]

Many of these same issues and concerns were echoed regionally. Efforts to organize workers at the Lakehead continued to lag behind those in other regions of the country. For example, calls in May 1928 for a meeting of the unemployed were largely ignored at the Lakehead (whereas thousands had attended a recent similar meeting in Winnipeg). John Carey, the CPC's Fort William organizer, accurately observed that the same issues facing workers in Winnipeg faced their comrades at the Lakehead. Unlike the Winnipeggers, however, workers at the

Lakehead "had not even learned that which is known even to wolves that hunt in packs, that many can do what one cannot, that in union lies strength." Carey blamed the inability to unite on the ethnic prejudice rampant in the region. One segment, he contended, viewed any form of organization as doomed to failure because it allowed "the foreigners into it." Others argued the opposite – that an organization without foreigners would be useless. Both, Carey pointed out, did not seem to have been issues in Winnipeg, even with its similar ethnic composition. "In short," he summed up the situation at the head of the lakes, "a combination of ignorance, cowardice and blind prejudice made the workers unwilling to take part in a scheme for their welfare, because forsooth there were among them those who spoke a different language."[17]

While the general lack of solidarity did not allow Communists to, for example, take advantage of the loss of 350 jobs when the Fort William Paper Company's mill closed, they still had some success in organizing young workers.[18] Building on the popularity among both Wobblies and Communists of "socialist summer camps" and educational classes geared towards children, a branch of the Young Communist League (YCL) had been organized in Port Arthur.[19] Twice-weekly meetings of the Young Pioneers in Fort William soon followed those in Port Arthur.[20]

The activities of the YCL caught the attention of government officials. As always, Finns bore the brunt of the increased scrutiny. Port Arthur educational authorities, for instance, reported to their Toronto superiors that "red" ideology was being taught in many Finnish schools and in the camps. According to one official: "Red literature runs in this vein. Don't listen to your teacher, he's only a tool working for the bosses. All honour to our brave comrades who would not salut [sic] the Union Jack." The official was further concerned about party meetings, which he thought closed with "the Red Flag and a pledge of readiness for world revolution." The teacher alone could overcome home influence, he warned. "The Red has been drilled in before he gets a chance. This is evident among the Finns more than any other class. If the government continues to dump them into the North it should see that they obey our laws."[21] The focus on the Finns was not without basis. By 1928, they constituted approximately 60 percent (2,640) of the CPC's 4,400 members.[22] In fact, the Finnish Organization of Canada (FOC), coupled with the Ukrainian Labour-Farmer Temple Association (ULFTA), had become the largest ethnically distinct demographic force within revolutionary left-wing politics in both Canada and the CPC.[23]

The IWW-affiliated Lumber Workers Industrial Union (LWIU) was, on the face of it, in a good position to capitalize on the CPC's problems, but its situation was actually a difficult one. Many of its members earnestly desired a merger with the Communist-affiliated Lumber Workers Industrial Union of Canada (LWIUC). Some thought that this merged union could simply follow the platform of the IWW.[24] Such a scenario flew in the face of the strategies of the CPC, all the more so as the party became increasingly subject to the Stalinist rigours of the Third Period. In this context, however logical and even obvious in theory it was, the merger of the two radical unions was at best a fantasy.

Union with the One Big Union (OBU) was not a new issue. Previous splits within the lumber unions had not been as clear-cut as the CPC and IWW wanted to believe. Many workers had become disillusioned with the Communists or had become nostalgic for the days when lumber workers spoke with a much more united voice.[25] Some hoped that a new union would eventually form a Canadian administration of the IWW, with an official publication in Winnipeg.[26] As early as 1925, J.D. Golden of the LWIU in Port Arthur and Sudbury had taken up the cause and could be found disseminating material favouring the creation of a separate Canadian administration. Vancouver members, perhaps sensing the General Executive Board's (GEB) shift in attention from the West Coast to Central Canada, took issue with Golden's suggestions. At a mass meeting in December 1925, they even called for all Canadian branches to go on record about whether they supported Golden and the creation of a Canadian administration.[27] It appears, however, that Wobblies in Canada felt that they were still not strong enough to go off on their own, despite growing concerns over a distant and seemingly aloof Chicago-based leadership.[28]

The organizational problems facing Wobblies at the Lakehead during this period appear to have been similar to those of their Communist brethren. As with the CPC and the LWIUC, the organization of French workers in eastern Canada had become a priority of the IWW's own LWIU. For example, the financially troubled Sudbury branch had been instructed at the Ninth Ontario District Conference in June to arrange for a French-speaking travelling delegate. Problems arose, however, when the largely Finnish and solvent Port Arthur branch was required to pay part of the expenses. Not surprisingly, Wobblies at the Lakehead were not happy with the decision to go ahead, as they had not been consulted.[29]

The Port Arthur branch also butted heads with the Ontario District and General Executive Board over its rule that workers who left the lumber industry for employment as harvesters had to transfer to the Agricultural Industrial Unit (AIU). The secretary of the Port Arthur branch argued that this left the LWIU in bad standing according to its bylaws, and ineligible to put forward nominations for any positions. In the past, this rule had prevented many of the most active LWIU members from either taking harvesting work or organizing on behalf of the union year-round. At the 1928 LWIU conference in Port Arthur, Golden presented a resolution that members of the LWIU, AIU, and the General Recruiting Union in Canada enter the harvest drive together, without their members being subject to transfer fees or loss of delegate status. The resolution passed without opposition.[30]

The GEB in Chicago made no comment on the unilateral decision of the Canadian Wobblies. In reality, it had little understanding of, and perhaps little interest in, the specific issues of Wobblies outside the United States. When asked in 1929 for a speaker to bolster recent gains in membership and to stave off Communist attempts to draw members away, the GEB declined "on account of [there] not being very many English speaking workers" at the Lakehead. "In this district at present," it argued, "we do not see any benefit for the organization." The GEB also pushed Canadian Wobblies to establish an English-language publication. Such was the tone of the Chicago leadership throughout much of the late 1920s. Like the CPC, it saw its future success as being dependent on establishing, in contrast to its earlier emphasis, a "non-foreign" membership base rather than supporting the initiatives of Finnish members.[31]

Ironically, both Lakehead Wobblies and Communists faced many of the same dilemmas. In each case, a distant leadership could only partially grasp the on-the-ground challenges of the local radicals. In the case of the CPC, it was – true to the spirit of the Third Period – intent on exposing and denouncing social democrats. Yet in the Lakehead context, the party's limited but real electoral successes in the 1920s had rested precisely on making appeals, through the Canadian Labour Party, to the very "soft leftists" it now denounced as so many "social fascists."[32]

The Ukrainian members of the party were another growing problem facing the CPC. Unknown to the Central Executive Committee, the National Ukrainian Agitprop had submitted a twenty-page document to the Anglo-American Secretariat criticizing the party's recent decisions, particularly the leaders' failure to consider the needs or heed the requests of its Ukrainian membership (the second-largest group within the party).[33] The Anglo-American Secretariat agreed and responded that the relationship between the Ukrainian membership and the rest of the CPC's units, especially the CEC and the YCL, was "far from healthy." The Ukrainians and Finns were recognized as playing an important role in industry. Yet they were also held to be problematic: "They hold onto their own previous modes of life" and tend to "lead their own social life. Do not speak English and in general, many of them submit only very slowly to ascimilation [sic]."[34]

The National Executive Committee of the YCL echoed the position of the party's leadership and placed sole blame on the Ukrainian leadership: "The accumulating pile of evidence strengthens our conviction that no attempt has been made by the Ukrainian leadership of our Party to put into evidence the conditions of the Fifth Convention of our Party."[35] Recognizing that the majority of its members were Finnish and Ukrainian, the CPC declared that the party must first embrace and then integrate them into the party. The CPC claimed that the language organizations were under Communist leadership, and had "considerable influence among the miners of Alberta, most of whom are Ukrainian, and the Lumber workers, most of whom are Finn." As such, it argued that "favourable conditions for drawing the broad masses of immigrants into the class struggle" existed.[36]

The CPC's conception of its "great task" of revolution, one strongly influenced by the Comintern and by graduates of the Lenin School in Moscow, entailed the party's more thorough Canadianization. It was directed by Moscow to draw more English-speaking "British and American immigrants," and more English- and French-speaking "native-born Canadians," into its ranks. How could this be balanced with the party's continuing reliance on the Finns and Ukrainians? The party was caught in a dilemma. Bolshevization and, later, Stalinization meant relegating the foreign-language groups to the periphery. Retaining the "red bases" it had so painstakingly built in Northwestern Ontario meant paying close attention to precisely these groups. The "new line" meant focusing intently on factories, but the "old realities" of the party stubbornly drew its attention back to its traditional bases in mining, forestry, and other resource industries. The party was being pulled in at least two directions.[37]

In response to Ukrainian concerns over the CPC leadership's desire to liquidate the ULFTA, the party "categorically repudiated the accusation." It determined in its resolution that "greater clarity" was necessary to defuse the increasing conflict between leading Ukrainians and the CPC leadership. The ULFTA was chastised for what the CEC saw as a blurring of the line between the Ukrainian Communists' "participation in the class struggle together with the Canadian proletariat" and a focus on the "socio-political struggles among the Ukrainians alone." Ukrainian Communists were urged to learn English "as a means of taking part in the general life of the party." The CEC further urged that "non-Party Ukrainian workers should be trained in the spirit of class solidarity with all other Canadian workers." Although the CPC declared that it recognized the impossibility of doing away with the "exclusiveness of immigrant groups in one sweep," it reaffirmed its dedication to the formation of a monolithic party organized along factory lines and from within trade unions.[38]

Following such declarations, the March District 6 (Port Arthur) conference agenda dealt with the anti-war position of the CPC, the condemnation by the national executive of Trotskyism and "its Canadian offspring (Spectorism)," and how to combat these tendencies within both the party and the district. The item that received the most attention was trade unionism and the CPC's relationship to it. The debate at the convention, one delegate reported to the *Worker*, clearly showed "the inability of a number of Party members to grasp the real issues of the Trade Union movement." In response, delegates passed a resolution supporting "strict disciplinary action against Party members who oppose or neglect to join in the Trade Union which exists in his or her trade." It appears that the cause of disagreement was "the slackness in our fractional work." Within the district, party members in what were described as "extra-Party organizations" – referring, in essence, to the continuing presence of the language federations – continued to openly oppose one another and what the district executive perceived as its central authority. While agreeing that the cooperative movement "is one of the most important weapons in the class struggle," delegates approved a resolution informing the CPC executive that it was composed of "various elements," not all of which were dedicated to furthering "proletarian interests in the class struggle."[39]

By the time of the Fifth National Convention of the LWIUC in April, the CPC's tactics in the region and continual conflict with the IWW had worn down workers. For example, although the LWIUC had financially supported strikers in a strike at Shabaqua, the strike committee consisting of both Wobblies and Communists forced the union to sign an agreement that it would make no attempt to organize any workers in the region during the conflict. In fact, all agreed that the strike was "under the leadership of rank and file strike committee which was paralyzed with fear of internecine war between the LWIU and the IWW disrupting the strikers, and anamoured [sic] with the idea (very popular among the lumber workers of Ontario) of exploiting all groups in the interest of their own particular struggle." This situation, coupled with a similar arrangement in a recent strike in Kapuskasing and a defeat in a South Porcupine strike, had left the union drained of financial resources and with no real gain in membership or influence. It was believed that the union's predominantly Finnish membership also limited its potential and success.[40]

A call by workers was made for the centralization of strike leadership with the LWIUC executive, rather than allowing "any local to pull a job strike."[41] This position appears to have reflected the growing belief by CPC leaders that the problems facing the union rested with its leader, Alf Hautamäki. Delegates argued that his presence had hindered the union's activities, as many workers tended "to avoid anything for the union undoubtly [sic] because it would have helped Hautamäki." The majority of delegates present were in favour of removing him whether or not a suitable replacement was available. Although the delegates agreed that the past two years had seen unprecedented losses, they also argued that the LWIUC had become the "real organizational expression of the main body of workers exploited in the logging camps of Ontario." The union had lost approximately 30 percent of its members due, according to the highly self-critical assessments of its organizers, to the tendency of the union towards "slackness in organizational matters, loss of interest by members, internal conflict, and general neglect of the essential work of maintaining and building up the union." Delegates were warned that "today the existence of the union is actually endangered."[42]

Although delegates credited Hautamäki with building up the union, his alleged recent personal conduct also came under fire. As the convention's report indicates, Hautamäki recognized "the opposition to his occupancy of the position, acknowledges that his personal conduct [particularly at the meeting in Timmins, where he appeared on the platform drunk] has at times been reprehensible, and has volunteered to decline nomination and support the candidatures of a comrade" who would be more successful. Given that no one suitable came forward who met the requirements laid out by the convention, it was decided to have him continue as General Secretary even though he "does not fully meet all of the requirements."[43] This was a slight exaggeration.

Hautamäki did possess most of the requirements, although not in exactly the way most would have hoped. Having been the cause of some of the current problems facing the LWIUC and the CPC in general, he definitely had "all the details of the organization and its problems at his finger tips." Having led a series of unsuccessful and financially draining initiatives since 1928, Hautamäki certainly had "a complete command of all necessary propaganda materials and channels." His long-standing involvement in the labour movement and the sheer fact that most lumber workers knew his name (even if they occasionally spat it out) clearly indicated that he had "the widest possible contact with the General Labor Movement." Although many had issues with him, Hautamäki was re-elected after making a full declaration that, "as a Communist," he acknowledged his errors.[44]

The convention also established new district LWIUC offices with full-time secretaries for the district of Northern Ontario (Porcupine District) and Sudbury. The general office in Port Arthur was instructed to function as the district office for the district of Thunder Bay. In the grand design, the new Lakehead office would generate new revenues and help the union regain its financial position. Montreal and Winnipeg were seen as the most problematic centres, and the convention decided that efforts needed to be redoubled in those two regions. Montreal (and Quebec more generally) was seen as an area where the union might recruit many new French Canadian lumber workers. Winnipeg was identified as a region notorious for generating the strikebreakers who so menaced the health of the union in Northwestern Ontario.[45]

Not all within the LWIUC were happy with the results of the convention. Many workers were appalled by the re-election of Hautamäki and the general disregard of the wishes of the rank and file by the leaders of the CPC. So disgusted was one member from Port Arthur that he wrote to Tim Buck and declared that it seemed to him that "there is a stronger machine in the [LWIUC] than there was in any of the AFL Unions." The delegates from Port Arthur, along with those from other regions, had gone to the convention determined to elect a new General Secretary. Considering this situation, George Sundqvist questioned how and why the convention could have re-elected Hautamäki. He also questioned Buck about why the executive committee remained an unelected body. In his view, this left Hautamäki with even more control and power than before the convention.[46]

Where could discontented radical workers go? Many at the Lakehead found an alternative in the IWW, which began to make substantial inroads in the region. In particular, the IWW appealed to the growing ranks of disgruntled Finnish Communists. As one Finnish member in Alberta wrote to A.T. Hill: "Everything is very bad," and the IWW "provides a place for all anti-Party Finns."[47] Although many did leave the union, under the guidance of Hautamäki it continued to be active. No fool, Hautamäki was well aware of what was occurring within the ranks of the Finnish socialists in the region, even if the CPC leadership was not. Writing to Tim Buck, he requested that the enlarged CEC and many of the CEC committees deal with the penchant of Finnish members in Port Arthur and other areas of District 6 for "fraternizing with the IWW group and its sustaining ring." Such a relationship with "the most rightist elements of Social Democracy," he contended, "are a danger to our Party life and to the life of the Finnish Organ."[48] With the return of the region's delegates and as the news of Hautamäki's re-election spread, workers began to leave the union, believing that its end was only a matter of time and vowing to return only if radical changes were made.[49]

Thus, as Sundqvist had so astutely predicted, Hautamäki's re-election breathed new life into both the IWW and the social democratic tendencies of many socialists in the region. Many in the region began corresponding with the Finnish Social Democratic Party, culminating in a speech by one of its leading members, Arthur Aalto, to a large gathering of Finns in the Finnish Labour Temple on 1 July. The IWW, seeking to capitalize on the internal rift, also began an active campaign to organize support rings among small farmers throughout the district. Many leading party members in the region began to declare that the IWW was "a brother organization" and should be treated as such. Although Hautamäki dismissed these efforts as moneymaking schemes and declared that the IWW had only sixty-five members, he wrote to Buck in July as a man deeply concerned about the IWW's renewed activity.[50]

Perhaps the most disconcerting developments in the eyes of Hautamäki and other Communists were the inroads being made by the Wobblies into previous strongholds of the Finnish Organization of Canada, "without the least opposition on the part of the leaders of the latter." As a result, Hautamäki and other Communists had been increasingly "the subject of some hostilities on the part of some Finnish comrades because we have denounced the anti-revolutionary policies of the IWW as seen at present." He requested that the CEC take up the issue and draft a resolution demanding that party members immediately sever all connection with the IWW or face expulsion. Ultimately, increasing unemployment and not the efforts of the CPC halted the expansion of the IWW in the region.[51]

Things were no better for the CPC, however. The same worsening economic conditions in the resource sector dramatically influenced its ability to operate at the Lakehead. In April, Hautamäki informed the CEC that membership within the LWIUC had decreased by approximately 20 percent since the previous year.

The most disconcerting losses were in the urban subdistricts within Port Arthur and Fort William. As a result, the union was now almost entirely composed of Finnish workers, since the bulk of the losses had come from "Slavic" and English members. By the time of the 1929 national convention, although Hautamäki was describing recent strikes as some of the best organized, he also was quite candid about the organizational problems facing the CPC at the Lakehead.[52]

Many of Hautamäki's criticisms pertained not only to the recent strike but also to the situation at the Lakehead in general. He contended that the attention paid to fighting the reformists in the party had been misguided, as it was easier to fight them than the IWW. It was syndicalism, he contended, that remained the party's primary roadblock in trying to organize the region's working class. Further, the CPC representative who came to advise the strikers had, like all "help" sent to the region in recent years, been ill prepared and knew nothing of the local situation. It is clear from Hautamäki's comments that he believed that most of the party's executive did not realize that "to fight in the wilderness is different than in the streets." For example, one telling mistake, according to Hautamäki, was a recent decision to bring the entire strike committee to the picket line. This had left the rest of the Port Arthur District "unprotected" as the district leadership became unavailable and other concerns were neglected.

The lumber workers were not the only segment of the CPC in dire need of help at the Lakehead. By the time of the convention, the YCL had made little recent progress due to the growing hesitation of many, particularly within the lumber industry, to lend their support. It did not help that organizers openly criticized the children of lumber workers for being "too feeble to do any real work." One organizer even suggested that they did not know the problems of the lumber workers and that the goal of the YCL should be to educate its members on the conditions and prepare them for life in camps.[53]

The convention also spent much of its time discussing the Ukrainian situation. Although Matthew Popovich's review of the Ukrainian Labour Temple argued that the reorganization followed the guidelines laid down in 1928 by the Politburo (or Pol Buro, in contemporary parlance), this was not the case in Fort William. Nationalist Ukrainian organizations, deemed fascist by Popovich, were reported to have become more active and focused on attacking the ULFTA. As a result, work in Fort William had been progressing at an unsatisfactory rate despite what Popovich believed was a favourable situation. The branch was described as "old fashioned." Although meetings were held and decisions made in line with the National Party Bureau, Comintern, and CEC, it was left to the fraction organizer alone to actually implement the party's decisions. This had resulted in a number of important initiatives not being instituted.[54]

The increasing loss of Ukrainian members at the Lakehead to the Provista Society was viewed as resulting from the left turn of the party and the unpopularity of Bolshevization in the region. According to Popovich, while the criticisms held true for the Finnish members of the party, almost no questions were now being raised aside from the best way to actually mobilize "the broadest mass organization for the purpose of building our revolutionary Trade Union Movement, and so on." Success was evident, for example, in the activities of Ukrainian party members in the Crowsnest Pass and Montreal. Even in Calgary, Sudbury, and Fort William, where the situation was "far from being satisfactory," no objections were being made "about the very new line in the Mass Organizations on general party work."[55]

Not all within the party were as confident. Many remained skeptical about the new strategy's overall success. Responding to Buck's report to the Sixth Convention, J. Carey, an organizer from Fort William, argued that a disunited and distracted leadership did "not understand the Party's tasks." He also agreed with comments made by Hautamäki that the language differences made the liquidation of federalism within the CPC impossible. He did not hesitate to suggest that the poor performance of many in the region had much to do with a poor understanding of theory.[56]

Hautamäki in particular argued that the party had lost a number of good chances to increase the strength of the LWIUC. Although over 15,000 workers were employed in the industries, the union numbered only 3,000. It was only through the Finnish organization, he contended, that any success had been achieved during the previous year. How could the party leadership attack the language organizations, when in recent campaigns the mass organizations at the Lakehead had treated the lumber workers as inferiors?[57] Both Carey and Hautamäki commented on, for example, a newly formed Unemployed Association of Port Arthur. Its policy and platform had "never [been] submitted to the unemployed but [had been] imposed upon them from above." In fact, the association was voicing none of the issues immediately facing workers in the region. Instead, it merely was a "mechanical recitation of about twenty-one points not most pressing to the immediate needs of the unemployed."[58]

Notwithstanding the election of Alex Gibson, a member of the CPC and the head of the local Pulp and Sulphite Workers Union, as secretary of the Port Arthur Trades and Labour Council, little positive news reached the CEC from the Port Arthur District during the first few months of 1929.[59] For these and other reasons, Carey declared, "large masses of workers still follow the IWW."[60] As one party member asked Buck: "How can the union progress when Party members refuse to join?"[61] Buck and the CPC leadership were in fact warned that the fight against the IWW, especially among the Finnish members, was extremely important. Hautamäki tried to explain to Buck that the IWW's sustaining rings in the region were, in contrast to the CPC branches, good at raising funds to support their activities. So successful were they in some areas that, he stated, "they are actually winning the ground from the Fin. Org'n [Finnish Organization of Canada] without the least opposition on the part of the leaders of the latter."[62]

Despite his complaints, Hautamäki believed that not all was lost for the CPC at the Lakehead. He was quick to point out that he was not "saying this attitude of the Finnish population is the main cause of the success of the IWW sustaining rings in this district." He contended that he merely "wish[ed] to show the tendencies prevalent, and the danger to the Party if these tendencies are not checked in some way." The situation, he suggested, was not entirely dire: "The IWW has nothing to do with the real proletariat of this district, its membership being, according to the highest estimate, less than 65 percent [of all workers]." Much of the problem resulted from the CEC's approach to the region and the lack of attention being paid to the lumber and camps workers by the Trade Union Educational League.[63]

As Hautamäki's correspondence to Buck reveals, by 1929 the attempts by the CPC leaders to centralize their power had been largely ineffectual in the region. In practice, the party was still at the mercy of the theoretically non-existent but actually potent language federations. The CPC adopted a much harder stance towards them following harsh criticism by the Comintern in late 1929. The CPC was strongly reminded that "the chief objectives of the language organizations must be to become real mass organizations which are to draw the foreign born workers into the general stream of the Canadian Labour Movement."[64]

The leaders of the FOC viewed their organization as much more than merely an auxiliary of the CPC, however. It provided a cultural, social, and often economic centre for Finnish Canadians. Its concerns, while often the same as those of the CPC, went beyond the single-minded goal of the CPC to first dominate Canadian unions and socialists and then lead workers into a social, political, and economic revolution. Due in part to the historical tensions between Finland

and Russia, Finns cherished their independence. Growing Soviet control of the CPC leadership made them uneasy. The FOC's executive, consisting of original party members John Wirta and J.W. Ahlqvist, refused to comply with the Politburo because, they argued, it did not and should not dictate the decisions of the organization.[65] On 7 November 1929, the executive of FOC Local #80 (Sudbury) passed a motion protesting against the leadership of the CPC. In response, the CPC sent Popovich to the region to placate the moderate element.[66] Shortly afterwards, things came to a head as the CPC attempted to censure *Vapaus,* the Finnish-language organ of the CPC.[67]

Vapaus had supported the CPC's decision in 1928 to expel members, most famously Maurice Spector, on grounds of Trotskyism. It had also supported MacDonald's continuing leadership of the party. Now the Finns found themselves at the centre of charges of "right-wing opportunism."[68] The conflict centred on *Vapaus*'s editor, Arno Vaara, only recently released from prison following publication of an article deemed by government officials to be treasonable.[69] Vaara's sedition trial had garnered national attention, served as a focal point for the grievances of Finnish socialists, and provided fuel for renewed attacks against them at the Lakehead.[70] The Fort William *Daily Times-Journal,* no doubt reflecting the views of many British-born and English-speaking residents, saw the trial as evidence that "Canada is piling up trouble by bringing in people who read foreign newspapers, defy her institutions and create a revolutionary hotbed. It is time to call a halt to bringing in more of them, and it is time to step heavily on those now here."[71] Vaara's release touched off a period of division within the Finnish membership of the CPC. It began when the CEC attempted to capitalize on the groundswell of rank-and-file support for him during his trial. For purely propaganda reasons, it appointed him as a party official. The problem, though, was that the party leadership had failed to consult with either Vaara or the FOC's executive committee. Responding to what its executive felt was a clear overstepping of the CPC's power, the FOC reappointed Vaara and declared that it and no one else had final control over *Vapaus.*[72]

The CEC, already cognizant that the overwhelming majority of the party's membership was Finnish and paranoid over losing control, viewed the FOC's stand as a direct challenge not only to its own authority but also to that of the Comintern. Completely misunderstanding the nature of the FOC's argument, the CPC leadership linked the FOC's actions to remaining right-wing elements in the party and those opposed to Stalin's Bolshevization plan.[73] Following the Sudbury local's decision to side with the FOC executive, the CEC instructed

Hill to tour Northwestern Ontario, where he spoke to enthusiastic and well-attended mass organization meetings in Port Arthur and Fort William.[74]

The paranoia towards the "right-wing element" had been developing in the CPC for some time. Even Hill had come under attack in early autumn for being part of an alleged plot by MacDonald, Popovich, and the language organizations to undermine the activities of the CPC.[75] These claims touched off a series of meetings where the loyalty of Hill and the ongoing difficulties with the Finns and Ukrainians were discussed. It should come as no surprise that Hill took exception to the accusation. In a lengthy letter, he outlined his position and declared: "My fight would be to see that the Comintern letter be carried out by collective work and stamp out factionalism." "Those opposing the CPC's position," he wrote, "were doing so from a position that was largely a holdover from Social Democratic ideology and were foreign to communist principles and tactics, which naturally could not accept the principles of democratic centralism." He had recently supported Popovich not because he believed in factionalism but because the Ukrainian members needed representation on the Political Committee. "I protest the damnable way of discrediting by comrades, and finally I protest against the way that my article of pre-convention discussion was kept out so that no English comrade is able to know my stand." He finished by demanding that a public correction be made and the larger issue of growing factionalism be discussed.[76]

No one in the CPC's leadership appears to have listened. Their decision to expel and suspend a number of Finnish members (including stalwarts Vaara, Ahlqvist, and Wirta) without input from the party's leading Finnish members, resulted in more, not less, factionalism.[77] A debate began immediately among the FOC locals over who should decide the position and actions of the FOC – its elected executive or the CPC leadership. For the CPC, the issue became a matter of the relationship between ethnic organizations and the party centre. Many formerly ardent supporters of the CPC within the FOC began questioning the objectives and policies of the party. Locals rallied behind their comrades in Sudbury in support of the FOC executive's autonomy, and soon began to attack the new Buck leadership of the CPC for a "false and dangerous attitude towards mass organizations."[78]

The Port Arthur local remained loyal to the party and actually led the attack against Ahlqvist and Wirta. Along with the Fort William and Intola locals, it passed a unanimous resolution condemning the anti-party actions of the FOC's executive and "demanding the calling of a special convention ... to oust the right wing executive Committee."[79] Such a position reveals the dedication of the local leadership to the party centre. Although the local leadership of Michael Biniowsky, Harry Bryan, and Alf Hautamäki had opposed Buck during the 1929 CEC election, they, along with the rest of the District Executive Committee, put aside their differences and joined with the local Finnish section to support the party's decision.[80]

The local leadership was also concerned, however, about the repercussions locally of supporting the CPC leadership's decision. It informed the CEC of its fear that its agreement with the decision would lead ultimately to a split in the region similar to the one that irrevocably damaged the OBU in 1920.[81] To prevent such an occurrence, the Finnish party stalwart S.G. Neil was sent to shore up support, as Vaara, Ahlqvist, and Wirta had been relatively popular among the Finnish party members in the region. As Neil reported, not all Finns were entirely convinced, and believed that the CEC was merely using the issue for its own aims.[82]

Most telling is that criticisms in the region were directed entirely towards the Anglo-dominated CPC leadership and not the Comintern. For example, one Finn questioned "whether the present leadership of the C.P. of C. has the confidence of the Comintern."[83] If not for the efforts of the FOC and the work of Hill, who came to the Lakehead following Neil's failure, the situation in Port Arthur would have resulted in a permanent schism within the party.[84] Hill, along with John Carey and Annie Galt of the YCL, local ULFTA organizer Mike Cosmishin, and George Sundqvist, had undertaken to organize in October a series of demonstrations intended both to promote the party line and protest the recent harassment of local workers by the police. Following a number of demonstrations attended by hundreds of workers, all five were arrested, but not before the groundwork had been laid for a mass lumber workers' convention.[85] Held at the Port Arthur Workers' Hall at 316 Bay Street in early October, the convention focused on two main issues. One was the decision by the LWIUC executive to enter the prairies. Such a move was seen by many to mean "a heavy drain on the resources of the union." The second issue, and the most pertinent to the membership at the Lakehead, was the prospect of a region-wide strike.[86]

On 22 October, workers at the Pigeon River Lumber Company's camps near the Shabaqua rail depot, fifty-six kilometres west of the Lakehead, went on strike for better wages and improved conditions. As in 1926, both the LWIUC and the LWIU participated in the strike, forming a joint strike committee with representatives from both unions on the executive and representing just under 1,000 workers.[87] Immediately, from many other parts of the country, calls arose for the "working class of Canada to rally to the assistance of the striking lumber workers."[88] Ontario Provincial Police reports from the period indicate that OPP members were used to harass the strike committee in Shabaqua, arrest pickets, and search them for weapons. Tensions rose and the situation became explosive as police, strikers, and strikebreakers all began carrying weapons. In addition, as Satu Repo states, the "trainloads of foreign-born workers coming from other parts of the country on false pretenses had little idea of the situation they were facing."[89] The strike was further complicated by the fact that some camps were under the control of recent immigrant nationalist Finns (White Finns), whose ideological position put them at the extreme other end of the political spectrum. The LWIUC adamantly insisted that it was responsible for directing the strike, notwithstanding the belief of many strikers that the Wobblies were the real leaders.[90] Although the strike represented an opportunity for the CPC to make inroads, the party appears to have been more interested in emasculating the IWW than in building on any success. As Anthony Rasporich has contended, the CPC leadership's ideologically pure determination to wipe out the IWW clashed with the strategy and tactics of Hautamäki, who as General Secretary of the LWIUC fully understood the Wobblies's deep roots in the Finnish community and the imperative for the CPC to form a united front with them.[91]

Many different conclusions have been reached about the strike. The most common one promoted by the Communists was that the IWW withdrew its support because it determined, following a supposed fact-finding mission on 20 November, that "the 15 camps, with an estimated worker capacity of 459, had 297 men working in them" and were not worth the time.[92] They blamed the IWW for rumours that the strike "had not started right and that it was only the scheming of the Communists by which they hoped to collect money for their own purposes." "They went so far," one correspondent to the *Worker* argued, "to state that there was no strike in existence while groundless slander was spread concerning the leaders."[93] "This 'once upon a time' revolutionary organization which contained the flower of the American working class," the Communist newspaper argued, "is reduced to a small coterie of syndicalist malcontents which, in order to get a foothold among the lumber workers of Ontario, will stop at nothing to gain their end."[94]

In contrast, J.D. Golden, a leading Wobbly organizer at the Lakehead, contended that the CPC had merely prolonged the strike to use appeals for financial contributions to deal with the LWIUC's financial crisis. As he reported in the *Industrial Worker,* "the Communist politicians have broken the strike in Ontario, but are still collecting funds although the strike is closed."[95] The IWW viewed the strike as a "flop." None of the demands had been met and damage had been done to the organizing spirit of the workers by the CPC. Chiefly responsible, according to Golden, was Hautamäki, whom he described as a "supreme wizard of this [the CPC] labour splitting and semi-bourgeois group." He argued that the CPC had alienated workers and decidedly repelled them from organized labour by not allowing them to "express their opinions" and by declarations that all those who did not join the strike were scabs (including those in the eight camps that were not involved). Golden also supported the rumour then circulating that Hautamäki had been seen carousing with the lumber bosses and even drinking privately with them while workers were picketing. Further, sworn testimonies from workers at a number of camps claimed that Hautamäki had arranged separate agreements.[96]

As for the IWW's official position on the strike, Golden stated in the *Industrial Worker* that the Wobblies in Port Arthur had refused to take action. "Past experience," he contended, "has taught their members that nothing can be obtained by cooperating with the officialdom of this group, who will only stab them in the back at their first opportunity, and betray the workers." As evidence, Golden referred to the incidents surrounding the 1926 pulp workers' strike. "'Corral the Dollars' seems to be the slogan of the LWIU of Canada. It reminds us of the old saying that 'Talk is cheap, but it takes money to buy booze.' And booze is necessary to the officials of the LWIU of Canada as gasoline is to a Ford; for, without it, they would not have the nerve to face the workers whom they are deceiving."[97]

The CPC maintained that both at the 20 November meeting of the IWW executive in Port Arthur and in the 27 November issue of the *Industrial Worker,* Golden and other prominent Wobblies had recognized the "good possibilities for winning the strike," reported that picketers had been sent to the strike area, and urged workers to provide funds so that the strikers could receive proper financial support.[98] The CPC further claimed that the IWW's picketers were in fact mostly recent strikebreakers who threatened the LWIUC leaders of the strike that, if they continued to lead it, the IWW "would declare it closed within a week and for this reason a new strikers Committee must be formed under the control of the IWW." The real reason the IWW wished to lead the strike was so that "they could more easily break it and betray the strikers."[99] The CPC also alluded to possible collusion between the IWW, lumber barons, and the police to break the strike.[100]

The remnants of the One Big Union (which had decided not to join the IWW) provide a third narrative of the events surrounding the strike. They contended that the men who initially went on strike decided to affiliate with neither the LWIUC nor the LWIU. Hautamäki had become a member of the strike committee through manipulation and, contrary to the desire of the workers, had printed strike notices claiming the strike to be a Communist-led one. In response, the strikers held another meeting, at which they not only reaffirmed their position and "unanimously agreed to call their strike an unorganized strike" but also resolved that only those involved in the strike could sit on the strike committee. This resulted in the expulsion from the committee of Hautamäki, who, incidentally, had also acted as its treasurer.[101]

Hautamäki, according to the *One Big Union Bulletin,* next organized another "gang" of workers unconnected in any way to the strike. They attended a mass meeting of the strikers and outvoted the actual participants, reinstating Hautamäki on the committee as its treasurer. The OBU claimed that he "cleaned up about $2,000 very quickly as a result of this move on the part of the gang." This manoeuvre changed an optimistic atmosphere to one of defeat. Workers went back to work, the *Bulletin* suggested, because they firmly believed that "when a grafter like Hautamäki has got charge of things there is no chance for us to win our fight." Workers were aware of both his and the CPC's past record in the camps of Northwestern Ontario. Specifically cited was his and the CPC's involvement in the 1928 Kapuskasing strike. During this strike, the strike committee headed by Hautamäki had collected over $3,000 but, it was alleged, the workers had seen none of it and the funds remained missing.[102]

The OBU also supported claims that Hautamäki and other Communists were misrepresenting the role of the IWW. In fact, even some within the LWIUC itself began to doubt Hautamäki's credibility. A joint committee composed of two members each of the IWW and LWIUC investigated his claims that the Port Arthur Branch of the IWW had been "acting as scab shippers." They reported that there was no evidence at all to support Hautamäki's claims and that workers had reported to them that they had, as the IWW had urged, gone back to work because of his involvement.[103]

As the Western nations descended into what subsequent generations would call the Great Depression, the Political Secretariat of the Executive Committee of the Communist International observed that the Communist Party of Canada continued to operate "mainly [as] a propagandist organization with small membership with weak connections with the broad masses of the Canadian workers."[104] As this chapter has suggested, despite attempts to diversify, approximately 90 percent of the CPC's membership was still composed of Finnish and Ukrainian immigrants.[105] Over half of its members were drawn from the FOC.[106] Even more disconcertingly, from a CPC perspective, was the actual decline in overall membership from 2,876 in 1928/29 to 1,385 in 1930.[107] Hill, echoing the party's leadership at the time, recalled that both the CPC's recent traumatic reorganization and the economic crisis necessitated a change in leadership and industrial strategy. As a result, when Tim Buck visited Russia again in December 1929, he did so as the newly anointed head of the CPC. He was also, however, the leader of a party embroiled in internal factionalism and facing increasing criticism from the Communist International.

Between 1921 and 1928, the CPC, John Manley states, "channeled its meager resources into a losing struggle to pull Canadian labour away from 'reactionary labour bureaucrats' and place it 'on the side of the proletarian revolution.'"[108] As Part 3 of this study will explore, with the introduction of the Workers' Unity League the Communist Party of Canada adopted the Third Period policies of the Communist International and began preparing for "imminent revolution" despite few tangible successes during the 1920s. The old penchant for boring from within and for the United Front, successfully used in strikes at the Lakehead but also the cause of much conflict, was replaced, ultimately to the detriment of local efforts, by an emphasis on the creation of separate "revolutionary industrial unions."[109]

PART 3
THE GREAT DEPRESSION AND THE THIRD PERIOD

7

"Class against Class"
Socialist Activities, 1930-32

With the onset of the Great Depression, many socialists believed that the time for radical social change in the Western world had finally come.[1] They saw the Depression, early signs of which could be seen at the Lakehead in 1928, as an indication that the Third Period, as the Communists called it, had begun and capitalism had finally run its course. The failure of farmers in the Canadian west to sell their wheat crop in 1928 marked the beginning of a period of massive unemployment.[2] Much of the Lakehead economy depended on moving the wheat crop. Wheat's collapse consequently triggered the region's crisis. As total production fell from 566 million bushels in 1928 to 293 million in 1929, the grain elevators on the waterfront of both Port Arthur and Fort William became increasingly still and hundreds lost their jobs.[3] The declining price of pulpwood, the region's other major industry, led to initial wage cuts and later unemployment for lumber workers as timber operators attempted to lower production costs.[4] Those workers who still had jobs faced increasingly poor working and living conditions on top of significant wage losses.[5]

On the surface, the situation at the Lakehead, combined with the growing popularity of socialist organizations, would seem to have been ideal for the expansion of left-wing groups throughout Northwestern Ontario. Accompanying the changing economic conditions was the further reorganization of the region's dominant socialist organization, the Communist Party of Canada (CPC). In line with decisions reached at the Communist International (Comintern) plenum of January 1930, the party disbanded the Trade Union Educational League and became directly involved in the organization of industrial unions in every sector of the economy. No longer was the focus of the CPC to be "boring from within"; rather, it pushed for the creation of separate Communist unions under the guidance of a central organization known as the Workers' Unity League (WUL).[6] Led by the enigmatic Tom McEwen, a blacksmith originally from Scotland, "the WUL sought to organize the unorganized into powerful industrial unions under rank and file control, unions which could mobilize workers for the defense and improvement of their living and working conditions and ultimately for the overthrow of the capitalist system."[7] The motivation for establishing the WUL came not from the changing conditions in Canada, as the party would later claim, but rather from directives from the Comintern. Although the WUL would eventually claim to have organized 40,000 workers by 1933, at the Lakehead tensions emerged between its leadership and the lumber workers' union.[8] One major reason can be traced back to the fact that, at the Lakehead, the vast majority of the CPC's membership continued to be Finnish and Ukrainian despite an intensive focus on diversification during the previous five years.[9]

The establishment of the WUL occurred during a period historians have regarded as "the Comintern's darkest hour, the moment when Stalinism triumphed in the International and Moscow's instructions politically disabled the working-class movement."[10] It was during this phase that "the slogan 'class against class' now fully characterized the struggle throughout the world."[11] Overall, although the CPC's adoption of the tactics of the Third Period achieved some political success, it had negative consequences for the CPC, as was particularly apparent in the party's Finnish-dominated Lumber Workers Industrial Union of Canada (LWIUC) at the Lakehead.

During this period, the CPC found itself immersed in a very ambiguous crisis. On the one hand, it had enormous potential; on the other, it was characterized by equally formidable internal contradictions. It was being asked to fulfill a seemingly impossible mandate to be, simultaneously, an ethnically focused party sensitive to the needs of a multiplicity of national groups. It was also being asked to be a homogeneous and monolithic battalion in the army of the world revolution. The situation at the Lakehead between 1930 and 1932 was that a plurality of interests operated within Port Arthur, Fort William, and the

Figure 9 IWW pamphlet advertisement, ca. 1930. *Courtesy of Lakehead University Library Archives*

surrounding region. Increasing competition from the Industrial Workers of the World (IWW) exacerbated tensions between the Finnish-dominated LWIUC and the Anglo-led unemployment associations and the leadership of the WUL. Although inter-organizational and extra-organizational conflict dominated the activities of socialist organizations in the region, all workers at the Lakehead shared a common plight. The situation would lead to moments of solidarity and demonstrated that, when united, socialists in the region could speak with a powerful voice. Such moments were all too fleeting, however.

Thousands from all ethnic backgrounds were on municipal relief rolls. In April 1931 alone, 200 families in Fort William, representing 1,000 people, were receiving goods in kind.[12] Over 90 percent of these people were non-Anglo-Saxon and 80 percent had been in Canada for less than five years. Such members of linguistic and cultural minorities confronted the local authorities' discriminatory practices. A Fort William relief officer informed one of the many unemployment organizations in the twin cities that preference was to be given first to Fort William-born applicants. Afterwards, the requests of Canadian-born and then British-born workers would be attended to. Only then, if there were still some goods or money left, would the non-British-born applicants be looked after.[13]

Such discrimination understandably led to significant unrest. Finnish workers, in particular, played an important role, as they had during the 1920s in both Fort William and Port Arthur and in the many lumber camps throughout the region. Those camps and organizations with Finns also tended to be more apt to dispute government initiatives and transform the threat of strikes into action.[14] The same Finnish workers who formed the bulk of the CPC and IWW membership were found more often, however, in the lines of the local soup kitchens than in the woods during this period. Not surprisingly, the focus of the WUL's early efforts in the region was on organizing the unemployed.[15]

The CPC played an unequalled part in the unemployment movement, and, as Lakehead Depression-era organizer Michael Fenwick claims, Communists were "the only ones who fought in the unemployed ranks."[16] The onset of the Depression provided the CPC with an opportunity to assume a greater leadership role within the Canadian left. In part, this resulted from the inability of the trades and labour organizations affiliated with the Trades and Labour Congress of Canada and the American Federation of Labor to deal with the growing unemployment throughout the country.[17] This does not mean, however, that the Communists stood alone or, conversely, that their activities were unanimously supported, either within or outside the party.

Next to the LWIUC, unemployed associations were the most active at the Lakehead. They were also increasingly the source of tension. The unemployed were often less concerned with the "politics of unemployment than with having *something* done about an exceedingly grim existence."[18] They also did not blindly defer to those with labour movement backgrounds; leadership became a major point of disagreement internally in the CPC and between competing interests. Alf Hautamäki's presentation (speaking as a Finn and as head of the LWIUC) to the CPC leadership at the 1930 plenum encapsulates the issues that dogged socialist organizations, particularly the CPC, at the Lakehead during this period.

Using the Port Arthur District as an example, Hautamäki argued that despite CPC rhetoric, in terms of organizing the unemployed the IWW was in fact ahead in the region. "The District Buro, myself included," he stated, "possibly had no time, possibly not even horse sense to prepare for this." In part, this was a result of the centre's being "unable to look after its own home."[19] He contended that too many members of the CPC were "trying to be leaders," and organizational efforts were being hampered by the party's not allowing the "the rank and filers to go among the unemployed and do the work." The party's failure to do so had led to a "great error" being made in the Port Arthur District.[20]

Hautamäki's critique of his comrades extended to the CPC's handling of the murder of Communist organizers Viljo Rosvall and Janne Voutilainen near Onion Lake in the winter of 1929. While visiting lumber camps in the region to persuade other workers to join the LWIUC, the two organizers disappeared.[21] In an increasingly rare show of solidarity, Communists, Wobblies, and unorganized workers combed the woods together looking for the bodies and, when that failed, watched the forests to ensure that the killer(s) did not spirit them away. When the bodies were found in early April 1930, socialists of all stripes stood shoulder to shoulder in condemning the actions of the lumber boss blamed for their deaths.[22] "As a visible sign of God's outrage at their comrades' dreadful fate," Alf Hautamäki pointed out, a three-quarter eclipse of the sun coincided with their funeral.[23]

However unifying the tragedy had been initially, by 1932 it had been transformed, under Third Period conditions, into a source of rancorous division. By December 1932, Communists regularly claimed that the Wobblies had participated in a campaign to stop workers from searching for Rosvall and Voutilainen. For its part, the IWW falsely argued that Hautamäki had "sent them [Rosvall and Voutilainen] to Russia and framed up their disappearance as a means of getting money and sympathy for the LWIUC."[24] There was a kernel of truth in the hyperbole. Citing their prior experiences with Hautamäki, the IWW initially did question, as the LWIUC claimed, the disappearance of the two men. Considering their much longer fight against both regional lumber bosses and White Finns (who were initially blamed), however, it is both laughable and inconceivable that they would have joined with them in the murder of two workers and its cover-up. The IWW was little better than its Communist brethren. It countered CPC accusations by arguing that the two workers had been tools of certain Communist leaders who, in sending them to the camps, had acted as "dangerous irresponsible creatures."[25]

Such an unedifying CPC/IWW dispute testified to the underlying political and structural problems confronting Lakehead leftists. The CPC in particular was initially unable to establish a normally functioning district council or a branch of the WUL in either of the twin cities.[26] Instead, Finnish and Ukrainian members undertook such activities. As a result, non-party members stigmatized the CPC and its activities as "foreign initiatives." Such a belief hampered attempts to recruit new members. The very Anglo-Saxon workers desired by the party viewed the continued dominance of the Finns as an indication of the party's lack of commitment to the region.[27] For the leadership of the CPC, such comments only served to reinforce their view that the continued existence of the language federations posed a problem for a revolutionary party that prided itself on science, discipline, and speed. Ethnic tensions ran high in the region. They influenced not only relations between Finns and Anglo-Canadians, but also those between Finns and Ukrainians.[28] Even the dispatch of veteran organizer Harvey Murphy to the Lakehead failed to re-energize a local labour movement apparently divided in membership and purpose.[29]

The inability of the CPC to mobilize the working class was first seen in the 1930 civic election. In Fort William, Andrew Heikkinen ran as an openly Communist candidate in the worker-dominated Ward 1. Many workers in the ward, such as Ukrainian leader Mike Cosmishin, had been "baptized" into the CPC during the Shabaqua strike, and many felt that the time had arrived for significant electoral gains.[30] Heikkinen's subsequent loss was attributed to his election manifesto. It called for the election to be used "as a preparation for future and sharper class struggles" and denounced Canada's involvement in Russia during 1919. Neither of these themes endeared him to voters, who re-elected the more moderate labour candidate Fred Moore to city council.[31]

Although not too much should be read into the election of Moore – he was, after all, the incumbent, popular among the unions and workers in the ward, and secretary of the Fort William Trades and Labour Council – the Communist response to Heikkinen's defeat reveals the deep divisions in the Lakehead left. The *Worker* drew on Third Period rhetoric to depict Moore as a "Labor-Faker," one of those who had "betrayed the workers." The Communists took particular aim at Moore's role in Fort William's Citizens' and Ratepayers' Unemployed Association (CRUA), a body that competed directly with them for influence among the unemployed.[32] CRUA aimed to provide relief for unemployed workers in all industries. It enjoyed some success. By early February 1930, it had established a variety of branches and even sponsored a sister organization in Port Arthur. It targeted long hours, the lack of workforce planning, and the particular problems of unemployed women. It won the respect of local councils and mayors and enjoyed the support of mainstream unions. For its supporters, it provided a tangible and direct response to the crisis.[33]

From the Communist perspective, CRUA was a dangerous adversary. Communists mobilized to restart their unemployed association and, under the prestigious leadership of A.T. Hill, sought to link the struggle of the unemployed to replacement of the existing economic system.[34] Their Unemployed Association of the Twin Cities (UATC) attained impressive dimensions, winning considerable support from diverse organizations, including labour organizations claiming 3,000 members in Fort William alone.[35] The UATC and CRUA jockeyed for influence in presentations to city councils, but the UATC was denounced and Mayor Darrell of Port Arthur declared that his council "did not intend to be dictated to [by] red propaganda."[36] Representatives from the Independent Labour Party (ILP) and trades and labour councils of both cities shared the mayor's anti-Communist position, but the Communists could more plainly articulate the outrage and anger of the unemployed. In March 1930, a large crowd of between 5,000 and 6,000 workers "paralyzed" Fort William and Port Arthur in a demonstration that denounced not only the plight of the jobless but also the "imperialist war."[37]

The UATC's troubles with the municipal councils of Port Arthur and Fort William were only one of a host of problems facing Communist organizers in the district. Finnish and Ukrainian members of the CPC had increasingly been under attack for being "leftists." Many Anglo members of the party were fond of criticizing them and their organizations for being "federalistic" and the root of the party's problems. Many, most often led by Hautamäki, countered by arguing that they were better geared towards organizing the unemployed and that the Bolshevization of the party could not, and should not, be carried out overnight. As Hautamäki stated to the CPC leadership: "Federalism cannot be done away with by resolutions alone, but by getting workers to work side by side of different nationalities, not as nationalities, but as members."[38]

Apparently, he was not alone in his criticisms. The Political Secretary of the Comintern in Moscow harshly criticized the CPC's executive for its recent expulsion of prominent Finns. Ostensibly for the sake of party unity, the CPC was instructed to reinstate all those Finnish members expelled during the Vaara incident in 1929. Characteristically, the CPC meekly accepted Moscow's critique.[39] To be fair, its leadership was caught between the Comintern's desire for larger numbers of English and French members and the reality that the vast majority continued to be neither. The Comintern had concluded, and the Canadian leadership accepted, that the continued lack of compliance by the language organizations was a "very strong basis for Right danger in Canada, and a very strong basis for Right tendencies."[40]

Finnish and Ukrainian organizations, being the largest and most prominent, came under the greatest scrutiny. Somewhat ironically, CPC leader Tim Buck argued that they had developed "a superiority complex ... in relation to other immigrant workers." This, he suggested, was a result of their inherent "petty bourgeoise [sic] attitude of superiority to those members who are not members of the revolutionary organizations, and partly a certain cultural superiority."[41] The attitude, he suggested, had little to do with the "Canadian" experience; rather, "foreign born workers in Canada" were "still to a great extent (mentally) living in their home countries. They still want to speak their own language, they cannot effectively participate in trade union meetings or Party meetings on the basis of their language, but in contradistinction to this, they are a decisive element in Canadian industry."[42]

As Buck's analysis suggests, it was difficult for the CPC to change its underlying demographic base. The Comintern strongly urged the party to develop its "growing mass influence" and to go beyond the ethnic communities historically identified with it. The Comintern was especially critical of the CPC for failing to translate large demonstrations into impressive membership increases.[43] In April 1930, the CPC launched an ambitious campaign to increase total membership in the party by 3,000 and to double the subscription list of the *Worker* from 5,000 to 10,000.[44] Members were informed that this campaign would focus on "Anglo-Saxon" and "Canadian-born" workers. Although they were told that this should not preclude the recruitment of "as many as possible revolutionary immigrant workers into its ranks, and must in no way be interpreted to mean that," district organizers knew what was expected of them.[45] They had also been warned, in vintage Third Period language, that anyone attempting "to destroy the party campaign by characterizing these aims as 'utopian and unrealizable' is a sabotageur [sic], who aims at disrupting and hindering the growth of the revolutionary movement."[46]

With the Finnish and Ukrainian organizations playing a huge role in the region and the bulk of local organizers being drawn from their ranks, it cannot be coincidental that Jim Barker, a Tim Buck loyalist, was sent to the Port Arthur District in April to shore up discipline and assist in the recruitment of English-speaking members.[47] Barker had been sent by the party to Cape Breton in November 1929 to assist in party organizational efforts and, one can assume, to keep an eye on Nova Scotia miner and union leader J.B. McLachlan, who was increasingly suspect for his alleged right-wing sympathies. McLachlan would later recall that Barker's "one consuming ambition" while in Nova Scotia had been "to get me out of the movement."[48] Although parades continued to draw thousands of workers in the twin cities, few of the 335 new members outside of the lumber industry recruited between July 1929 and July 1930 were English-speaking or trade union members, despite Barker's best efforts.[49] Barker could hardly be blamed for the lack of progress, however. The WUL continued to have no offices in either of the twin cities. Communists in the region also had to deal with the re-emergence of the IWW in the lumber camps and its growing prominence in demonstrations in Port Arthur. Unlike the CPC's organizers, the Wobblies tended to focus more on regional issues rather than those half a world away. This tactic, Hautamäki reported, resonated better with workers than did the national and international platforms advocated by the CPC's organizers.[50]

Concerns over the IWW had became so pronounced that by the time of the Seventh Annual Convention of the LWIUC, it was resolved that members should have no connection with the IWW or with its restaurants and auxiliaries.[51] Finns in the region were known to participate in both CPC and IWW cultural, sporting, and social activities, and the CPC was concerned that such activities had contributed to its membership losses.[52] The Central Executive Committee was particularly harsh: "All workers shall be thoroughly acquainted with the betrayal that the leadership of the IWW committed in Port Arthur [Shabaqua] strike last fall, in directly acting in the interests of the employers by serving as an agent of lumber jobbers and petty businessmen."[53]

The IWW attempted to organize the unemployed, the unorganized, and the lumber workers, but these efforts met with limited success. To deal with the situation, the LWIUC opted to reorganize to allow for the inclusion of unorganized workers at the convention. Such a move was also an attempt to rectify the confusion resulting from the seasonal nature of lumber work and the lumber workers' need to seek additional employment during the harvest season. To reflect this change, the union changed its name to the Lumber and Agricultural Workers Industrial Union of Canada (LAWIU), and affiliated with the WUL shortly after. It also became the sole WUL presence in the region.[54]

The new union also made the situation facing young workers a priority. Building on the successful participation of the CPC during the strikes of 1929, the Young Communist League (YCL) had begun establishing branches throughout Northwestern Ontario and holding regular meetings. By 1931, highly active branches could be found in Kenora, Sioux Lookout, Fort Frances, Fort William, Nipigon, Port Arthur, and Kivikoski. The LAWIU also established its own youth section, since lumber camp bosses were increasingly using young workers in the Port Arthur District as a form of cheap labour. This move was seen as a natural outgrowth of the union's goal of organizing all of the unorganized in the district.[55]

The new prominence of the YCL and the LAWIU was reflected in their leading role in the 1930 May Day demonstrations, the largest the twin cities had seen in years. Thousands of residents participated in the parades or came out to support them.[56] Various police inspectors followed the estimated 1,000 marchers from the Ukrainian Labour Temple. Fearing trouble, additional officers, members of the local militia, and Royal North-West Mounted Police officers descended on the crowd. Strengthened by "a battalion" of Canadian Legion members, authorities arrested dozens, including parade leaders Frank Bruce, Peter Bolotynuk, Waino Hakala, Mike Cosmishin, and Elsie Danalinski.[57] Notwithstanding the efforts of the newly established Finnish branch of the Canadian Labour Defence League and of noted lawyer J.L. Cohen, all the accused were found guilty of unlawful assembly and, with one exception, sent to jail. The exception, seventeen-year-old Elsie Danalinski, was given the option of paying a $100 fine. Danalinski stalwartly refused to pay the fine, because she wished to stand shoulder to shoulder with her comrades and not receive special treatment as a woman. It proved a fatal choice. She was placed in close contact with a prisoner with tuberculosis, contracted the disease, and died after her release.[58]

Despite the visible support in the region for the causes promoted by the CPC, the Port Arthur District continued to be racked with turmoil. The growing number of demonstrations in the region had not translated into support for the CPC's political platform. The provincial election of 1930, for example, saw A.E. Smith run once again, but this time he chose the riding of Fort William over Port Arthur.[59] The decision was not an arbitrary one. After consulting with district organizers, the Political Committee had decided that this constituency, unlike the faction-ridden and Finnish Port Arthur, offered the prospect of building a more stable working-class base.[60] Nonetheless, Smith received fewer than half of the votes he had won in his previous run for office.[61] One reason could have been that Port Arthur, with its higher population of Finns, was more demographically and politically "red" than Fort William.

Mobilizing workers in Fort William had become just as problematic as in Port Arthur. While the strength of the CPC in the latter city remained the Finns, in Fort William it was dependent on the participation of local Ukrainian workers. The souring relationship between the Ukrainian Labour-Farmer Temple Association (ULFTA) and the CPC resulted in the branches in Port Arthur and Fort William cutting off communication with the district executive. Only a few of the ULFTA's members had recently attended party functions. As Hautamäki complained to McEwen in the spring of 1930, a recently planned WUL campaign could not be effectively prepared without the ULFTA executive's assistance.[62]

The CPC attributed Smith's dismal results to poor campaign financing and to the fact that he was the first Communist candidate ever to run in the constituency.[63] His lack of success was also a result of the region's increasingly acting as "the junction between eastern and western Canada." As Lita-Rose Betcherman suggests, "the twin towns of Port Arthur and Fort William were the stopping-off place for all of the unemployed single men who rode the rails from one end of the country to the other." While "this drifting mass of migratory workers was grist for the communist mill," the population's transience also contributed to the difficulties of establishing a stable party structure.[64] The potential was apparent. As one local Communist organizer suggested, "if we are successful in lining up the harvesters when they are penniless and, in spite of that, in good spirits and in a fighting mood we will be able to get all the westerners interested in this important and great movement."[65]

In an attempt to reinvigorate the district, the leadership underwent a change in August. The District Secretary and Agit-Prop Organizer had been forced to leave the region to find work, and new and relatively inexperienced members replaced them. As a result of the shuffle, YCL member Mary Gilbert became much more active in the region.[66] Gilbert's rise through the local CPC ranks was evidently very rapid. When seventeen delegates from all over the Port Arthur District met in September for the first youth section of the LAWIU conference, she opened the proceedings. Frank Bruce represented the WUL (nationally), Hautamäki greeted the conference on behalf of the General Executive Board of the LAWIU, and Dan Parnega represented the YCL.[67]

More demonstrations meant more police surveillance. Tensions climaxed on 28 October 1930 when local police, the RCMP, and members of the Canadian Legion raided the Port Arthur headquarters of the LAWIU and the offices of the CLDL. Everything was seized and those who protested were arrested.[68] Officials at all levels also increasingly let it be known that any infractions by the "foreign-born" would lead to deportations.[69] As the work of Barbara Roberts has demonstrated, the threat of deportation during the Depression years was hardly a phenomenon unique to the Lakehead.[70] "The techniques used for the political deportations of the 1930s were similar to those developed during the period of the First World War," Roberts argues. "In both instances, political deportation was made easier by special legal powers to deport radicals overtly for political 'crimes' as enemies of the state." Those arrested at the Lakehead were frequently charged with lesser crimes such as vagrancy.[71] Two very notable deportation cases involved Akselt Panttaja and Eric Holm. Panttaja, a Finnish labourer, was arrested on a charge of vagrancy. On the advice of his lawyer, he pleaded "not guilty" to the charge, but the court translator put down his plea as "guilty." Despite the best efforts of his lawyer, and a signed affidavit from Panttaja, he was deported to Finland on 23 March 1931, to certain imprisonment. Holm's offence was to have demanded "work or bread" from city officials. In both cases, the Canadian Labour Defence League argued that the system was discriminating against workers on political grounds.[72]

Changes in leadership and in the migratory patterns of many workers meant institutional chaos. Each unit operated autonomously and in isolation, without a centralizing authority providing either guidance or information. As one local member advised Buck, even though a "fairly strong section of the unemployed workers" had been established in Port Arthur, it was "merely an accident and not through any fault of the party."[73] Hautamäki argued that many locals had also been getting the wrong impression of the party as, without any form of explanation, money sent for meeting the cost of speakers in the region was not being used for that purpose.[74]

For its part, the LAWIU National Executive Committee argued, "our union is an economic organization of great importance as it includes the most exploited sections of the working class. Because of the unstable economic conditions, an intensive fight *must* be carried on in the streets as well as in the camps. For this reason, our union is much nearer to the revolutionary political activities than many of the other unions."[75] Disappointed with the efforts of Gilbert and the WUL, and fearing what further absorption would mean locally, the LAWIU actively sought to become the "decisive factor" in the region. It argued that "those who are traveling in the freight trains" must become the "rallying centre of the jungle gangs, and the talk of those who are filling the skid rows and the flop houses." "It must also be guiding spirit among the loggers and the camp workers," Hautamäki wrote to a colleague in British Columbia. "We have a strong enough union to create our own ideas, psychology of fight and revolt based on communist principles."[76] The LAWIU's financial problems continued to prevent it from orchestrating successful organizing and educational campaigns, however. The National Executive Committee estimated in 1930 that at least 5,000 dues-paying members would be required to ensure stable activities.[77]

As Communists grappled with internal issues, external forces also threatened to destabilize the party. Local authorities had not been blind to the growing militancy in the area and to Communist attempts to mobilize workers for demonstrations. In response, they beefed up the local police force, asked that the militia be on standby, and requested an enlarged detachment of the Royal Canadian Mounted Police in the area. In order to "curb mob scenes," the Port Arthur police board also organized a permanent auxiliary force composed largely of officers from the Canadian Legion.[78] The auxiliary force was used indiscriminately to quash demonstrations through the rest of the 1930s. For example, when at the end of October 1930 a group of peaceful marchers led by Frank Bruce and Mary Gilbert neared the Port Arthur city hall to present a petition to the council, policemen began to harass and physically abuse them. As was often the case at the Lakehead, things turned violent. After being assaulted, Gilbert called for assistance and a brawl broke out. Police attacked the marchers and a number of onlookers responded by attacking the police, knocking Chief George Taylor to the ground and injuring him.[79] In retaliation, the police raided the Communist and Wobbly halls on Bay Street. Specifically targeted were Gilbert, the Unemployed Association of Port Arthur, and the offices of the local branch of the CLDL.[80] The situation had become so tense that Hautamäki believed the police would arrest him at any moment.[81]

Despite the growing militancy in the region and the successful establishment of an unemployed association affiliated with the WUL, the situation did not look so good when the November 1930 District 6 conference took place. Recent recruitment efforts had resulted in only minor gains in membership (although the LAWIU reported five new locals in the region). A. Skarra, chair of the Organization Department, attributed this to the "lack of the party machinery in groups carrying out the party work."[82] Those groups and units that submitted some form of report indicated that a culture of indifference had taken hold. There was much misunderstanding among the units.[83] The District Executive Committee suspected, in classic Third Period style, that some of the party's numerous groups had succumbed to "pacifist ideas and manners," and feared that many members were indifferent to the party.[84]

While membership numbers in unions may have been down, the UATC had begun to see considerable progress.[85] By December, it had become so large that it was divided into two separate organizations, one operating in each city. The Port Arthur Unemployment Association (PAUA) appears to have been the more active. For example, the soup kitchens it ran provided between 350 to 400 single men in Port Arthur with coffee and food daily.[86] So successful were such initiatives which, in reality, were initiated and led by Mary Gilbert that McEwen suggested she take advantage of the situation and that those who had received some form of relief be "hunted out by committee and brought back into the fight."[87]

Tensions between Gilbert and Hautamäki split the local Communists. Gilbert thought that Hautamäki and his lumber workers were overstepping their authority by recruiting unemployed workers. Hautamäki pragmatically considered that organizing the unemployed was more important than the particular organization or organizer claiming credit for it. It was, he told Gilbert, "quite unnecessary to get warmed up as to who did the work."[88] Hautamäki, in some WUL interpretations, was confusing revolutionary trade unionism with organizing the unemployed.[89] Gilbert, in the eyes of her critics, was dabbling with concepts of monetary reform in the PAUA newspaper the *Bulletin*, and even Tom McEwen, who was generally supportive of her, thought she was in danger of sinking into a "swamp of false ideology."[90] Many of these conflicts appeared to stem from the CPC's being caught in a contradictory position, that of suddenly being required to undertake the complicated tasks of constructing a comprehensive unemployment organizing program in a region that did not conform to its underlying conception of how a revolutionary movement should be built. In this setting, Hautamäki could draw on long-standing Finnish bonds of unity and the organizational history of his union to do something with the unemployed, but in doing so, he ran up against the ostensibly more inclusive alternative strategy of the WUL, which, organizers and members of the LAWIU were told by the National Secretary, was to be placed at "the forefront of every question."[91]

For his part, Hautamäki made the situation worse by attacking and condemning the tactics of the WUL in the region. Spurred by the inability of the PAUA to protect "foreign" workers, he blamed the regional failures of the association and the WUL on the "two Anglo-Canadian organizers with the WUL [Barker and Gilbert] for their destruction of the ethnic mass protest" cultivated since the death of Rosvall and Voutilainen.[92] Workers in the region knew that it was through the mostly Finnish membership of the LAWIU that Port Arthur, or more specifically 316 Bay Street, had become "the talk in every freight and in all the hang outs" throughout the country.[93]

To change the situation, the WUL began actively planning to move the LAWIU's headquarters to Montreal. As McEwen suggested, "a greater concentration could be carried on in the Maratime [sic] Provinces, which in connection with Ontario, would direct its energies towards the organization of the entire pulp cutting industry."[94] For historians such as Anthony Rasporich, this summed up "two decades of intra-party factionalism between Finns and Anglo-Saxons in the Left."[95] Such mishandling of lumber workers in the region contributed, Hautamäki argued, to the continued presence of the IWW.[96] Although the WUL did support maintaining a district office to keep up organizing efforts in the region, it favoured Winnipeg over Port Arthur as the location because of the potential to recruit agricultural workers in Manitoba and, no doubt, to decrease the power of the members from Northwestern Ontario. The CPC also continued to attribute the growing unrest within its ranks to the "problem of ironing out one of the most important questions facing our Party – that of determining the role of the proletarian revolution in Canada – and the question of Canadian imperialism, the status of Canada itself."[97] According to Ian

Radforth, the "hands-off approach" to both the LAWIU and Port Arthur District, the adoption of the policy of Bolshevization, the rise of Tim Buck, and the subsequent aggressive attack against the autonomy of the language federations led the party to take a much more direct role in Northwestern Ontario during 1931.[98] Alex Gibson joined Mary Gilbert as the WUL's leading figure in the region.

Of the five "labour" candidates endorsed by the Port Arthur Trades and Labour Council during the 1930 civic election, the Communists had backed only Gibson, and only he had been elected.[99] President of the Pulp and Sulphite Workers local and a well-known member of the local branch of the Communist Party, his nomination was a coup for the CPC, as his endorsement by the Trades and Labour Council indicated a certain amount of success in appealing to the trade unionists in the region.[100] Unlike in Fort William, where labour candidates (in the vein of the Lib-Labs a decade before) were elected based on centre-left campaigns, Gibson capitalized on "his Marxist sympathies and support for radical unions among the bushworkers, [which] made him a fairly popular candidate while other more moderate trade unionists were unable to make an impact."[101] As Tom McEwen told Gilbert, however, although the CPC publicly remained quiet about Gibson's connection to Moore and other centre-left politicians, privately it believed that Gibson was "not worth a damn" and was useful only for his position in the Pulp and Sulphite Workers Union.[102]

With Gibson's dedication in question, it was decided that Barker should be the District 6 organizer.[103] He and the Organizing Secretary of the CPC realized, however, that to have any chance at success, it was essential to gain the support of Finnish members. The party instructed the Finnish National Party Fraction Bureau in Toronto to assist in the mobilization of the Finnish members and their mass organizations in the region, as they were essential in the fight for the unemployed. The Central Executive Committee also stuck to the Comintern's directive. As the Organizing Secretary stated, "a step in the direction of carrying out the decisions of the recent Enlarged Plenum on the tasks of the language mass organizations" had to be carried out.[104]

Barker had "concrete tasks" to carry out under the direction of the district and local WUL councils. Central was the participation of Finnish Organization of Canada (FOC) locals and the need for them to concentrate on workers other than those from their communities. "This campaign," the FOC was instructed, "must result in thousands of contacts for our Party especially among the Anglo-Saxon and French Canadian workers in the factories. Every Finnish Party member must concentrate on the establishment of these contacts in his or her own place of work."[105] These initiatives posed a number of problems. First, as discussed previously, the WUL did not operate a local council and the PAUA and LAWIU continued to perform its duties. In fact, the WUL had little direct influence, even among the lumber workers in the district. Further, the WUL leadership was concerned at the prospect of someone (possibly Gibson or Gilbert) whom it described as "a representative of 'The Reformist Unions,' NOT A PARTY MEMBER" becoming the new Secretary of the "District Committee."[106] Finally, much to the chagrin of McEwen and Gilbert, Hautamäki continued to be the most visible leader in the region, organizing unemployment demonstrations and frequently being arrested and fined for his role.[107] In terms of leadership, the WUL continued play a decidedly subservient role vis-à-vis the LAWIU.[108]

By the end of 1930, another factor began to influence the CPC's activities in the region. The formation of the Karelia Autonomous Soviet Republic, a socialist utopia in the historic Finnish homeland of Karelia, led to what historians have called "Karelia fever."[109] Thousands of Finnish workers were driven, perhaps in equal parts by cultural nostalgia, a utopian impulse to finally live in a socialist society, and a sharp sense of alienation from a rejecting and unemployment-ridden Canadian society, to explore this distant, alluring option. Unemployment was undoubtedly a driving force for many. In 1931, approximately 10,000 of Canada's estimated 70,000 Finns were unemployed.[110] This migration worried the CPC and Comintern leadership, as it threatened to deprive the party of the bulk of its most ardent organizers and much of its rank and file.

It should come as no surprise that the unemployment situation, combined with the increased persecution and arrests and the constant threat of deportation, meant that the CPC executive was receiving literally thousands of applications from Finnish members for transfers to the USSR. At the Lakehead, hundreds of Finnish Communists, such as prominent YCL member Aate Pitkänen, told their District Executive Committees that they intended to go to Karelia. Many of them were among the most valuable workers of the CPC and the LAWIU. Between 2,000 and 3,000 Finnish socialists opted to leave Canada.[111] Many CPC locals ceased to exist. In the summer of 1931, no fewer than 200 workers left the Lakehead for Karelia;[112] by 1932, much of the regional leadership of the LAWIU had emigrated.[113]

Karelia only served to heighten the CPC's concern about its dependence on non-Anglo-Saxon workers. The problem was that it also realized that they were necessary for the financial and political success of the party.[114] Over twelve mass Ukrainian and Finnish organizations were operating in the district, providing the bulk of the operating funds even if they did not send reports to the national headquarters.[115] The FOC remained the most active, financially supporting and providing the largest number of participants for demonstrations, rallies, and presentations by touring and local speakers. In short, the Finns remained the glue that held the CPC together in the region during a time when the district was in shambles.[116] The Finns's often-criticized "federalistic tendencies" had reportedly begun to reassert themselves in the region and to dominate CPC activities. Some Finnish party members in Fort William, for example, crippled efforts to hold demonstrations by refusing to work with their Ukrainian comrades.[117] The reason for this position remains unknown, but the ULFTA's three branches had recently become more active under the guidance of Michael Biniowsky, and had been showing a greater interest in developing the platform of the WUL than in its own cultural initiatives. It even appears that the ULFTA branches were beginning to fall more in line with the party's directives than the associations in Winnipeg. Under Biniowsky's leadership, however, the ULFTA remained firm in its desire to operate autonomously.

Such factional disputes between the Ukrainian and Finnish Communists appear to have been rare. For example, Hautamäki and Biniowsky worried that the WUL was unsuited, and perhaps unable, to organize farm labourers and harvesters in the region. The two men cautioned Tom McEwen that the local branch of the ULFTA had "been quite passive," opposing, for instance, the creation of committees for fear that the WUL and LWIUC would become a competitive organization.[118] Demonstrations held in Port Arthur and Fort William in February featured both Finnish and Ukrainian mass organizations, with Hautamäki and Biniowsky playing prominent roles along with Gilbert.[119] For their roles, Hautamäki and another Finnish agitator, Emil Wilen, were arrested and served brief jail sentences.

By April, the Political Bureau of the CPC and District 6 organizer Jim Barker wanted to have Alf Hautamäki and his wife, Ailiane (head of the Finnish Women's Labour League branch in Port Arthur), thrown out of the party for their stubborn refusal to comply with the party's directives. Barker viewed Hautamäki, much as he had McLachlan in Nova Scotia – as the impediment to success in the region. He was not alone in this opinion. Many party loyalists, both nationally and in the region, had become dissatisfied with Hautamäki's performance as leader of the LAWIU. His lack of enthusiasm for CPC policies and the recent inactivity in the bush camps was blamed on his diminishing personal popularity.[120] The Kivikoski and Tarmola locals, for example, wrote to Tim Buck that he had even been seen drinking with opponents of the party, and that this and other indiscretions had cost him the confidence of workers in the region.[121]

Officially, Hautamäki was also blamed for the failure of Bolshevization to take hold within the Finnish membership of the LAWIU. McEwen and the WUL, in particular, lashed out at him for his "pessimism and defeatism" and for "his policy of concentrating on educational work among the unemployed bushworkers," to cite the words of Ian Radforth. In contrast, McEwen argued that the LAWIU should focus on "the camps, at the work place, organizing them for strikes, rather than serving as a propaganda organization."[122] Hautamäki's position as National Secretary of the LAWIU complicated matters, however. Conscious of the Comintern's reaction to such decisions in the Vaara scandal of 1929, the party executive suspended Hautamäki for three months on the pretext that he missed a district convention of the LAWIU.[123]

During his suspension, a LAWIU convention was held in May and Emil Wilen, despite being a poor English speaker, was nominated by the Finnish lumber workers to become secretary of the union. While agreeing that an alternate plan would be prudent, McEwen disagreed and advised Barker to use the convention to elect the WUL's preferred Finn, a man named Sillanpaa. The membership's choice carried the day, even getting Hautamäki's support. The long-desired replacement of Hautamäki occurred as Wilen took over as National Secretary of the union.[124] Clearly, the WUL was attempting to manipulate the district into supporting its choice, despite growing support for another candidate.[125]

McEwen's direct intervention was preceded in March by his declaration at the Port Arthur district conference of the LAWIU that the WUL "must assume equal responsibility with the leadership" of the union. This assumption of power was supposed to accompany a transformation of the union into a mass organization and mark a material change in the union's organization. The WUL argued that rather than operating at the point of production (the lumber camps), it operated instead in those areas where workers were unemployed. The present form of organization "renders the ideological development of the membership of the [LAWIU] for the economic struggles on the job extremely difficult, and reduces their contact with the poor farmers throughout the district to nil during the course of these preparations."[126] The CPC had also become concerned that the LAWIU was "sinking its identity in the Unemployed Association, where its membership have become unemployed." As a result, many LAWIU locals had become defunct and ceased to exist.[127] An attempt to rectify this situation occurred in March when a mass conference was held ostensibly to establish among all party units and members a basis for the WUL.[128]

The decision to have the WUL play a more direct role in the organizing efforts of the LAWIU was made at the centre without any consultation with or consideration of the district. As no Industrial Department or WUL branch existed and all agitation was being carried out by Ukrainian and Finnish members (aside from Barker, Gilbert, and occasionally Bryan), the CPC continued to appeal to few beyond the Finnish community. By taking a greater role in the LAWIU, the WUL hoped to increase its presence, using its infrastructure while not having to provide for a separate organizer.[129] The LAWIU itself, however, was experiencing more and more problems. By March, only about 100 of the 1,000 members were paying dues; as many were unemployed or had become increasingly involved with the IWW. Similarly, the YCL branches at the Lakehead reported no activity due to increasing competition from both inside and outside the party. The Ukrainians in the district were described as being "tied down with work in the mass organization" and, outside of Kivikoski and Murillo, many Finns were opting to send their children to Junior Wobbly meetings instead. The problem, from the perspective of the Finns and Ukrainians, had to do with the CPC's leadership in the region.

Local members of the Ukrainian fraction, for example, described the head of the district's Women's Branch as anti-ULFTA and dictatorial. Mary Gilbert was now also being described as someone who had "antagonized all members" in the district.[130] The grounds for this negative perception of Gilbert were that, as one of the few Communist leaders not imprisoned in the February disturbances, she had failed to maintain accustomed levels of activity among the Finns. In Gilbert's defence, the WUL appears to have spread her too thin. As Barker wrote to McEwen, she was frequently called away on party business, and in her absence the non-Finnish and non-Ukrainian activity in Port Arthur and the surrounding region would cease.[131]

Emil Wilen's attempts to strengthen the Finnish base of support in the LAWIU were hampered by the Central Organization Department's (COD) emphasis on Anglo-Saxon and French Canadian workers. In the May recruiting drive, for example, the COD informed all organizers that the main task of the drive was to ensure that 60 percent of new recruits came from these two ethnic groups. Further, the COD informed district organizers that whereas the "foreign-born" membership "to a certain degree retards mass recruiting among Anglo-Saxon workers, we must decisively reject now the claim that foreign-born comrades cannot recruit from among the basic sections of the working class."[132] As Stewart Smith remarked, "the general impression here [in Moscow] is that there is not sufficient blending between the new comrades in the leadership ... and the older and more experienced comrades." This had resulted in "un-thought-out statements" and a "weakening of [the] Party line."[133]

Even Hill, a party member seemingly above reproach, felt the impact of the party's new turn when Smith, the young rising star, criticized him for comments made about the party's purpose and program. At issue, however, was not the eventual organization of the party. Both Hill and Smith agreed on the fundamental principles, yet Smith was out of touch with Lakehead realities. Operating from his Lenin School perspective, he attributed divisions within the Lakehead left to ideological battles between left and right, or to errors in carrying out the "tactical line" of the party, and seemed oblivious to the underlying ethnic or organizational realities that had intensified the left's personal and political differences.[134]

By 1931, the leadership of the WUL still failed to understand the local situation. With Hautamäki gone, Barker was chastised for the "bloody crime" of obtaining only 500 signatures for the recent unemployment insurance campaign. As McEwen remarked, "that amount could be got by a mere visit to a few factories alone." Further, Barker was warned to be leery of those who dismissed claims that non-English workers could not organize Anglo-Saxons. "[We] will have to fight continually against this 'not speaking English' crap," he argued. "We have a Finnish girl here who hardly speaks a damn word of it, and who had collected more English signatures than any other single member in Toronto. The reason is that she is determined to collect rather than to speak."[135] Comparing Toronto to the situation at the Lakehead speaks to his inability to grasp the local situation, and the general failure of the WUL and the CPC to come to grips with the growing unrest in the region.[136]

Was the LAWIU in danger of losing its identity when it came to the Finnish issues articulated by the FOC? Yes, some Communists worried. In response, they acted to make the LAWIU less Lakehead-centred. They established new districts from Montreal to Vancouver. They even diminished Port Arthur as the union's headquarters by establishing a joint headquarters in Sudbury, apparently in the hope of appealing to French Canadian workers. All such measures appeared aimed at making the Finnish Canadians less central to the LAWIU.

Certainly, the vast majority of the local CPC members belonged to the union, but other departments continued to be active even if only in a limited fashion. For example, the 25 February demonstrations resulted in 2,000 demonstrators participating in Port Arthur and another 3,000 in Fort William.[137] Over 1,400 had turned out in March for the International Women's Day demonstrations in Fort William, West Fort William, Intola, Tarmola, and Port Arthur organized by District 6 organizer Jim Barker.[138] These demonstrations also served to underscore the issues facing the region, however. The CPC's Political Bureau admitted that it had little direction of the events and that the lack of party organization had resulted in little, if any, recruitment.[139]

Working under the aegis of the PAUA during the spring of 1931, the WUL did succeed in organizing a series of demonstrations. In April, mass rallies in both Port Arthur and Fort William featured over 4,000 and 1,000 workers, respectively.[140] The May Day celebrations of 1931 saw some of the largest crowds in years. Local Finnish and Ukrainian Communists came out by the thousands to listen to speeches by leading members of their communities.[141] Local food workers also rallied to the cause, as twenty-nine working in the Finnish restaurants and cooperatives joined the WUL and created the Food Workers' Union of Canada's first local.[142] That same month, the Workers' Unity League federated the increasingly unwieldy unemployed associations into the National Unemployed Workers' Association (NUWA).[143] Shortly after, NUWA councils were running in Port Arthur, Fort William, West Fort William, Kenora, Fort Francis, and Sioux Lookout, with a total of approximately 1,000 members.[144]

In reality, it was national in name only. With the attention of McEwen and the WUL focused on the creation of "red" unions, little attention was paid to providing national leadership.[145] This left local associations largely without guidance from the party centre – and such guidance and support were badly needed at the Lakehead. Independent Labour Party supporters on both city councils continued to block attempts by the Communists to advance their issues in each of the city councils. Fred Moore, in particular, as secretary of the Citizens' Unemployed Association (CUA) and secretary of the Fort William Trades and Labour Council, began a campaign to convince workers not to take part in the NUWA.[146] Only the LAWIU, thanks to its largely Finnish membership, remained active. The number of union locals had increased since the last plenum from fifteen to seventeen. Its continued activity and success was believed to have been more the result of the lessons learned following the deaths of Rosvall and Voutilainen than due to the WUL leadership.[147]

To be fair, the organizing ability of the LAWIU had been complicated by the presence of farmers in the union. As farmers were nonmigratory, their inclusion had created a problem. The LAWIU leadership was unsure how they could best be mobilized, as the union's previous strategies were geared towards the seasonal nature of the lumber camps. Even McEwen questioned the connection that farmers had to the lumber industry. "At what point," he argued, "do these dairy and stump farmers meet the system of capitalism, certainly not in the lumber camp but as farmers, their problems are mortgages, taxes (school, road, post, etc)." Blame was laid at the feet of Hautamäki, who, although no longer head of the LAWIU, remained an active organizer for the union and the FOC branch in Port Arthur. Despite following the desires of the party, he was criticized for "organizing anyone but lumber jacks."[148]

McEwen proposed that a Farmers' Unity League (FUL) be formed whose foundation could be the farmers currently in the LAWIU in the Thunder Bay District.[149] His argument made some sense. Although many farmers in the region, especially those within communities dominated by Finnish and Ukrainian immigrants, were sympathetic to the CPC and had a long history of providing both moral support and food to striking lumber workers, they had fought numerous attempts by the local organizers to have them join the LAWIU. Would it not make more sense to fully organize the Long Lac workers, McEwen wondered, than to persist in attempts to squeeze money from the farmers? Here was a pattern that would be paralleled elsewhere in Northwestern Ontario.[150]

The CPC's influence among youth workers, women, and agricultural workers was waning. No functioning women's department or shop presence could be found in District 6.[151] Despite the large number of small farmers in the district, the FUL remained virtually unknown in the region. All of this, the 1931 plenum concluded, resulted from "the state of affairs in the party itself."[152] To solve the organizational problems and specifically to recruit Anglo-Saxon farmers, the WUL convinced Harry Bryan to work as an unpaid organizer. He used his contacts among the English unionists and the Finns to recruit workers in both the lumber and agricultural industries.[153] Despite Bryan's efforts, organizing workers in other fields still fell to the LAWIU due to the lack of WUL leadership. For example, the LAWIU successfully organized a section of transport workers when 200 and 300 dockworkers joined in Port Arthur and Fort

William, respectively. A short-lived publication called the *Great Lakes Transport Worker* was even established.

The inability of the CPC to attract members from industries outside the lumber camps continued through the summer and fall. For example, at the June district convention, Barker reported that thirty-two units were operating in the region, with only 239 members in twenty-seven of the units, fifty-four of whom were women.[154] It was only because of the personalities of Gibson and Gilbert that the numbers had not decreased further. In late 1931, Gibson managed to organize a small number of food workers in Port Arthur. Working with Harry Bryan, Gilbert had likewise reorganized over 30 workers and YCL members at the Thunder Bay Dairy into the newly established Food Workers' Union (the first dairy in Canada where this occurred).[155]

The arrest in August of nine of the CPC's leaders under Section 98 of the Criminal Code (belonging to an "unlawful association") led to renewed activity. Local demonstrations drew an estimated 4,000 workers and caused so much alarm that Attorney General William Price described the Lakehead as being in the midst of "an uprising."[156] Although total party membership (in all WUL-affiliated unions) in the district had fallen to only 700 members, fewer than 50 of whom were actually working, clearly the Communist labour movement could still respond strongly to a challenge.[157] By the beginning of 1932, however, the WUL had exacerbated many of the CPC's internal problems in the region.

The much more established and largely non-English sections, such as those in Fort William, West Fort, and Port Arthur, continued to "have great remnants of the past passivity, resistance to the turn on the part of the leading circles, inability to break with old forms of activity, hiding behind excuse of persecution and victimization."[158] Secret meetings and demonstrations of those opposing the WUL were reportedly occurring across the region in what was seen as a degeneration of the CPC in the area.[159] As one official commented, although the differences in the party had apparently been "partially overcome ... we still have plenty of carry over of Federalism from the past."[160]

It is significant that, at the CPC's February 1932 party plenum, some delegates admitted to being involved in "splitting tactics," which had led the party into "mistakes" in its struggle against the supposed right danger. The typically self-flagellating Third Period jargon captured some grains of truth: District 6, although plainly the CPC's heartland, was not flourishing. The party had made some gains in visibility and organizational presence, but in Port Arthur and

Fort William, no shop or factory group could be found, and the WUL existed in name only.[161] Hautamäki had been marginalized, Gilbert was thought by some to be ideologically unsound and only intermittently effective, and the controversial Jim Barker had been deported.[162] There was a palpable sense within the party as a whole that the pattern of "obligatory membership" in the Communist Party for those who joined the Finnish Organization for cultural or personal reasons was diluting the party.[163]

While admitting that the district reflected many of the problems facing the party nationally, the local leadership was blamed by the CPC executive for utterly failing to capitalize on a local situation pregnant with the possibilities of growth. As we have seen, the WUL and its activities in the first few years of the 1930s alienated many workers at the Lakehead. Alf Hautamäki, for one, remained adamant that the destruction of the ethnic solidarity that had resulted from the murder of Rosvall and Voutilainen owed more to the work of Anglo-Canadian organizers than to the trade unionists or the IWW, as the CPC executive suggested.[164]

By 1932, the CPC firmly believed that "the present system of obligatory membership of the CP [Communist Party] for those workers who join the Finnish Society for social reasons must be abandoned." Considering the ongoing issues, the leadership believed that "only those who are convinced Communists can be recruited into the Party. The Finnish Society must become a mass organization and be utilized by the Party fraction as a recruiting ground for the Party."[165] The LAWIU had become more widespread and the number of locals at the Lakehead had increased from eleven to thirty-four, but total national membership in the union fell 30 percent during this period, due in part to growing unemployment.[166] Although the LAWIU,the largest Communist union at the Lakehead, would affiliate with the WUL in 1930, its initiatives and large Finnish membership would place it and its leadership increasingly at odds with the goals of the national leadership. By 1932, ongoing tensions, rooted in many cases in ethnic differences, once again fuelled the desire of many to find alternatives.[167]

As the next chapter will discuss, the LAWIU leadership realized that the key to achieving this goal at the Lakehead lay in undermining the activities of the IWW and, in essence, stripping 314 Bay Street of its allure. Despite recent successes in recruiting new members (especially among the unemployed), the leaders remained concerned about the activities of the IWW – even though they dismissed their rivals as "quite like a bunch of rabbits under the leadership of the well-known pie artist – [J.D.] Golden [the new head of the IWW in Canada]."[168] Underlying the words, one senses a worried acknowledgment that the Lakehead left was far from a homogeneous CPC stronghold.

8

Wobbly Relations

The Communist Party of Canada, the Industrial Workers of the World, and the Lakehead, 1932-35

Between 1932 and 1935, the Lakehead was gripped by a series of strikes that not only nearly crippled the already weakened economy of the region but also gravely affected the workers' organizations still existing in Port Arthur and Fort William. The year 1933 alone saw ten strikes in Northwestern Ontario logging camps, involving over 3,000 workers. According to the federal Department of Labour, such disputes accounted for one-third of the total time lost in Canada, including two of the ten largest non-coal-mining strikes in the entire country.[1] This number increased in 1934 to sixteen strikes involving over 6,107 workers.[2] The Workers' Unity League (WUL), through the Lumber and Agricultural Workers Industrial Union of Canada (LAWIU), played a prominent role in the unrest. It was a movement, however, that extended far beyond the Communists. By 1933, only 500 of an estimated 3,500 workers in the heavily Finnish-dominated lumber industry in the Thunder Bay District actually belonged to the LWIUC.[3] It is even more startling that despite the role played by the Communist Party of Canada (CPC) in this period's momentous wave of unrest, by July 1935 only about 400 members could be found in District 6, despite total party membership of 7,390.[4]

The CPC at the Lakehead faced many of the same challenges in 1932 that it had faced in 1926. Notwithstanding the efforts of the WUL, and the vigorous attempts by the party's leaders to implement the directives of the Communist International (Comintern), not much had actually changed. The language groups and lumber workers' unions remained vital. As one party official told the Comintern's Anglo-American Secretariat, "our sectarian approach to the masses," combined with glaring weaknesses in trade union work, had confined the party to its traditional bases of support.[5] At the same time, the CPC faced a new element in a revived and combative Industrial Workers of the World (IWW). Although sworn enemies, the CPC and the IWW evolved a curiously symbiotic relationship on the ground that was very different from the somewhat abstract revolutionary doctrines enunciated in Moscow or Chicago. Both revolutionary socialist organizations were unable to expand much beyond their Finnish-Canadian base, however. In the end, their inability to do so meant that they did not survive, as powerful shapers of the Lakehead left, the vast sea change in the Canadian and international socialist movement in 1935.[6]

The first few months of 1932 did not bode well for the aspirations of Communists at the Lakehead. The year began with the deportation of district organizer Jim Barker (alias Sam Langley). According to the *Canadian Labour Defender,* he "was picked up on the street in Port Arthur, thrown around by two detectives, handcuffed and placed in the cells." He was on an eastbound train by ten o'clock that same night, and, at the time of the article, on the ship *Ascania* heading for Europe.[7] While deportations had become a common occurrence for immigrant workers in the immigrant-heavy timber industry, the sudden deportation of the British-born Barker was no doubt an attempt to deprive the already weakened District Bureau of its most active member,[8] and the CPC national leadership of its most faithful local servant.

Barker's arrest and deportation was just one of many instances of a dramatic campaign of official repression. Provincial and city police frequently searched the residences of known and suspected Communists in both Fort William and Port Arthur. Specifically targeted were the Ukrainian Labour Temple in Fort William and both the Communist and IWW Finnish Labour Temples in Port Arthur. Also singled out were the local offices of the Canadian Labour Defence League (CLDL) and the WUL. The police often seized "suspicious" literature and threatened those in the workers' and Finnish halls with arrest and deportation. In a few instances, they even apprehended those they found present at the time of the search, in an attempt to force the CPC to spend its time and resources in litigation rather than in rallying workers to their cause out in the camps or on the streets.[9]

Under these conditions, left-wing activism was fraught with danger and difficulty. Yet Lakehead leftists kept working.[10] The Young Communists, for example, organized strike support in Nipigon and initiated a Thunder Bay membership drive.[11] Youthful members of the WUL organized a Finnish Workers' Sports Club, and those in the Ukrainian Labour-Farmer Temple Association (ULFTA) in Fort William and Intola maintained a vibrant presence.[12] All the while, such young leftists were intensively surveilled by the RCMP. In such an environment, many Finnish Communists realized ever more sharply how important it was to combine with Ukrainian and other "ethnic" socialists, as evidenced in a joint slate of candidates in the 1932 Port Arthur civic election.[13] As the Canada-wide pattern of anti-Communist repression took hold, CPC insiders thought that many at the Lakehead had succumbed to a "great terror." In May 1932, the Anglo-American Secretariat was told that the membership had become "panic-stricken and somewhat passive," and even the region's many left demonstrations were not generating solid growth for the party.[14] State repression and Bolshevization together, it seemed, had worked to demoralize the Lakehead left.

Added to these CPC woes was another: the re-emergence of a much more active and enthusiastic IWW. Finns disquieted by Bolshevization, some of them perhaps already inclined towards syndicalism, began to abandon the LAWIU for the IWW's Lumber Workers Industrial Union (LWIU) and the IWW-affiliated Finnish support circle *Canadan Teollisuusunionistinen Kannatus Liitto* (the Support League of Canadian Industrial Unionists, or CTKL), which functioned under a newly created Canadian Administration (CA) of the IWW. Doubtless to the chagrin of some Communists, the Wobblies, not the Communists, held centre stage in the struggle against the Pigeon River Timber Company in 1932.[15] The Communists, however, through the WUL, lent their support to the strikers in the form of cash contributions and food, and when the strikers were beaten, they placed the blame not on the IWW but on the repressive tactics of the RCMP.[16]

It would be hard to exaggerate the traumatic results of the RCMP crackdown. According to the CLDL, 200 members of the CPC were arrested on minor charges in 1930. By 1931, this number had increased to 720, ranging from charges under Section 98 of the Criminal Code such as sedition, unlawful assembly, and inciting to riot. In the first six months of 1932 alone, the CLDL reported 456 arrests.[17] The issues facing the district received a significant amount of attention at the August plenum of the CLDL.[18] Primarily, delegates expressed optimism about gains in the district's Anglo-Saxon membership. According to the plenum report, the arrest and trial of the eight CPC leaders had resulted in unprecedented support from across the country. "In Toronto, Vancouver, and Port Arthur districts," it was suggested, "there is already a decided turn towards the Anglo-Saxon masses." In Port Arthur, this included the participation of many leading trade unionists.[19] The Lakehead's members constituted 1,000 of the CLDL's 13,042 members. They came from local workers' organizations that included LWIU locals, Pulp and Paper Workers locals, Building Union Trade locals, the Trades and Labour Council (Port Arthur), ULFTA, unemployed associations, and the Workers' Benevolent Association.[20]

The plenum also resolved that the Port Arthur District should establish a Finnish *Patronati*. The *Patronati* was a structure first used as a committee among Italian immigrants in France in 1927. "The Patronati," the CLDL informed districts, "constitute a wide mass movement with a very loose organizational form." The CLDL's purpose in establishing them in certain districts was to tap into the ranks of various immigrant groups in order to raise funds for the support of political prisoners in specific jails or in their countries of origin. The CLDL's enthusiasm for the *Patronati* suggested a creative new flexibility in the face of the repression, and prefigured in some respects the Popular Front tactics that were to become popular after 1935.[21]

Many of the same issues dealt with at the CLDL plenum also appeared at the LAWIU convention held in the same month in Sudbury. Delegates from the Lakehead were among those who discussed the "heroic support given to the unemployed workers during the strike struggles." They learned how various Communist organizations "had supported the lumber and sawmill workers in their fight against the common enemy."[22] At the conference, the Port Arthur District was instructed to focus its attention and resources on four key tasks: (1) further organize the unemployed lumber workers into the union; (2) strengthen itself by including more Swedish, Ukrainian, and Slovakian workers; (3) keep in close contact with organized workers to ensure that they remain with the party; and (4) remain vigilant in carrying on an ideological campaign and in "skillfully handling" the White Finn question.[23]

The schism that had occurred within the party following the expulsion of Maurice Spector and Jack MacDonald in the late 1920s also figured in the discussion of the general stagnation of both the LAWIU and the CPC in the region. The failure of the strike at Onion Lake in 1929 came to be viewed as an example of the "leftist tendency" within the party. The new guard believed that this tendency had found expression in the strikes and that it, rather than any of the strategies and tactics involved in the disputes, was responsible for the failure of workers to adopt the program and policy of the LAWIU. To combat the supposedly leftist tendency the CPC urged members to reflect on the centrality of "united front forms of struggle." Its Lakehead policy was inherently contradictory, however. The CPC was seeking a base within a working class historically inclined to support the IWW, the One Big Union, and the Independent Labour Party, among other non-Communist organizations, but rather than articulating a program that might address such other forms of leftism, it focused on perfecting its own internal ideological development. The CPC also remained preoccupied with the predominance of the foreign-born and the relative absence of Anglo-Saxon and French Canadian workers, without really suggesting how, without abandoning its longtime stalwarts, it could effectively reach out to these other Canadians.[24]

Just as the CPC was undergoing internal changes, so was the structure of the IWW. Sometime between July and August 1932, members in Canada had chosen Port Arthur as the home for its newly formed Canadian Administration. A *pro tempore* Canadian Executive Branch (CEB) was established under the leadership of Finnish Wobbly H.J. Lindholm. The *pro tem* CEB quickly launched a Canadian IWW publication, the *Organizer,* and began a series of attacks on capitalism in general and on trade unions and Communists in particular.[25] It also blamed the inability of the unemployed to receive relief on Canadian Communists, "Labour Parties, Unions, Liberals, Conservatives, Churches, and many other organizations."[26] It claimed that the only way the situation could be changed was for one industrial union to be formed in such a way that "all its members in any one industry, or in all industries, if necessary, cease work whenever a strike or lockout is on in any department."[27] As the *Organizer* proclaimed in its inaugural issue, "we of the IWW, who have tasted of both victory and defeat, know of old that our tactics and our principles are sooner or later to be recognized by the great mass of workers, both employed and unemployed."[28]

As the IWW undertook its own organizing activities, it also began to lend moral support to all activities of other organizations attempting to undermine conventional trade unionism. An example of this emphasis was the formation of the Amalgamated Mine Workers of Nova Scotia (AMW of NS) under the leadership of Michael McNeil in 1932. The CEB viewed the AMW of NS campaign as inspirational: it had "all the ear marks of the kind of tactics used by the IWW." Such support for the formation of the AMW of NS provided some indication of the IWW's plan for Canada. The CEB was quick to assert that the formation of the AMW of NS demonstrated that "the day is not far distant when the coal miners of Nova Scotia and all Canada are organized into the same Union with our brother miners in the United States, who are fast signifying their choice of organization by joining the IWW." The *Organizer* called on Nova Scotia miners "to study the structure of the IWW and how it is so built that out of its industrial units is built the model ONE BIG UNION."[29]

On 12 September 1932, members of the IWW met in the Finnish Labour Temple in Port Arthur to officially establish the Canadian Administration. H.J. Lindholm presided over the meeting of seventeen delegates representing branches and industrial unions from across Canada. Besides delegates from the Port Arthur Branch and General Recruiting Union (GRU), representatives from Kingston, Ontario and the Vancouver and Merritt branches of British Columbia attended the conference. Several other localities also sent resolutions, minutes, and correspondence even though their delegates could not attend. The goal of the meeting, according to the *Organizer,* was to "put the Industrial Workers of the World on the map in Canada," and to lay the foundation for the First Annual Convention of the Canadian Administration, which was to be held in June 1933.[30]

Although the minutes of the September 1932 convention lack any reference to the Canadian IWW's struggle against Communists, the pages of the IWW's official organ reveal a deep mistrust of CPC activities in Northwestern Ontario and of their alleged "dirty lies." The CEB contended, for instance, that "the Definition of a Bigot ... [was] the Canadian Communist."[31] Often going beyond the Canadian experience for fodder, it attempted to create a rift between the Finnish members and the leaders of the CPC. It sought to draw in some of those lumber workers who had elected to join the recently renamed Communist Lumber Workers Industrial Union of Canada (LWIUC).[32] Frequently, contemporary and historical events in Europe were invoked to suggest that Communists in Canada were now colluding in the camps with the hated nationalist "White Finns" who had killed thousands of Finnish socialists during the Finnish civil war in 1918.[33] The perceived failure of the American Communist party in Michigan was also used as an example of the growing lack of revolutionary policies and tactics within the North American Communist movement. How, the CEB wondered, could Communists consider themselves revolutionary, when it was in fact the Wobblies, not the Communists, who were demanding that workers possess the complete value of their labour, whereas the Communists were content to fiddle with such reforms as unemployment insurance?[34]

Despite attempts to portray itself as moderate, principled, and revolutionary, the CEB, like its prewar manifestation, still advocated the general strike. "Nothing less than the thunder-bolt of the General Strike," argued the CEB, "can uproot the profit system and destroy it, branch and limb." Using the short-lived socialist republic in Chile during the summer of 1932 as inspiration, in October that year the CEB renewed calls for a general strike and industrial unionism. It argued that the events in Chile were just another example showing that "the dream of a Socialist Commonwealth is – but a dream, without the strength of Industrial organization." Moreover, the CEB argued, "no armed insurrection or revolution has yet changed the social system."[35]

Although the CEB acknowledged that both the Paris Commune and the Russian Revolution had changed material conditions, it considered that "both of them were failures insofar as freedom from slavery was the objective." The French, the article continued, were "still slaves of capitalism" and the Russians were "slaves of State Capitalism." Revolutionary Industrialism, "with its well developed plan for control of the state through control of industries, is the only logical answer to our prayers or salvation. Make your laws in the Union Hall."[36] The CEB also took issue with what it perceived to be the CPC's manipulation of the plight of the unemployed, especially recent immigrants. When the unemployed in Hearst, Ontario, facing starvation, took action into their own hands and "served several ultimatums" to local authorities, the CPC took credit despite its lack of involvement. Outraged, Wobblies claimed that this was merely another example of Communists throughout Northern Ontario taking credit for the successes of others. The CEB also attacked the Communists for their lack of internationalism. "Real revolutionary labour movements," the *Organizer* wrote, "are international, but really Communism is falling in line with the R.B. Bennett regime in Canada: 'Run those dam [sic] foreign agitators out of the country.'"[37]

It was a sharp critique, but in reality the IWW was in many respects little better than its Communist adversary. Between 1924 and 1935, only a handful of general conventions had taken place, and many of these had little or no Canadian or other non-American representation. In addition, the conventions held in the 1930s tended to focus more on the survival of the General Executive Board (GEB) than on any new initiatives to organize workers.

These ideological battles took place against a backdrop of intensifying state repression. In October, unemployed workers in Port Arthur began weeklong rotating demonstrations throughout the city to protest the actions of local officials. Einar Nordstrom, a well-known Communist who participated in the demonstrations, recalled that things became violent when fifty protesters gathered peacefully outside the residence of Port Arthur mayor Percy Victor Ibbetson.[38] Informed by an insider of the protesters' plans, the police, according to Nordstrom, were waiting in nearby bushes and trees. When the protesters arrived, the police surprised them and proceeded to attack them with clubs and fists. At a pre-arranged signal, the local RCMP detachment joined in and the protesters were beaten, overpowered, and arrested. Many demonstrators suffered such severe beatings that they became unconscious and later woke up in the local jail without having received any medical attention.

In one such incident, a rally of approximately 1,000 unemployed workers in October turned ugly when a dozen mounted officers swinging batons rode into the ranks of demonstrators. A number were injured and knocked unconscious, the most serious case being that of a Finnish worker named K. Jaaska (also spelled Jaaski), who eventually died.[39] Those demonstrators who escaped the initial charge by the mounted police and fled to Bay Street were run down by police, who also forced their way into the Communist hall and arrested all present. Police also raided the Scandinavian Workers' Society Hall and arrested and ordered deported its chairman, Emil Sandberg, for his alleged role in masterminding the march.[40]

Although the death of Jaaska resulted in an inquest, local officials trivialized the sworn testimony of workers and accepted the statements of police without question. The final verdict determined that Jaaska had died of lockjaw resulting from a cut on his nose, and as his body "showed no evidence of blows or other violence" when examined, claims of police brutality were unfounded. The hundreds of socialists who had showed up for the verdict were visibly angered, but their "branding [of] the Port Arthur cossacks as murderers" appears to have had little bite.[41] Jaaska's death resulted in a massive funeral reminiscent of the one held for Rosvall and Voutilainen in April 1930. Over a thousand workers took part, marching behind his red-flag-draped coffin and a banner that read: "The future belongs to toilers. Comrade Jaaska died demanding bread."[42]

Jaaska's death created a sense of solidarity among workers in the twin cities and caused civic officials concern. Employment agencies in both Port Arthur and Fort William began to refuse work to Finnish and Ukrainian workers in an attempt to stem the growth of both the CPC and the IWW. In no other industry was this more apparent than in the lumber industry. Companies hired men to watch workers, and liaised closely with the employment agencies to ensure that known Communists or Wobblies did not get work.[43] Anti-Communist "White Finns," such as Kosti Koivukoski, president of the Loyal Sons of Canada and an official with the dreaded Pigeon River Timber Company, were placed in positions of authority within both the employment agencies and the camps. Their goal of "preserving the good name of the Finns, fighting the Reds by all means and helping the authorities in whatever way they can," presented them "with an ideal opportunity to exploit the antagonisms within the Finnish community and the divisions within the working class as a whole to their own advantage."[44]

The minutes of the November 1932 District Organization Conference of the Young Communist League (YCL) in District 6 reveal that little information about the activities of the YCL's National Executive Committee or about what had been occurring in the region had been reported to members.[45] Although an effort was made to rectify the situation, this was cut short by police raids and the arrest and conviction of Walter Waywood, secretary of the Fort William Unemployed Council and a member of the District 6 YCL. Waywood was at first arrested for allegedly holding up a local gasoline station and then, when the local magistrate dismissed these charges, for being a counterfeiter.[46] The real purpose of these arrests appears to have been for the local police to gather information on "the Young Communist League, its activities, and many other such questions." Although the *Young Worker* assured its readers that the secretary "was too loyal to tell them more," shortly after Waywood's arrest the YCL district organizer was incarcerated along with a host of other non-Anglo members in the region.[47]

In an attempt to win over current and former Wobblies, the CPC began to take a more conciliatory tone, even admitting that in the past the IWW had "combined the best elements of the fighting trade unionists, and much of the theoretical knowledge of the Social-Democrats. They helped to radicalize sections of workers." Yet, "the fatal weakness that makes the IWW anti-working class was their ignorance of the political nature of the class struggle ... Industrial organization with the general strike as the weapon to emancipate the workers was the beginning and the end of their theory and practice." Finally, "the magnificent struggles put up by the IWW in the past taught them no lessons."[48]

They might have added that the Wobblies were equally struggling to balance centralism with grassroots power. Communists at the Lakehead were by no means the only socialists having trouble with their central authorities. The CA's submission to the 1932 General Convention of the IWW reveals a growing distance between the two administrative branches. According to the report, between 1931 and 1932, only one IWW-supported speaker had visited Canada, and he had stopped only in Vancouver. In fact, except for the CA's secretary-treasurer, no IWW speaker (English or Finnish) had visited many regions, such as Northern Ontario, for nearly eight years. Since the September conference in Port Arthur, the Canadian Administration had taken it on itself to give two travelling delegates the task of "invading" Eastern and Northern Ontario. The CA claimed that, through the efforts of Fred Anderson and George MacAdam, Sault Ste. Marie had been brought back into the fold and over forty new members enrolled in the final weeks of October alone.[49]

According to the CA, total IWW membership in Canada had increased by almost 50 percent since the CA's establishment in July 1932. This was in direct contrast to the GEB's report of decreasing membership during that same period. The Vancouver, Port Arthur, Sault Ste. Marie, and Timmins LWIU branches, and the Port Arthur GRU, were all reported to be holding regular meetings and exchanging minutes. Membership meetings were also being held in Kingston and Nipigon. The CTKL continued to be active.[50] In November alone, the Port Arthur branch signed up thirty new dues-paying members. Besides Sault Ste. Marie, other regions expressed a growing need for members in order to stay active.[51]

By November, the CA also reported on two initiatives being undertaken solely at its discretion. Delegates at the General Convention were informed that Anderson, MacAdam, and all Canadian Wobblies had begun a campaign to organize the unemployed into industrial unions throughout Canada. While the Canadian Administration acknowledged that organizing the unemployed was "a seemingly unsound financial step ... [that] will turn into a sound step with the acquiring of a larger membership."[52] The General Convention was also informed that the Canadian Administration planned to submit resolutions calling for alterations to the constitution of the IWW to reflect the realities of the current situation in Canada. The two most significant changes, intensely debated in Canada and eventually made the foci of a referendum, were a reduction in the size of the Executive Board from seven to five and the lowering of initiation fees for unemployed members.

The CA reaffirmed its commitment to industrial unionism ("as it was an idea no more ... [but] a living factor"), but it also made it clear to the delegates that it would be actively attempting to "stay on good terms with such revolutionary Unions as the OBU [Canada] and the newly formed Amalgamated Mine Workers of Nova Scotia, that efforts to combine all Canadian revolutionary workers into a real ONE BIG UNION can be consummated without difficulty, or with as little difficulty as possible."[53] The CA also reported, however, that the biggest obstacle to its making "immediate big gains" was the "anti-IWW propaganda carried on by Finnish Communists."[54]

Although Communists may have been generally unwilling to work with the Wobblies, during the 1933 municipal elections they participated with other organizations in a "United Front Election Conference." The conference was organized to put forth candidates to fight "not only against the out-and-out capitalist politicians, who are supported by the Chamber of Commerce, but more so the candidates and the program of the League for Municipal Progress." The league had been established by Fred Moore in the 1920s and was now led by on-again, off-again Communist Alex Gibson. Local Communists were concerned with this organization as, they contended, it "put up candidates who spout revolutionary phrases about 'organization,' 'Control by the workers,' etc. etc." Local Communists argued that such ill-defined "leagues" sought to persuade workers to take the easy path of elections rather than the more difficult but rewarding route of class struggle. And they also criticized the explicit nativism of the Fort William Ratepayers' Association, which seemed (in the words of the *Young Worker*) determined to stir up "hatred against the foreign-born workers."[55]

Although they intended to run three candidates in each city on the United Front ticket, regulations forced them to run only one man (named Nayda) in Fort William and a labourer named Emil Roukalla in Port Arthur. Nayda polled 306 votes in Ward One and Roukalla garnered 700 votes in Port Arthur. The "relatively high vote," according to the *Worker*, resulted from the increased presence of the CPC in the region, particularly during unemployment demonstrations. The inability to win a seat was attributed, however, to the "poor apparatus" in the region. Three aldermen belonging to the League for Municipal Progress were elected, including Gibson in Port Arthur and Fred Moore in Fort William. Their success in winning the votes of workers was due, local organizers admitted quite candidly, to their getting the support of the trade unions and forming a united front. Neither man received as many votes as in the previous year, however.[56] For many, the election highlighted the need for the "full mobilization of ALL MASS ORGANIZATIONS."[57]

Over the next few months, relief efforts increased dramatically, as did the number of threatened and actual strikes.[58] Workers building the Northwestern Ontario section of the Trans-Canada Highway walked off the job over wages. Unemployment demonstrations also continued unabated. The Workers' Unity League claimed to be taking a prominent role in each.[59] Authorities clearly believed this to be the case, as surveillance increased and, as was the case in April, the CLDL offices in Port Arthur and the Ukrainian Labour Temple in Fort William were raided and workers were arrested.[60]

The raids may have prompted the renewed sense of solidarity that began just before May Day in 1933. Wobblies, Communists, and assorted trade unionists joined to form a committee to organize demonstrations in both cities. A reported 2,500 workers attended the parade and accompanying outdoor mass meeting.[61] Cooperation was most apparent, however, in June 1933, when over 1,300 workers in the Thunder Bay and Nipigon districts began a strike under the leadership of a committee composed of both Communists and Wobblies.[62]

The LWIUC would claim that it had organized the joint strike committee. Many signs, however, such as the central role of the Wobbly-controlled Labour Temple and the prominence of key figures, point to its formation through the united efforts of Wobblies, Communists, and even Finnish nationalists.[63] In this instance, as in many others, the IWW and Communists could achieve things together that eluded them separately. Finnish and Ukrainian workers leery of Communists, especially given recent controversies regarding their language federations, could be brought into the struggle through the Wobblies. Thus, seemingly opposed forces – the Port Arthur Trades and Labour Council, the YCL, the Finnish Organization of Canada (FOC), the LWIUC, and the IWW – all contributed to this epochal strike of the 1930s.[64]

It was a large (1,300-strong), dramatic, and violent strike. It brought crowds of people into the streets of Port Arthur, and although it resulted in a disappointing wage settlement, below that demanded by the workers, such concrete achievements as the recognition of camp committees, no-discrimination agreements, and the reform of the truck system in the camps allowed the LWIUC to claim a moral victory.[65] At the same time, the LWIUC blamed the IWW for the settlement's limitations, and emerged from the strike as its clear beneficiary – with a growth in its membership from 500 to 1,300 over the first six months of

1933.[66] Moreover, because the CPC union, unlike the Wobblies, was willing to take part in government-imposed collective bargaining, it was left in a stronger, more permanent position.

Throughout the summer and fall of 1933, the CPC continued to experience success in the forests of Northwestern Ontario.[67] "An estimated 25,000 meals," according to Mary Veltri, "were distributed to the strikers through the seven kitchens which were set up in the Lakehead, Tarmola, Lappi, Nipigon, North Branch, and Long Lac."[68] Donations and foodstuffs flowed from both the Communist and Wobbly halls in Port Arthur and Fort William. Much of this cooperation resulted from a mass conference held in August 1933. The LWIUC, IWW, unemployed and unorganized workers, and farmers from the region surrounding the Lakehead all participated and agreed on a strategy for the upcoming harvest and lumber season. A uniform piece rate of $2.50 per cord, a minimum monthly wage of $40, and a 75-cent daily charge for board were established.[69] This solidarity ensured that when timber operators increased wages from the previous year, the mass committee rejected the offer.

The strike gained strength despite an attempt by the LWIUC representatives to take control of the joint IWW/CPC strike committee. By the middle of November, over 4,500 lumber workers were participating, most of them in the Thunder Bay District.[70] In response, the police in Fort William and Port Arthur began to arrest strike fundraisers in an attempt to weaken the strike effort. In one incident, forty-seven picketers were arrested and thirty-three of them were sent to jail for two months or more.[71] One outcome of the strikes was a change in tactics by the Canadian Administration of the IWW. The Canadian Executive Branch began to vigorously push forward the changes that its newly elected leader, George MacAdam, thought necessary for the survival of the IWW in Canada. Financially, MacAdam had inherited an administration no better off than that of the Communists. Writing to the other members of the CEB, he outlined the board's priorities as he saw them. Foremost was a commitment to the establishment of the Canadian Defence Organization (CDO). MacAdam viewed the CDO as a necessity because, he argued, "if the IWW functions with success in the economic field, it will incur the hostility of the masters and their tools."[72]

While rational, the desire for the CDO demonstrates that the IWW was not acting as an innovative and forward-thinking organization. It was also trying to compete with the recent activities of the CPC's Canadian Labour Defence

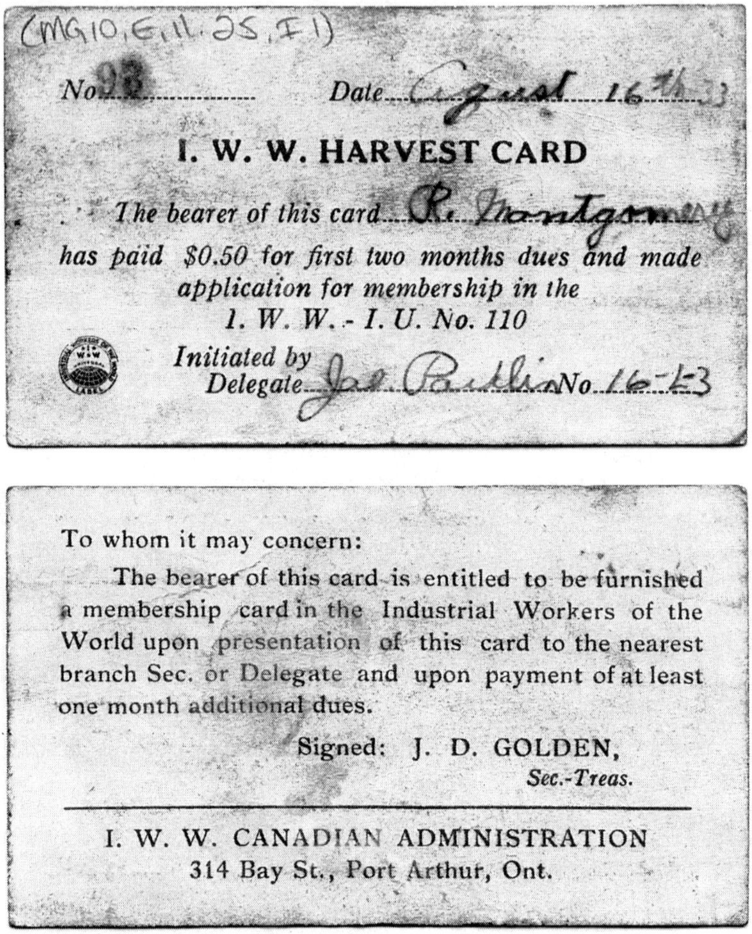

No. .... Date ....

I. W. W. HARVEST CARD

The bearer of this card ....

has paid $0.50 for first two months dues and made application for membership in the I. W. W. - I. U. No. 110

Initiated by Delegate .... No. ....

To whom it may concern:

The bearer of this card is entitled to be furnished a membership card in the Industrial Workers of the World upon presentation of this card to the nearest branch Sec. or Delegate and upon payment of at least one month additional dues.

Signed: J. D. GOLDEN,
Sec.-Treas.

I. W. W. CANADIAN ADMINISTRATION
314 Bay St., Port Arthur, Ont.

Figure 10 (Top) IWW Harvest Card for Agricultural Workers Industrial Union #710. *Courtesy of Lakehead University Library Archives*

League, which had failed to address the needs of all workers. MacAdam was concerned that "cases would be thrown upon us by the rival defence organization [the CLDL] and if we do not have a clear cut policy, we could not turn them down without losing prestige."[73] The CDO was ambitious in design and difficult to implement. A chronic lack of money meant that members were limited to the CEB and the CTKL.[74] The CEB and MacAdam also proposed to model the CDO after the General Defence Committee. Funds would be generated through membership cards and stamps patterned after those currently used by the CTKL and Junior Wobblies Union, but as these were unavailable in 1933 and the cost was prohibitive, it was decided that a 25-cent stamp would be made compulsory for members one year and over and voluntary for those under one year. "Older members," MacAdam argued, "thoroly [sic] understand the necessity of raising monies."[75]

The inability of the IWW General Executive Board to provide support for the defence of Canadian Wobblies also reveals a lack of interest in and understanding of the plight of workers in Canada by the American administration. In fact, the GEB was surprisingly ignorant of events in Canada. For example, despite the fact that the *OBU Bulletin* was sent to both the GEB and the *Industrial Worker* so that members could keep abreast of events in Canada, GEB Secretary-Treasurer Herbert Mahler himself admitted, "I seldom see it and none are kept on file, so it has gone the waste basket route." Responding in the same letter sent to H.J. Lindholm in July 1932, he further showed the GEB's lack of information by requesting "the clippings, then we can look it over and take a shot at them. Perhaps you could accompany the clippings with an article. That would be better as you know the local situation."[76]

This lack of commitment sometimes also manifested itself in competition within the IWW for scarce resources such as speakers. In 1932, the GEB expressed concern over the CA's attempts to get Canadian expatriate Fred Thompson from the United States to go on tour throughout Canada. Joseph Wagner, head of the IWW GEB, refused, declaring that they needed him themselves and "will try to keep him here as long as we can, although if he should be deported, we cheerfully turn him over to you."[77] The need for an organizer in Northwestern Ontario was paramount, however, as, according to one relief camp worker who had recently moved to British Columbia, the Communists had managed to "create enough friction between the anti-communists and pro-communists that it is almost impossible to hold a camp organization together once the word communist is mentioned."[78]

Although many of MacAdam's desired reforms would have made the Canadian Administration less dependent on the GEB, the establishment of a Canadian Wobbly press was not high on his list. Although less than a month earlier the First Annual Convention had empowered the CEB to establish a Canadian IWW paper, MacAdam voiced his personal dislike for the proposal. In contrast, many, including CA Secretary-Treasurer H.J. Lindholm, strongly urged members to support an IWW paper "chuck full of Canadian and World Wide labor news." Lindholm suggested that, although the *Industrial Worker* left "nothing to be desired for our fellow workers across the line," the success of the *Organizer* clearly demonstrated a "crying need" for a "nice little paper" printed at the Lakehead. Such a paper, he argued, would appeal to both former and current members of the IWW and provide food for the increasingly radical labour movement.[79]

The proposed content of the paper provides a window on how Wobbly leaders in both Canada and the United States viewed the world around them.[80] Lindholm, for instance, argued that a Canadian-based paper would satisfy the growing appetite for information on Technocracy and Technology. He encouraged Canadian Wobblies "to bring the matter of subscribing for a paper which advocates practical Technocracy to them and see how soon they will buy a subscription." Even the new GEB Secretary-Treasurer Joseph Wagner, who would neither support nor condemn the establishment of a Canadian-based paper, agreed that "the IWW should profit as much by the development of the Technocrats' moves as possible."[81] The interest of Lindholm and Wagner in "Technocracy," an approach to the crisis of the Depression derived from the scientific management writings of Howard Scott, an admirer of Thorstein Veblen, suggested that Canadian Wobblies shared some of the utopian aspirations of their American counterparts for a post-capitalist, scientifically managed society informed by the most advanced concepts of expertise and efficiency.[82]

Despite claims by Lindholm that the CA already had 200 subscribers lined up by July, MacAdam, citing once again the financial crisis that faced the CA, argued that a Canadian paper could not succeed when the *Industrial Worker*, despite its large subscription base, was teetering on the brink of financial collapse and dragging the GEB down with it.[83] Many Wobblies, such as August Torttila, agreed, and it was decided instead to petition the *Industrial Worker* to create a "special space for Canadian news."[84] The situation facing the IWW in Canada only worsened in the coming months as members increasingly perceived that the CA had done "little or nothing" during the last few years. Foremost was the issue of language. August Torttila's resignation in Sault Ste. Marie on 12 July 1933, for example, demonstrated that the issue was hardly settled. Torttila argued that although wholly committed to the IWW, he wanted someone to take his place on the CEB "as it is a handy cap for me as I cant Read or write English and it is Hard to get a interprtor [sic] all ways that can exsplane [sic] them."[85]

Echoing the thoughts of many Wobblies, MacAdam argued that the IWW in general "had been living on our reputation too long now." He also challenged the CEB and the membership in general "to get busy and lay the ground work for a drive this winter that will put the IWW on its feet in Canada ... Either we change our tactics and get down to the facts that are confronting us or [we] will be relegated to the ranks of 'spittoon philosophers.'"[86] One of the biggest obstacles to success, however, was the "lack of efficient organizers who have the ability to hold meetings, especially outdoor meetings." The need for good organizers was paramount in MacAdam's view as, he aptly observed, the IWW lacked "the pep that the 'commies' have. They are always on the go and manage to get a lot of publicity which is essential to a labour union that is just growing." By stealing the "thunder and publicity" of the CPC, MacAdam reasoned, the IWW could draw away workers disillusioned by the "brass band bally-hoo" of a party that was still dominated by Moscow.[87]

Hostility to both the CPC and the IWW following the 1933 strikes provided many of these disillusioned workers with an alternative, however. Affiliated with the All Canadian Congress of Labour, the Canadian Bushmen's Union (CBU) was dominated by anti-Communist and "White," or non-socialist, Finnish lumber workers. The union and its members acted as informants for the RCMP and the Ontario Provincial Police (OPP) on the activities of local Communists.[88] The union disappeared sometime during 1934, but it created difficulties during its brief existence. Formed under the leadership of George Salverson, a Port Arthur alderman and prominent member of the newly formed Co-operative Commonwealth Federation (CCF), the union's executive also included a local timber subcontractor, L. Maki, and the local Finnish consul, a man named Koivukoski.[89] The executive's composition, and the role of Salverson in mediating an end to recent strikes, led the CPC and IWW to attack the CBU as a company union.[90] In response, Salverson, using local newspaper coverage of a spurious plot by the Soviet Union to undermine Canadian timber production, attacked the LWIUC for its use of professional agitators who were more loyal to the CPC and Russia than to the region.[91] Even though his accompanying claims that there was little dissatisfaction over working conditions were utterly false, his appeal to regional patriotism did strike a chord.

Workers at the Lakehead, especially within the lumber industry, had seen a continuous parade of organizers and agitators from the CPC tour the region for nearly a decade. These individuals would appear, organize, and then move on. During provincial and federal elections, the CPC would use the region – deemed one in which Communist sympathies ran high and success was a real possibility – to supplant the local leadership and parachute in candidates such as A.E. Smith in an attempt to win a seat for a member of the party's cadre. Once the election was lost, Smith would leave and not return until the next election, and the region would go back to being neglected by the CEC and having to beg for speakers. Although the CBU failed to attract more than a few supporters (aside from the White Finns, who did not share the ideological beliefs of members of either the LWIUC or LWIU), its existence proved to be an irritant for both the CPC and the IWW in the region until it disappeared in 1934.[92]

Violence broke out again in early December, when, after nearly a month of labour unrest in the bush camps, police attempted to break the ranks of strikers blocking strikebreakers from gaining access to the Pigeon Timber Company's stables. Over fifty police officers armed with guns and batons attacked the unarmed strikers but were repelled. Undaunted, they next fell on a nearby workers' hall and, with the assistance of a number of citizens, proceeded to enter and beat the men found asleep inside. Additional officers outside ambushed those who managed to escape.[93] So indiscriminate did the police become that, according to one witness, they "did not distinguish strikers from bystanders and several onlookers and passersby in the vicinity received a cudgeling."[94] The next day, even the most ardently anti-Communist unions at the Lakehead added their voices to those protesting the city of Port Arthur's involvement in the violence and demanding that the strike be resolved. Eight days after the police attack, many smaller operations bowed to pressure, reaching a settlement on wages and recognizing the unions involved. The larger companies agreed to align their wage scale with that of the other companies but continued refusing to recognize any unions.[95] The CPC won renown in its fight against the timber companies, despite incurring the anti-Communist and anti-foreign wrath of the local media. Up to the end of 1933, the party was prominent in the extraordinary struggles unfolding in Northwestern Ontario.

Certainly, many young people were attracted by the party's fighting record. In November, Communist youth staged a major youth conference that drew participants from a host of socialist and non-socialist organizations.[96] Yet, from the standpoint of the Junior Wobblies, even this opening up to non-Communist progressives needed to be pushed further: in a fascinating issue of their paper, the *Junior Recruit,* they drew on the example of Marx himself in urging the Communists to reconsider their disparaging attitudes towards students, teachers, and the petty trades.[97] It was a foreshadowing of the new "common sense" on the left that would flourish fully only after 1935.

Predictably, just as the fortunes of the party appeared to be improving at the Lakehead, the nature of the Communist movement underwent another change. The policy of separate unions, which had consolidated with the creation of the WUL, gave way to renewed efforts to create a united front to tackle the growing concerns over fascism. As Leslie Morris indicated to the First Congress of the League against War and Fascism in October 1934: "In Canada before the fascist avalanche comes down the mountain-side we must forge this united front through which fascism cannot break."[98] Although for many the fight for the legality of the CPC and the release of the leaders arrested in 1931 remained a priority, the weakened position of the party also necessitated a change in tactics. The CPC realized that, aside from the odd strike victory, its efforts to form a mass movement had been a dismal failure. Even party strongholds such as the Finnish lumber workers at the Lakehead had suffered near-crippling losses in membership. By 1934, the attempts by the LWIUC to organize some form of united mass conference had increasingly met with mistrust and scorn. The IWW, still a force that the CPC could not dismiss in the region, refused to participate, and the remaining workers who attended either belonged to camps too small to have a great influence or merely followed the decisions of the LWIUC representatives.[99]

The decisions made at the conference were also hollow. Many companies, including the region's largest, had already signed agreements with the CBU. In effect, the CBU had managed to block both the LWIUC and the LWIU from organizing in the largest camps.[100] Members of the Fort William Ukrainian Labour Temple Association – comprising the second-largest number of members after the Finns – were also more concerned with the famine in Soviet Ukraine than with domestic issues. This situation, coupled with increasing – although often discredited – reports of "Stalinist terror" in the Ukraine, led many party faithful to openly question the Communist International and the Canadian leadership, and to leave both the CPC and ULFTA.[101] The Ukrainian community had also split into a number of factions. Many in such "nationalist organizations" as the Provista Society (founded in 1923), ardently opposed the CPC.[102]

While the lumber unions and the remnants of the former language organizations were experiencing inner turmoil, Jack Quinn, head of the Single Men's Section of the Unemployed Workers' Protective Association (UWPA), reported that the association had been especially active in camps connected with the construction of the Northwestern Ontario section of the Trans-Canada Highway. The UWPA was a YCL-supported organization representing hundreds of single men in Port Arthur alone. It had won relief concessions shortly after being established.[103] The activities of the UWPA were complemented by the WUL-affiliated Relief Camp Workers' Union (RCWU).[104] With over 7,000 men employed in relief camps located in Northwestern Ontario, the RCWU had been established as a means of mobilizing the workers and providing a unified voice to advocate for better conditions and wages in the camps. Interestingly, the YCL continued its attempts to establish its own nucleus in the camps, enjoying a certain amount of success as well.[105]

The YCL, RCWU, and UWPA played major roles in the May Day activities of 1934.[106] An attempt to coordinate workers in the relief camps was made throughout the Thunder Bay District. Linked to these events were anti-war and anti-fascism meetings to stir up support for a series of mass rallies in the coming months.[107] The *Young Worker* reported in mid-May that the Port Arthur YCL had approached the Junior Wobblies and the Youth Section of the Fort William ULFTA to form a mass committee. This proposed committee would "conduct its activity by approaching all bourgeois youth organizations, sport organizations and church clubs." The purpose was to make them aware of the importance of the anti-war activity and, by "using all available statistics ... link our agitation with the economic position" facing young workers.[108] One of the CPC's most interesting cultural challenges arose in its struggles with the Junior Wobblies, which performed a significant cultural and social role in promoting the ideal of the general strike and direct action at the Lakehead.[109]

As Communists and Wobblies jockeyed for position, other political parties took advantage of the situation. When the writ was dropped for the 1934 provincial election, Jack Gillbanks, national organizer of the LWIUC, received the nomination for Port Arthur at the United Workers and Farmers Convention. The choice of Gillbanks cannot be seen as anything but a calculated attempt to appeal to the hundreds of unemployed lumber workers in the region, as both the Liberal and Conservative candidates were timber barons whose mistreatment of workers had become synonymous with the problems facing the working class in the region. Nevertheless, Gillbanks's candidacy and his ties to the LWIUC did appeal to many voters.

"A Vote for Gillbanks is a Vote Against Poverty, fascism, War," wrote Peter Zakar, a lumber worker serving time in the Fort William jail farm for his participation in recent lumber strikes and unemployment demonstrations.[110] The entry of a candidate for the Co-operative Commonwealth Federation, a newly established western-based political party composed of socialist, farm, cooperative, and labour organizations, hampered the Communists' ability to secure the labour vote. Gillbanks won 634 votes, but this total was down significantly from the left tally in the previous election. The CCF carried the majority of rural polls.[111]

Although politically unsuccessful, the Tenth Annual Convention of the LWIUC held in Port Arthur in August demonstrated the growing strength of the CPC in the region. Unlike past conventions, Gillbanks focused on the union's positive aspects and underlined its position within the industry and within the WUL. "Since its formation fifteen years ago," he reported, "it has grown from a small sectarian group to one of the biggest [Workers'] Unity League unions." The conference focused mostly on the presence and need for more French Canadian workers, but also on the recent activities of the CBU and the IWW. The report from the conference clearly indicates that a sustained united front with either of these two organizations was viewed as highly improbable.[112]

Whereas twenty-four delegates attended the LWIUC convention, only members from the local branch of the LWIU and the Port Arthur GRU had attended the Second Annual Convention of the Canadian Administration of the IWW held in the Finnish Labour Temple in June. Perhaps indicative of the troubles facing the CA was the first resolution carried following the appointment of committee representatives. Article 6, section 6(a), of the constitution, which stipulated that delegates to the Canadian convention were required to have been members for twelve months and in continuous good standing six months prior, was declared void by a majority vote because of the large number of delegates who did not meet its requirements.[113]

When CA Secretary-Treasurer J.D. Golden presented his report, it revealed much about the activities of the IWW over the past year. In November, a number of strikes had broken out in the region surrounding the Lakehead. Both the Communist LWIUC and the LWIU had taken part. The LWIUC claimed that the settlement of the Pigeon River Timber Company strike was a success; Golden and the CA viewed the results as "shameful" and as a settlement reached between operators and "perfect leaders" who "were more interested in the welfare of the scabs than the betterment of conditions for the actual strikers."[114]

Despite these setbacks, Golden's report did have some positive aspects. Between July 1933 and July 1934, funds acquired through entertainments and dances had resulted in the Canadian Administration's being able to provide financing to the Junior Wobblies and to pay all its own outstanding bills. Revenue had doubled since July 1933 and, Golden suggested, "with the proper efforts now on the part of the members the organization will grow steadily in the future as the sentiment for industrial unionism, especially amongst the Finnish workers of Ontario and on the west coast and the Scandianavian [sic] workers of BC is better than it has been for several years."[115] As a result, during the winter of 1934-35, the Workers' Unity League was once again forced to call on the IWW to ensure that strikes could take place once called. Both the District Committee and the YCL took part. The Port Arthur YCL was one of the nine active districts reported across the country. Most groups found in the Port Arthur District were located in predominantly Finnish communities surrounding the Lakehead, such as Kivikoski, Nolalu, and Intola.[116] According to Tolvanen, "the united front policy of the WUL which created confusion on the strike front was part of the groundwork for a concerted drive to elect Communist candidates in the Federal election in 1935, for which co-operation between the unions was deemed desirable."[117] Port Arthur mayor Charlie Cox had also discovered the potency of the "ethnic" vote in Port Arthur, and now extended this discovery to the rural hinterland. For his 1934 campaign, he recruited Intola Finnish homesteader Anna Koivu, who acted as a translator and "ethnic liaison" for Cox and his campaign.[118] This worked and Cox, on the strength of the Finnish vote, doubled the results of his closest competitor, Tory Don Clarke, 7,449 votes to 4,249.[119] The Communist-backed Gillbanks received only 456 votes.[120] It probably did not help that throughout the year a rumour had persisted that relief jobs were more likely to go to young workers who belonged to the Liberal Youth Club.[121]

The second half of 1934 saw a series of strikes and demonstrations sweep the Lakehead and the lumber camps in Northern Ontario. Some of the hardest fought occurred in the Thunder Bay District and in Sioux Lookout. In total, more than 2,045 men were involved.[122] In one memorable moment, 150 men, women, and children paraded on the evening of 1 October through the business section of Port Arthur, carrying, according to RCMP reports, "a Union Jack, the Red Flag and a number of banners" and singing the *Internationale* in support of the strikers.[123] Attempts by Peter Heenan, Member of Parliament for Kenora and Minister of Lands and Forests, to negotiate a settlement failed. (Outside of Northwestern Ontario, French Canadians, at least according to the RCMP, were the "back-bone" of the labour insurgency.[124]) The efforts of Heenan and the RCMP were ultimately unnecessary. The strikes were poorly organized and run, and fell apart when many strikers left for other camps.[125]

Similar actions in other regions of the province may have been successful, but the party suffered from "a lack of organization among the Lakehead strikers."[126] During the winter of 1934-35, the WUL needed to call on the IWW once again to ensure that strikes could take place once called. To underscore this, the LWIUC executive argued that, nationally, the United Front was necessary for any hope of success, an interesting acknowledgment of the necessity of the IWW.[127] According to Tolvanen, "the united front policy of the WUL which created confusion on the strike front was part of the groundwork for a concerted drive to elect Communist candidates in the Federal election in 1935, for which co-operation between the unions was deemed desirable."[128]

By 1935, the Lakehead's Unemployed Association had been integrated into a national framework and, in John Manley's estimation, was one of the strongest such units in the country.[129] Yet, the strength of the association did not derive from the Lakehead CPC alone. It arose from the unique symbiosis of Communists and Wobblies at the Lakehead – the inadvertent, often explosive yet paradoxically functional unity of seeming opposites that made this region such a fascinating and puzzling zone for the left. As Peter Campbell has remarked, "the Communists could not conduct an effective strike without Wobbly support."[130] The point can be extended further into other forms of left activism. Whether it was among young people debating the finer points of the general strike or rival strategies of unemployed organizing, the CPC/IWW dynamic was richer and more productive than either side was willing to concede at the time.

No single group of revolutionary socialists at the Lakehead could dominate the left between 1932 and 1935. The IWW might disparage the Communists as Moscow-liners, but they needed their expertise and their cross-Canada support system. The Communists might officially write off the Wobblies as yesterday's radicals, but they still needed them as they fought strikes and mounted resistance movements against a repressive state. Moreover, both drew unacknowledged strength from the resilient and feisty immigrant cultures, especially from the Finns, who found ways to combine both forms of radicalism in many of their day-to-day activities. The Third Period was in many respects a dire time for the Canadian left, but the Lakehead case suggests that beneath the often icy surface of dogmatism and rigidity stirred powerful new currents of left solidarity and purpose.

Epilogue
1935

The nature of socialism in Canada changed irrevocably in 1935 as the rise of fascism came to dominate left policy and actions well into the 1940s.[1] Between the decision by the Communist International (Comintern) to direct the Communist Party of Canada (CPC) to dissolve the Workers' Unity League (WUL) and the creation of the Committee for Industrial Organization in 1935 (later renamed the Congress for Industrial Organization, or CIO), the nature and characteristics of trade unionism in Canada and at the Lakehead underwent another fundamental shift.[2] The new watchwords for Canadian Communists became "Toward a Canadian People's Front."[3] The year saw the consolidation of "Radical Plannism," which would come to dominate the Canadian left between 1935 and 1960.[4] Rather than the revolutionary overthrow of the existing state and the capitalist order, which was a vibrant unifying thread of much of the "second formation" of the Canadian left between 1919 and 1935, many leftists now looked to the reform of the existing Canadian state system. Such a goal was not conceptualized as a minor adjustment in social relations but rather as part of a comprehensive program of egalitarianism. Moreover, while revolutionaries would continue to fight past 1935, other leftists whose struggles and strategies were quite different from theirs would increasingly drown out their voices.

The shift in policy of the CPC resulted from decisions made at the Seventh World Congress of the Communist International held in November 1935. The focus of the CPC and the Communist movement throughout the world shifted from that of revolutionary class struggle to fighting the rise of fascism. National parties were instructed to "discard all doctrinaire attitudes and all dogmatic positions and to recognize that the decisive key to defeat of Fascism was working class unity, and that the only possibility for broad parliamentary advance required working class unity, and that the trade union movement needed working class unity."[5] By 1934, the rise of Hitler and the menace of fascism throughout Europe and in North America, A.T. Hill later recalled, "became an all-embracing political fight, to defend the living standards, and also to defend the democratic organizations, free institutions, and national independence of various countries."[6]

In reality, the move to the new paradigm had already been underway at the Lakehead. In early January 1935, Charles Stewart, recently appointed secretary of the Port Arthur District Council of the Canadian Labour Defence League (CLDL), had spoken to the Unemployed Association of the Twin Cities urging it "to become organized and fight for unemployed insurance and against Fascism."[7] As a result, "between 1935 and 1939 Popular Front imperatives forced the indefinite postponement of socialist revolution and made the party's main objective the construction of cross-class alliances to defend bourgeois democracy."[8]

The dismantling of the WUL was ostensibly designed "to strengthen the trade union ranks and to lay a solid foundation for a broad united front against fascism and against another imperialist war." It also effectively alienated thousands of socialists and threw the Communist movement in Canada into chaos.[9] The decision to dissolve the much-maligned but now established WUL occurred just as non-socialists went on the attack at the Lakehead. For example, the theme of the speech given by Robert Manion, Port Arthur MP and future leader of the Conservative Party of Canada, to inaugurate the completion of the Trans-Canada Highway paid little attention to the event itself. Instead, he spoke about the conflict between police and the On to Ottawa Trekkers occurring in Regina and the radical atmosphere he felt was present at the Lakehead.[10] "On a day like this and at a time when subversive activities are so apparent," Manion declared, "all true Canadians should be prepared to take their part in maintaining law and order and the respect for those in authority that has made Canadian life and citizenship worthwhile. Let us guard our country and its institutions against any revolutionary groups' doctrines."[11] As local authorities, with support from many trade unions, moved to crush the unemployed workers' movement in Port Arthur, Communist leaders increasingly believed it "is better to retreat now than be crushed altogether." The rank and file were informed that a need existed "to consolidate our organization, that we must mobilize all workers, employed and unemployed, trade unions, churches, etc. for our support."[12]

The change in position of the CPC also signified an end to the idea of revolution as the party's main goal. While the WUL's position had been "revolutionary," the American Federation of Labor (AFL) and the Trades and Labour Congress of Canada (TLC) favoured concessions and industrial harmony over militancy. The decision, Douglas Thur suggests, was also "in complete contradiction to the resolutions adopted at the Seventh Annual Convention of the [Lumber Workers Industrial Union of Canada (LWIUC)] which was held in Port Arthur in April 1930."[13] At the convention, delegates had condemned the actions of the AFL as differing little from the policy of "American imperialists."[14] As bushworker and CPC member Tulio Mior later recalled, the demise of the two lumber workers' unions was spurred by the rise of fascism, and "the results of the Spanish Civil War demonstrated clearly what could be expected if it was left unchecked."[15] Ironically, renewed talk of a united front occurred just as the RCMP was reporting a substantial increase in the WUL's membership due to the disintegration of the ineffectual Canadian Bushmen's Union.

The turn to the Popular Front also coincided with a heightening of Stalin's intolerance towards Finns and Finnish nationalism. As Oiva W. Saarinen suggests: "With no basis in fact, he charged that Finns were planning a counter-revolution in Karelia in an effort to rejoin Finland. Branded as traitors of the fatherland, Finns in the Sudbury area became victims of the purges."[16] The same held true for Finns at the Lakehead. Many Communists in Canada were unwilling to believe that Moscow would actively persecute ardent supporters. Instead, those who suggested such things, as reflected in the pages of *Vapaus,* were dismissed as "'servants of capitalism." Their allegations of hunger and death in the Soviet Union were only "foolish talk."[17] Unfortunately, such "foolish talk" turned out to underestimate the severity of the sufferings of the Finns, especially those who had gone to construct a new and better society in Soviet Karelia.

The shift to the Popular Front did influence the position of the Finnish Organization of Canada (FOC). Just as the CPC abandoned its extreme radicalism and calls for immediate revolution, the FOC returned to its prewar roots. It became once again a largely cultural and educational organization (two things it had never truly abandoned) that favoured non-political activities.[18] The influence of the Karelian exodus and gradual improvements in economic conditions led to a gradual decline in the FOC membership during the mid-1930s. Although an estimated eighty locals still operated throughout the country, membership decreased from a peak of 4,000 to 6,000 in 1933 to below 2,700 after 1935.[19]

"The year 1935," Ian Radforth writes, also "marked the end of an era in the history of the Ontario bushworkers' union movement," the main source of socialist agitation in the region. While Communists and Wobblies would continue to fight for the allegiance of bushworkers, the rise of Bruce Magnuson at the Lakehead signified a fundamental change in both leadership and purpose. The strikes of 1933 had marked the twenty-four-year-old Magnuson's first appearance at the Lakehead. "I got involved in the Port Arthur strike," he later recalled, "by acting as recording secretary at the striker's [sic] meetings ... It was a big strike and I was blacklisted after it was over." Through his involvement in the strike, he "started to read books on socialism and the Communist Manifesto and to think about political activity and the working class struggle."[20] The last strikes involving the LWIUC took place in June and July 1935.[21] In 1936, the union, under the leadership of Magnuson, entered into an affiliation with the AFL and became the Lumber and Sawmill Workers Union Local 2693, with links to the International Carpenters and Joiners of America.[22] What had once been a revolutionary union, pugnaciously devoted to fighting capitalism and less radical labour movements, became part of the mainstream "house of labour." In addition, Finns "would play a somewhat less prominent role and, more significantly, its leaders would begin to pursue a less confrontational approach within a different union structure."[23]

A sign of the CPC's strength was evident during the 1935 civic and federal elections. The Trades and Labour Council in Port Arthur refused to run joint candidates in the civic election because of certain passages describing the role of labour leaders in the council in the Communist election manifesto.[24] In Port Arthur, Garfield Boulter and D.S. Reid ran under the Communist banner.[25] Although Boulter received 741 votes, a modest gain from the previous year, it was nowhere near the number achieved by Alex Gibson. Gibson, running openly for the Co-operative Commonwealth Federation (CCF), was re-elected to city council. The *Worker* made much of the fact that another CCF-backed candidate, Sam Wright, received only twenty-one votes more than Boulter; no other openly Communist candidate would come that close to winning.[26]

Local Liberals, riding a wave of national support, swept both federal ridings encompassing Port Arthur and Fort William. The election of 1935 was a pivotal moment in the history of Canada, the Lakehead, and the Canadian left. Nationally, the election swept into power William Lyon Mackenzie King's Liberals and ushered in a new era in federal politics. At the Lakehead, it launched the career of newly elected Port Arthur MP C.D. Howe, one of this country's most significant and influential politicians. For the left, at least regionally, it signified the accession of the CCF as the socialist political party of choice. It also signalled a shift in the Finnish vote in the region. Even combined, the CCF and CPC vote among Finns in Port Arthur, the "heart" of the Lakehead left, did not come close to the 1925 total. Instead, Finns overwhelmingly voted for the Liberals and, based on poll results, actual helped propel their candidate to victory.[27]

Formed in 1932, the CCF fundamentally altered the socialist landscape in Canada. When the Port Arthur Unemployment Association sponsored a meeting in 1933 entitled, "The Role of the CCF in Class Struggle," it marked a significant change in the structure of the socialist movement at the Lakehead. This period was characterized by open hostility between those who had turned to the CCF following its foundation in 1932 and the revitalized Communist Party. The latter, Jean Morrison states, viewed the CCF as equivalent to "social fascists" and argued that "the CCF is the more dangerous to the workers than the capitalists."[28] As Joan Sangster has suggested, the entry of the CCF resulted in "two parties differing in approach to socialism and often quarrelling with each other."[29] On the youth question, for example, the CPC claimed that the CCF was attempting to delude workers "with glib phrases about 'ordinary British justice,' 'democracy,' 'and constitutions.'"[30] "For the non-Marxist Left between the wars," J.S. Woodsworth's biographer Allen Mills suggests, "the founding of the Co-operative Commonwealth Federation (CCF) stood out as a beacon of hope in an otherwise tenebrous political landscape."[31]

The CCF was able to make inroads into a segment of the working class at the Lakehead that had long eluded the Communist Party of Canada and the Industrial Workers of the World. "At the Lakehead," contends Jean Morrison, "its early supporters were mainly British- and Canadian-born skilled workers or tradesmen, small proprietors, and union leaders." It also had support from most of those who had at one time or another managed to be elected on the labour ticket in Fort William or Port Arthur. This was no more apparent than in the federal election of 1935, when Alex Gibson opposed A.E. Smith and ran as a CCF candidate.[32]

Support for socialism, particularly the brand espoused by the CPC, was a significant phenomenon in the atmosphere of 1935. When the CPC held a mass meeting in the Port Arthur Arena on 26 September 1935, over 2,500 attended to hear the recently released Tim Buck. A combination of old guard and new guard in the region appeared onstage:[33] Bruce Magnuson had replaced Alf Hautamäki (who appears to have vanished) as head of the LWIUC in the region and now spoke for the YCL. Harry Bryan had moved over to head the Farmers' Unity League (FUL). The Independent Labour Party (ILP) was also present in the form of Alfred Batters, although the party later informed the press that he was there on his own. CPC ideologue Stewart Smith was also present, speaking at some length after welcoming Buck. He criticized other national and local politicians, saving his appeals for members of the newly formed CCF. Interestingly, no mention of Mary Gilbert is found in the available documents.

Those in attendance as well as those tuning in to radio station CKPR heard Buck speak at some length on the role of the CPC if elected to Parliament and, most importantly, the need for a united front, specifically between the CPC and CCF. This message received an enthusiastic response, with hundreds in attendance carrying banners reading "Towards Soviet Canada" and "For the United Front of the Communist Party and the CCF."[34] Buck's speech mattered little in the end, however. Although electing only seven MPs despite running candidates in 119 of 294 seats in the 1935 federal election, the CCF received 10.8 percent of the popular vote in Port Arthur, edging out Smith by 1.6 percent. In Fort William, where no Communist candidate ran, CCF candidate Garfield Anderson obtained 11.8 percent of the popular vote.[35] These results at the Lakehead and elsewhere showed that the CCF had now become the political party of choice for many radicals within the working class.[36]

A new moderation could be found even among the Finns, whose tenacious radicalism had set so much of the tone of Canadian and Lakehead leftism since the first years of the twentieth century. Most Finnish Wobblies slowly left the IWW, caught up in the renewed Communist movement or turning away from revolutionary politics and joining the newly formed Finnish Workers' and Farmers' Federation (FWFF), an organization with close ties to the CCF.[37] Although the Finns remained important players in Lakehead politics – even

Robert Manion would attribute his defeat in 1935 in part to the weight of the "foreign" vote against him – they would no longer be the Reds of old.[38] Many of them would find their way into the CCF or even the Liberal Party.

During the years following the change in tactics of the CPC, the virtual disappearance of the IWW, and the rise of the CCF as the political voice of the left at the Lakehead, the Trades and Labour Council of Fort William experienced revitalization. Over twenty-three unions joined, including previously Communist-controlled ones such as the Lumber and Sawmill Workers Union Local 2693. J.R. Pattison was one of only a few leftists from the 1920s. Fred Moore was no longer active in the council, and A.H. Dennis, William Welsh, Ed Smith, and many others had passed away. Magnuson, shortly elected head of the local Carpenters' Union, was the only real success for the Popular Front before the Second World War.

Even those who remained dedicated to the socialist cause, be it Wobbly or Communist, became increasingly disillusioned with Canada. The real fight for change, many believed, was occurring elsewhere in the world. Much as many Finns left North America for Karelia hoping to create a socialist utopia, so hundreds of socialists in the 1930s went to fight for their beliefs in Spain, the new theatre in the fight against both capitalism and the much more sinister threat of fascism. In 1937, socialists from the Lakehead joined the Canadian Communist-oriented Mackenzie-Papineau Battalion and the syndicalist-oriented union militia in Spain.[39]

What can be learned from the first thirty-five years of socialist activity at the Lakehead? Lakehead socialists fought hard and won important victories. They reined in the unbridled ferocity of exploitation in the woods, and they fed the poor, sheltered the homeless, and fought for democratic rights of assembly and organization. They brought a measure of justice to the outlying lumber camps. To an extent unusual in North America, they evolved a sturdy, resilient, multifaceted, and often lively left-wing counterculture. Like Prometheus, they displayed an enormous resilience and strength, qualities at times bound by the shackles of ethnic intolerance and doctrinal narrowness. In sum, the circumstances and actions of Lakehead labour, especially those related to ideology, ethnicity, and personality, worked simultaneously to empower and to fetter workers in their struggles against capitalism.

The Lakehead of the first thirty-five years of the twentieth century never lacked for a population of enthusiastic, energetic, and talented left-wingers, even though the movement never truly solidified and took hold. Socialist organizations, organizers, and organs came and went, leaving behind an enduring legacy, although paradoxically the sum of their efforts came to less than the immense sacrifices and energies they had poured into them. Yet, sometimes inadvertently, and sometimes with a winning combination of pragmatism and idealism, the movement they created at the Lakehead at its best reworked the politics of difference into a politics of solidarity. The next socialist formation would have much to learn from them.

Notes

INTRODUCTION

1 The stunning symbolic nature of this statue is apparent in the Gemini-nominated documentary film *Letters from Karelia,* directed by Kelly Saxberg (Montreal: National Film Board of Canada, 2004). Saxberg uses the statue as a starting point for her story of one Finnish Communist from Port Arthur who went to Karelia and was never heard from again.

2 The literature on Canadian involvement in Soviet Karelia is quite extensive and is discussed as part of Chapters 7 and 8. A more recent overview is found in Ronald Harpelle, Varpu Lindström, and Alexis Pogorelskin, eds., *Karelian Exodus: Finnish Communities in North America and Soviet Karelia during the Depression Era* (Beaverton, ON: Aspasia Books, 2004).

3 For this study, I will use the term "Lakehead" to refer to a region located at the head of Lake Superior in Northwestern Ontario and defined primarily by the municipal boundaries of the former cities of Port Arthur and Fort William (present-day Thunder Bay) between 1902 and 1935. Written use of the term "Lakehead" to describe the region can be found in the writings of the earliest European explorers.

4 *Port Arthur News-Chronicle,* 1 May 1919. Some historians have argued that these "breeding places" were found primarily in western Canada, flourishing in the months following the First World War. See David J. Bercuson, *Fools and Wise Men: The Rise and Fall of the One Big Union* (Toronto: McGraw-Hill Ryerson, 1978), ix. For more on the argument that the Lakehead had a "western orientation" during this period, see A.W. Rasporich, "Faction and Class in Modern Lakehead Politics," *Lakehead University Review* 7, 1 (Summer 1974): 33.

5 For the most recent overview history of Northwestern Ontario, see Michel S. Beaulieu and Chris Southcott, *North of Superior: An Illustrated History of Northwestern Ontario* (Toronto: James Lorimer, 2010).

6 Recently, Desmond Morton highlighted the abundance of scholarship in his contribution to the millennium edition of *Labour/Le Travail.* See Desmond Morton, "Some Millennial Reflections on the State of Canadian Labour History," *Labour/Le Travail* 46 (Fall 2000): 20-23.

7 A recent exception is David M. Quiring's *CCF Colonialism in Northern Saskatchewan: Battling Parish Priests, Bootleggers, and Fur Sharks* (Vancouver: UBC Press, 2004).

8 *Port Arthur Daily News,* 20 March 1906.

9 The literature dealing with the region's role in the fur trade is mountainous. For overviews, see Jean Morrison, *Superior Rendezvous-Place: Fort William in the Canadian Fur Trade* (Toronto: Natural Heritage Books, 2001), and Jean Morrison, ed., *Lake Superior to Rainy Lake, Three Centuries of Fur Trade History: A Collection of Writings* (Thunder Bay: Thunder Bay Historical Museum Society, 2003).

10 Jean Morrison, "Community and Conflict: A Study of the Working Class and Its Relationship at the Canadian Lakehead, 1903-1913" (MA thesis, Lakehead University, 1974), 4. Morrison's MA thesis remains the definitive history of the working class during the first three decades of the twentieth century. A shorter, less detailed version was published as *Labour Pains: Thunder Bay's Working Class in Canada's Wheat Boom Era* (Thunder Bay: Thunder Bay Historical Museum Society, 2009). See also Bruce Muirhead, "The Evolution of the Lakehead's Commercial and Transportation Infrastructure," in *Thunder Bay: From Rivalry to Unity,* ed. Thorold J. Tronrud and A. Ernest Epp (Thunder Bay: Thunder Bay Historical Museum Society, 1995), 78.

11 Joseph M. Mauro, *A History of Thunder Bay* (Thunder Bay: City of Thunder Bay, 1981), 104.

12 See, for example, Thorold J. Tronrud, *Guardians of Progress: Boosters and Boosterism in Thunder Bay, 1870-1914* (Thunder Bay: Thunder Bay Historical Museum Society, 1993).

13 Ibid., 86.

14 James Stafford, "A Century of Growth at the Lakehead," in *Thunder Bay: From Rivalry to Unity*, 41, and Tronrud, *Guardians of Progress,* 13.

15 Muirhead, "Evolution," 85.

16 For an overview of immigrant workers and the Canadian economy before 1914, see Donald Avery, *"Dangerous Foreigners": European Immigrant Workers and Labour Radicalism in Canada, 1896-1932* (Toronto: McClelland and Stewart, 1979), and *Reluctant Host: Canada's Response to Immigrant Workers, 1896-1994* (Toronto: McClelland and Stewart, 1995). For a general discussion of immigration policy during this period, see Ninette Kelley and Michael Trebilcock, *The Making of the Mosaic: A History of Canadian Immigration Policy* (Toronto: University of Toronto Press, 1998).

17 See Ian McKay, "For a New Kind of History: A Reconnaissance of 100 Years of Canadian Socialism," *Labour/Le Travail* 46 (Fall 2000): 78, fn. 31. In addition, this regional approach to working-class and left history is not new. This has included a spirited discussion in the Autumn 1996 edition of *BC Studies,* where regionalism, class, and the writing of history are debated by Mark Leier, Bryan Palmer, Veronica Strong-Boag, and Robert A.J. McDonald.

18 See, for example, *Polyphony* 9, 2 (1987). See also Anthony W. Rasporich's examination of the role of ethnicity in local politics, "Twin City Ethnopolitics: Urban Rivalry, Ethnic Radicalism and Assimilation in the Lakehead, 1900-1970," *Urban History Review/Revue d'histoire urbaine* 18, 3 (February 1990): 210-30.

19 B.W. Muirhead, "A Short History of Thunder Bay," *Polyphony* 9, 2 (1987): 7.

20 Thorold J. Tronrud, "Building an Industrial City," in *Thunder Bay: From Rivalry to Unity,* 106.

21 Morris Zaslow, *Opening of the Canadian North, 1870-1914* (Toronto: McClelland and Stewart, 1971), 192. Studies on the Lakehead reveal that those of British and French descent peaked in 1901 at 78.5 percent and gradually declined over the next three decades. "Of the 65 Canadian cities, with over 10,000 population, listed in the 1911 census, Fort William and Port Arthur show the two greatest percentages of 'foreign born.'" See Marvin MacDonald, "An Examination of Protestant Reaction towards the Non-English Speaking Immigrant in Port Arthur and Fort William, 1903-1914" (MA thesis, Lakehead University, 1976), 18.

22 See Chris Southcott, "Ethnicity and Community in Thunder Bay," *Polyphony* 9, 2 (1987): 17, and his "Introduction," in *Provincial Hinterland: Social Inequality in Northwestern Ontario,* ed. Chris Southcott (Halifax: Fernwood Publishing, 1993), 1.

23 These percentages are based on total populations of 15,634 in Port Arthur and 22,800 in Fort William: A.W. Rasporich, "Ethnicity in Lakehead Politics, 1900-1930," *Polyphony* 9, 2 (1987): 61-62.

24 For more on Finnish migration to North America, see Reino Kero, *Migration from Finland to North America in the Years between the United States Civil War and the First World War* (Turku, Finland: Institute for Migration Studies, 1974); Keijo Virtanen, *Settlement of Return? Finnish Emigrants (1860-1920)* (Helsinki: Migration Institute 1979); Varpu Lindström, *The Finns in Canada* (Ottawa: Canadian Historical Association, 1985); and the first chapter of Varpu Lindström, *Defiant Sisters: A Social History of Finnish Immigrant Women in Canada,* 2nd ed. (Beaverton, ON: Aspasia Books, 2003).

25 Rasporich, "Twin City Ethnopolitics," 213-15.

26 Morrison, "Community and Conflict," 2.

27 Ian McKay, *Rebels, Reds, Radicals: Rethinking Canada's Left History* (Toronto: Between the Lines Press, 2005), 145-218, and his "For a New Kind of History," 69-125.

28 Thomas Dunk, for instance, has argued that working-class men in Thunder Bay actively construct sets of meaning and values in opposition to what they see as the dominant culture. See *It's a Working*

Man's Town: Male Working-Class Culture (Montreal and Kingston: McGill-Queen's University Press, 1991; reprinted 1994).

29 For discussions of the role of ethnicity in Canadian labour history, see Avery, *"Dangerous Foreigners"*; Gregory S. Kealey, *Workers and Canadian History* (Montreal and Kingston: McGill-Queen's University Press, 1995), 112; Ian Radforth, "Finnish Radicalism and Labour Activism in Northern Ontario Woods," in *A Nation of Immigrants: Women, Workers, and Communities in Canadian History, 1840s-1960s*, ed. Franca Iacovetta with Paula Draper and Robert Ventresca (Toronto: University of Toronto Press, 1998), 293; and Norman Penner, *Canadian Communism: The Stalin Years and Beyond* (Toronto: Methuen, 1988). For recent international discussions, see Marcel van der Linden, "Introduction," in *Class and Other Identities: Gender, Religion and Ethnicity in the Writing of European Labour History*, ed. Marcel van der Linden and Lex Heerma van Voss (New York and Oxford: Berghahn Books, 2002), 18. The classic discussion of the relationship between class and ethnicity in Canada is John Porter's *The Vertical Mosaic: An Analysis of Social Class and Power in Canada* (Toronto: University of Toronto Press, 1965).

30 For more on the treatment of the issues of "ethnicity" in Canadian history, see Jorgen Dahlie and Tissa Fernando, eds., *Ethnicity, Power and Politics in Canada* (Toronto: Methuen, 1981), and Robert Harney, "Ethnicity and Neighbourhoods," in *Gathering Place: People and Neighbourhoods in Toronto*, ed. Robert Harney (Toronto: Multicultural History Society of Ontario, 1985), 1-23.

31 Avery's *"Dangerous Foreigners,"* for example, demonstrates the stigmatization that occurred. For more on the "Anglo" or "English" ethnicity in Canada, see A.B. Anderson, "'The Invisible Minority' in Canada: In Search of the Anglo-Canadian Ethnic Group," *Canadian Ethnic Studies Association Bulletin* 9, 3(1982): 17-18, and R. McCormack, "Cloth Caps and Jobs: The Ethnicity of English Immigrants in Canada 1900-1914," in *Ethnicity, Power and Politics*, 38.

32 The works of Ian Radforth and Varpu Lindström have established that within the rural areas, in particular regions involved in the lumber industry, immigrants played important social, cultural, and political roles. See Radforth, *Bushworkers and Bosses: Logging in Northern Ontario, 1900-1980* (Toronto: University of Toronto Press, 1987), and Lindström, *Defiant Sisters*.

33 For more on the concept of Canada as a project of liberal order, see Ian McKay, "The Liberal Order Framework: A Prospectus for a Reconnaissance of Canadian History," *Canadian Historical Review* 81, 3 (September 2000): 617-45. For the classic exploration of the rise of multiculturalism in Canadian society, see Howard Palmer, *Immigration and the Rise of Multiculturalism* (Toronto: Copp Clark, 1975).

34 Charles Taylor, "The Politics of Recognition," in *Multiculturalism and "The Politics of Recognition": An Essay by Charles Taylor*, ed. Amy Gutman et al. (Princeton, NJ: Princeton University Press, 1992), 64.

35 Jean Morrison, "The Organization of Labour at Thunder Bay," in *Thunder Bay: From Rivalry to Unity*, 120. For some important work by Morrison, see "Community and Conflict"; "Ethnicity and Class Consciousness: British, Finnish, and South European Workers at the Canadian Lakehead before World War I," *Lakehead University Review* 9, 1 (Spring 1976): 55-65; "Labour in Fort William and Port Arthur, 1903-1913," Thunder Bay Historical Museum Society *Papers and Records* 1 (1973): 23-30; and "Ethnicity and Violence: The Lakehead Freight Handlers Before World War I," in *Essays in Canadian Working Class History*, ed. Gregory S. Kealey and Peter Warrian (Toronto: McClelland and Stewart, 1976), 143-60.

36 See, for example, Dave Adams, "1919 in Canada: The Birth of a New Left," *Socialist Worker* (December-January 1991).

37 McKay, "For a New Kind of History," 95.

38 For more on this period, see John Manley, "Communism and the Canadian Working Class during the Great Depression: The Workers' Unity League, 1903-1936" (PhD dissertation, Dalhousie University, 1984); "Does the International Labour Movement Need Salvaging? Communism,

Labourism and the Canadian Trade Unions, 1921-1928," *Labour/Le Travail* 41 (Spring 1998); and "'Starve, Be Damned!': Communists and Canada's Urban Unemployed, 1929-1939," *Canadian Historical Review* 79, 3 (September 1998).

39 McKay, *Rebels, Reds, Radicals,* 157.

40 Roy Piovesana, *Robert J. Manion: Member of Parliament for Fort William, 1917-1935* (Thunder Bay: Thunder Bay Historical Museum Society, 1990), 33-34. A.E. Smith had also been the Port Arthur candidate in the 1925 and 1926 federal elections, under the banner of the Canadian Labour Party.

41 Irving Abella's *Nationalism, Communism, and Canadian Labour: The CIO, the Communist Party, and the Canadian Congress of Labour, 1935-1956* (Toronto: University of Toronto Press, 1973) remains the most thorough look at the activities of the CIO and labour's relationship with the Communist Party of Canada and the fledgling CCF.

42 See Ian McKay and Suzanne Morton, "The Maritimes: Expanding the Circle of Resistance," in *The Workers' Revolt in Canada, 1917-1925,* ed. Craig Heron (Toronto: University of Toronto Press, 1998), 43-86.

CHAPTER 1: EARLY SOCIALIST ORGANIZATIONS AT THE LAKEHEAD, 1900-14

1 See *Port Arthur Daily News* (hereafter *PADN*), 21 March 1906.

2 See Martin Robin, *Radical Politics and Canadian Labour, 1880-1930* (Kingston: Queen's University Industrial Relations Centre, 1968), 79-91. This notion is shared in the work of Craig Heron. See, for example, *The Canadian Labour Movement: A Short History* (Toronto: James Lorimer, 1989), 47.

3 Robin, *Radical Politics and Canadian Labour,* 104.

4 A. Kari, "Imatra Yhdesksäs in *Canadan Suomalainen Järjestö 24 Vuotta* (Sudbury: Vapaus Publishing, 1936), 10; Marc Metsaranta, "The Workingmen's Associations 1903-1914," in *Project Bay Street: Activities of Finnish-Canadians in Thunder Bay before 1915,* ed. Marc Metsaranta (Thunder Bay: Thunder Bay Finnish Canadian Historical Society, 1989), 66.

5 Jean Morrison, "The Organization of Labour at Thunder Bay," in *Thunder Bay: From Rivalry to Unity*, ed. Thorold J. Tronrud and A. Ernest Epp (Thunder Bay: Thunder Bay Historical Museum Society, 1995), 122. The United Brotherhood of Railway Employees was crushed between Winnipeg and Port Arthur following the suppression of UBRE-led strikes in 1902. Nothing is known about this early Finnish carpenters' union. For more on the topic, see Lakehead University Archives (hereafter LUA), Thunder Bay Finnish-Canadian Historical Society Collection, 1870-1970 (hereafter TBFCHS), MG8, Series B, 7, 30, Item 2, Tape 4, Interview with Einar Nordstrom, 15 and 19 March, 2 April, 7 May 1979.

6 For brief overviews of Harry Bryan, see LUA, Jean Morrison Labour History Collection (hereafter JMLHC), GS186a, Tape 5, Harry Bryan Reminiscences, 1972; Michel S. Beaulieu and Bruce Muirhead, "Harry Bryan, a Man of Fanatical Convictions," in *Essays in Northwestern Ontario Working Class History: Thunder Bay and Its Environs,* ed. Michel S. Beaulieu (Thunder Bay: Lakehead University Centre for Northern Studies, 2008); and Jean Morrison, "Community and Conflict: A Study of the Working Class and Its Relationships at the Canadian Lakehead, 1903-1913" (MA thesis, Lakehead University, 1974).

7 For more on the Knights of Labor, see Gregory S. Kealey and Bryan Palmer, *Dreaming of What Might Be: The Knights of Labor in Ontario, 1880-1900* (New York: Cambridge University Press, 1982).

8 For more on Bryan's relationship with Gompers, see Morrison, "Community and Conflict," 28. Her sources are the *Gompers Letterbooks* held at the Library of Congress. For more on Gompers in Canada, see Robert H. Babcock's *Gompers in Canada: A Study in American Continentialism before the First World War* (Toronto: University of Toronto Press, 1974), and his much more useful "The AFL in Canada, 1896-1908: A Study in American Labor Imperialism" (PhD dissertation, Duke University, 1970).

9 See Bruce Muirhead, "The Evolution of the Lakehead's Commercial and Transport Infrastructure," in *Thunder Bay: From Rivalry to Unity*, 76-97.

10 *Fort William Daily Times-Journal* (hereafter *FWDTJ*), 20 January 1903.

11 Morrison, "The Organization of Labour at Thunder Bay," 121; *FWDTJ*, 12 October 1903.

12 Bruce Muirhead points out that this number has been disputed by Jean Morrison and others. See his "Harry Bryan," 37, fn. 2 for further information.

13 LUA, JMLHC, Tape 5, Harry Bryan Reminiscences, 1972.

14 For a thorough discussion of municipal ownership see F.B. Scollie, "The Creation of the Port Arthur Street Railway 1890-95: Canada's First Municipally-Owned Street Railway," Thunder Bay Historical Museum Society *Papers and Records* 18 (1990): 40-58; Mark Chochla, "Sabbatarians and Sunday Street Cars," Thunder Bay Historical Museum Society *Papers and Records* 17 (1989): 25-36; Thorold J. Tronrud, *Guardians of Progress: Boosters and Boosterism in Thunder Bay, 1870-1914* (Thunder Bay: Thunder Bay Historical Museum Society, 1993).

15 Steven C. High, "'A Municipal Ownership Town': The Organization and Regulation of Urban Services in Port Arthur, 1875-1914" (MA thesis, Lakehead University, 1994), 4.

16 For more on the Bell Telephone incident, see Morrison, "Community and Conflict," 40-46. For a perspective on why Bryan was blacklisted, see LUA, JMLHC, Tape 5, Harry Bryan Reminiscences, 1972.

17 *FWDTJ*, 15 May 1902.

18 Ibid., 24 April 1902.

19 G.R. Weller, "Hinterland Politics: The Case of Northwestern Ontario," in *Provincial Hinterland: Social Inequality in Northwestern Ontario*, ed. Chris Southcott (Halifax: Fernwood Publishing, 1993), 14; Don Scott, "Northern Alienation," in *Government and Politics of Ontario*, ed. Donald C. MacDonald (Toronto: Macmillan, 1975), 247.

20 See Ian McKay, *Reasoning Otherwise: Leftists and the People's Enlightenment in Canada, 1890-1920* (Toronto: Between the Lines Press, 2008). For differing views, see Robin, *Radical Politics and Canadian Labour*, 34; Norman Penner, *The Canadian Left: A Critical Analysis* (Scarborough, ON: Prentice Hall Canada, 1977), 40. For the CSL's development in British Columbia, see Ross Alfred Johnson, "No Compromise – No Political Trading: The Marxian Socialist Tradition in British Columbia (PhD dissertation, University of British Columbia, 1976). For the activities of the CSL and its most prominent member, Jimmy Simpson, see Gene Homel, "James Simpson and the Origins of Canadian Social Democracy (Socialism in Toronto, 1890-1914)" (PhD dissertation, University of Toronto, 1978).

21 Robin, *Radical Politics and Canadian Labour*, 35.

22 Ibid., 37. For quoted material, see the *Port Arthur Western Clarion*, 24 October 1903. For the general CSL platform, see Johnson, "No Compromise – No Political Trading," 70-71. Johnson himself references *Citizen and Country*, 28 October 1899.

23 *Port Arthur Western Clarion*, 24 October 1903.

24 For an examination of the life and career of Louis Peltier, see F.B. Scollie, "Louis Lawrence Peltier (1853-1939): Railway Labour Leader, Mayor of Fort William 1909-10," Thunder Bay Historical Museum Society *Papers and Records* 32 (2004): 10-30.

25 *FWDTJ*, 20 January 1904; Morrison, "The Organization of Labour at Thunder Bay," 123.

26 *FWDTJ*, 28 October 1904.

27 Jean Morrison, "Labour in Fort William and Port Arthur, 1903-1913," Thunder Bay Historical Museum Society *Papers and Records* 1 (1973): 23.

28 Jean Morrison, "Frederick Urry, Architect: The Wage-Earner's Advocate," Thunder Bay Historical Museum Society *Papers and Records* 14 (1986): 11.

29 Morrison, "Community and Conflict," 51.

30 *FWDTJ*, 9 June 1904.

31 Morrison, "The Organization of Labour at Thunder Bay," 122.

32 For more information on the Socialist Party of America, see Anthony V. Esposito, *The Ideology of the Socialist Party of America, 1901-1917* (New York: Garland, 1997).

33 LUA, TBFCHS, Series B, 7, 30, Item 2, Tape 4, Interview with Einar Nordstrom, 15 and 19 March, 2 April, 7 May 1979.

34 For more on this period, see Toivo Nygård and Veikko Kallio, "Rajamaa," in *Suomen historian pikkujättiläinen*, ed. Seppo Zettergerh (Porvoo, Finland: WSOY, 1978); Tuomo Polvinen, *Valtakunta ja rajamaa: N.I. Bobrikov Sumomen kenraalikuvernöö 1898-1904* (Helsinki: WSOY, 1984); Päiviö Tommila, *Suuri adressi* (Helsinki: WSOY, 1999); Osmo Jussila, *Maakunnasta valtioksi: Sumomen valtion synty* (Helsinki: WSOY, 1978); Osmo Jussila, "Suomi suuriruhtinaskuntana," in *Suomen poliittinen historia*, ed. Osmo Jussila, Seppo Hentilä, and Jukka Nevakivi (Helsinki: WSOY, 2000), 66-67, 148-59; and Osmo Jussila, "Die russische Reichsgesetzgeburng in Finnland in den Jahren 1809-1898," *Jahrbücher für Geshichte Osteuropas* 33 (1985): 345-65.

35 Ahti Tolvanen, "Population Development of Finns in Port Arthur," *Polyphony* 9, 2 (1987): 43, and *Finntown: A Perspective on Urban Integration. Port Arthur Finns in the Inter-war Period: 1918-1939* (Helsinki: University of Helsinki, 1985).

36 Christine Kouhi, "Labour and Finnish Immigration to Thunder Bay: 1876-1914," *Lakehead University Review* 9, 1 (Spring 1976): 41-55.

37 See Christine Kouhi, "The Finnish Church in Thunder Bay, 1876-1916," and Tellervo Kahara, "The New Attempt Temperance Society, 1902-1909," in *Project Bay Street*, 31-43 and 44-58.

38 Morrison, "Community and Conflict," 84.

39 LUA, Finlandia Club Collection (hereafter FCC), MG3, 2, Minutes of *Imatra #9*, 24 May 1903; Arja Pilli, *The Finnish-Language Press in Canada, 1901-1939: A Study in the History of Ethnic Journalism* (Turku, Finland: Institute for Migration Studies, 1982), 34; A. Kari, "Imatra Yhdeksas," in *Canadan Suomalainen Järjestö 25 vuotta: Kuvauksia ja muistelmia 25-vuotiselta toimintataipaleelta 1911-1936* Sudbury: Vapaus Publishing, 1936), 9; and Kouhi, "Labour and Finnish Immigration to Thunder Bay," 29-31. For the most extensive examination of Finnish workingmen's associations at the Lakehead prior to 1914, see Metsaranta, "The Workingmen's Associations," 66-99.

40 Kari, "Imatra Yhdekas," 9; Christine Kouhi, "Finnish Immigrants in Thunder Bay: 1876-1914" (Honours thesis, Lakehead University, 1975), 24; and LUA, TBFCHS, A, I, 1, 10, Varpu Lindström-Best, "The Unbreachable Gulf: Division of the Finnish Community of Toronto before the First World War (unpublished presentation for Finn Forum, 1979).

41 LUA, FCC, 2, Minutes of *Imatra #9*, cited in Kouhi, ibid., 24. See also Kouhi, "Labour and Finnish Immigration to Thunder Bay," 28-29. For more on the *Amerikan Suomalainen Työväenliito Imatra*, see Michael G. Karni, "Yhteishyvä – or, for the Common Good: Finnish Radicalism in the Western Great Lakes Region 1900-1940" (PhD dissertation, University of Minnesota, 1975); and Auvo Kostiainen, "Finnish-American Workingmen's Associations" in *Old Friends – Strong Ties*, ed. V. Niitemaa et al. (Vaasa, Finland: Institute of Migration, 1976).

42 Metsaranta, "The Workingmen's Associations," 89.

43 LUA, FCC, 2, *Imatra #9* Minutes, "*Vuosikertomus* 1903," and Minutes of *Imatra #9*, "*Vuosikertomus* 1906" [Annual report], quoted in Kouhi, "Finnish Immigrants in Thunder Bay," 27 and 29, and Varpu Lindström, *Defiant Sisters: A Social History of Finnish Immigrant Women in Canada*, 2nd ed. (Beaverton, ON: Aspasia Books, 2003), 143. Although the executive was composed of both men and women, the former held the key positions.

44 In 1905, for instance, membership in the Port Arthur Temperance Society numbered 224. See LUA, FCC, 2, U.Y.R. Minutes, 2 April 1905.

45 Metsaranta, "The Workingmen's Associations," 89.

46 LUA, FCC, 2, Minutes of *Imatra #9*, 10 July and 30 October 1904; Kouhi, "Finnish Immigrants in Thunder Bay," 28; Pilli, *The Finnish-Language Press in Canada*, 34.

47 LUA, FCC, ibid., 2 December 1906, quoted in Kouhi, ibid., 29.

48 Metsaranta, "The Workingmen's Associations," 76; Kouhi, "Labour and Finnish Immigration to Thunder Bay," 30. For the Finnish connection to the Socialist Party of Canada, see LUA, TBFCHS, A, I, 1, 9, Varpu Lindström-Best, "The Socialist Party of Canada and the Finnish Connection, 1905-1911" (unpublished Canadian Ethnic Studies Association Conference paper, October 1970).

49 For more on the rise of the Social Democratic Party in Finland and the issues surrounding the Finnish Civil War, see Jussila, "Suomi suuriruhtinaskuntana," 91-96, and Seppo Hentilä, "Itsenäistymisestä jatkosodan päättymiseen," in *Suomen poliittinen historia,* 98-104.

50 For more on "hall socialism," see Ian Radforth, "Finnish Radicalism and Labour Activism in the Northern Ontario Woods," in *A Nation of Immigrants: Women, Workers, and Communities in Canadian History, 1840s-1960s,* ed. Franca Iacovetta, Paula Draper, and Robert Ventresca (Toronto: University of Toronto Press, 1998), 293; and his *Bushworkers and Bosses: Logging in Northern Ontario, 1900-1980* (Toronto: University of Toronto Press, 1987).

51 LUA, FCC, 2, Minutes of *Imatra #9,* "*Vuosikertomus* 1903," cited in Kouhi, "Finnish Immigrants in Thunder Bay," 28. See also Minutes of *Imatra #9,* 27 February and 20 March 1904.

52 Penner, *The Canadian Left,* 41, and John Saywell, "Labour and Socialism in British Columbia: A Historical Survey of Historical Developments before 1903," *British Columbia Quarterly* 15 (July-October 1951): 129-50. For overviews of the Socialist Party of Canada, see Peter Campbell, *Canadian Marxists and the Search for a Third Way* (Montreal and Kingston: McGill-Queen's University Press, 1999); Peter Campbell, "In Defence of the Labour Theory of Value: The Socialist Party of Canada and the Evolution of Marxist Thought," *Journal of History and Politics* 10 (1992): 61-86; A. Ross McCormack, *Reformers, Rebels, and Revolutionaries: The Western Canadian Radical Movement, 1899-1919* (Toronto: University of Toronto Press, 1977), 53-76; and Robin, *Radical Politics and Canadian Labour,* 92-103.

53 Johnson, "No Compromise – No Political Trading," 10.

54 Ibid., 10-11.

55 *PADN,* 30 April 1906.

56 English's lecture brought out fifty individuals, many of whom had supported the OSP, from both Port Arthur and Fort William.

57 *Port Arthur Western Clarion,* 26 September 1908.

58 Ibid., 30 November 1907.

59 Kouhi, "Finnish Immigrants in Thunder Bay," 31.

60 See LUA, FCC, 2, Minutes of *Imatra #9,* 15 January 1905. Although the exact date of the name change is unknown, the last use of the name *Imatra* occurred on 22 October 1907. By 3 November 1907, the name *Suomalainen Sosialisti Osasto* was in use. See Kouhi, ibid., 32.

61 LUA, TBFCHS, A, I, 2, 10, Nick Viita, "Origins of the Finnish Labour Movement," trans. Ahti I. Tolvanen, *Industrialisti,* 75-76 (9 and 13 October 1970): 4; Metsaranta, "The Workingmen's Associations," 89; Kouhi, "Labour and Finnish Immigration to Thunder Bay," 32.

62 J.W. Ahlqvist, "Jarjestamme Toiminta Vuoteen 1920," in *Canadan Suomalainen Järjestö: 25 Vuotta* (Sudbury: Vapaus Publishing, 1936), 33. The author would like to thank Samira Saramo for translating the section used.

63 See Lindström-Best, "The Socialist Party of Canada and the Finnish Connection," 2; and Pilli, *The Finnish-Language Press in Canada,* 35.

64 Lindström-Best, 3, and McCormack, *Reformers, Rebels, and Revolutionaries,* 65-66.

65 For more on the 1906 freight handlers' strike, see Morrison, "Ethnicity and Violence: The Lakehead Freight Handlers before World War I," in *Essays in Canadian Working Class History,* ed. Gregory S. Kealey and Peter Warrian (Toronto: McClelland and Stewart, 1976), 143-60.

66 *PADN,* 1 October 1906. For more on the Italian communities at the Lakehead, see John Potestio, *The Italians of Thunder Bay* (Thunder Bay: Lakehead University, Chair of Italian Studies, 2005).

67 *PADN*, 30 April 1907; *FWDTJ*, 8 June 1907.

68 *PADN*, 10 April 1908.

69 *FWDTJ*, 14 March 1908.

70 Morrison, "Frederick Urry, Architect," 11.

71 Ibid., 8. See also *Port Arthur Western Clarion*, 26 September 1908, for Urry's response.

72 Interestingly, one of the first members of the Port Arthur Trades and Labour Council was the Ministerial Association of Thunder Bay.

73 Leo T. English, quoted in Morrison, "Labour in Fort William and Port Arthur," 28.

74 *PADN* and *FWDTJ*, 5 April 1908. For the platform of the Socialist Party of Canada, see *PADN*, 27 May and 5 June 1908.

75 *PADN*, 27 April 1908.

76 Morrison, "Community and Conflict," 100-1.

77 *Port Arthur Western Clarion*, 21 August 1909.

78 Morrison, "Community and Conflict," 102-4. Even the *Port Arthur Daily News* provided favourable coverage of English's campaign, if only to assist in the election of Conservative J.J. Carrick by splitting the labour vote between English and Mooring, who still ran. See Morrison, "Labour in Fort William and Port Arthur," 28.

79 *PADN*, 20 December 1907. The combined votes for the seven candidates running for positions as aldermen totalled 182 of 5,878, and Matt Ulvila's attempt to become mayor resulted in only 43 of a total of 1,104 votes cast. See *PADN*, 7 January 1908, for the results.

80 Ibid., 20 October 1908.

81 For the quotation, see ibid., 24 April 1908.

82 Ibid., 22 and 24 August 1908; A.W. Rasporich, "Twin City Ethnopolitics," *Urban History Review/Revue d'histoire urbaine* 18, 3 (February 1990): 215; and Kouhi, "Labour and Finnish Immigration to Thunder Bay," 32.

83 Johnson, "No Compromise – No Political Trading," 461.

84 Morrison, "Community and Conflict," 88, and *FWDTJ*, 28 March and 11 April 1908.

85 Morrison, "Frederick Urry, Architect," 10-11.

86 Ibid., 10.

87 *PADN*, 16 October 1908.

88 While in Winnipeg in April 1907, Goldman, for instance, criticized "organized labour, urging more frequent, harder, longer strikes, building towards a general strike." See Theresa Moritz and Albert Moritz, *The World's Most Dangerous Woman: A New Biography of Emma Goldman* (Vancouver and Toronto: Subway Books, 2001), 12.

89 See Lindström, *Defiant Sisters*, 75-77.

90 Morrison, "Frederick Urry, Architect," 11.

91 *Port Arthur Western Clarion*, 14 November 1908.

92 Ibid., 20 February 1909.

93 For an extensive examination of the strike, see Morrison, "Community and Conflict," 115-39; and Morrison, "Ethnicity and Violence," 143-60. For Italian involvement, see Antonio Pucci, "Thunder Bay's Italian Community 1880s-1940s," in *The Italian Immigrant Experience*, ed. John Potestio and Antonio Pucci (Thunder Bay: Canadian Italian Historical Association, 1988), 89-90; and Antonio Pucci, "Canadian Industrialization versus the Italian Contadini in a Decade of Brutality, 1902-1912," in *Little Italies in North America*, ed. Robert F. Harney and J. Vincenza Scarpaci (Toronto: Multicultural History Society of Ontario, 1981), 191-97.

94 *Industrial Banner*, September 1909.

95 *Cotton's Weekly*, 2 September 1909.

96 Morrison, "Labour in Fort William and Port Arthur," 27.

97 Morrison, "The Organization of Labour at Thunder Bay," 126.

98 *FWDTJ,* 12 August 1909. For more on the response to the strike, see David Ratz, "Aid to Civil Power: The 96th 'Lakehead Superior Regiment' 1909 and 1912," Thunder Bay Historical Museum Society *Papers and Records* 19 (1991): 51-64; and Thomas F. Beasley, "The 1909 Freight Handlers' Strike: Col. Sam Steele Searches Strikers for Guns," Thunder Bay Historical Museum Society *Papers and Records* 17 (1989): 18-20.

99 Sam Steele, quoted in Morrison, "Community and Conflict," 154-55.

100 *Industrial Banner,* September 1909. In one notable half-hour incident, CPR police were driven back and captured, with eight known causalities. See *FWDTJ,* 13 August 1909.

101 LAC, Department of National Defence (hereafter DND), RG24, Acc. 69440, File 363/17, Steele to Militia Council, 20 August 1900.

102 *PADN,* 17 August 1909, and *Cotton's Weekly,* 2 September 1909.

103 *FWDTJ,* 19 August 1909.

104 *Labour Gazette* 10 (September 1909): 344, quoted in Morrison, "Labour in Fort William and Port Arthur," 27.

105 A testament to his position within the socialist community, Harry Bryan joined the managing editor of *Työkansana* and chairman of the local Finnish socialist club, Moses Hall, in making the opening speeches. See LUA, TBFCHS, Series B, 7, 30, Item 2, Tape 3, Interview with Einar Nordstrom, 15 and 19 March, 2 April, and 7 May 1979. A local Finnish builder named Alex Beck originally drew up plans for the hall, which were later refined by a professional architect.

106 *FWDTJ,* 14 September 1910.

107 McCormack, *Reformers, Rebels, and Revolutionaries,* 71.

108 *Port Arthur Western Clarion,* 30 October 1909.

109 Viita, "Origins of the Finnish Labour Movement," 8.

110 For example, prominent Finnish Social Democratic Party member Frans Syrjälä toured Finnish communities in Ontario shortly after his immigration in 1903 and became a leading member of the Toronto Finnish socialist community. He often lectured throughout the province on the political situation in Finland and Russia, and the ideals and theories of socialists such as German Social Democratic Party leader Karl Kautsky. For more on Kautsky, see Dick Geary, *Karl Kautsky* (Manchester, UK: Manchester University Press, 1987); Patrick Goode, ed., *Karl Kautsky: Selected Political Writings* (London: Macmillan, 1983); and Massimo Salvadori, *Karl Kautsky and the Socialist Revolution, 1880-1938* (London: New Left Books, 1979).

111 Penner, *The Canadian Left,* 45.

112 For an example of such an appeal, see the *Port Arthur Western Clarion,* 26 September 1908.

113 Penner, *The Canadian Left,* 43.

114 See Robin, *Radical Politics and Canadian Labour,* 112-13; Lindström-Best, "The Socialist Party of Canada and the Finnish Connection, 1905-1911," in *Ethnicity, Power and Politics in Canada,* ed. Jorgen Dahlie and Tissa Fernando (Toronto: Methuen, 1981), 116-17; Jacqueline F. Cahan, "A Survey of the Political Activities of the Ontario Labour Movement, 1850-1935" (MA thesis, University of Toronto, 1945), 28-29; and William Eklund, "The Formative Years of the Finnish Organization of Canada" in *Finnish Diaspora I: Canada, South America, Africa, Australia and Sweden,* ed. Michael G. Karni (Toronto: Multicultural History Society of Ontario, 1981), 56. For primary Finnish sources, see *Canadan Sosialistipuolue ja sosialidemokratia* 1909 and *Raivaajan Työvainioilta IV* 1908 (J.V. to Kannasto, Canadan sosialistiliikkeen suunta), 96-97.

115 Rasporich, "Twin City Ethnopolitics," 215; Kouhi, "Labour and Finnish Immigration to Thunder Bay," 33.

116 Kouhi, "Finnish Immigrants in Thunder Bay," 35; Edward W. Laine, "Finnish Canadian Radicalism and Canadian Politics: The First Forty Years, 1900-1940," in *Ethnicity, Power and Politics in Canada,* 97 and 105; Lindström-Best, "The Socialist Party of Canada and the Finnish Connection," 116-17; and Pilli, *The Finnish-Language Press in Canada,* 35.

117 Johnson, "No Compromise – No Political Trading," 283. For the Canadian Socialist Federation and the Port Arthur Finns, see *Cotton's Weekly,* 20 July 1911; Viita, "Origins of the Finnish Labour Movement," 8; Cahan, "A Survey of the Political Activities of the Ontario Labour Movement," 30; Norman Penner, "The Socialist Idea in Canadian Political Thought" (PhD dissertation, University of Toronto, 1975), 117-18; and Laine, ibid., 97.

118 *Cotton's Weekly,* 4 May 1911. Bryan represented his new hometown of Kakabeka Falls (located thirty-seven kilometres from Fort William), while George Mekela represented Port Arthur and C. Kukkel represented Fort William. Other delegates were also reported from Nipigon, Fort Frances, and Kenora.

119 Johnson, "No Compromise – No Political Trading," 112-13.

120 SDPC platform, quoted in Penner, *The Canadian Left,* 47, and also quoted in George R. Troop, "Socialism in Canada" (MA thesis, McGill University, 1922), 57-58.

121 Penner, *The Canadian Left,* 46 and 50; Paul W. Fox, "Early Socialism in Canada," in *The Political Process in Canada,* ed. J.H. Aitchison (Toronto: University of Toronto Press, 1963), 96.

122 *Työkansa,* 12 and 16 January 1912; Pilli, *The Finnish-Language Press in Canada,* 37.

123 These statistics are from Metsaranta, "The Workingmen's Associations," 88. See also *Canada Suomalaisen Sosialistijärjeston Ensimmäisen Edustajakokouksen Pöytäkirja,* Port Arthuissa, Ont. (Port Arthur: Työkansa Publishing, 1914), 25-30; and *Canadan Suomalainen Järjestö 25 Vuotta, 1911-1936* (Sudbury: Vapaus Publishing, 1936), 8.

124 Metsaranta, "The Workingmen's Associations," 84. By 1914, branches established in Northwestern Ontario included Port Arthur, Fort William, Nolalu, Nipigon, Kivikoski, Intola, Wolf Siding, and Fort Frances. Many more communities contained locals that were affiliated with those listed. The Finnish branches also brought with them to the SDPC the newspaper *Työkansa.* Throughout its existence, it remained editorially and organizationally autonomous and reported to the Finnish publishing company, not the SDPC executive.

125 Bryan D. Palmer, *Working-Class Experience: The Rise and Reconstitution of Canadian Labour, 1800-1980* (Toronto: Butterworth, 1983), 164; and Robin, *Radical Politics and Canadian Labour,* 101.

126 A.W. Rasporich, "Faction and Class in Modern Lakehead Politics," *Lakehead University Review* 7, 1 (Summer 1974): 39; and Morrison, "The Organization of Labour at Thunder Bay," 124-25.

127 *Fort William Morning Herald,* 17 October 1911.

128 George B. Macgillivray, *A History of Fort William and Port Arthur Newspapers from 1875* (Toronto: Bryant Press, 1968), 88.

129 *FWDTJ,* 7 September 1911.

130 Morrison, "Community and Conflict," 180-81.

131 *PADN,* 4 and 12 December 1911.

132 Rasporich, "Faction and Class in Modern Lakehead Politics," 39.

133 *PADN,* 11 June 1910.

134 For Port Arthur, see Kouhi, "Labour and Finnish Immigration to Thunder Bay," 31; for Fort William, see Rasporich, "Faction and Class in Modern Lakehead Politics," 39.

135 Tronrud, *Guardians of Progress,* 58.

136 *PADN,* 30 July 1912.

137 Morrison, "Community and Conflict," 168, and "Ethnicity and Violence," 143-60.

138 See Morrison, "Community and Conflict," 190-91, and "The Organization of Labour at Thunder Bay," 127. For more on McGuire and Hicks, see Morrison, "Cobalt Agitators Stir Up Lakehead Union Interest," *Highgrader Magazine* (Fall 2005): 24-26, and "Cobalt Agitators Played a Part in Lakehead Labour Battles," *Highgrader Magazine* (Christmas 2005): 22-23. Lockhead's prior involvement can be gleaned from his infrequent mention in *Cotton's Weekly.* See, for example, the 13 April 1911 issue.

139 Archives of Ontario (hereafter AO), Fred E. Moore fonds (hereafter FEM), F1274, Frederick Urry to W. Hicks, 7 June 1912.

140 Morrison, "Community and Conflict," 193-95.
141 Ibid., 197.
142 Morrison, "Frederick Urry, Architect," 14.
143 AO, FEM, W. Mantus to Fred E. Moore, 7 May 1915.
144 Ibid., Frederick Urry to W. Hicks, 7 June 1912.
145 *PADN,* 1 August 1912.
146 Jean Morrison, "Ethnicity and Class Consciousness: British, Finnish and South European Workers at the Canadian Lakehead before World War 1," *Lakehead University Review* 9, 1 (1976): 51.
147 *Voice,* 12 October 1912.
148 AO, FEM, Frederick Urry to W. Hicks, 7 June 1912.
149 *Cotton's Weekly,* 7 November 1912.
150 Ibid., 14 November 1912.
151 Morrison, "The Organization of Labour at Thunder Bay," 127. Over the course of the next few months, Ukrainian and Scandinavian locals were established in Fort William and a Russian local was reportedly in the works. No more is known about them, however. See *Cotton's Weekly,* 5 June 1913.
152 The total number of SDPC locals reported throughout Canada was 126. The number of locals reported by province was Quebec (3), Ontario (58), Manitoba (22), Saskatchewan (8), Alberta (11), and British Columbia (24). In contrast, the SPC had 144 locals in good standing. The number reported by province was New Brunswick (1), Quebec (1), Ontario (4), Manitoba (3), Alberta (56), and British Columbia (77). See *Cotton's Weekly,* 10 April 1913.
153 See Morrison, "Community and Conflict," 231; and *PADN,* 20 December 1912 and 2 January 1913.
154 Morrison, "The Organization of Labour at Thunder Bay," 127.
155 AO, FEM, Frederick Urry to W. Hicks, 7 June 1912; Morrison, "Colbalt Agitators Played a Part in Lakehead Labour Battles," 23.
156 Morrison, "Community and Conflict," 233-36.
157 D.J. Bercuson, *Fools and Wise Men: The Rise and Fall of the One Big Union* (Toronto: McGraw-Hill Ryerson, 1978), 53. For a thorough overview of the strike, see Morrison, "Community and Conflict," 239-48.
158 *FWDTJ,* 10 May 1913; Morrison, "Labour in Fort William and Port Arthur," 27; and LUA, TBFCHS, A, I, 2, 11.
159 They had even, much to the chagrin of Major John Oliver, also wrecked the police station. Morrison, "Community and Conflict," 241.
160 *PADN* and *Cotton's Weekly,* 22 May 1913. For more on the strike, see LAC, Department of Labour, RG27, vol. 302, Box 73.
161 *PADN,* 22 May 1913; *Cotton's Weekly,* 22 May 1913; Morrison, "Community and Conflict," 243.
162 LUA, TBFCHS, A, I, 2, 11, Mayor J. Oliver to Edmund Leslie Newcombe, Deputy Minister of Justice, 6 June 1913. Oddly enough, no mention was made of Harry Bryan, who appears to have, for unknown reasons, temporarily left the region.
163 Bryce M. Stewart, comp., *Report of a Preliminary and General Social Survey of Fort William,* directed by the Department of Temperance and Moral Reform of the Methodist Church, and the Board of Social Service and Evangelism of the Presbyterian Church (n.p., 1913), 10-11. See also their *Report of a Preliminary and General Social Survey of Port Arthur* (n.p., 1913).
164 *PADN,* 22 May 1913; Morrison, "Community and Conflict," 256.

CHAPTER 2: REPRESSION, REVITALIZATION, AND REVOLUTIONS, 1914-18

1 Desmond Morton with Terry Copp, *Working People: An Illustrated History of Canadian Labour* (Ottawa: Deneau and Greenburg Publishers, 1980), 101.

2 Ibid., 101. Robert Rutherdale's recent work, for example, demonstrates how the everyday lives of people in three cities affected their perceptions of the war. See *Hometown Horizons: Local Responses to Canada's Great War* (Vancouver: UBC Press, 2004).

3 Martin Robin, *Radical Politics and Canadian Labour, 1880-1930* (Kingston: Queen's University Industrial Relations Centre, 1968), 119.

4 Morton, *Working People*, 101.

5 Ibid., 102.

6 Gregory S. Kealey, "State Repression of Labour and the Left in Canada, 1914-1920: The Impact of the First World War," in *A Nation of Immigrants: Women, Workers, and Communities in Canadian History, 1840s-1960s*, ed. Franca Iacovetta with Paula Draper and Robert Ventresca (Toronto: University of Toronto Press, 1998), 385. See also Craig Heron and Myer Siemiatycki, "The Great War, the State, and Working-Class Canada," in *The Workers' Revolt in Canada, 1917-1925*, ed. Craig Heron (Toronto: University of Toronto Press, 1998), 11-42.

7 A. Ross McCormack, *Reformers, Rebels, and Revolutionaries: The Western Canadian Radical Movement, 1899-1919* (Toronto: University of Toronto Press, 1977), 118. See 118-64 for his discussion of "western radicals" during the First World War.

8 For more on the effect the Russian Revolution had on the western radical movement, see ibid., 137-64.

9 Morton, *Working People*, 101.

10 Jean Morrison, "The Organization of Labour at Thunder Bay," in *Thunder Bay: From Rivalry to Unity*, ed. Thorold J. Tronrud and A. Ernest Epp (Thunder Bay: Thunder Bay Historical Museum Society, 1995), 128.

11 *Labour Gazette* 15 (1914-15), and Morrison, ibid., 128.

12 City of Thunder Bay Archives (hereafter TBA), Fort William fonds (hereafter FWF), City of Fort William Annual Reports (hereafter FWAR), Series 16, vol. 207, 71, and James Stafford, "A Century of Growth at the Lakehead," in *Thunder Bay: From Rivalry to Unity*, 44.

13 Bryan Palmer, *Working-Class Experience: The Rise and Reconstitution of Canadian Labour, 1800-1980* (Toronto: Butterworth, 1983), 170-71.

14 Franca Iacovetta, "Encountering the 'Other': Society and Responses, 1900s-1930s," in *A Nation of Immigrants*, 360-61.

15 The lone strike in May 1914, involving fifty-two barkeepers, lasted only three days and the only terms were the recognition of Local 761, Bartenders' Union. This was a far cry from the violence that had surrounded the streetcar workers' strike a year before. See LAC, Department of Labour (hereafter DL), RG27, vol. 303, Strike 19; *Fort William Daily Times-Journal* (hereafter *FWDTJ*), 1 May and 2 May 1914; and *Port Arthur Daily News* (hereafter *PADN*), 1 May 1914. For national coverage, see *Cotton's Weekly*, 14 May 1914, and *Edmonton Journal*, 1 May 1914. Frederick Urry also reported to the Department of Labour that four or five structural ironworkers refused to work but their terms were agreed quickly on. See *FWDTJ* and *PADN*, 1 May 1914.

16 *Voice*, 10 July 1914, and Robin, *Radical Politics and Canadian Labour*, 115.

17 Nationally, the SDPC opposed the war and it, along with its newspaper, the *Canadian Forward*, would be subject to persecution and banning by war's end. For the SDPC's position, see *Canadian Forward*, 24 May 1917.

18 Unfortunately, no other information explaining this position has been located. For more on Wilson, see Morrison, "The Organization of Labour at Thunder Bay," 129.

19 *Cotton's Weekly*, 25 June 1914.

20 Ibid., 23 June 1914. According to *Cotton's Weekly*, the total provincial SDPC vote was 6,326. See 6 August 1914.

21 Ibid., 30 July 1914.

22 Louis Peltier, quoted in Frederick Brent Scollie, "Louis Lawrence Peltier (1853-1939), Railway Labor Leader, Mayor of Fort William 1909-10," Thunder Bay Historical Museum Society *Papers and Records* 32 (2004): 25. The election is perhaps most notable as it marked the first time that a Swedish resident of the Lakehead received public support from the SDPC and the Independent Labour Party. Although he lost the election, his candidacy demonstrated a growing desire for electoral participation on the part of the non-Anglo population. See *PADN,* 6 January 1914, and Elinor Barr, "Swedes at the Lakehead 1900-1930," Thunder Bay Historical Museum Society *Papers and Records* 20 (1992): 50-62.

23 Robin, *Radical Politics and Canadian Labour,* 115.

24 *Cotton's Weekly,* 30 July 1914.

25 Candidates for alderman included Sid Wilson, Rod Young, George Bell, Ernest Mann, and Peter Katainen. The three candidates nominated for school board trustees were T.H. Wynn, H. Barker, and A.E. Kettridge. At the last minute, James Dunbar, the Independent Labour candidate for council, and James Booker, the Independent Labour candidate and member of the SDPC, pulled out of the race for public commissioner. See *PADN,* 26 December 1914.

26 Ibid., 9 January 1915.

27 For a discussion of enemy aliens in Fort William, see Gerald Ross, "Fort William's Enemy Alien 'Problem' during the First World War," Thunder Bay Historical Museum Society *Papers and Records* 22 (1994): 1-22. For examples of reports in local papers on this fear, see, for example, *FWDTJ,* 26 November and 27 November 1914. The Lakehead is also discussed in Joseph A. Boudreau, "1914-1919: Interning Canada's 'Enemy Aliens,'" *Canada: An Historical Magazine* 2, 1 (September 1974): 15-27. On internment, see W.A. Waiser, *Park Prisoners: The Untold Story of Western Canada's National Parks, 1915-1946* (Calgary: Fifth House, 1995).

28 See Robert Craig Brown and Ramsay Cook, *Canada 1896-1921: A Nation Transformed* (Toronto: McClelland and Stewart, 1974), 224.

29 See, for example, *PADN,* 25 June 1915.

30 Joseph M. Mauro, *A History of Thunder Bay* (Thunder Bay: City of Thunder Bay, 1981), 263. Another well-documented incident involved the arrest and deportation of two men on the suspicion that they were coming to Northwestern Ontario to cause havoc after having been involved in a similar plot in Detroit. For more on the apparent sabotage carried out in Port Arthur, see LAC, Department of National Defence (hereafter DND), RG24, vol. 4588, File 15-69-22, vol. 1, Military District 10 Files – Aliens; and *PADN,* 14 August 1914. On the concern over Austrians and Germans in Northwestern Ontario, see LAC, DND, vol. 4588, File 15-69-22, vols. 2 and 3, "Canadian Government In re Germans and Austrians, Operative S-11," various dates, 28 August to 8 October 1914. For more on the belief that a German invasion was imminent, see Martin Kitchen, "The German Invasion of Canada in the First World War," *International History Review* 7, 2 (May 1985): 175-346.

31 Mauro, *Thunder Bay,* 263.

32 Ross, "Fort William's Enemy Alien 'Problem' during the First World War," 4.

33 Donald Avery, *"Dangerous Foreigners": European Immigrant Workers and Labour Radicalism in Canada, 1896-1932* (Toronto: McClelland and Stewart, 1979), 68. For the best extant description of this phenomenon, see Waiser, *Park Prisoners.* For an assortment of Fort William records pertaining to the internment of enemy aliens, see TBA, FWF, Index to Council Minutes, 1901-68, Series 2. For more on Ukrainian internment, see, for example, Orest Martynowych, "The Ukrainian Socialist Movement in Canada, 1900-1918," *Journal of Ukrainian Graduate Studies* 1 (1976): 27-44; "The Ukrainian Socialist Movement in Canada, 1900-1918," *Journal of Ukrainian Graduate Studies* 2 (1977): 22-31; Peter Melnycky, "The Internment of Ukrainian Canadians in Canada," in *Loyalties in Conflict: Ukrainians in Canada during the Great War,* ed. Frances Swyripa and John Herd Thompson (Edmonton: Canadian Institute of Ukrainian Studies, University of Alberta, 1985), 1-24. First-hand experiences of internment can be found in Helen Potrebenko, *No Streets of Gold: A*

Social History of the Ukrainians in Alberta (Vancouver: New Star Books, 1977), 131-36; and Watson Kirkconnell, "Kapuskasing – An Historical Sketch," *Queen's Quarterly* 28 (1921): 264-78.

34 *PADN*, 18 December 1914.

35 See LAC, DND, vol. 4744, File 2, Major A.E. Hopkins, commandant of the Jasper internment camps, to Sir W.H. Otter, cited in Lubomyr Luciuk, *A Time for Atonement: Canada's First National Internment Operations and the Ukrainian Canadians, 1914-1920* (Kingston: Limestone Press, 1988), 19, fn. 7.

36 *FWDTJ*, 2 September 1914; *PADN*, 27 and 30 November 1914.

37 Luciuk, *A Time for Atonement*, 7. See also J.B. Gregorovich, ed., *Ukrainian Canadians in Canada's Wars: Materials for Ukrainian Canadian History* (Toronto: Ukrainian Canadian Research Foundation, 1983), 74-94.

38 Ross, "Fort William's Enemy Alien 'Problem' during the First World War," 7. A total of 2,078 of those designated as enemy aliens in Fort William were immigrants from the Austro-Hungarian Empire.

39 TBA, Port Arthur fonds (hereafter PAF), Series 72: Licence, Police, and Relief Committee Minutes (hereafter LPRC), Police Department 1917 and 1918; TBA, FWF, Series 4: Fort William City Clerk's Files (hereafter FWCCF), Watkins, Acting Chief Constable, to J.T. Horne, Chairman of Alien Committee of Fort William, 25 June 1915; S.C. Young et al. to the Mayor and Council, City of Fort William, 25 June 1915; and Ross, "Fort William's Enemy Alien 'Problem' during the First World War," 7.

40 *PADN*, 27 November 1914.

41 Nothing is known about this branch and it appears to have been relatively inactive and eclipsed by the more dominant English and Finnish branches.

42 In 1906, for example, a railyard worker by the name of Nykola Haidiuk was run over by a locomotive in the Fort William yards, a mere three days after coming to Canada. For this incident, see *Svoboda*, 17 May 1906, cited in Orest T. Martynowych, *Ukrainians in Canada: The Formative Period, 1891-1924* (Edmonton: Canadian Institute of Ukrainian Studies Press, 1991), 133-34.

43 *PADN* and *FWDTJ*, 14 June 1915.

44 J.W. Ahlqvist, "Jarjestamme Toimina Vuoteen 1920," in *Canadan Suomalainen Järjestö: 25 Vuotta* (Sudbury: Vapaus Publishing, 1936), 38. The 3,062 members were drawn from sixty-four locals from across the country.

45 Lakehead University Archives (hereafter LUA), Finlandia Club Collection (hereafter FCC), MG3, Executive Minutes of the Port Arthur Finnish Socialist Local of the SPC (*Suomalainen Sosialisti Osasto*), 1911.

46 LUA, Thunder Bay Finnish-Canadian Historical Society Collection (hereafter TBFCHS), MG8, A, I, 3, 3, A.T. Hill, "All People Should Accept the Truth and Reject Lies and Misrepresentations," n.d. (c. 1970), 4. Hill claims his information is directly from the FSOC minute books in his possession at the time of writing.

47 Ibid., 5-6; and LUA, *Canadan Teollisuusunionistinen Kannatus Liitto* fonds (hereafter CTKL), MG10, Series D, 8, 10, A.T. Hill, untitled manuscript, n.d., 6-7.

48 *Port Arthur News-Chronicle* (hereafter *PANC*), 3 March 1916.

49 TBA, PAF, LPRC, Series 72, File 2, "Aliens 1913-1915," S.C. Young (Chairman), J.T. Horne, Douglas [unclear], and A. Snelgrove to Mayor and Council, City of Fort William, 25 June 1915. This letter was forwarded to Prime Minister R.L. Borden, C.J. Doherty, Minister of Justice, General letter, Aliens, Maj. Gen. Hughes, Minister of Militia, R. Rogers, Minister of Public Works, and W.H. Hearst, Premier of Ontario.

50 See TBA, Series 3, File 82, Superintendent of Immigration to A.M.F. Naughton, Fort William City Clerk, 20 August 1914. For more on the "great fear" of enemy aliens and deportations during the war, see Barbara Roberts, *Whence They Came: Deportations from Canada, 1900-1935* (Ottawa: University of Ottawa Press, 1988).

51 LUA, TBFCHS, A, 1, 2, 10, J. Oliver to Minster of Justice, 6 June 1913, 2-3.

52 Ibid., 3-4.

53 *PANC*, 3 March 1916.

54 Ahlqvist, "Jarjestamme Toimina Vuoteen 1920," 38.

55 Marc Metsaranta, "The Workingmen's Associations 1903-1914," in *Project Bay Street: Activities of Finnish-Canadians in Thunder Bay before 1915*, ed. Marc Metsaranta (Thunder Bay: Thunder Bay Finnish Canadian Historical Society, 1989), 90.

56 The experience of the Finnish-language newspaper *Työkansa* highlights the issues facing all Finnish socialists throughout 1914 and 1915. See *Työkansa*, 15 June 1915, and Aku Paivo, *Canadan Suomalainsen Sosialisti jarjeston Ensimmainen Edustaja-Kokouksen Poytakirja* (Port Arthur: Työkansan Kirjapaino, 1914), 123.

57 Archives of Ontario (hereafter AO), Fred E. Moore fonds (hereafter FEM), F1274, W. Manthus to Fred E. Moore, 7 May 1915.

58 Ibid., Moore to Fred E. Moore, 6 and 13 June 1915.

59 *PADN*, 19 June 1915.

60 Ibid., 25 June 1915.

61 A.T. Hill, "Historic Basis and Development of the Lumber Workers Organization and Struggle in Ontario," unpublished manuscript, Studies Resource Centre, Lakehead University (c. 1952), 1.

62 The literature on the early years of the IWW is mountainous. The standard works on the Wobblies, though, remain Melvyn Dubofsky, *We Shall Be All: A History of the Industrial Workers of the World* (Chicago: Quadrangle Books, 1969); and Philip S. Foner, *History of the Labor Movement in the United States. Vol. 4: The Industrial Workers of the World, 1905-1917* (New York: International Publishers, 1965). For more on the activities of the IWW in Canada before the First World War, see Mark Leier, *Where the Fraser River Flows: The Industrial Workers of the World in British Columbia* (Vancouver: New Star Books, 1990); and Jack Scott, *Plunderbund and Proletariat* (Vancouver: New Star Books, 1975).

63 Harry Bryan appears to have been very active throughout the eastern part of Northwestern Ontario. After moving to Dorion, approximately 100 kilometres away, he continued to make the journey into the twin cities for meetings. For a discussion of his leadership in the formation of the SDPC branch in Dorion, see *Cotton's Weekly*, 6 February and 6 March 1913.

64 For more on Finnish activity in the Great Lakes region and within the IWW, see Matti E. Kaups, "The Finns in the Copper and Iron Ore Mines of the Western Great Lakes Region, 1864-1905: Some Preliminary Observations," and Douglas Ollila, "From Socialism to Industrial Unionism (IWW): Social Factors in the Emergence of Left-Labor Radicalism among Finnish Workers on the Mesabi, 1911-1919," in *The Finnish Experience in the Western Great Lakes Region: New Perspectives*, ed. Michael G. Karni, Matti E. Kaups, and Douglas J. Ollila Jr. (Turku, Finland: Institute for Migration Studies, 1975), 55-88 and 156-71.

65 Gary Jewell, *The History of the IWW in Canada* (Chicago: Industrial Workers of the World, 1975), 2. Jewell puts the date at 1916, but Hill recalls organizing workers as early as 1913.

66 According to historian Oiva W. Saarinen, the FSOC in the Sudbury region differed as it was focused on the mining industry. For example, it "worked closely with the WFM [Western Federation of Miners], a Colorado-based radical union formed in the United States in 1893 that fought strenuously for better mine regulation, the eight-hour day, and workmen's compensation and trade union rights." See *Between a Rock and a Hard Place: A Historical Geography of the Finns in the Sudbury Area* (Waterloo, ON: Wilfrid Laurier University Press, 1993), 188. See also Allen Seager, "Finnish Canadians and the Ontario Miners' Movement," *Polyphony* 3, 2 (1981): 38; and Morrison, "The Organization of Labour at Thunder Bay," 130.

67 Martha Isobel Gerard Allen, "A Survey of Finnish Cultural, Economic, and Political Development in the Sudbury District of Ontario" (MA thesis, University of Western Ontario, 1954), 79. For

information on the Copper Country Strike of 1913, see Arthur Puotinen, "Copper Country Finns and the Strike of 1913," in *The Finnish Experience in the Western Great Lakes Region*, 143-55.

68 In his memoirs, Hill claims to have worked for Debs in the 1916 campaign. Debs ran for President of the United States in the 1904, 1908, 1912, and 1920 (the final time from jail) elections, however. As Hill is known to have been in the United States only during the period of the 1912 election, this is most likely the election he refers to.

69 Avery, *"Dangerous Foreigners,"* 53.

70 A.T. Hill, "Historic Basis and Development of the Lumber Workers' Organization and Struggles in Ontario" (unpublished manuscript, 1952), 2; and Thunder Bay Historical Museum Society (hereafter TBHMS), A.T. Hill fonds, Series A17, 2/1-16, A.T. Hill, "Thank You," 1.

71 Morrison, "The Organization of Labour at Thunder Bay," 130.

72 Hill, "Historic Basis and Development," 1. Hill recalled from his experiences that "the organization of the workers in these camps was not an easy task, because workers were distributed to various lumber camps, workers did not know where they would be going for the next season, and then their movements were easily noted by the bosses and stool pigeons ready and handy."

73 For more on the IWW's use of sabotage, see Dubofsky, *We Shall Be All*, 160-64; and Elizabeth Gurley Flynn, *Memories of the Industrial Workers of the World* (New York: American Institute for Marxist Studies, 1977), 35-37.

74 McCormack, *Reformers, Rebels, and Revolutionaries*, 106-11. For more on strikes in 1916, see LAC, DL, vol. 305, Strike 62.

75 *PANC*, 26 August 1916, 1. On railway labour shortage, see 17 August 1916, 1.

76 For an overview of conscription in Ontario, see Paul Maroney, "'The Great Adventure': The Context and Ideology of Recruiting in Ontario, 1914-1917," *Canadian Historical Review* 77, 1 (March 1996): 62-98; and W.R. Young, "Conscription, Rural Depopulation, and the Farmers of Ontario," *Canadian Historical Review* 53 (September 1972): 289-320.

77 *PANC*, 26 August 1916.

78 Morrison, "The Organization of Labour at Thunder Bay," 129; and *Labour Organizations in Canada* (Ottawa: Department of Labour, 1917), 49. For the Trades and Labour Congress's reaction, see Charles Lipton, *The Trade Union Movement of Canada, 1827-1959* (Montreal: Canadian Social Publications, 1966); and Kenneth McNaught and David J. Bercuson, *The Winnipeg Strike: 1919* (Don Mills, ON: Longman Canada, 1974), 15-16.

79 *PANC*, 5 January 1917.

80 For more on the meeting in the Walker Theatre, see J.M. Bumsted, *The Winnipeg General Strike of 1919: An Illustrated History* (Winnipeg: Watson Dwyer Publishing, 1994), 17-19; Lipton, *The Trade Union Movement of Canada*, 187; and Harold Logan, *Trade Unions in Canada* (Toronto: Macmillan, 1948), 304-5.

81 *PANC*, 5 January 1917.

82 William Rodney, *Soldiers of the International: A History of the Communist Party of Canada, 1919-1929* (Toronto: University of Toronto Press, 1968), 13.

83 *PANC*, 17 March 1917.

84 Ibid., 28 March 1917.

85 See Gregory S. Kealey, "State Repression of Labour and the Left in Canada, 1914-1920: The Impact of the First World War," *Canadian Historical Review* 73, 3 (September 1992): 281-314; and Jeffrey Keshen, "All the News That Was Fit to Print: Ernest J. Chambers and Information Control in Canada, 1914-1919," *Canadian Historical Review* 73, 3 (September 1992): 315-43. For more on the Russian Revolution's effect in Canada, see Theresa Baxter, "Selected Aspects of Canadian Public Opinion on the Russian Revolution and on Its Impact on Canada, 1917-1919" (MA thesis, University of Western Ontario, 1973); and Elliot Samuels, "The Red Scare in Ontario: The Reactions of the Ontario Press to the Internal and External Threat of Bolshevism, 1917-1918" (MA thesis, Queen's University, 1972).

86 *PANC*, 26 November 1917.

87 TBA, FWF, FWCCF, File 148, F.H. Bole, Mutual Elevator Co. Ltd., to Fort William City Clerk, 5 October 1917.

88 See Seppo Hentilä, "Itsenäistymisestä jatkosodan päättymiseen," in Osmo Jussila, Seppo Hentilä, and Jukka Nevakivi, *Suomen poliittinen historia* (Helsinki: WSOY, 2000), 98-104.

89 For overviews of Finnish-Russian relations, see Austin Goodrich, *Study in SISU: Finland's Fight for Independence* (New York: Ballantine Books, 1960); and LA. Puntila, *The Political History of Finland, 1809-1966*, trans. David Miller (Helsinki: Otava Publishing, 1974).

90 See Anthony F. Upton, *The Finnish Revolution, 1917-1918* (Minneapolis: University of Minnesota Press 1980).

91 For more on the German support of the "White" Finnish faction, see A. Harding Ganz, "The German Expedition to Finland, 1918," *Military Affairs* 44, 2 (April 1980): 84-91; Jackson J. Hampden, "German Intervention in Finland, 1918," *Slavonic and East European Review* 18 (July 1939): 93-101; Kalervo Hovi, "The Winning of Finnish Independence as an Issue in International Relations," *Scandinavian Journal of History* 3 (1978): 47-73; Taisto Matti Kaipio, "German War Aims in Finland, 1918" (PhD dissertation, University of Toronto, 1976); Jay Smith, "Russia and the Origins of the Finnish Civil War of 1918," *American Slavic and East European Review* 14, 4 (December 1955): 481-502; and John H. Wuorinen, "Finland's War of Independence, 1918," *American Scandinavian Review* 51 (1963): 389-95. For more on the civil war, see Osmo Jussila, "Suomi suuriruhtinaskuntana," in *Suomen poliittinen historia*, ed. Osmo Jussila, Seppo Hentilä, and Jukka Nevakivi (Helsinki: WSOY, 2000), 66-67, 91-96; and Hentilä, "Itsenäistymisestä jatkosodan päättymiseen," 98-104.

92 Upton, *The Finnish Revolution*, 312.

93 Those who settled in Northern Ontario included, according to Ian Radforth, the prime minister of Finland's short-lived socialist government and some members of his cabinet. They "found temporary refuge in a logging camp near New Liskeard in northeastern Ontario." See Radforth, "Finnish Radicalism and Labour Activism in Northern Ontario Woods," in *A Nation of Immigrants*, 297.

94 Peter Kivisto, *Immigrant Socialists in the United States: The Case of Finns and the Left* (Rutherford, NJ: Fairleigh Dickinson University Press; Cranbury, NJ: Associated University Presses, 1984), 16.

95 A.T. Hill, "Historic Basis and Development," 3. Hill's comments on the IWW are hardly unique. For more on the IWW's response to the Russian Revolution, see Dubofsky, *We Shall Be All*, 349-422.

96 See Roy MacLaren, *Canadians in Russia, 1918-1919* (Toronto: Macmillan of Canada, 1976); John Swettenham, *Allied Intervention in Russia 1918-1919 and the Part Played by Canada* (Toronto: Ryerson Press, 1967), 54 and 128; and Robert Jackson, *At War with the Bolsheviks* (London: Tandem, 1974).

97 A.T. Hill, "Historic Basis and Development," 3.

98 See *One Big Union Monthly* (hereafter *OBUM*) (Chicago), May 1919, 7.

99 Ibid., April 1919, 56.

100 LUA, Jean Morrison Labour History Collection (hereafter JMLHC), GS186a, Tape 4, Interview with Holmer Borg, 1972.

101 Avery, *"Dangerous Foreigners,"* 53.

102 Mary Veltri, "Labour Radicalism among Finnish Bushworkers at the Lakehead, 1916-1936" (Honours thesis, Lakehead University, 1981), 64.

103 A.W. Rasporich, "Faction and Class in Modern Lakehead Politics," *Lakehead University Review* 7, 1 (Summer 1974): 39; and Arja Pilli, "Finnish-Canadian Radicalism and the Government of Canada from the First World War to the Depression," in *Finnish Diaspora I: Canada, South America, Africa, Australia and Sweden*, ed. Michael G. Karni (Toronto: Multicultural History Society of Ontario, 1981), 23.

104 LUA, TBFCHS, A, 1, 3, 3, A.T. Hill, "All People Should Accept the Truth and Reject Lies and Misrepresentation," 17 June 1974, 1.

105 Avery, *"Dangerous Foreigners,"* 73.

106 *PANC,* 30 April, 5 and 25 May 1917.

107 Joining Harry Bryan to speak to those in attendance (a cross-strata of the region included returned soldiers) were Herbert Barker, A.E. Kettridge, and William Welsh. See *Canadian Forward,* 24 May 1917.

108 *PANC,* 4 June 1917, and *Canadian Forward,* 12 June 1917.

109 *PANC,* 4 June 1917.

110 Ibid.

111 Ibid., 21 July 1917.

112 Ibid., 12 September 1917.

113 *PANC* and *FWDTJ,* 1 October, 2 October, and 6 October 1917.

114 *PANC* and *FWDTJ,* 9 October 1917.

115 Morton, *Working People,* 111.

116 *PANC,* 2 November 1917.

117 For more on the Ontario Labour Party and its role in the 1917 federal election, see Robin, *Radical Politics and Canadian Labour,* 140-42.

118 *PANC,* 26 November 1917.

119 Ibid., 21 November 1917.

120 Ibid., 5 December 1917.

121 Ibid., 5 December 1917.

122 Ibid.

123 Ibid., 30 November 1917; *FWDTJ,* 12 December 1917; and Roy Piovesana, *Robert J. Manion: Member of Parliament for Fort William, 1917-1935* (Thunder Bay: Thunder Bay Historical Museum Society, 1990), 12.

124 *PANC,* 30 November 1917. Interestingly, the list of delegates to the joint convention at Kenora for the nomination meeting include A. Mustonen, editor of *Canadan Uutiset,* and A. Kyro, a former member of the Finnish branch of the SDPC. See *PANC,* 12 November 1917. On Gompers and trade unionism in Canada during the war, see Samuel Gompers, *American Labor and the War* (New York: George H. Doran, 1919), 141-58 and 197-205.

125 Francis Henry Keefer received 5,990 votes compared with James Asher Dunbar's 2,476. Robert James Manion received 5,943 votes compared with Albert Hugh Dennis's 2,560. Parliament of Canada, "History of Federal Ridings since 1867," http://www.parl.gc.ca/information/about/process/house/hfer/hfer.asp?Language=E&Search=Gres&genElection=13&ridProvince=9&submit1=Search.

126 *Canadian Forward,* 10 February 1918. Bryan's connections to the IWW are unclear at this point.

127 LAC, Robert L. Borden fonds (hereafter RBF), MG26-H, File OC 519, 56639-56640, Chief Commissioner of Police to F.A. Acland, Deputy Minister of Labour, 9 May 1918.

128 For more on the activity in May, see LAC, DL, vol. 309, Strike 107 and 120; *FWDTJ,* 5 May 1918.

129 Donald Avery, *Reluctant Host: Canada's Response to Immigrant Workers, 1896-1994* (Toronto: McClelland and Stewart, 1995), 75; and Rodney, *Soldiers of the International,* 17. C.H. Cahan belongs to a long list of wartime bureaucrats that had the ear of the more hawkish members of the Borden government.

130 Avery, *Reluctant Host,* 74-75.

131 LAC, RBF, File OC 519, 56657-56658, Cahan to C.J. Doherty, Minster of Justice, 20 July 1918; 56665-56681, Cahan to C.J. Doherty, Minster of Justice, 14 September 1918; Rodney, *Soldiers of the International,* 17-18; and Arja Pilli, *The Finnish-Language Press in Canada, 1901-1939: A Study in the History of Ethnic Journalism* (Turku, Finland: Institute for Migration Studies, 1982), 91.

132 Hill, "Historic Basis and Development," 4; Lorne and Caroline Brown, *An Unauthorized History of the RCMP* (Toronto: James Lorimer, 1973), 37-38; and Nick Viita, "The Origins of the Canadian Finnish Labour Movement," trans. Ahti Ilmari Tolvanen, *Industrialisti,* 75-76 (9, 13 October 1970): 9.

133 The exception was the Sudbury-based *Vapaus,* established in 1917. See Pilli, "Finnish-Canadian Radicalism," 23. The ban, interestingly, also included the right-wing Port Arthur–based Finnish newspaper *Canadan Uutiset,* a paper started in 1915 geared to the more conservative "White Finns" of Northern Ontario. For more on press censorship during the war, see George D. Kerr, "Canadian Press Censorship in WW I," *Journalism Quarterly* 59, 2 (1982): 235-39; Jeffery A. Keshen, *Propaganda and Censorship during Canada's Great War* (Edmonton: University of Alberta Press, 1996).

134 Luciuk, *A Time for Atonement,* 25; and D. Morton and G. Wright, *Winning the Second Battle: Canadian Veterans and the Return to Civilian Life 1915-1930* (Toronto: University of Toronto Press, 1987), 74-75.

135 LAC, Records of the Privy Office, RG2, Series 1, PC 2384, 30 September 1918; *Canada Gazette,* 30 September 1918; 5 October 1918, 1277-1278; *Statutes of Canada, 1919,* 9-10 Geo. V, vols. 1-11, 77-78; and Rodney, *Soldiers of the International,* 35.

136 LAC, RBF, vol. 104, File OC 519, 56665-56682, Reel C-4334, C.H. Cahan to Charles J. Doherty, 14 September 1918; and Pilli, *The Finnish-Language Press in Canada,* 38-39.

137 Edward E. Laine, "Finnish Canadian Radicalism and Canadian Politics: The Forty Years, 1900-1940," in *Ethnicity, Power and Politics in Canada,* ed. Jorgen Dahlie and Tissa Fernando (Toronto: Methuen, 1981), 98-99.

138 Viita, "The Origins of the Canadian Finnish Labour Movement," 10. For a discussion of the FSOC position, see J. Donald Wilson, "The Finnish Organization of Canada, the 'Language Barrier' and the Assimilation Process," *Canadian Ethnic Studies* 9, 2 (1977): 106; and Ahti Tolvanen, *Finntown: A Perspective on Urban Integration. Port Arthur Finns in the Inter-war Period: 1918-1939* (Helsinki: University of Helsinki, 1985), 42-43.

139 Ian Radforth, *Bushworkers and Bosses: Logging in Northern Ontario, 1900-1980* (Toronto: University of Toronto Press, 1987), 113.

140 Ibid., 113; Pilli, "Finnish Canadian Radicalism," 19-32; and Hill, "Historic Basis and Development," 4.

141 See Viita, "The Origins of the Canadian Finnish Labour Movement," 7.

142 Antonio Pucci, "Thunder Bay's Italian Community 1880s-1940s," in *The Italian Immigrant Experience,* ed. John Potestio and Antonio Pucci (Thunder Bay: Canadian Italian Historical Association, 1988), 93.

143 Penny Petrone, *Breaking the Mould* (Toronto: Guernica, 2001), 77.

144 Lipton, *The Trade Union Movement of Canada,* 175.

145 Ivan Avakumovic, *The Communist Party in Canada: A History* (Toronto: McClelland and Stewart, 1975), 14.

146 Luciuk, *A Time for Atonement,* 13 and 20. For example, in the 1916 riot in the Kapuskasing internment camp, 1,200 prisoners squared off against 300 guards. There is no doubt that, owing to the high percentage of Ukrainians involved in workers' and socialist organizations, they were detrimentally affected. See Luciuk, ibid., 8; and W.D. Otter, *Internment Operations, 1914-1920* (Ottawa: n.p., 1921), 20. Unfortunately, as Melnycky has discovered, determining the nationality of the internees or of those registered as "enemy aliens" is difficult, since relevant archival materials were destroyed at the National Archives of Canada after the Second World War. See Melnycky, "The Internment of Ukrainians in Canada," 23-24.

CHAPTER 3: "THE HOG ONLY HARMS HIMSELF IF HE TOPPLES HIS TROUGH"

1 The Winnipeg General Strike has been the focus of numerous studies, plays, and films. Especially useful are David Jay Bercuson, *Confrontation at Winnipeg,* rev. ed. (Montreal and Kingston:

McGill-Queen's University Press, 1990); Gerald Friesen, "'Yours in Revolt': The Socialist Party of Canada and the Western Labour Movement," *Labour/Le Travail* 1 (1976): 139-57; Harry Gutkin and Mildred Gutkin, *Profiles in Dissent: The Shaping of Radical Thought in the Canadian West* (Edmonton: NeWest Press, 1997); Gregory S. Kealey, "1919: The Canadian Labour Revolt," *Labour/Le Travail* 13 (1984): 11-44; D.C. Masters, *The Winnipeg General Strike* (Toronto: University of Toronto Press, 1950); Kenneth McNaught and David J. Bercuson, *The Winnipeg Strike: 1919* (Don Mills, ON: Longman Canada, 1974); and Norman Penner, ed., *Winnipeg 1919: The Strikers' Own History of the Winnipeg General Strike,* 2nd ed. (Toronto: James Lorimer, 1975).

2 Merrily Weisbord, *The Strangest Dream: Canadian Communists, the Spy Trials, and the Cold War* (Montreal: Véhicule Press, 1983; reprint, 1994), 27. Although this opinion was shared by most of the media, the work of Michael Dupuis argues that the *Toronto Star* was more moderate in its assessment. See Dupuis, "The Response of the Toronto Daily Press to the Winnipeg General Strike" (MA thesis, University of Ottawa, 1973); and "Winnipeg's Red Scare," *Beaver* (August-September 2007): 38-43.

3 The source of this quotation is William Eklund, *Builders of Canada: History of the Finnish Organization of Canada, 1911-1971,* trans. Vappu Tyyskä (Toronto: Finnish Organization of Canada, 1987).

4 See D.J. Bercuson, *Fools and Wise Men: The Rise and Fall of the One Big Union* (Toronto: McGraw-Hill Ryerson, 1978), 134-36; Stuart Jamieson, *Industrial Relations in Canada,* 2nd ed. (New York: St. Martin's Press, 1974), 20-21; H.A. Logan, *Trade Unions in Canada* (Toronto: Macmillan, 1948), 306-16, 320-27; Paul A. Phillips, *No Power Greater: A Century of Labour in British Columbia* (Vancouver: BC Federation of Labour; Boag Foundation, 1967), 82-85; and Arja Pilli, *The Finnish-Language Press in Canada, 1901-1939: A Study in the History of Ethnic Journalism* (Turku, Finland: Institute for Migration Studies, 1982), 138.

5 Bercuson, *Fools and Wise Men,* 136.

6 Lakehead University Archives (hereafter LUA), Thunder Bay Finnish-Canadian Historical Society (hereafter TBFCHS), MG8, Series B, 7, 10, Item 2, Tape 2, Interview with William Holder, 31 March 1977.

7 Bercuson, for example, describes the workers at the Lakehead as "perhaps the most militant in the country." See *Fools and Wise Men,* 42.

8 As Craig Heron and others have concluded, while the revolt "was a cross-country phenomenon that emerged in similar ways across Canada ... [it] nonetheless took a different course and faced different obstacles in each region." See Craig Heron, "Introduction," in *The Workers' Revolt in Canada, 1917-1925,* ed. Craig Heron (Toronto: University of Toronto Press, 1998), 7.

9 See, for example, Heron, *The Workers' Revolt in Canada.*

10 For an overview of the Lakehead response to the Winnipeg General Strike, see Michel S. Beaulieu, "Reacting to the Workers' Revolt: The Lakehead and the Winnipeg General Strike," *Left History* 14, 2 (2009): 18-32; and "A Proletarian Prometheus: Socialism, Ethnicity, and Revolution at the Lakehead, 1900-1935" (PhD dissertation, Queen's University, 2007), 134-63.

11 Bercuson, *Confrontation at Winnipeg,* 78; Bercuson, *Fools and Wise Men,* 68-74; Logan, *Trade Unions in Canada,* 430-31; and Martin Robin, *Radical Politics and Canadian Labour, 1880-1930* (Kingston: Queen's University Industrial Relations Centre, 1968), 160-61.

12 Larry Gambone, *The Impossibilists: Selections from the Press of the Socialist Party of Canada and the One Big Union, 1906-1938* (Montreal: Red Lion Press, 2002). Online excerpt: Socialist History Project, http://socialisthistory.ca/Docs/Imposs/Impossibilists1.htm.

13 Gerald Friesen, "'Yours in Revolt': The Socialist Party of Canada and the Western Canadian Labour Movement," *Labour/Le Travail* 13 (Spring 1984): 146.

14 The Finnish Socialist Organization of Canada had been renamed in 1919 after being allowed to reform following its ban under the War Measures Act in 1918.

15 See, for example, Todd McCallum, "The Strange Tale of Tom Cassidy and Catherine Rose, or Free Love, Heterosexuality, and the One Big Union," *Journal of the Canadian Historical Association* 9 (1998): 125-54; and "Not a Sex Question? The One Big Union and the Politics of Radical Manhood," *Labour/Le Travail* 42 (1998): 15-54.

16 Examples of regional studies include, but are not limited to, James R. Conley, "Frontier Labourers, Crafts in Crisis, and the Western Labour Revolt: The Case of Vancouver, 1900-1919," *Labour/Le Travail* 23 (1989): 9-37; Gillian Creese, "Exclusion or Solidarity? Vancouver Workers Confront the 'Oriental Problem,'" in *Canadian Working Class History: Selected Readings,* 2nd ed., ed. Laurel Sefton MacDowell and Ian Radforth (Toronto: Canadian Scholar's Press, 1992), 311-32.

17 No single note could encompass all of the works dealing with the One Big Union and the events of 1919. The following are the major works consulted for this study: Bercuson, *Fools and Wise Men;* Peter Campbell, *Canadian Marxists and the Search for a Third Way* (Montreal and Kingston: McGill-Queen's University Press, 1999); Heron, *The Workers' Revolt in Canada;* Larry Peterson, "The One Big Union in International Perspective: Revolutionary Industrial Unionism 1900-1925," *Labour/Le Travail* 7 (1981): 41-66; and Peter Warrian, "The Challenge of the One Big Union Movement in Canada, 1919-1921" (MA thesis, University of Waterloo, 1971).

18 Bercuson, *Confrontation at Winnipeg,* 51. See also his "Labour in Winnipeg" (PhD dissertation, University of Toronto, 1971).

19 Although it is clear that delegates attended, who exactly they were remains unknown. A letter from William Checkley, later a prominent OBU organizer in the region, appears to indicate that J.P. Harris, a street railway worker, attended. See Provincial Archives of Manitoba (PAM), One Big Union fonds (hereafter OBU), MG10, A3, William Checkley to Unknown, 20 May 1919.

20 PAM, OBU, Fred E. Moore, Secretary Fort William Trades and Labour Council to V.R. Midgley, Secretary Labour Temple, Vancouver, 14 December 1918. One such individual was Fred Moore, a local printer and former city councillor whose business was responsible for the printing of political materials not only for socialist organizations such as the SPC, SDPC, IWW, ILP, and OBU but also for the Liberal and Conservative parties. Because of his association with socialists, the RCMP suspected Moore of being a Bolshevik. See "Register of Bolshevist and Agitator Investigations 1920," 6 and "Fort William, Fred E. Moore, Suspect," in *RCMP Security Bulletins: The Early Years, 1919-1929,* ed. Gregory S. Kealey and Reg Whitaker (St. John's: Canadian Committee on Labour History, 1994), 675.

21 Robin, *Radical Politics and Canadian Labour,* 174. Robin himself is quoting directly from "The Origin of the OBU," in *Verbatim Report of the Calgary Labour Conference* (Winnipeg: One Big Union, 1919). See also Warrian, "The Challenge of the One Big Union Movement in Canada," 56.

22 J.B. McArthur, secretary of the Port Arthur Trades and Labour Council, reported that this included (number of members in parentheses): the Brotherhood of Railway Carmen #344 (70); Sheet Metal Workers #580 (10); Canadian Brotherhood of Railway Employees (17); Brotherhood of Pulp, Sulphite, and Paper Mill Workers #40; Steam Operating Engineers (50); Plumbers and Pipe Fitters #378 (60); Brotherhood of Boiler Makers and Iron Shipbuilders (600); Bricklayers and Masons #25 (50); United Brotherhood of Carpenters and Joiners #498 (206); Amalgamated Section of Carpenters #2610 (80); Electrical Workers #360 (10); Structural Iron Workers #33 (25); Machinists #820 (80); and Amalgamated Postal Workers of Canada (20). See PAM, OBU, 114-15, J.B. McArthur, Secretary Port Arthur Trades and Labour Council to V.R. Midgley, 31 March 1919.

23 Robin, *Radical Politics and Canadian Labour,* 175.

24 Ibid., 181.

25 LUA, *Canadan Teollisuusunionistinen Kannatus Liitto* fonds (hereafter CTKL), MG10, Series D, 8, 10, "A.T. Hill Biography," n.d., 12.

26 Bercuson, *Fools and Wise Men,* 136.

27 *One Big Union Bulletin* (hereafter *OBUB*), 27 December 1919, 3.

28 Ibid.

29 See, for example, ibid., 20 September 1920, 3.

30 For example, see M. Phillips Price, "The Truth about Soviet Russia," *OBUB*, 20 September 1919, 4.

31 *OBUB*, 18 October 1919, 7; and Gordon Hak, "British Columbia Loggers and the LWIU, 1919-1922," *Labour/Le Travail* 23 (Spring 1989): 67-90. For reference to an early progress report being filed with the Winnipeg Central Labour Council, see PAM, Robert Boyd Russell Collection (hereafter RBR), MG10, A14-2, 15, Minutes, Winnipeg Central Labour Council, 21 October 1919.

32 Donald Avery, *"Dangerous Foreigners": European Immigrant Workers and Labour Radicalism in Canada, 1896-1932* (Toronto: McClelland and Stewart, 1979), 79; and Ahti Tolvanen, *Finntown: A Perspective on Urban Integration. Port Arthur Finns in the Inter-war Period: 1918-1939* (Helsinki: University of Helsinki, 1985), 43. The Port Arthur Labour Temple had been closed by the Canada Permanent Mortgage Company after the Finnish Building Company defaulted on its loan in late 1918. The newly established Finnish support ring of the One Big Union bought control of the temple for $29,000. See Nick Viita, "Origins of the Finnish Labour Movement," trans. Ahti I. Tolvanen, *Industrialisti*, 75-76 (9 and 13 October 1970): 7.

33 *Fort William Daily Times-Journal* (hereafter *FWDTJ*), 10 and 11 October 1919.

34 The Executive Board consisted of J. Lyones (Port Arthur), Harry Bryan (Port Arthur), R. Christie (Port Arthur), W. Arnberg (Port Arthur), M. Cerutti (Fort William), S. Janatuinen (Fort William), H.M. Eames (Fort William), and E.E. Sykes as Secretary. LUA, CTKL, Series C, 4, 1, "Executive Board," n.d.

35 *OBUB*, 25 October 1919, 6.

36 *FWDTJ*, 10 and 11 October 1919, and *Port Arthur News-Chronicle* (hereafter *PANC*), 11 October 1919. Ollikkala was eventually fined $2,000 but appealed his conviction. See *PANC*, 17 November 1919.

37 *FWDTJ*, 10, 11, and 14 October 1919, and *PANC*, 10, 17, and 18 October 1919. According to the RNWMP, the searches had occurred after a prolonged period of surveillance and the recent movement of the prohibited material from the hall to houses in the region to avoid confiscation. Those arrested in the Port Arthur raid included Allie Kiovisto, Karl Hyman, William Koivu, John Nelson, Carl Nyman, Andrew Pannanen, and Victor Saikula. All were eventually convicted and fined amounts ranging from $500 to $2,000. See *FWDTJ* and *PANC*, 31 October 1919.

38 *FWDTJ*, 20 October 1919.

39 *OBUB*, 8 November 1919, 2.

40 *OBUB*, 8 November 1919, 2. Varley's meeting with the Port Arthur Trades and Labour Council met with the same scorn and ridicule. See *FWDTJ*, 8 November 1919.

41 There were sixteen votes in favour and two against. See *FWDTJ*, 15 November 1919, and *PANC*, 14 November 1919.

42 *OBUB*, 8 November 1919, 4.

43 *FWDTJ*, 25 October 1919.

44 *OBUB*, 15 November, 1, and 13 December 1919, 1.

45 Ibid., 25 October 1919, 1.

46 Ian Radforth, *Bushworkers and Bosses: Logging in Northern Ontario, 1900-1980* (Toronto: University of Toronto Press, 1987), 116-18.

47 Bercuson, *Fools and Wise Men*, 136.

48 Hak, "British Columbia Loggers and the LWIU," 76.

49 Tolvanen, *Finntown*, 47.

50 Viita, "Origins of the Finnish Labour Movement," 10.

51 Library and Archives Canada (hereafter LAC), Canadian Security Intelligence Service (hereafter CSIS), RG146, vol. 2, File 1025-9-9018. The IWW had remained a factor in the British Columbia lumber industry throughout 1919.

52 *OBUB*, 29 November 1919, 2.

53 Ibid., 13 December 1919, 1.

54 These included unions consisting of bakers, coal handlers, starch workers, carpenters, civic employees, and lumber workers. See Bercuson, *Fools and Wise Men*, 164.

55 Jean Morrison, "The Organization of Labour at Thunder Bay," in *Thunder Bay: From Rivalry to Unity* (Thunder Bay: Thunder Bay Historical Museum Society, 1995), 130.

56 Bryan D. Palmer, *Working-Class Experience: The Rise and Reconstitution of Canadian Labour, 1800-1980* (Toronto: Butterworth, 1983), 167.

57 For more on the growing hostility towards non-Anglo-Saxon immigrants during the 1920s, see, for example, Donald Avery, *"Dangerous Foreigners,"* 90-115, and *Reluctant Host: Canada's Response to Immigrant Workers, 1896-1994* (Toronto: McClelland and Stewart, 1995), 82-107. For a general discussion of immigration policy during this period, see Ninette Kelley and Michael Trebilcock, *The Making of the Mosaic: A History of Canadian Immigration Policy* (Toronto: University of Toronto Press, 1998), 164-215.

58 *OBUB*, 25 October 1919, 6.

59 Archives of Ontario (hereafter AO), Ontario Provincial Police (hereafter OPP), RG23, Series E, E30, Campbell to Major J.E. Rogers, Superintendent of Provincial Police, 8 June 1919. The OPP knew much more than just their names. In his report, the OPP official even indicated the delegate number of each man. See also J. Peter Campbell, "The Cult of Spontaneity: Finnish-Canadian Bushworkers and the Industrial Workers of the World in Northern Ontario, 1919-1934," *Labour/Le Travail* 41 (Spring 1998): 127.

60 AO, OPP, ibid., Campbell to Major J.E. Rogers, ibid.

61 Ibid., [Illegible], Acting Chief of Police, to Major Jos. E. Rogers, Superintendent of Provincial Police, 24 September 1919, for a report on the IWW-led unrest in lumber camps along the Algoma Central Railway.

62 Bercuson, *Fools and Wise Men*, 166-67.

63 Royal Canadian Mounted Police, "Notes of the Work of the CIB Division for the Week Ending 30th September, No. 43, 30 September 1920, V Ontario, OBU Convention," in *RCMP Security Bulletins: The Early Years, 1919-1929*, 176.

64 Ibid.

65 *One Big Union Monthly* (hereafter *OBUM*), May 1919, 7 and 13.

66 Ibid., 7.

67 Ibid.

68 Ibid., 7 and 8.

69 Ibid., 8.

70 Ibid., 10.

71 Ibid.

72 Ibid., July 1919, 13.

73 Ibid., September 1919, 13.

74 Ibid., April 1920, 14.

75 Ivan Avakumovic, *The Communist Party in Canada: A History* (Toronto: McClelland and Stewart, 1975), 14; Avery, *"Dangerous Foreigners,"* 86-89; and William Rodney, *Soldiers of the International: A History of the Communist Party of Canada, 1919-1929* (Toronto: University of Toronto Press, 1968), 25-27.

76 AO, OPP, Series E, E30, Campbell to Major J.E. Rogers, Superintendent of Provincial Police, 18 December 1919. The strike, it appears, never materialized and, despite the best attempts of the police, the OBU remained highly active in Northwestern Ontario, particularly in the lumber camps formerly organized by A.T. Hill and the IWW around Fort Frances and elsewhere in the Port Arthur district, such as Ignace. See *Le Travailleur/The Worker* (Montreal), 15 May and 15 June 1920. In Fort Frances, much of the radical activity could be found in the Shelvin Clark Lumber Mill.

77 AO, Fred E. Moore fonds (hereafter FEM), MV2160, F1274, E.J. McMurray to Fred E. Moore, 29 January 1920.

78 Ibid., Mrs. Zura to Hon. the Minister of Justice, 4 August 1920. The specific works in his possession included: *Novyi Svit 1918, The Russian Workers' Union, Rabotchy, Narod, Nove Evangelie, Russian Social Revolutionist, Rovitnyk, Khller Volja, Vsemrny Soyuse,* and twelve copies of an unnamed IWW publication. See *FWDTJ* and *PANC,* 29 September 1919.

79 *FWDTJ,* 25 October 1919.

80 AO, FEM, E.J. McMurray to Fred E. Moore, 29 January 1920. Eventually released, Zura and her child were destitute, with no means of support. They had to rely on what was granted from the City Relief Committee to survive. See ibid., Mrs. Zura to Hon. the Minister of Justice, 4 August 1920.

81 *OBUB,* 29 November 1919, 4.

82 *OBUM,* January 1920, 58.

83 Ibid., May 1919, 8.

84 *Le Travailleur/The Worker,* 15 June 1920.

85 See ibid., 1 July 1920, for some responses to E. Maki's 15 July article.

86 Ibid., 1 September 1920.

87 Disagreements at the February convention of lumber workers in the Port Arthur district, for example, had led to a referendum on the issue and a break from the Vancouver headquarters in March. See Radforth, *Bushworkers and Bosses,* 118. The Winnipeg Central Labour Council, for example, discussed the issue of industrial versus geographic organization, and the issue of the lumber workers' fee, in earnest in August. See PAM, RBR, 15, "Special Meeting of Central Labour Council," 31 August 1920.

88 *FWDTJ,* 22 and 24 September 1920, and *PANC,* 20, 21, and 22, September 1920.

89 Royal Canadian Mounted Police, "Notes of the Work of the CIB Division for the Week Ending 30th September," 175-76.

90 For overviews of the convention, see Robin, *Radical Politics and Canadian Labour,* 193; Bercuson, *Fools and Wise Men,* 166-69; and Logan, *Trade Unions in Canada,* 327-29. See also Royal Canadian Mounted Police, "Notes of the Work of the CIB Division for the Week Ending 14 October, No. 45, 14 October 1920," in *RCMP Security Bulletins,* 207-13; "Notes of the Work of the CIB Division for the Week Ending 2nd September, No. 39, 2 September 1920," in *RCMP Security Bulletins,* 81; and "Notes of the Work of the CIB Division for the Week Ending 23rd September, No. 42, 23 September 1920," 92-93, 94-95, and 143.

91 For an overview of Winch's life and career, see Peter Campbell, *Canadian Marxists and the Search for the Third Way* (Montreal and Kingston: McGill-Queen's University Press, 1999), 31-72.

92 Avery, *"Dangerous Foreigners,"* 119; Royal Canadian Mounted Police, "Notes of the Work of the CIB Division for the Week Ending 2nd September," 82.

93 Bercuson, *Fools and Wise Men,* 167.

94 For more on the activities of the IWW in Canada before the First World War, see Mark Leier, *Where the Fraser River Flows: The Industrial Workers of the World in British Columbia* (Vancouver: New Star Books, 1990).

95 See Avery, *"Dangerous Foreigners,"* 119. The question of the nature of the One Big Union had been formally discussed as early as January 1920 in Winnipeg. See One Big Union, *What Is the OBU? Constitution and Laws Amended at Winnipeg Convention, January 1920* (Vancouver: OBU, 1920; Ottawa: Canadian Institute for Historical Microreproductions, CIHM/ICMH series 65198, 1997).

96 Bercuson, *Fools and Wise Men,* 166-67.

97 Avery, *"Dangerous Foreigners,"* 119.

98 *OBUB,* 19 February 1921, 4. For detailed discussions of the convention, see 2 October 1920. The Convention Credentials Committee's report can also be found at LAC, Communist Party of Canada fonds (hereafter CPC), MG28-IV4, vol. 51, File 90.

99 See *OBUB,* 2 October 1920, 1; and PAM, RBR, 15, "Meeting of Central Labour Council," 15 June 1920.

100 *OBUB,* 2 October 1920, 1. Carl Berg, the Labour Council of Edmonton delegate, was the only non-LWIU representative to accompany them (although he was also a member of the LWIU).

101 For an alternative perspective, see Bercuson, *Fools and Wise Men,* ch. 6.

102 Radforth, *Bushworkers and Bosses,* 118. During the CLC's annual election of officers in December, many of the leadership, such as J. Dixon, declined to run again. See *OBUB,* 8 January 1921, 3.

103 *OBUB,* 6 November 1920, 3.

104 *Le Travailleur/The Worker,* 15 November 1920.

105 *OBUB,* 6 November 1920, 3.

106 *Le Travailleur/The Worker,* 15 November 1920. Those unemployed included F.W. Sykes, the financial secretary of the Central Labour Council, and F.W.M. Eamer, the recording secretary of the council. This was exacerbated by the decision of the CPR in late November to reduce its staff by 40 percent.

107 On the second Thursday of every month, meetings were held in the Finlayson Street Labour Hall in Fort William, and on the fourth Thursday of every month in the Port Arthur Finnish Labour Temple at 314 Bay Street.

108 *OBUB,* 23 October 1920, 1.

109 For example, see *British Columbia Federationist,* 15 October 1920, and *OBUB,* 30 October 1920, 2, for a response by F. Woodward.

110 *OBUB,* 13 November 1920, 4.

111 Ibid., 27 November 1920, 1; 25 December 1920, 2; and 15 January 1921, 3.

112 Ibid., 13 November 1920, 4, and 27 November 1920, 1.

113 Ibid., 4 December 1920, 3.

114 Ibid., 13 November 1920, 4.

115 Ibid., 11 December 1920, 4.

116 Ibid., 4 December 1920, 3.

117 The District Executive Committee results were: William Brown, 147; Hugo Morrell, 145; Edward Stanley, 143; and J. Jaakkola, 130. See also ibid., 19 February 1921, 2. Results for the position of secretary-treasurer were Richard Lockhead, 144; Harry A. Bryan, 54; and Adam Beck, 16.

118 LAC, CSIS, vol. 2, File 1025-9-9019, RCMP "Investigation Committee," 2.

119 *Le Travailleur/The Worker,* 15 December 1920.

120 *OBUM,* December 1920, 41.

121 *OBUB,* 18 December 1920, 1.

122 See, for example, a report in ibid., 25 December 1920, 3.

123 Bryan was often also accompanied by other members of the Port Arthur District LWIU. During the Fort Frances LWIU convention in December 1920, he was accompanied, for instance, by John Ursin. See *OBUB,* January 1921, 3.

124 See LAC, CPC, MG28-IV4, vol. 52, File 21, Jakka Toivar to Dad, 8 July 1921.

125 A.T. Hill, "Highlights of Labour History – Lakehead and Canada" (unpublished manuscript, c. 1973), 1.

126 Organized in both the United States and Canada in 1921, the TUEL was created to spearhead action among the trade unions in the hopes of compelling the American Federation of Labor to pursue more militant policies. See Tom McEwen, *The Forge Glows Red: From Blacksmith to Revolutionary* (Toronto: Progress Books, 1974), 138-41.

127 Midgley referred to the lumber workers as "a mass of undigested syndicalist propaganda," and, according to David Bercuson, "predicted the Lumber Workers' experiment would fail because 'an effective working class organization cannot recognise divisions of either craft or industry.'" See Bercuson, *Fools and Wise Men,* 169. His source for this quotation is PAM, OBU, Midgley circular letter, 2 February 1921.

128 See, for example, *OBUB*, 19 March 1921, 1, and 26 March 1921, 4.

129 Radforth, *Bushworkers and Bosses*, 118; Bercuson, *Fools and Wise Men*, 169; *OBUB*, 20 March, 17 April, 1 October, and 6 November 1920; and *Le Travailleur/The Worker*, 1 July and 1 October 1920.

130 Warrian, "The Challenge of the One Big Union Movement in Canada," 103.

131 *OBUM*, December 1920, 41.

132 J.W. Ahlqvist and A.T. Hill, cited in Pilli, *The Finnish-Language Press in Canada*, 138.

133 Charles Lipton, *The Trade Union Movement of Canada, 1827-1959* (Montreal: Canadian Social Publications, 1966), 220.

134 Many of the OBU's leadership, including R.B. Russell, attended the founding convention of the Communist Party of Canada even if they eventually did not support the new organization. See Warrian, "The Challenge of the One Big Union Movement in Canada," 103-4.

135 Logan, *Trade Unions in Canada*, 328. For information on the OBU's role in the freight handlers' strike in 1922, see *OBUB*, 24 August, 31 August, and 7 September 1922; and *PANC* and *FWDTJ*, 22 August to 8 September 1922.

CHAPTER 4: "INTO THE MASSES!"

1 Ian Angus, *Canadian Bolsheviks: The Early Years of the Communist Party of Canada* (Montreal: Vanguard, 1981), 76. See also Ian McKay, *Rebels, Reds, Radicals: Rethinking Canada's Left History* (Toronto: Between the Lines Press, 2005), 155-69.

2 For discussions of this period, see Ian Angus, *Canadian Bolsheviks: The Early Years of the Communist Party of Canada*, 2nd ed. (Vancouver: Trafford Publishing, 2004), 2-166; John Manley, "Communism and the Canadian Working Class during the Great Depression: The Workers' Unity League, 1930-1936" (PhD dissertation, Dalhousie University, 1984), 1-62; and William Rodney, *Soldiers of the International: A History of the Communist Party of Canada, 1919-1929* (Toronto: University of Toronto Press, 1968). For more on the period internationally, see Geoff Eley, *Forging Democracy: The History of the Left in Europe, 1850-2000* (New York: Oxford University Press, 2002), 152-65; François Furet, *The Passing of an Illusion: The Idea of Communism in the Twentieth Century*, trans. Deborah Furet (Chicago: University of Chicago Press, 1999); Robert Service, *Comrades! A History of World Communism* (Cambridge, MA: Harvard University Press, 2007), 49-50.

3 V.I. Lenin, *Left-Wing Communism: An Infantile Disorder* (Moscow: Foreign Languages Publishing House, 1952). In particular, see ch. 6.

4 E.H. Carr, *The Russian Revolution from Lenin to Stalin, 1917-1929*, with a new introduction by R.W. Davis (New York: Palgrave Macmillan, 2004), 16.

5 F. Borkenau, *World Communism: A History of the Communist International* (Ann Arbor: University of Michigan Press, 1962), 168; Milorad M. Drachkovitch, ed., *The Revolutionary Internationals, 1864-1943* (Palo Alto, CA: Stanford University Press, 1966), 162; and Peter Kivisto, *Immigrant Socialists in the United States: The Case of Finns and the Left* (Rutherford, NJ: Fairleigh Dickinson University Press; Cranbury, NJ: Associated University Presses, 1984), 68-69. For more on the Third World Congress, see J.L. Black, *Canada in the Soviet Mirror: Ideology and Perception in Soviet Foreign Affairs* (Ottawa: Carleton University Press, 1998), 31-32; Borkenau, *World Communism*, 221; and Tim Rees and Andrew Thorpe, eds., *International Communism and the Communist International, 1919-1943* (Manchester, UK: Manchester University Press, 1998), 3-4.

6 Norman Penner, *Canadian Communism: The Stalin Years and Beyond* (Toronto: Methuen, 1988), 272.

7 Donald Avery, *"Dangerous Foreigners": European Immigrant Workers and Labour Radicalism in Canada, 1896-1932* (Toronto: McClelland and Stewart, 1979), 68. See also Donald Avery, "Ethnic Loyalties and the Proletarian Revolution: A Case Study of Communist Political Activity in Winnipeg, 1923-1936," in *Ethnicity, Power and Politics in Canada*, ed. Jorgen Dahlie and Tissa Fernando (Toronto: Methuen, 1981), 71; Penner, ibid., 272; and Rodney, *Soldiers of the International*, 41.

8 See Auvo Kostiainen, *The Forging of Finnish-American Communism, 1917-1924: A Study in Ethnic Radicalism* (Turku, Finland: Turun Yliopisto, 1978), 191; and Ivan Avakumovic, *The Communist Party in Canada: A History* (Toronto: McClelland and Stewart, 1975), 35.

9 For more on Lenin's trade union policy, see Lenin's *Collected Works*, 2nd English ed., vol. 33 (Moscow: Progress Publishers, 1965), 188-96.

10 For more on syndicalism in France, see Duncan Gaillie, *Social Inequality and Class Radicalism in France and Britain* (Cambridge: Cambridge University Press, 1983), 189-204; Jeremy Jennings, *Syndicalism in France: A Study of Ideas* (New York: Palgrave Macmillan, 1990); F.F. Ridley, *Revolutionary Syndicalism in France: The Direct Action of Its Time* (Cambridge: Cambridge University Press, 1970); P. Stearns, *Revolutionary Syndicalism and French Labor: A Cause without Rebels* (New Brunswick, NJ: Rutgers University Press, 1971).

11 Gary Jewell, "The History of the IWW in Canada," *Our Generation* 11, 3 (1976): 40.

12 Contrary to popular lore, this was not the first attempt to form a Communist party. Between 1919 and 1922, a number of organizations operated in Canada purporting to be Communist in either name or actions. None, however, was affiliated with the Communist International, formed in March 1919. The Anglo-American Colonial Group of the Comintern, for example, recognized that an illegal Communist party with an auxiliary legal body known as the "Canadian Labour Alliance" was at work in Canada in 1921. For the early attempts, see Library and Archives Canada (hereafter LAC), Communist International fonds (hereafter CI), MG10-K3, Reel 3 [K-271], 495, 98, 1, Report of Organizer Atwood to the American Agency of the Communist International," 18 April 1921; Angus, *Canadian Bolsheviks* (2004); Rodney, *Soldiers of the International*, 31-36; and Tim Buck, *Thirty Years: 1922-1952: The Story of the Communist Movement in Canada* (Toronto: Progress Books, 1952), 21.

13 Hill was not alone in his gravitation towards the Communist movement. As Donald Avery argues, over the course of the first few years of the WPC, many of the country's leading socialist activists joined. See Avery, *"Dangerous Foreigners,"* 119.

14 Lakehead University Archives (hereafter LUA), *Canadan Teollisuusunionistinen Kannatus Liitto* fonds (hereafter CTKL), MG10, Series D, 8, 10, "A.T. Hill Biography," n.d., 13.

15 A.T. Hill, "Highlights of Labour History – Lakehead, Canada and World" (unpublished manuscript, c. 1973), 3; and LUA, ibid., 13-14. See also LAC, Canadian Security Intelligence Service fonds (hereafter CSIS), RG146, vol. 21, File [1025-9-9019] 92-A-00099, pt. 2, 018-019, 027-028, and 039-040; Ahti Tolvanen, *Finntown: A Perspective on Urban Integration. Port Arthur Finns in the Inter-war Period: 1918-1939* (Helsinki: University of Helsinki, 1985), 30; and Ravio Yrjö, *Kanadan Suomalaisten Historia*, vol. 1 (Sudbury: n.p., 1979), 464-82.

16 LAC, CI, Reel 3, [K-271], 495, 98, 4, 47, "CEC Minutes," 9 December 1921; and O.W. Kuusinen, letter to the Communist Party of Canada, 28 December 1921, cited in *Canada's Party of Socialism: History of the Communist Party of Canada, 1921-1976* (Toronto: Progress Books, 1982), 18. For the Winnipeg council's reaction to the formation of the CPC, see Provincial Archives of Manitoba (hereafter PAM), Robert Boyd Russell Collection (hereafter RBR), MG10, A14-2, 17, "Special Meeting of Central Labour Council," 14 November 1922. See also 10-13.

17 For Angus's discussion of the underground party, see *Canadian Bolsheviks* (2004), 89-93.

18 *Canada's Party of Socialism*, 19-20. In particular, this was in keeping with Lenin's twenty-one conditions for entry into the Communist International. See V.I. Lenin, *Collected Works*, vol. 31 (Moscow: Foreign Languages Publishing House, 1960-70), 206-12. According to William Rodney, this distinction was actually meaningless as the underground party was the driving force and made all the decisions for the legal party. See Rodney, *Soldiers of the International*, 53-54.

19 Manley, "Communism and the Canadian Working Class," 6.

20 Ibid., 9.

21 David Frank, *J.B. McLachlan: A Biography* (Toronto: James Lorimer, 1999), 252. For more on the founding of the CPC, see Angus, *Canadian Bolsheviks* (2004), 2-119; Penner, *Canadian Communism,* 44-69; and Rodney, *Soldiers of the International,* 28-40.

22 Rodney, ibid., 41.

23 Ibid.

24 Ibid., 42-44.

25 This also applied to the CPC's leadership during its first decade. For example, John MacDonald had been heavily involved with the Independent Labour Party in Ontario and William Moriarty with the Socialist Party of Canada, Maurice Spector was on the executive of the SDPC, and A.T. Hill was a leading member of the Industrial Workers of the World in Canada. A number of officials had also been involved in a variety of socialist organizations in Europe. Interestingly, aside from MacDonald and Tim Buck, none of the early leadership had much actual experience in the trade union movement. See Avakumovic, *The Communist Party in Canada,* 11.

26 Letter, O.W. Kuusinen to the Communist Party of Canada, 28 December 1921, cited in *Canada's Party of Socialism,* 18.

27 For material on meetings of the Anglo-American Secretariat dealing with Canada, see LAC, CI, Reel 1, [K-269], 495, 72, 1-176; Avakumovic, *The Communist Party in Canada,* 23; Black, *Canada in the Soviet Mirror,* 32; and Robert C. Tucker, "The Emergence of Stalin's Foreign Policy," *Slavic Review* 36, 4 (December 1977): 571.

28 See LAC, CI, ibid.; and Rodney, *Soldiers of the International,* 61.

29 "Decisions and Activities of the Central Executive Committee of the Communist Party of Canada," June-July 1921, cited in *Canada's Party of Socialism,* 20. See also 18-20. According to Ian Angus, the conference was composed of 63 delegates (43 from Ontario, 16 from western Canada, 5 from Quebec, and a host of fraternal delegates from organizations such as the Finnish and Ukrainian language groups). See Angus, *Canadian Bolsheviks* (2004), 88-89.

30 Ian Angus, "A Party of a New Type, the Socialist Party of Canada and the Birth of Canadian Communism," *Marxism: A Socialist Annual* 4 (2006): 66.

31 For the Socialist Party of Canada's role, see Angus, ibid., 66-73, and *Canadian Bolsheviks;* and Rodney, *Soldiers of the International,* 37-39.

32 *Canada's Party of Socialism,* 18. English-speaking members were not considered to form a language group despite being numerically one of the smallest groups from the beginning. In fact, at times during the next ten years, paid English-language members would have been hard-pressed to meet the minimum requirement for the formation of a section.

33 LUA, Thunder Bay Finnish-Canadian Historical Society Collection (hereafter TBFCHS), MG8, A, I, 3, 3, A.T. Hill, "All People Should Accept the Truth and Reject Lies and Misrepresentations," n.d. (c. 1970), 7; Avakumovic, *The Communist Party in Canada,* 27; and Rodney, *Soldiers of the International,* 51. A.T. Hill and John Ahlqvist (both former residents of the Lakehead) were in Guelph during the meeting. Whereas Ahlqvist actually participated, Hill remained with John Slup, future treasurer and office manager of the Communist Party of Finland, in a restaurant not too far away, no doubt discussing the way in which the new social order would be brought into existence. Hill and Slup remained in more or less constant contact until Hill's death. See Hill, ibid.

34 See Ian Radforth, *Bushworkers and Bosses: Logging in Northern Ontario, 1900-1980* (Toronto: University of Toronto Press, 1987), 110, 120, and 123-26.

35 See LAC, Finnish Association (*Suomalainen Osasto*) of Port Arthur fonds (hereafter SOP), MG28-V137, *Suomalainen Osasto* of Port Arthur Minute Book, 80, 18 January 1920 to 15 November 1921, 80-129 for the early years of this relationship. See also Arja Pilli, *The Finnish-Language Press in Canada, 1901-1939: A Study in Ethnic Journalism* (Turku, Finland: Institute for Migration Studies, 1982), 138-39.

36 For the quotation, see Manley, "Communism and the Canadian Working Class," 14. For a discussion of the TUEL and its activities, see Angus, *Canadian Bolsheviks* (2004), 104-5, 118-22, 159-60, 163-64, and 253-59; Manley, ibid., 14-16.

37 Paul Yuzyk, *Ukrainians in Manitoba: A Social History* (Toronto: University of Toronto Press, 1953), 99; and Michael H. Marunchak, *The Ukrainian Canadians: A History* (Winnipeg and Ottawa: Ukrainian Free Academy of Science, 1970), 403-5. For more on the ULFTA and its relationship with the CPC, see Angus, *Canadian Bolsheviks* (2004), 276-80 and 285-86.

38 Avery, *"Dangerous Foreigners,"* 79 and 120-21.

39 A. Ernest Epp, "The Achievement of Community," in *Thunder Bay: From Rivalry to Unity,* ed. Thorold J. Tronrud and A. Ernest Epp (Thunder Bay: Thunder Bay Historical Museum Society, 1995), 196. For more on the Workers' Benevolent Association, see Marunchak, *The Ukrainian Canadians,* 403-7; John Kolasky, *The Shattered Illusion: The History of Pro-Communist Organizations in Canada* (Toronto: PMA Books, 1979), 1-26; and Orest T. Martynowych, *Ukrainians in Canada: The Formative Period, 1891-1924* (Edmonton: Canadian Institute of Ukrainian Studies Press, 1991), 496-501.

40 Workers' Benevolent Association of Canada, *Friends in Need: The WBA Story, a Canadian Epic in Fraternalism* (Winnipeg: Workers' Benevolent Association of Canada, 1972), 101-2.

41 Angus, *Canadian Bolsheviks* (1981), 75.

42 For the impact of the WPC's formation on other socialist organizations, see Avery, *"Dangerous Foreigners,"* 116-17, 119; Penner, *Canadian Communism,* 66-67; and Paul W. Fox, "Early Socialism in Canada," in *The Political Process in Canada,* ed. J.H. Aitchison (Toronto: University of Toronto Press, 1963), 97.

43 Pilli, *The Finnish-Language Press in Canada,* 142. For an in-depth discussion of Finnish-American Communism, see Auvo Kostiainen, *The Forging of Finnish-American Communism, 1917-1924: A Study of Ethnic Radicalism* (Turku, Finland: Turun Yliopisto, 1978).

44 *One Big Union Bulletin* (hereafter *OBUB*), 4 December 1920, 3.

45 Radforth, *Bushworkers and Bosses,* 120.

46 The relatively little organization occurring in Ontario is evident in correspondence between Tim Buck and LWIUC head J.M. Clarke in April 1923. See Radforth, ibid.; A.T. Hill, "Highlights of Labour History – Lakehead and Canada" (unpublished manuscript, c. 1973), and "Highlights of Labour History – Lakehead, Canada and World" (unpublished manuscript, c. 1973); and Douglas Thur, "Beat around the Bush: The Lumber and Sawmill Workers Union and the New Political Economy of Labour in Northern Ontario, 1936-1988" (MA thesis, Lakehead University, 1990), 39.

47 Organized in both the United States and Canada in 1921, the TUEL was created to spearhead action among the trade unions in hopes of compelling the American Federation of Labor to pursue more militant policies. See Tom McEwen, *The Forge Glows Red: From Blacksmith to Revolutionary* (Toronto: Progress Books, 1974), 138-41.

48 LAC, CI, Reel 3 [K-271], 495, 98, 4, 22, "Minutes of CEC Meeting," 5 August 1921. For more on the CPC reports to the Comintern about the OBU during this period, see Reel 3 [K-271], 495, 98, 6, 12, William Moriarty, "Report on Canada," August 1922.

49 LUA, TBFCHS, Series B, 7, 1, I3, 2.

50 LUA, Jean Morrison Labour History Collection (hereafter JMLHC), GS186a, Tape 5, Harry Bryan Reminiscences, 1972.

51 LAC, CI, MG3-K3, Reel 3 [K-271], 495, 98, 4, 18, "CEC Minutes of the CPC," 3 July 1921, 3. District 2 consisted of Manitoba, Alberta, and Ontario west of Fort William. This included many of the small Finnish communities such as Finland, Ontario, and larger centres within the influence of Port Arthur and Fort William, such as Fort Frances. District 3 consisted of branches in Ontario between Fort William and Ottawa.

52 See ibid., 495, 98, 4, 109, "To Presidium of the Executive Committee of the Comintern," August 1922, and 495, 98, 3, 6. These numbers, though, are not entirely accurate. The total number of Ukrainian members in Fort William is derived from estimates, as the party had received no definite figure. In several cases, figures received from district and local organizers did not match. Figures given by district organizers were used more often, but in the case of those reporting Finnish members, the figures of their bureaus were used according to the documents consulted, as they reported members in several places not previously reported in both District 2 and District 3.

53 *Worker,* 15 March 1922; and Rodney, *Soldiers of the International,* 51. See also Information Access Section, Canadian Security Intelligence Service, File 88-A-25, "Political Activities, Maurice Spector." Accessed at the office of the Access to Information and Privacy Co-ordinator, Solicitor General of Canada, Ottawa: "Re – Workers Party of Canada – Morris Spector – Tour through Western Canada. Port Arthur, Ont. 31 May 1923." I would like to thank Ian McKay for providing this information.

54 Kolasky, *The Shattered Illusion,* 115. See *Ukrainski Robitnychi Visti,* 18 March 1922. M. Popowich, I. Navizivsky, V.N. Kolisnyk, M. Shatulsky, and D. Lobay were put in charge of organizing the Ukrainian section of the WPC. Elected as delegates to the WPC convention were I. Hlady, J. Zradowsky, I. Boychuk, I. Hobatiuk, I. Lilitsak, R. Komar, S. Prokopa, I. Marchak, Gelych, and Kachala. See also John Kolsky, ed. and trans., *Prophets and Proletarians: Documents on the History of the Rise and Decline of Ukrainian Communism in Canada* (Edmonton: Canadian Institute of Ukrainian Studies Press and University of Alberta, 1990), 114.

55 Kolasky, ibid., 115.

56 Ibid., 113.

57 LUA, JMLHC, Tape 6, Interview with Mike Cosmishin, 1972.

58 LAC, Communist Party of Canada fonds (hereafter CPC), MG28-IV4, Reel M-7376, 1A 0003, [unclear], "To All Party Branches and Members," c. 1922 [date unclear].

59 Ibid., 1A 0004-0005, J. MacDonald and W. Moriarty, "To Branches of the W.P. of C.," c. 1922.

60 Ibid.

61 LAC, CI, Reel 3 [K-271], 495, 98, 3, "The Communist Party of Canada Brief sent by A. Kent to President of Comintern," 15 August 1922.

62 Ibid., 495, 98, 6, 12, William Moriarty, Report on Canada, August 1922.

63 Ibid., 495, 98, 3, 19, "The Communist Party of Canada, Brief sent by A. Kent to President of Comintern," 15 August 1922, 4; and 495, 98, 3, 34, Report to Presidium, August 1922, 6.

64 Rodney, *Soldiers of the International,* 55 and 68.

65 LAC, CPC, Reel M-7376, 1A 0008, "General Instructions to Districts for Guidance in Municipal Elections," 25 September 1922.

66 Ibid.

67 *Worker,* 1 and 15 December 1922.

68 Ibid., 15 March 1923.

69 Ibid.

70 Radforth, *Bushworkers and Bosses,* 120; and J. Peter Campbell, "The Cult of Spontaneity: Finnish-Canadian Bushworkers and the Industrial Workers of the World in Northern Ontario, 1919-1934," *Labour/Le Travail* 41 (1998): 133-34. This occurred despite the fact that a referendum on the issue was not going to be held until December 1923.

71 LAC, CI, Reel 3 [K-270], 495, 98, 9, "Report of the Second Annual Convention of the Workers' Party of Canada (22 February 1923)," 3 April 1923; and *Worker,* 15 March 1923.

72 Ibid., Reel 4 [K-271], 495, 98, 13, 7, and 11, "Report of the Proceedings of the Second Annual Convention of the Workers' Party of Canada, 22-25 February 1923." For a discussion of the convention, see also Rodney, *Soldiers of the International,* 54-55.

73 LAC, CI, ibid., 495, 98, 13.

74 Rodney, *Soldiers of the International*, 69.

75 LAC, SOP, *Suomalainen Osasto* of Port Arthur Minute Book, 30 March 1923.

76 Information Access Section, Canadian Security Intelligence Service, File 88-A-25, "Political Activities, Maurice Spector." Accessed at the office of the Access to Information and Privacy Co-ordinator, Solicitor General of Canada, Ottawa: "Re – Workers Party of Canada – Morris Spector – Tour through Western Canada. Port Arthur, Ont. 31 May 1923." I would like to thank Ian McKay for providing this information.

77 Jean Morrison, "The Organization of Labour at Thunder Bay," in *Thunder Bay: From Rivalry to Unity*, 133. For more on early Communist attacks on the One Big Union, see "OBU Bulletin and Industrial Unionism," *Worker*, 1 August 1922.

78 City of Thunder Bay Archives (hereafter TBA), Fort William fonds (hereafter FWF), Series 4: Fort William City Clerk's Files (hereafter FWCCF), File 209, H.P. Hansen, Secretary, Building Trades Unit to the OBU Fort William to Mayor of the City of Fort William and members of the City Council, 28 February 1923.

79 LAC, CI, Reel 4 [K-271], 495, 98, 14, 10, "Minutes of the CEC Meeting," 24 March 1923 and "Minutes of the CEC Meeting," 27 June 1923; *Worker*, 8 December 1923. Very little is actually known about the activities of Italian Communists at the Lakehead. Due to the stigma and repression they experienced during the First World War, most Italian workers in the twin cities preferred to keep within their ethnically based fraternal organizations. Often nationalistic and cultural in orientation, such organizations were dedicated to showing patriotism to Canada. As a result, the *bandiera rosa*, as they were often called, were "marginalized and considered to be nuisances as they had 'funny ideas.'" See John Potestio, *The Italians of Thunder Bay* (Thunder Bay: Chair of Italian Studies, Lakehead University, 2005), 88-89, fn. 32. For a first-hand recollection of the activities of Italian Communists in Port Arthur, see Penny Petrone, *Breaking the Mould* (Toronto: Guernica, 2001), 87.

80 *Worker*, 20 June 1923.

81 LAC, CI, Reel 4 [K-272], 495, 98, 14, 39, "Report of Enlarged Session of the Central Executive Committee of the Workers' Party of Canada, Edmonton," 26 September 1923, and 495, 98, 14, 39, 51, "Workers Party of Canada – Minutes," 24 November 1923. Hill reported at the November meeting that the Finnish section of the WPC now had approximately 2,600 members nationally.

82 For examples of the discussions, see LAC, SOP, *Suomalainen Osasto* of Port Arthur Minute Book, 13 and 30 March 1923.

83 See Edward W. Laine, "The Finnish Organization of Canada, 1923-1940, and the Development of Finnish Canadian Culture," *Polyphony* 3, 2 (Fall 1981): 81-90.

84 Rodney, *Soldiers of the International*, 81-89; Pilli, *The Finnish-Language Press in Canada*, 139-40; Michael Karni, "Struggle on the Cooperative Front: The Separation of Central Cooperative Wholesale from Communism, 1929-1930," in *The Finnish Experience in the Western Great Lakes Region: New Perspectives*, ed. Michael G. Karni, Matti E. Kaups, and Douglas Ollila Jr. (Turku, Finland: Institute for Migration Studies, 1975), 230-39; and Auvo Kostiainen, "The Finns and the Crisis over 'Bolshevization' in the Workers' Party, 1924-1925," in *The Finnish Experience in the Western Great Lakes Region*, 171-85.

85 Avery, *"Dangerous Foreigners,"* 122.

86 *Fort William Daily Times-Journal* (hereafter *FWDTJ*), 7 April 1923; and Workers' Benevolent Association of Canada, *Friends in Need*, 102-4; A.W. Rasporich, "Ethnicity in Lakehead Politics, 1900-1930," *Polyphony* 9, 2 (1987): 63; and "Twin City Ethnopolitics: Urban Rivalry, Ethnic Radicalism and Assimilation in the Lakehead," *Urban History Review* 18, 3 (February 1990): 216. As the work of Donald Avery has indicated, this situation was paralleled in Winnipeg and other areas of western Canada where vibrant and active Ukrainian cultural societies existed before the establishment of the ULFTA. Donald Avery, "Ethnic Loyalties and Proletarian Revolution: A Case Study of Communist Political Activity in Winnipeg, 1923-1936," in *Ethnicity, Power and Politics in*

Canada, ed., Jorgen Dahlie and Tissa Fernando (Toronto: Methuen, 1918), 71. The factionalism within the local Ukrainian community received considerable attention in the local press. See, for example, *Port Arthur News-Chronicle* (hereafter *PANC*), 28 March 1923 and 12 January 1924.

87 *FWDTJ*, 7 April 1923, and *Worker*, 12 January 1924.

88 Epp, "The Achievement of Community," 196.

89 Workers' Benevolent Association of Canada, *Friends in Need*, 102-4; and Rasporich, "Twin City Ethnopolitics," 216.

90 LUA, TBFCHS, B, 7, 1, I3, 2, and *Worker*, 19 January 1924, 3. The early leaders of the Young Communist League were S. Lehto, J. Carlson, Lahti, Miss Hiltunen, Niemi, Miss Lukas, Mendellon, and Arnold Beck.

91 *Worker*, 9 February 1924, 3.

92 *Worker*, 16 February 1924, 4. Local newspapers downplayed the meeting, describing it as medium-sized and providing no other details. See *FWDTJ* and *PANC*, 4 and 5 February 1924.

93 *Worker*, 29 March 1924.

94 Thunder Bay Historical Museum Society (hereafter TBHMS), Finnish-Canadian Labour History Interview Project, Interview with Arvo Matson, 1979.

95 For more on the Finnish cooperative movement in Canada and the United States, see A.J. Gedick, "Working Class Radicalism among Finnish Immigrants in Minnesota and Michigan Mining Communities" (PhD dissertation, University of Wisconsin, 1979); and Mauri A. Jalava, "The Finnish-Canadian Cooperative Movement in Ontario," in *Finnish Diaspora I: Canada, South America, Africa, Australia, and Sweden*, ed. Michael G. Karni (Toronto: Multicultural History Society of Ontario, 1981), 93-100. The standard work on the cooperative movement in English Canada remains Ian MacPherson, *Each for All: A History of the Co-operative Movement in English Canada, 1900-1945* (Toronto: Macmillan, 1979). MacPherson briefly discusses Finnish and Ukrainian cooperatives on 113-15.

96 LAC, CI, Reel 4 [K-272], 495, 98, 21a, 22, "Third Convention of the Workers' Party of Canada, 18-20 April 1924." For more on the convention, see Reel 4 [K-271], 495, 98, 21a, "Bulletin – Report of Preparation for the Third National Convention of the Workers' Party of Canada, 18-20 April 1924," and 495, 98, 22, "Resolutions of the Third National Convention of the Workers' Party of Canada," c. April 1924. At the Third National Convention, the name of the party was also officially changed to the Communist Party of Canada. See LAC, CPC, Reel M-7380, 8C 0114, J. MacDonald, "Secretary's Report to the Third National Convention of the Workers' Party of Canada," 18 April 1924, 3.

97 LAC, CPC, vol. 11, File 11-11, "Submitted by DEC District #6 to the 3rd national Convention of W.P. of C.," c. April 1924, 1.

98 See PAM, RBR, 18, "Minutes of GEB meeting," 28 April 1924; 19, "Joint Executive Board Meeting," 12 September 1924; "Meeting of the Resident Members of the GEB," 5 May 1924; 20, "Minutes of Central Labour Council Meeting," 1 April 1924. Something similar occurred in Sudbury later in the year, when lumber workers decided to turn over all monies and property to the IWW. The Sudbury lumber workers were directed by the Winnipeg executive to instead transfer their assets to the Port Arthur branch. They ignored the directive.

99 For Russell's report of his trip to Port Arthur, see ibid., "Report of Trip to Port Arthur," c. 10 March 1924. Not all Finnish socialists were happy with this turn of events. William Arnberg, best known for his debates with A.T. Hill in the early 1920s, continued to organize on behalf of the OBU despite the increasing loss of Finns to either the IWW or the WPC/CPC. See, for example, ibid., 18, "Meeting of GEB," 6 January 1924.

100 Ibid., 21, "Minutes Winnipeg Central Labour Council Meeting," 7 December 1926. During the previous year, a couple of organizers had been sent to the region, at the expense of OBU members in the region. Requests for teachers for educational purposes were refused. For mention of these requests and those of other members for organizers, see a variety of minutes found in ibid., 22.

101 Jalava, "The Finnish-Canadian Cooperative Movement in Ontario," 84-85.
102 LUA, JMLHC, Tape 12, Interview with L. Friberg, 1972.
103 Ibid., Tape 4, Interview with Holmer Borg, 1972.
104 LAC, CSIS, vol. 2, File 1025-9-9018, pt. 2, p. 871, RCMP, "E" Division, Re: Lumber Workers Industrial Union, 24 April 1923.
105 LAC, CPC, vol. 11, File 11-11, "Submitted by DEC District #6 to the 3rd national Convention of W.P. of C.," c. April 1924, 2.
106 Ibid., 3.
107 According to William Rodney, originally Port Arthur and Fort William resided in the newly formed District 5 (Port Arthur-Kenora). Shortly after, however, District 5 was reorganized to include the region surrounding Sudbury and Sault Ste. Marie, and the Lakehead formed the nucleus of District 6. See Rodney, *Soldiers of the International,* 84 and 188, cf. 11.
108 Avakumovic, *The Communist Party in Canada,* 33.
109 Rodney, *Soldiers of the International,* 55; Avakumovic, *The Communist Party in Canada,* 31.
110 Rodney, ibid., 64-65.
111 LAC, CPC, Reel M-7380, 8C 0112, J. MacDonald, "Secretary's Report to the Third National Convention of the Workers' Party of Canada," 18 April 1924, 1.
112 Ibid.
113 *Worker*, 17 May 1924.
114 Ibid., 17 May 1924; *PANC,* 1 May 1924.
115 *Worker*, 14 and 21 June 1924. This may have been the same organization attributed by Captain E.M. MacBrayne to the One Big Union and whose formation he blamed on "outside agitators from Winnipeg." See LAC, Department of External Affairs (hereafter DEA), RG25, vol. 2669, Captain E.M. MacBrayne, Military District No. 10, "Report: Labour Unrest at Port Arthur, Ontario," 16 June 1924, quoted in Tolvanen, *Finntown,* 57.
116 Tolvanen, ibid., 74.
117 LAC, CI, Reel 4 [K-272], 495, 68, 21, 41, "Communist Party of Canada – Minutes of the CEC," 7 December 1924.
118 Gary Jewell, *The History of the IWW in Canada* (Chicago: Industrial Workers of the World, 1975), 2-3.
119 LAC, DEA, vol., 2669, Captain E.M. MacBrayne, Military District No. 10, "Report: Labour Unrest at Port Arthur, Ontario," 16 June 1924, quoted in Tolvanen, *Finntown,* 56.
120 *Worker,* 1 November 1924.

CHAPTER 5: BOLSHEVIZATION AND THE REORGANIZATION OF THE LAKEHEAD LEFT, 1925-27

1 Ian Angus, *Canadian Bolsheviks: The Early Years of the Communist Party of Canada* (Montreal: Vanguard, 1981), 154.
2 Robert C. Tucker, "The Emergence of Stalin's Foreign Policy," *Slavic Review* 36, 4 (December 1977): 570.
3 Norman Penner, *Canadian Communism: The Stalin Years and Beyond* (Toronto: Methuen, 1988), 73.
4 See John Manley, "Communism and the Canadian Working Class during the Great Depression: The Workers' Unity League, 1930-1936" (PhD dissertation, Dalhousie University, 1984), 27. For more on this period, see 62-93 and Penner, ibid., 89. Bolshevization preceded the accession to power of Joseph Stalin, but he undoubtedly refined and radicalized the doctrine. The most notable use of Stalin's policy of Bolshevization to alter the structure of the Russian Communist Party and the Comintern is seen in his attacks on and eventual expulsion of Leon Trotsky and his followers. See, for example, E.H. Carr, *Socialism in One Country. Vol. 3: 1924-1926* (London: Macmillan, 1964); Geoff Eley, *Forging Democracy: The History of the Left in Europe, 1850-2000* (New York: Oxford

University Press, 2002), 235-60; Robert Service, *Comrades! A History of World Communism* (Cambridge, MA: Harvard University Press, 2007), 97-153; and the relevant sections of Albert Glotzer, *Trotsky: Memoir and Critique* (Buffalo: Prometheus Books, 1989).

5 For the situation within the American Communist movement, see Theodore Draper, *American Communism and Soviet Russia: The Formative Period* (New York: Viking Press, 1960); and Harvey Klehr and John Earl Haynes, *The American Communist Movement: Storming Heaven Itself* (New York: Twayne Publishers, 1992).

6 Interestingly, although Stalin and his proponents supported Bolshevization, the United Front continued for some time. See, for example, J.L. Black, *Canada in the Soviet Mirror: Ideology and Perception in Soviet Foreign Affairs* (Ottawa: Carleton University Press, 1998), 48.

7 William Rodney, *Soldiers of the International: A History of the Communist Party of Canada, 1919-1929* (Toronto: University of Toronto Press, 1968), 81.

8 This was a concern especially for the Finns as they comprised over 60 percent of the party's membership. With the addition of Ukrainian members and their organizations, "foreign-born" workers accounted for over 90 percent of the party's membership. See Ivan Avakumovic, *The Communist Party in Canada: A History* (Toronto: McClelland and Stewart, 1975), 35; and Donald Avery, *"Dangerous Foreigners": European Immigrant Workers and Labour Radicalism in Canada, 1896-1932* (Toronto: McClelland and Stewart, 1979), 116. For the situation in the United States, see Auvo Kostiainen, "The Finns and the Crisis over 'Bolshevization' in the Workers' Party, 1924-25," in *The Finnish Experience in the Western Great Lakes Region: New Perspectives*, ed. Michael Karni, Matti E. Kaups, and Douglas J. Ollila Jr. (Turku, Finland: Institute for Migration Studies, 1975), 174.

9 Rodney, *Soldiers of the International*, 82-84.

10 Draper, *American Communism*, 154 and 159.

11 Some historians have challenged Draper's position. See, for example, Hugh Wilford, "The Communist International and the American Communist Party," in *International Communism and the Communist International, 1919-43*, ed. Tim Rees and Andrew Thorpe (Manchester, UK: Manchester University Press, 1998); and Auvo Kostiainen, *The Forging of Finnish-American Communism, 1917-1924: A Study in Ethnic Radicalism* (Turku, Finland: Turun Yliopisto, 1978).

12 Draper, *American Communism*, 159. See also Rodney, *Soldiers of the International*, 95; and Avery, *"Dangerous Foreigners,"* 128.

13 Kostiainen, "The Finns and the Crisis Over 'Bolshevization' in the Workers' Party," 172.

14 *Worker*, 30 March 1929, and *Canada's Party of Socialism: History of the Communist Party of Canada, 1921-1976* (Toronto: Progress Books, 1982), 57.

15 Avakumovic, *The Communist Party in Canada*, 38; Avery, *"Dangerous Foreigners,"* 129; Kostiainen, "The Finns and the Crisis Over 'Bolshevization' in the Workers' Party," 174-75; and Rodney, *Soldiers of the International*, 81-84. For American opposition, especially those led by William Z. Foster, consult Draper, *American Communism*, 158; and Edward P. Johanningsmeier, *Forging American Communism: The Life of William Z. Foster* (Princeton, NJ: Princeton University Press, 1994), 221-25.

16 Avery, *"Dangerous Foreigners,"* 116.

17 *Worker*, 14 February 1925.

18 Ibid., 21 February 1925.

19 Ibid., 30 May 1925. Moore's lead role in these events is somewhat puzzling. It remains unknown whether he was actually a member of the Communist Party of Canada or, as in the past, a supporter of all working-class initiatives in the region.

20 *Fort William Daily Times-Journal* (hereafter *FWDTJ*) and *Port Arthur News-Chronicle* (hereafter *PANC*), 14 May and 19 May 1919.

21 Margaret Hobbs and Joan Sangster, eds., *The Woman Worker, 1926-1929* (St. John's: Canadian Committee on Labour History, 1999), 9. For a discussion of the involvement of women within the

Communist Party of Canada, see ibid., 7-13; Joan Sangster, *Dreams of Equality: Women on the Canadian Left, 1920-1950* (Toronto: McClelland and Stewart, 1989), 26-90; and Joan Sangster, "The Communist Party and the Woman Question, 1922-1929," *Labour/Le Travail* 15 (Spring 1985): 25-56.

22 For more on the organization of Finnish domestic servants, see Varpu Lindström, *Defiant Sisters: A Social History of Finnish Immigrant Women in Canada,* 2nd ed. (Beaverton, ON: Aspasia Books, 2003).

23 *Worker,* 23 May 1925 and 30 May 1930. As late as 1923, Moore was still a member of the Thunder Bay Central Council. While little information has been found on the council's activities between late 1922 and 1925, Winnipeg Central Labour Council minutes reveal that he was still involved. See, for example, Provincial Archives of Manitoba (hereafter PAM), Robert Boyd Russell fonds (hereafter RBR), MG10, A14-2, 18, "Minutes of meeting of the GEB," 14 September 1923.

24 Ahti Tolvanen, *Finntown: A Perspective on Urban Integration. Port Arthur Finns in the Inter-war Period: 1918-1939* (Helsinki: University of Helsinki, 1985), 51-52; and A.T. Hill, "Historic Basis and Development of the Lumber Workers Organization and Struggle in Ontario," unpublished manuscript, Northern Studies Resource Centre, Lakehead University (c. 1952), 7.

25 *Industrial Pioneer,* July 1925, 5; and November 1925, 29. For reports of increased activity in Montreal, Calgary, Saskatchewan, British Columbia, Timmins, Nova Scotia, and South Porcupine, see *Industrial Unionist,* 25 April; 13 June; 4 and 18 July; 1, 8, 15, 22, and 29 August; 5, 12, 16, and 30 September; 7 October; 4, 18, and 25 November; 9 and 16 December 1925; and 27 January 1926.

26 Lakehead University Archives (hereafter LUA), Jean Morrison Labour History Collection (hereafter JMLHC), GS186a, Tape 4, Interview with Holmer Borg, 1972. See also *Industrial Unionist,* 29 August 1925. For more on the activities of the LWIUC and the LWIU during the 1925-26 logging season, see Ian Radforth, *Bushworkers and Bosses: Logging in Northern Ontario, 1900-1980* (Toronto: University of Toronto Press, 1987), 120-21; and J. Peter Campbell, "The Cult of Spontaneity: Finnish-Canadian Bushworkers and the Industrial Workers of the World in Northern Ontario, 1919-1934," *Labour/Le Travail* 41 (Spring 1998): 134-39.

27 See, for example, *Industrial Unionist,* 12 September 1925.

28 *Worker,* 17 October 1925.

29 Jean Morrison, "The Organization of Labour at Thunder Bay," in *Thunder Bay: From Rivalry to Unity,* ed. Thorold J. Tronrud and A. Ernest Epp (Thunder Bay: Thunder Bay Historical Museum Society, 1995), 133-34. See also *FWDTJ,* 26 October 1919.

30 LUA, JMLHC, Tape 7, Interview with George Andrew Cotter, 1972.

31 *PANC,* 24 and 26 October 1925. The quotations used are from 26 October. Just before the election, Smith made a last appeal to the working class in the riding. See *PANC,* 18 October 1925. No labour or Communist candidate ran in the Fort William–Kenora riding.

32 Parliament of Canada, "History of Federal Ridings since 1867," http://www.parl.gc.ca/information/about/process/house/hfer/hfer.asp?Language=E&Search=Gres&genElection=15&ridProvince=9&submit1=Search; and *PANC,* 30 October 1925. The newspaper reported his total as 1,353. Smith's results clearly show that his strength lay in the city of Port Arthur. He garnered 775 within the city, but only 576 in the rural areas. In Dorion, Smith polled 39 votes, compared with 40 for Langworthy, 41 for Mathews, and 13 for Carrick.

33 *FWDTJ,* 30 October 1925; LUA, JMLHC, Tape 7, Interview with George Andrew Cotter; A.W. Rasporich, "Twin City Ethnopolitics: Urban Rivalry, Ethnic Radicalism and Assimilation in the Lakehead," *Urban History Review/Revue d'histoire urbaine* 18, 3 (February 1990): 65; and Mary Veltri, "Labour Radicalism among Finnish Bushworkers at the Lakehead, 1916-1936" (Honours thesis, Lakehead University, 1981), 58.

34 *FWDTJ* and *PANC,* 30 October 1925; LUA, JMLHC, ibid.; A.W. Rasporich, "Ethnicity in Lakehead Politics, 1900-1930," *Polyphony* 9, 2 (1987): 65; and Veltri, ibid., 58.

35 Smith lost by one vote in two urban polls in the Bay Street area. The rural polls he won included McIntyre, Nakina, and Hydro. Significantly, the Finnish vote played a decisive role. See *FWDTJ*, 30 October 1925; and Tolvanen, *Finntown*, 105-6.

36 Radforth, *Bushworkers and Bosses*, 120-21.

37 Avery, *"Dangerous Foreigners,"* 116.

38 *Young Worker*, April 1925, 2.

39 *Worker*, 20 February 1926.

40 Ibid., 27 February 1926.

41 Library and Archives Canada (LAC), Communist International fonds (hereafter CI), MG10-K3, Reel 6 [K-274], 495, 98, 40, 9, "Minutes of the Organization Committee of the C.P. of C.," 20 April 1926; *Worker*, 15 May 1926; and *PANC*, 1 May 1926.

42 See, for example, *Worker*, 17 July 1926.

43 *PANC*, 1 May 1926.

44 *Worker*, 15 May 1926.

45 For commentary on the Fifth Convention, see Melvin Leonard Pelt, "The Communist Party of Canada, 1929-1942" (MA thesis, University of Toronto, 1964), 28.

46 Tim Buck, *Thirty Years: 1922-1952: The Story of the Communist Movement in Canada* (Toronto: Progress Books, 1952), 58.

47 Avery, *"Dangerous Foreigners,"* 129; and Veltri, "Labour Radicalism among Finnish Bushworkers at the Lakehead," 80. For Hill, see LAC, CI, Reel 6 [K-274], 495, 98, 40, 37, "Report of Enlarged Session of the Central Executive Committee of the Workers' Party of Canada," 24-26 September 1926.

48 LAC, CI, Reel 6 [K-274], 495, 98, 40, 43, "Communist Party of Canada, Minutes of the CEC," 31 September 1926.

49 *Worker*, 21 August 1926; *FWDTJ*, 27 August 1926; *PANC*, 11 and 25 August 1926; and Royal Canadian Mounted Police, "Weekly Summary, Notes Regarding Revolutionary Organizations and Agitators in Canada Report, No. 333, 2 September 1926," in *RCMP Security Bulletins: The Early Years, 1919-1929*, ed. Gregory S. Kealey and Reg Whitaker (St. John's: Canadian Committee on Labour History, 1994), 345.

50 Ian Angus, *Canadian Bolsheviks: The Early Years of the Communist Party of Canada*, 2nd ed. (Vancouver: Trafford Publishing, 2004), 95. For overviews, see 20-21, 95-100, and 164-65; Avakumovic, *The Communist Party in Canada*, 51-53, 67, 102; and Martin Robin, *Radical Politics and Canadian Labour, 1880-1930* (Kingston: Industrial Relations Centre, 1968), 119-37 and 237-67.

51 Avakumovic, ibid., 51.

52 Ibid., 52.

53 Angus, *Canadian Bolsheviks* (2004), 21.

54 A.T. Hill, "Highlights of Labour History – Lakehead and Canada" (unpublished manuscript, c. 1973), 5.

55 Tolvanen, *Finntown*, 31.

56 *PANC*, 17 September 1926.

57 Radforth, *Bushworkers and Bosses*, 123.

58 *FWDTJ*, 6 October 1926. Interestingly, the strikers, according to Bryan, were not asking for the recognition of their unions. Hautamäki and James Dixon, general secretary of the Trades and Labour Council of the Thunder Bay District, made it very clear that the strike had nothing to do with the One Big Union. See *PANC*, 17 September 1926.

59 LAC, Department of Labour (hereafter DL), RG27, vol. 337, Strike 76, Alf Hautamäki to Department of Labour, 29 November 1926. The initial numbers reported were 1,300 men and 15 women. For coverage of the strike, see *Worker*, 2, 16, 23, and 30 October 1926; and *Industrial Solidarity*, 6 October 1926. See also Avery, *"Dangerous Foreigners,"* 124.

60 *FWDTJ*, 6 October 1926.

61 *Worker,* 13 November 1926.

62 *Metsätyöläinen* 5 (1926): 12 and 20.

63 See Avery, *"Dangerous Foreigners,"* 124-25. Reports of strikebreakers being imported can be found in *FWDTJ* and *PANC,* 22 October 1926. Finnish cooperatives also played a pivotal role. Throughout the strike, they made meals for workers and sold them at cost, with the LWIUC and LWIU paying half the cost for each worker. The Communist *Tarmo* and IWW *Hoito* fed the bulk of those workers within Port Arthur and Fort William. See *Worker,* 16 and 28 October 1926; *Industrial Solidarity,* 6 October 1926; and *One Big Union Bulletin* (hereafter *OBUB*), 4 October 1926.

64 LAC, CI, Reel 6 [K-274], 495, 98, 40, "Minutes of the Organization Committee of the C.P. of C. held 13 April," 9 May 1926.

65 Campbell, "The Cult of Spontaneity," 135.

66 See Hill, "Historic Basis and Development of the Lumber Workers Organization and Struggle in Ontario."

67 *Worker,* 16 October 1926.

68 *PANC,* 29 October 1926.

69 Tolvanen, *Finntown,* 52-53; and *PANC,* 4 November 1926.

70 LAC, DL, vol. 337, Strike 76, A.E. Grant, Correspondent *Labour Gazette* to Department of Labour, 11 December 1926.

71 Radforth, *Bushworkers and Bosses,* 123.

72 Archives of Ontario (hereafter AO), Fred E. Moore fonds (hereafter FEM), F1274, "Election Announcement," c. 1926.

73 Ibid. For more on the origins of the Canadian Labour Defence League, see J. Petryshyn, "Class Conflict and Civil Liberties: The Origins and Activities of the Canadian Labour Defence League, 1925-1940," *Labour/Le Travail* 10 (Autumn 1982): 39-64.

74 *Toronto Star,* 25 April 1925; and *Edmonton Forum,* 21 June 1925.

75 Bruce Muirhead, "Harry Bryan, a Man of Fanatical Conviction," Thunder Bay Historical Museum Society *Papers and Records* 17 (1989): 42; and LUA, JMLHC, Tape 5, Harry Bryan Reminiscences, 1972.

76 *Worker,* 4 September 1926.

77 Ibid., 11 September 1926; and *PANC,* 8, 9, and 13 September 1926.

78 Parliament of Canada, "History of Federal Ridings since 1867." For federal election results between 1917 and 1940, see Roy Piovesana, *Robert J. Manion: Member of Parliament for Fort William, 1917-1935* (Thunder Bay: Thunder Bay Historical Museum Society, 1990), 33-34. For the returns for each poll in the Port Arthur-Thunder Bay riding, see *PANC,* 15 September 1926. Within the city of Port Arthur, Smith's total was 831. See *PANC,* 24 September 1926.

79 *FWDTJ,* 20 October 1926.

80 AO, FEM, W.N. Welsh to the Electors of the Fort William Constituency, 14 September 1926; and Parliament of Canada, "History of Federal Ridings since 1867."

81 *Worker,* 20 November 1926.

82 LAC, Communist Party of Canada fonds (hereafter CPC), MG28-IV4, vol. 143, File 6, "Lumber Workers Industrial Union of Canada Annual Report March 8, 1926 to March 5, 1927," 5 March 1927, 2-3.

83 *Worker,* 27 November 1926.

84 Ibid., 13 November 1926.

85 *Industrial Solidarity,* 14 July 1926; Campbell, "The Cult of Spontaneity," 135; and Tolvanen, *Finntown,* 56-57. Nick Viita became general secretary and E.M. Jouppi the editor for the local branch.

86 For a summary of Wobbly activity in Vancouver during the first few months of 1926, see LAC, CI, Reel 6 [K-274], 495, 98, 40, "Minutes of the Organization Committee of the C.P. of C. held 13 April," 9 May 1926.

87 LUA, JMLHC, Tape 4, Interview with Holmer Borg, 1972.

88 Avery, *"Dangerous Foreigners,"* 53.

89 *Worker*, 13 November 1926. See also LAC, CPC, vol. 143, File 6, "Lumber Workers Industrial Union of Canada, Annual Report March 8, 1926 to March 5, 1927," 5 March 1927.

90 *Industrial Solidarity,* 6 October 1926.

91 LUA, *Canadan Teollisuusunionistinen Kannatus Liitto* fonds (hereafter CTKL), MG10, F, 15, 10, "Lumber Workers Organize Camp Committees in Every Camp."

92 See LAC, DL, vol. 338, Strike 87, Reverse of a Report to Harold G. Garner, *Labour Gazette,* from unknown.

93 *FWDTJ,* 6 October 1926.

94 *Industrial Solidarity,* 6 October 1926.

95 Campbell, "The Cult of Spontaneity," 130; and Royal Canadian Mounted Police, "Weekly Summary, Notes Regarding Revolutionary Organizations and Agitators in Canada Report, No. 334, 9 September 1926," in *RCMP Security Bulletins: The Early Years,* 356.

96 LAC, CI, Reel 1 [K-269], 495, 72, 21, 5, "Report of Comrade Tim Buck to the National Secretary of America and Canada," 12 January 1927, 3; and 495, 72, 34, 50, "Report of the Communist Party of Canada for the Period of 1927," 6 March 1928, 11.

97 For commentary on the reorganization of the party, see, for example, *Worker,* 25 December 1926 and 26 March 1927.

98 LAC, CI, Reel 1 [K-269], 495, 72, 21, 5, "Report of Comrade Tim Buck," 3; and 495, 72, 34, 50, "Report of the Communist Party of Canada for the Period of 1927," 11.

99 Ibid.

100 Ibid., 495, 72, 21, 5, "Report of Comrade Tim Buck," 1. See also Reel 6 [K-274] 495, 98, 49, 1-13.

101 Ibid., 495, 72, 34, 50, "Report of the Communist Party of Canada for the Period of 1927," 5. This report is also found on Reel 6 [K-274] 495, 98, 49, 11 and 14-22.

102 *Worker,* 26 March 1927; and LAC, Department of Citizenship and Immigration (hereafter DCI), RG76, vol. 219, File 95027, List of Fort William Finnish Members c. 1927-28. This item also contains lists for Fort Frances, Port Arthur, South Porcupine, Timmins, Porcupine, Nipigon, and Port Arthur. In Northern Ontario, branches could be found in Port Arthur, Nipigon, Sault Ste. Marie, Beaver Lake, Wanup, Cobalt, Rosegrove, Kirkland Lake, Connaught Station, Pottsville, South Porcupine, and Timmins.

103 Edwin Suksi interviewed by Lennard Sillanpaa, Multicultural History Society of Ontario, Oral History Collection, 1977, quoted in Radforth, *Bushworkers and Bosses,* 122.

104 LAC, CPC, Reel M-7378, 5B 0458, Beckie Buhay to Harry Bryan, 19 April; and *Worker,* 16 April 1927.

105 *Worker,* 16 April 1927.

106 LUA, JMLHC, Tape 5, Harry Bryan Reminiscences, 1972.

107 Having organized the Finnish Women's Federation, among the Finnish women in Port Arthur, Sanna Kannasto spent 1927-28 in Sudbury, organizing women in the nickel district. See Lempi (Makela) Maki, "Activities of the Women of the Labouring Class in the Nickel District," n.d., originally published in *Suomalaiset Nikkelialuella* (n.p., 1937) and translated into English by Mr. V. Rinne. My source for this document is the Shebandowan Films research files for the National Film Board of Canada's *Letters from Karelia* (2004).

108 *Young Worker,* December 1927, 3.

109 *Worker,* 4 June 1927.

110 LAC, CPC, Reel M-7378, 5B 0464, Michael Biniowsky to the *Worker,* 11 February 1927; and 5B 0473, George Eleudiuk, Secretary, Ukrainian Agitprop of Fort William, to Business Manager of the *Worker,* 11 April 1927. The Ukrainian Agitprop operated out of an office located at 612½ Simpson Street.

111 LUA, CTKL, F, 14, 25, Port Arthur "Branch News Letter," 1 April 1927; *Worker*, 4 June 1927.

112 LAC, CPC, vol. 143, File 6, "Lumber Workers Industrial Union of Canada Annual Report March 8, 1926 to March 5, 1927," 5 March 1927, 3. See also Campbell, "The Cult of Spontaneity," 135.

113 LUA, CTKL, F, 14, 25, Port Arthur "Branch News Letter," 1 April 1927.

114 Ibid., Ed Peterson [?], Secretary-Treasurer, LWIU No. 120, IWW, to Thomas Hill, 25 June, 1 July, 11 July, and 17 October 1927; and By-Laws Committee to the Members, LWIU No. 120, IWW, 18 April 1927.

115 Ibid., Ed Peterson [?], Secretary-Treasurer, LWIU No. 120, IWW, to Thomas Hill, 22 and 24 October 1927.

116 Ibid., F, 14, 17, "Regular IU 120 of the IWW Port Arthur Branch Business Meeting," 2 May 1927; and F, 15, 4, "Regular Business Meeting of LWIU 120 Port Arthur," 1 March 1931.

117 LAC, CPC, Reel M-7380, 8C 0092, "DEC No. 6 CP Minutes of Meeting Held on Dec. 13th 1927."

118 In December 1927, this included Biniowsky, Stenrees, Kari, Neimi, Stolberg, Antila, A. McLeod, and Lewis. See ibid.

119 Ibid., Reel M-7380, reverse of 7B 2033, "Canadian Labour Defence League," 16 December 1927. For his efforts, Fred Moore was appointed by the CPC as the local CLDL's secretary pro tempore.

120 Total union membership (25 of 28 branches reporting) was 1,673 in Fort William and 1,643 in Port Arthur (22 of 27 branches reporting). See ibid., 7B 1892, "Trade Unionists Increase: Report Issued by Department of Labour Shows Gain in Membership in Canada in 1928," 2.

CHAPTER 6: TURNING TO THE LEFT, 1928-30

1 See John Manley, "Communism and the Canadian Working Class during the Great Depression: The Workers' Unity League, 1930-1936" (PhD dissertation, Dalhousie University, 1984), 94-157.

2 Tim Rees and Andrew Thorpe, "Introduction," in *International Communism and the Communist International, 1919-1943*, ed. Tim Rees and Andrew Thorpe (Manchester, UK: Manchester University Press, 1998), 4. See also Geoff Eley, *Forging Democracy: The History of the Left in Europe, 1850-2000* (New York: Oxford University Press, 2002), 249-61.

3 See Ivan Avakumovic, *The Communist Party in Canada: A History* (Toronto: McClelland and Stewart, 1975), 54.

4 For more on the Third Period, see John Manley, "Canadian Communists, Revolutionary Unionism, and the 'Third Period': The Workers' Unity League, 1929-1935," *Journal of the Canadian Historical Association*, New Series 5 (1994): 167-91; and John McIlroy and Alan Campbell, "'Nina Ponomareva's Hats': The New Revisionism, the Communist International, and the Communist Party of Great Britain, 1920-1930," *Labour/Le Travail* 49 (Spring 2002): 147-88.

5 Ian Angus, *Canadian Bolsheviks: The Early Years of the Communist Party of Canada*, 2nd ed. (Vancouver: Trafford Publishing, 2004), 233.

6 Ian McKay, *Rebels, Reds, Radicals: Rethinking Canada's Left History* (Toronto: Between the Lines Press, 2005), 157.

7 *Canada's Party of Socialism: History of the Communist Party of Canada, 1921-1976* (Toronto: Progress Books, 1982), 29; Ian Angus, *Canadian Bolsheviks: The Early Years of the Communist Party of Canada* (Montreal: Vanguard Publications, 1981), 199; and Manley, "Communism and the Canadian Working Class during the Great Depression," 41.

8 Library and Archives Canada (hereafter LAC), Communist Party of Canada fonds (hereafter CPC), MG28-IV4, Reel M-7370, 1A0066, no title, and 1A0088, no title, signed A. Skarra. For example, of the thirteen members of the District 6 Trade Union Department, only three were not Finnish or Ukrainian. In 1929, the District 6 Trade Union Department included the following: A. McLeod (Port Arthur), A. Skarra (Port Arthur), J. Carey (Port Arthur), A. Hautamäki (Port Arthur), J. Chepusiak (Fort William), Steve Manaryk (Fort William), W. Perunuk (Fort William), A. Gibson

(Fort William), M. Benouski (Fort William), G. Sonquist (Port Arthur), N. Law (Fort William), William Boyce (Fort William), and B. Nicolaichuk (Port Arthur).

9 J. Donald Wilson, "Matti Kurikka and A.B. Mäkelä: Socialist Thought among Finns in Canada, 1900-1932," *Canadian Ethnic Studies* 10, 2 (1978): 17.

10 William Rodney, *Soldiers of the International: A History of the Communist Party of Canada, 1919-1929* (Toronto: University of Toronto Press, 1968), 115-16.

11 LAC, Communist International fonds (hereafter CI), MG10-K3, Reel 1 [K-269], 495, 72, 34, 78, "Meeting of the Anglo-American Secretariat," 23 April 1928, 1.

12 Ibid., 495, 72, 34, 86, "Draft Letter to the Communist Party of Canada," n.d., c. 23 April 1928, 2. This letter went through several drafts until it was eventually sent. I have used the material from the initial draft, unless otherwise indicated, that did not differ from the final copy. The reason is pragmatic; it was clearer than some of the others.

13 Ibid., 495, 72, 34, 88, "Draft Letter to the Communist Party of Canada," c. 23 April 1928, 4.

14 Ibid., 495, 72, 34, 91, "Draft Letter to the Communist Party of Canada," c. 23 April 1928, 7.

15 Ibid., 8.

16 Ibid., 495, 72, 34, 107, "Draft Resolution of Decision of the Canadian Question," c. 23 April 1928, 3.

17 *Worker,* 26 May 1928.

18 Ibid., 30 June and 14 July 1928.

19 For an overview of the Young Pioneers and radical summer camps, see Paul C. Mishler, *Raising Reds: The Young Pioneers, Radical Summer Camps, and Communist Political Culture in the United States* (New York: Columbia University Press, 1999).

20 See, for instance, *Young Worker,* March 1928, April 1928, and May 1929.

21 George Gault to Colquhoun, 2 January 1928; unsigned to unsigned, Finland, Ontario, 19 April 1928, quoted in A.W. Rasporich, "Ethnicity in Lakehead Politics, 1900-1930," *Polyphony* 9, 2 (1987): 65; and "Twin City Ethnopolitics: Urban Rivalry, Ethnic Radicalism and Assimilation in the Lakehead," *Urban History Review* 18, 3 (February 199): 216.

22 J. Donald Wilson and Jorgen Dahlie, "Introduction," *Canadian Ethnic Studies* 10, 2 (1978): 4; and Mauri Amiko Jalava, "'Radicalism or a "New Deal"?' The Unfolding World View of the Finnish Immigrants in Sudbury, 1883-1932" (MA thesis, Laurentian University, 1983), 61.

23 Jalava, ibid., 61; and Michael H. Marunchak, *The Ukrainian Canadians: A History* (Winnipeg and Ottawa: Ukrainian Free Academy of Sciences, 1970), 405.

24 Lakehead University Archives (hereafter LUA), *Canadan Teollisuusunionistinen Kannatus Liitto* fonds (hereafter CTKL), MG10, F, 14, 30, "Minutes of Eighth Semi-Annual Ontario District Conference of the Lumber Workers IU of the IWW," 1 April 1928.

25 Ibid., F, 14, 20, J.D. Golden Resolution dated 30 March 1927 to "Sixth Semi-Annual Ontario District Conference of Lumber Workers Industrial Union #120 of the IWW," 3 April 1927.

26 Ibid., F, 14, 31, "Minutes of the LWIU of the IWW Ninth Ontario District Conference," 7 October 1928.

27 Ibid., F, 14, 6, "Mass Conference of the IWW Members at Vancouver, BC," 27 December 1925.

28 See an assortment of branch minutes in ibid., F, 14, 19 and F, 14, 10, "Minutes of Ontario District Conference of IU 120, IWW," 26 December 1926.

29 Ibid., F, 14, 31, "Minutes of the LWIU of the IWW Ninth Ontario District Conference," 7 October 1928. See also F, 14, 30, Dave Dubé, Camp #5, Dean Lake, Ontario to IU 120 Conference, Port Arthur, 1 April 1928, and "Minutes of Eighth Semi-Annual Ontario District Conference of the Lumber Workers IU of the IWW," 1 April 1928.

30 Ibid., F, 14, 30, J.D. Golden, Resolution No. 2 to LWIU Conference, 1 April 1928, and "Minutes of Eighth Semi-Annual Ontario District Conference of the Lumber Workers IU of the IWW," 1 April 1928.

31 Ibid., E, 10, 5, "Minutes of the Regular General Membership Meeting," 18 August 1929, 1-2.

32 LAC, CPC, Reel M-7380, 8C 0136, "Synopsis of Proceedings of Enlarged Executive Meeting," 20-22 October 1928, 5.

33 Ibid., 8C 0140, "Synopsis of Proceedings of Enlarged Executive Meeting," 20-22 October 1928, 9.

34 Ibid., 8C 0158, "Resolution of Communist International on the Question of Communist Workers in the Ukrainian Workers' Organizations in Canada," c. October 1928, 1.

35 Ibid., 8C 0154, "Synopsis of Proceedings of Enlarged Executive Meeting," 20-22 October 1928," 24.

36 Ibid., 8C 0158, "Resolution of Communist International on the Question of Communist Workers in the Ukrainian Workers' Organizations in Canada," c. October 1928, 1.

37 Ibid.

38 Ibid., 8C 0159, "Resolution of Communist International on the Question of Communist Workers in the Ukrainian Workers' Organizations in Canada," c. October 1928, 2.

39 *Worker,* 23 March 1929.

40 LAC, CPC, Reel M-7376, 1A 0111, "Report of Fifth Convention of the Lumber Workers Industrial Union of Canada," 6-8 April 1929, 1.

41 *Worker,* 27 April 1929.

42 LAC, CPC, Reel M-7376, 1A 0111, "Report of Fifth Convention of the Lumber Workers Industrial Union of Canada," 6-8 April 1929, 2.

43 Ibid., 1A 0112, "Report of Fifth Convention of the Lumber Workers Industrial Union of Canada," 6-8 April 1929, 3.

44 Ibid., 1A 0113, "Report of Fifth Convention of the Lumber Workers Industrial Union of Canada," 6-8 April 1929, 3 and 4.

45 Ibid., 1A 0115, "Report of Fifth Convention of the Lumber Workers Industrial Union of Canada," 6-8 April 1929, 6.

46 Ibid., 1A 0120, George Sundqvist to Tim Buck, 21 April 1929. In addition to questions regarding Hautamäki's leadership of the LWIU, he also faced personal criticism. For example, a motion was presented that he be disciplined "on the matter of drink, and censured." See ibid., Reel M-7380, 8C 0170, "Minutes of Joint Meeting of the Trade Union Department of the CEC – CP of Canada, with Party Fraction of the LWIU of Canada," 3 April 1929.

47 Ibid., Reel M-7376, 1A 0144, H.M. to Tom [Hill], 15 January 1929.

48 Ibid., 1A 0121, A. Hautamäki to Tim Buck, 9 July 1929.

49 Ibid., 1A 0120, G. Sundqvist to Tim Buck, 21 April 1929.

50 Ibid., 1A 0121, Alf Hautamäki to Tim Buck, 9 July 1929.

51 LUA, CTKL, F, 14, 44, Ed Peterson, Secretary-Treasurer LWIU 120, to J.D. Golden, 26 March 1929.

52 LAC, CPC, Reel M-7380, 8C 0170, "Minutes of Joint Meeting of the Trade Union Department of the CEC – CP of Canada, with Party Fraction of the LWIU of Canada," 3 April 1929. Reflecting the ethnic composition of the district membership, Harry Bryan, Michael Biniowsky, and Alf Hautamäki represented District 6 at the convention. Unfortunately, no reports or additional information dealing with either Bryan or Biniowsky have been located.

53 Ibid., Reel M-7376, 8C 0384, A. Hautamäki, "Discussion on Ewan's Report," c. 31 May to 7 June 1929, 13.

54 Ibid., 8C 0314, Matthew Popovich, "General Review of Work of Ukrainian Labour Temple and Fraction Bureau," c. 31 May to 7 June 1929, 8.

55 Ibid.

56 Ibid., 8C 0334, J. Carey, "Discussion T. Buck's Report," c. 31 May to 7 June 1929. See also 8C 0317, Mikhalenki, "Sub-Report on Fraction Buros and Preparation for Convention," c. 31 May 1929, 3.

57 Ibid., 8C 0384, A. Hautamäki, "Discussion on Ewan's Report," c. 31 May to 7 June 1929, 13.

58 Ibid., 8C 0385, J. Carey, "Discussion on Ewan's Report," c. 31 May to 7 June 1929, 14.

59 Ibid., 1A 0121, Alex Gibson to Tim Buck, 4 September 1929; and ibid., Reel M-7380, 8C 0394, K. Salo, "Discussion on Ewan's Report," c. 31 May to 7 June 1929, 23.

60 Ibid., Reel M-7376, 8C 0385, J. Carey, "Discussion on Ewan's Report," c. 31 May to 7 June 1929, 14.

61 Ibid., 8C 0395, K. Salo, "Discussion on Ewan's Report," c. 31 May to 7 June 1929, 24.

62 Ibid., 1A 0121, Alf Hautamäki to Tim Buck, 9 July 1929.

63 Ibid.

64 Donald Avery, *"Dangerous Foreigners": European Immigrant Workers and Labour Radicalism in Canada, 1896-1932* (Toronto: McClelland and Stewart, 1979), 129.

65 LAC, CI, Reel 10 [K-278], 495, 98, 81, 47, A.T. Hill to Political Committee, CPC, 25 August 1929; and LAC, CPC, Reel M-7380, 8C 0220 to 8C 0222, "Minutes Special Joint Meeting of the Secretariat, National Finnish Fraction Buro and Leading Members of 'Vapaus' Staff," 2 November 1930.

66 *Sudbury Star,* 30 November 1929.

67 Avakumovic, *The Communist Party in Canada,* 54-55; Melvin Leonard Pelt, "The Communist Party of Canada, 1929-1942" (MA thesis, University of Toronto, 1964), 17; Arja Pilli, *The Finnish-Language Press in Canada, 1901-1939* (Turku, Finland: Institute for Migration Studies, 1982), 162-63; and Rodney, *Soldiers of the International,* 136-46.

68 *Worker,* 16 November 1929; and Pilli, *The Finnish-Language Press in Canada,* 164-65. For more context on the situation, see Angus, *Canadian Bolsheviks* (2004), 185, 186-202, 204, and 312-19. For a general overview of Spector and Trotskyism, see Bryan D. Palmer, "Maurice Spector, James P. Cannon, and the Origins of Canadian Trotskyism," *Labour/Le Travail* 56 (Fall 2005): 91-148.

69 LAC, CPC, Reel M-7380, 8C 0220 to 8C 0222, "Minutes Special Joint Meeting of the Secretariat, National Finnish Fraction Buro and Leading Members of 'Vapaus' Staff," 2 November 1930; Lita-Rose Betcherman, *The Little Band: The Clashes between the Communists and the Political and Legal Establishment in Canada, 1928-1932* (Ottawa: Deneau Publishers, 1982), 29-41; Lita-Rose Betcherman, "Lèse Majesté: The Trial of Aaro Vaara," *Beaver* 78, 5 (October/November 1998): 12-18; and Pilli, *The Finnish-Language Press in Canada,* 174-78. For the Sudbury reaction, see *Worker,* 29 December 1928; and A.D. Gilbert, "The 1920s," in *Sudbury: Rail Town to Regional Capital,* ed. C.M. Wallace and Ashley Thomson (Toronto: Dundurn Press, 1993), 115-17.

70 For the Port Arthur and Fort William reaction, see *Worker,* 23 March 1929.

71 *Fort William Daily Times-Journal* (hereafter *FWDTJ*), 22 and 29 December 1928, 29 January and 7 March 1929; and Rasporich, "Ethnicity in Lakehead Politics," 65.

72 *Vapaus,* 8 November 1929; Avery, *"Dangerous Foreigners,"* 129-30; and Pilli, *The Finnish-Language Press in Canada,* 164-65.

73 LAC, CPC, Reel M-7380, 8C 0209, "Minutes of Political Committee," 16 November 1929, 2. The ethnic tension in the Sudbury local was apparent at an early meeting discussing the CPC's actions. One speaker at the meeting, for example, objected to the CPC CEC's attempts to have "Englishmen from other localities" attending this meeting. She did not want "impotent speakers." For more on this issue, see LAC, CI, Reel 10 [K-278], 495, 98, 81, 27, "Minutes of General Membership Meeting of Sudbury Organization, CP of C," 8 November 1929; 495, 98, 81, 34, "Notice to All District Executive Committees, Communist Party of Canada," 23 November 1929; and 495, 98, 81, 35, "Right Wing Splitters Disgrace Twelfth Anniversary of Russian Revolution and Launch Attack on CPC and CI," 18 November 1929.

74 LAC, CPC, Reel M-7380, 8C 0208, "Minutes of Political Committee," 16 November 1929, 1.

75 LAC, CI, Reel 10 [K-278], 495, 98, 81, 47, A.T. Hill to Political Committee, CPC, 25 August 1929; and John Williamson, *International Press Correspondence* 38 (9 August 1929), quoted in ibid.

76 Ibid., 495, 98, 81, 50, A.T. Hill to Political Committee, CPC, 25 August 1929, 4.

77 LAC, CPC, Reel M-7380, 8C 0209, "Minutes of Political Committee," 16 November 1929, 2. See also *Worker,* 16 and 30 November, and 7 December 1929; and *Vapaus,* 21 November 1929. For

secondary interpretations, see Pelt, "The Communist Party of Canada," 46; and Pilli, *The Finnish-Language Press in Canada,* 165.

78 *Vapaus,* 8 and 9 November 1929; Pilli, *The Finnish-Language Press in Canada,* 166.

79 LAC, CI, Reel 10 [K-278], 495, 98, 84, 43, S.C. Neil to Secretariat of CPC, 3 December 1929.

80 LAC, CPC, Reel M-7380, 8C 0257 to 8C 0268, "Report of the Sixth Convention of the Communist Party of Canada," 31 May to 7 June 1929, 1-2 and 137-38; Angus, *Canadian Bolsheviks* (2004), 222-23. For the district support of the decision, see *Worker,* 16 November 1929, and *Canada's Party of Socialism,* 59.

81 *Vapaus,* 21 November 1929; *Worker,* 30 November 1929; and Pilli, *The Finnish-Language Press in Canada,* 166-68. The CPC also received support from the Finnish bureau of the Communist Party of the United States as it broke off contact with the opposing locals, essentially leaving them isolated.

82 LAC, CI, Reel 10 [K-278], 495, 98, 84, 43, S.C. Neil to Secretariat of CPC, 3 December 1929.

83 Ibid.

84 LAC, CPC, Reel M-7377, 2A 1323, A.T. Hill to the Full Secretariat, 17 February 1931. Unlike Neil's short visit, Hill spent much of December touring the rural parts of the region and speaking to even the smallest of gatherings.

85 *Worker,* 19 and 26 October 1929.

86 Ibid., 26 October 1929.

87 *Labour Gazette* 30 (1930): 14-15. Peter Campbell has argued that the IWW took no official role during the strike, but this appears to be inaccurate. Although the CPC did little to promote their involvement, local press reports and IWW records clearly show their involvement. For Campbell's interpretation, see his "The Cult of Spontaneity: Finnish-Canadian Bushworkers and the Industrial Workers of the World in Northern Ontario, 1919-1934," *Labour/Le Travail* 41 (1998): 139. For coverage of the strike, see *Worker,* 2, 9, and 16 November 1929.

88 Archives of Ontario (hereafter AO), Attorney General of Ontario Files (hereafter AGO), RG4-32, 1929/3738, "Resolution on the Disappearance of Voutilainen and Rosvall, Two Organizers of the Lumber Workers Industrial Union, Winnipeg, Manitoba," 30 December 1929. Additional resolutions came from the ULFTA in East Kildaman, Manitoba; a mass meeting of workers from Brandon; YCL, Winnipeg; the Left Poale Zion, Winnipeg; the Polish Workers Association, Winnipeg; and the Toronto Women's Labour League.

89 Satu Repo, "Rosvall and Voutilainen: Two Union Men Who Never Died," *Labour/Le Travail* 8/9 (Autumn/Spring 1981/82): 83.

90 LAC, Department of Labour fonds (hereafter DL), RG27, vol. 344, Strike 98, Thomas Falls to Deputy Minister of Labour, 29 October 1929. For more on the "White Finns," see Chapter 3.

91 A.W. Rasporich, "Faction and Class in Modern Lakehead Politics," *Lakehead University Review* 7, 1 (Summer 1974): 43-44.

92 Repo, "Rosvall and Voutilainen," 84.

93 *Worker,* 11 January 1930.

94 Ibid., 28 December 1929.

95 *Industrial Worker,* 9 November 1930.

96 Ibid., 23 November 1930.

97 Ibid.

98 Ibid., 27 November 1930; *Worker,* 11 January 1930; and also LAC, CPC, Reel M-7382, 10C 1989, "Is the IWW to blame for the breaking up of the strike in the Port Arthur district?", n.d.

99 *Worker,* 11 January 1930.

100 See, for example, ibid., 28 December 1929, and 11 and 18 January 1930.

101 *One Big Union Bulletin,* 26 December 1929.

102 Ibid.

103 Ibid.

104 LAC, CPC, Reel M-7382, Political Secretariat ECCI [Executive Committee of the Communist International], to Central Committee, CPC, 3 October 1930.

105 Pelt, "The Communist Party of Canada," 28.

106 Avery, *"Dangerous Foreigners,"* 120.

107 Avakumovic, *The Communist Party in Canada,* 66; Pelt, "The Communist Party of Canada," 28; and Norman Penner, *Canadian Communism: The Stalin Years and Beyond* (Toronto: Methuen, 1988), 93.

108 Manley, "Communism and the Canadian Working Class during the Great Depression," 46.

109 Radforth, *Bushworkers and Bosses,* 126.

CHAPTER 7: "CLASS AGAINST CLASS"

1 Ian McKay, "For a New Kind of History: A Reconnaissance of 100 Years of Canadian Socialism," *Labour/Le Travail* 46 (Fall 2000): 95.

2 Desmond Morton with Terry Copp, *Working People: An Illustrated History of Canadian Labour* (Ottawa: Deneau and Greenburg, 1980), 139.

3 John Manley, "Communism and the Canadian Working Class during the Great Depression: The Workers' Unity League, 1903-1936" (PhD dissertation, Dalhousie University, 1984), 159.

4 A.E. Safarian, *The Canadian Economy in the Great Depression* (Toronto: McClelland and Stewart, 1970), 44.

5 For first-hand accounts of the working and living conditions in the camps, see Lakehead University Archives (hereafter LUA), Jean Morrison Labour History Collection (hereafter JMLHC), GS186a, Tape 4, Interview with Holmer Borg, 1972; Tape 14, Interview with William Holder; Tape 25 (1 and 2), Interview with Einar Nordstrom; and Tape 30, Interview with Ivar Seppala. For secondary discussions, see Ian Radforth, *Bushworkers and Bosses: Logging in Northern Ontario, 1900-1980* (Toronto: University of Toronto Press, 1987), 88-106; and Edmund W. Bradwin, *The Bunkhouse Man* (Toronto: University of Toronto Press, 1972).

6 Although established on Christmas Day 1929, the Workers' Unity League was made public only in March 1930. According to John Manley, the CPC created the WUL only on Moscow's intervention. See Library and Archives Canada (hereafter LAC), Communist Party of Canada fonds (hereafter CPC), MG28-IV4, Reel M-7382, 10C 1813 to 10C 1814, "CPC, National Trade Union Department, Minutes," 25 December 1929; and John Manley, "Moscow Rules? 'Red' Unionism and 'Class against Class' in Britain, Canada, and the United States, 1928-1935," *Labour/Le Travail* 56 (Fall 2005): 14. The most thorough study of the WUL remains Manley's "Communism and the Canadian Working Class during the Great Depression." See also the succinct version of his argument in "Canadian Communists, Revolutionary Unionism and the 'Third Period': The Workers' Unity League, 1929-1935," *Journal of the Canadian Historical Association* 5 (1994): 167-94.

7 *Canada's Party of Socialism: History of the Communist Party of Canada 1921-1976* (Toronto: Progress Books, 1982), 85. For more on Tom McEwen, see his autobiography, *The Forge Glows Red: From Blacksmith to Revolutionary* (Toronto: Progress Books, 1974). For purposes of consistency, I have opted to use the spelling of his name that he used in his autobiography. Documents from this period use a variety of spellings.

8 Ivan Avakumovic, *The Communist Party in Canada: A History* (Toronto: McClelland and Stewart, 1975), 71 and 94; and Leslie Morris, *The Story of Tim Buck's Party, 1922-1939* (Toronto: New Era Publishers, 1939), 22.

9 This assessment does not apply to Canada only. See, for example, Matthew Worley, *Class against Class: The Communist Party in Britain between the Wars* (London: I.B. Tauris, 2002). Membership in the party during the first years of the Depression dropped from a reported 2,900 paid members in 1929 to only 1,400 in 1931. Total membership (both paying and non-paying socialists who claimed

party affiliation) has been estimated at between 4,000 and 5,000. See Avakumovic, ibid., 66; Melvin Leonard Pelt, "The Communist Party of Canada, 1929-1942" (MA thesis, University of Toronto, 1964), 85; and Arja Pilli, *The Finnish-Language Press in Canada, 1901-1939: A Study in Ethnic Journalism* (Turku, Finland: Institute for Migration Studies, 1982), 179-80.

10 Manley, "Moscow Rules?" 9.

11 Avakumovic, *The Communist Party in Canada*, 54.

12 Thunder Bay Historical Museum Society (hereafter TBHMS), City of Fort William fonds (hereafter CFW), G3/4/18, Mayor, Fort William, to Ralph H. Webb, Mayor of Winnipeg, 1 April 1931. Although no statistics on Port Arthur have been located, it is safe to assume that a similar situation existed when one considers the higher number of Finnish bushworkers in that city. For more information on Canada's response to immigrants during the Great Depression, see Donald Avery, *"Dangerous Foreigners": European Immigrant Workers and Labour Radicalism in Canada, 1896-1932* (Toronto: McClelland and Stewart, 1979), 116-41; and *Reluctant Host: Canada's Response to Immigrant Workers, 1896-1994* (Toronto: McClelland and Stewart, 1995), 108-25. For a general discussion of immigration policy during this period, see Ninette Kelley and Michael Trebilcock, *The Making of the Mosaic: A History of Canadian Immigration Policy* (Toronto: University of Toronto Press, 1998), 216-49.

13 TBHMS, CFW, G3/6/6, Fort William Relief Officer [names unclear] to Citizens' and Ratepayers' Unemployed Organization of Fort William, 11 December 1931. Copies of the letter were sent to the Northern Development Branch, Mr. Powers, Employment Service, and Mr. McNaughton, Fort William City Clerk.

14 See, for example, Livio Ducin, "Unrest in Algoma Lumber Camps: The Bushworkers' Strikes of 1933-1934," in *50 Years of Labour in Algoma*, ed. Livio Ducin et al. (Sault Ste. Marie: Algoma University College, 1978), 82. For more on relief strikes during the 1930s, see Carmela Patrias, *Relief Strike: Immigrant Workers and the Great Depression in Crowland, Ontario, 1930-1935* (Toronto: New Hogtown Press, 1990).

15 A number of scholars have explored the unemployed organizations during this period. For example, see Manley, "Communism and the Canadian Working Class during the Great Depression," and Gordon Hak, "The Communists and the Unemployed in the Prince George District, 1930-1935," *BC Studies* 68 (Winter 1985-86): 45-61.

16 Manley, "Communism and the Canadian Working Class during the Great Depression," 535. For an overview of the CPC's attempts to organize the unemployed, see 535-606.

17 J. Petryshyn, "R.B. Bennett and the Communists, 1930-1935," *Journal of Canadian Studies* 9, 4 (1974): 44.

18 Manley, "Communism and the Canadian Working Class during the Great Depression," 538-39.

19 LAC, CPC, Reel M-7381, 8C 0566, "Response of Com. Hautamäki," c. February 1930, 1. The IWW claimed to have organized the unemployed through its Finnish support circle members in Port Arthur, Nipigon, Sioux Lookout, Sault Ste. Marie, Hearst, and Cochrane. In addition, a General Recruiting Union #310 was operating in Port Arthur. See ibid. and LUA, *Canadan Teollisuusunionistinen Kannatus Liitto* fonds (hereafter CTKL), MG10, F, 14, 46, "Minutes of Regular IU 120 Business Meeting," 6 January 1930.

20 LAC, ibid.

21 The story surrounding the deaths of Rosvall and Voutilainen is one of the best known in Canadian labour history. For competing interpretations, see Satu Repo, "Rosvall and Voutilainen: Two Union Men Who Never Died," *Labour/ Le Travail* 8/9 (Autumn/Spring 1981-82): 79-102; and Peter Raffo, "Oral Witness versus Documentary Evidence: The Case of Rosvall and Voutilainen," Thunder Bay Historical Museum Society *Papers and Records* 29 (2001): 3-34.

22 Archives of Ontario (hereafter AO), Attorney General of Ontario Files (AGO), RG4-32, 1929/3738, Constable James Higgins to Ontario Provincial Police District 9 Headquarters, Port Arthur, Ontario, 23 April 1930; and E. Baley, Deputy Attorney General, to J.L. Cohen, 2 May 1930. The funeral of

the two men covered two miles and was attended by an estimated 5,000 to 10,000. It remains one of the largest public gatherings in the history of the Lakehead. See Repo, ibid., 95; Laurel Sefton MacDowell, "The Mysterious Deaths at Onion Lake," *Beaver* (April/May 1995): 34; and *Thunder Bay Chronicle-Journal,* 24 February 1979.

23 Raffo, "Oral Witness versus Documentary Evidence," 4.

24 *Lumber Worker,* December 1932, 5. The Canadian Labour Defence League in particular used the men to create the Canadian equivalent of the "Sacco-Vanzetti Day," for mass demonstrations against deportation. See LAC, CPC, Reel M-7383, 11C 2871, "Resolution on the Defence of Foreign Born Workers," c. 11-12 July 1930, 1; *Worker,* 28 December 1929. For a discussion of the development of the "myth," see Peter Raffo, "'Murder' in the Bush: The Making of a Modern Myth," in *Karelian Exodus: Finnish Communities in North America and Soviet Karelia during the Depression Era,* ed. Ronald Harpelle, Varpu Lindström, and Alexis Pogorelskin (Beaverton, ON: Aspasia Books, 2004), 87-104.

25 *Lumber Worker,* December 1932, 4.

26 For example, although 300 freight shed workers had organized under the WUL banner shortly after its creation, they quickly disappeared due to inadequate organizational support.

27 LAC, CPC, Reel M-7380, 8C 0385, J. Carey, "Discussion on Ewan's Report," c. 31 May to 7 June 1929, 14; and LUA, JMLHC, Tape 6, Interview with Mike Cosmishin, 1972.

28 Manley, "Communism and the Canadian Working Class during the Great Depression," 175.

29 Ibid., 167. According to the National Development Bureau's *The Industrial Survey of Port Arthur, Part One, Survey of General Conditions,* 15 December 1931, Port Arthur and Fort William combined possessed 29 unions. Membership in Port Arthur totalled 2,152 (22 of the 29 unions) and in Fort William 1,538 (24 of the 29 unions). This was out of a combined population of approximately 46,000. See National Development Bureau, Department of the Interior, *The Industrial Survey of Port Arthur, Part One, Survey of General Conditions,* 15 December 1931, 6 and 56.

30 LUA, JMLHC, Tape 6, Interview with Mike Cosmishin, 1972.

31 City of Thunder Bay Archives (hereafter TBA), Fort William fonds (hereafter FWF), Series 4: Fort William City Clerk's Files (hereafter FWCCF), vol. 124, File 209, "Communist Party Election Manifesto," c. 1930. For a breakdown of the results in Port Arthur, see *Port Arthur News-Chronicle* (hereafter *PANC*), 7 January 1930.

32 *Worker,* 26 April 1930.

33 See, for example, TBA, FWF, FWCCF, vol. 124, File 209, Leslie Howard, Secretary, Citizens' and Ratepayers' Unemployed Organization of Fort William, to Fort William Relief Committee, 24 February 1930; Leslie Howard, Secretary, Citizens' and Ratepayers' Unemployed Organization of Fort William, to Fort William Mayor and Council, 20 February 1930 and 24 February 1930. By 1932, the organization was known as the Citizens' and Ratepayers' Association of Fort William. Miscellaneous material can also be found in TBHMS, CFW, G3/6/5 and G3/6/6.

34 TBA, FWF, FWCC, 124, File 209, Unemployed Association of the Twin Cities to the Mayor and Council of the City of Fort William, 25 January 1930.

35 TBA, FWF, FWCCF, vol. 124, File 209, Unemployed Association of the Twin Cities to the Mayor of Fort William, 27 January 1930. According to the *Worker,* delegates representing the CPC, YCL, CLDL, Freight Shed Workers' Union, Musicians' Union, Finnish Organization of Fort William, Finnish Organization of Port Arthur, Finnish Organization District Executive Committee, ULFTA of Fort William, ULFTA of West Fort William, and the Port Arthur Trades and Labour Council attended the meeting. See *Worker,* 8 March 1930. A second session in March did not include the Port Arthur Trades and Labour Council as it refused to participate. See *Worker,* 29 March 1930.

36 *PANC,* 25 and 27 January 1930; and TBA, FWF, FWCCF, vol. 124, File 209, "Program of the Organized Unemployed of the Twin Cities," c. January 1930.

37 *Worker,* 15 March 1930.

38 LAC, CPC, Reel M-7381, 8C 0566, "Response of Com. Hautamäki," c. February 1930, 3.

39 LAC, Communist International (hereafter CI), MG10-K3, Reel 11 [K-279], 495, 98, 98, 10-11, "Minutes of the POLCOM Meeting," 26 March 1930, 1-2; and *Worker*, 12 April 1930.

40 LAC, ibid., 495, 98, 101, 80, "Draft Report by Tim Buck on Canadian Situation (1930) for CEC of CPC," c. 1930, 2-4.

41 Ibid., 4. In the following years, Buck would paint a picture of unanimous support by all members for party initiatives. See, for example, his *Thirty Years: 1922-1952: The Story of the Communist Movement in Canada* (Toronto: Progress Books, 1952), 69-116.

42 LAC, ibid., 4.

43 See LAC, CPC, Reel M-7380, 7B 2116 and 7B 2117, Communist Party of Canada, Central Agitation and Propaganda Department, "Party Recruiting Campaign," 1 April 1930, 2-3.

44 Ibid. The main party pamphlets listed included: "The Triumph of Socialism in the Soviet Union," "The Communist Manifesto," "The Programme of the Communist International," Lenin's "On the Road to Insurrection," "The Constitution of the Communist Party of Canada," and Lenin's "State and Revolution."

45 LAC, ibid., 7B 2120, Communist Party of Canada, Central Agitation and Propaganda Department, "Party Recruiting Campaign," 1 April 1930, 6.

46 Ibid., 7B 2115, Communist Party of Canada, Central Agitation and Propaganda Department, "Party Recruiting Campaign," 1 April 1930, 1.

47 Ibid., Reel M-7376, 1A 0449, Jim Barker to Tom Ewen, 3 April 1930. There has been a suggestion that Barker was in fact Sam Langley, who, following his arrest during May Day demonstrations in Toronto, was deported sometime in the summer of 1929. The chronology does not make sense, though. Langley was arrested in Port Arthur while walking with A.E. Smith, but the dates do not seem to add up. It is more likely that it was the summer of 1931, as Barker mysteriously disappears from the Lakehead and Communist files around this time. See Lita-Rose Betcherman, *The Little Band: The Clashes between the Communists and the Canadian Establishment 1928-1932* (Ottawa: Deneau and Greenburg, 1982), 50; *Worker*, 25 May 1929; *PANC*, 20 April 1932; and A.E. Smith, *All My Life: An Autobiography* (Toronto: Progress Books, 1977), 109.

48 "J.B. McLachlan Resigns from the Communist Party (1936), a Letter to Tim Buck, 13 June 1936," Social History Project, http://www.socialisthistory.ca/Docs/StalBirth/McLachlanResigns.htm. For more on the relationship between Barker and McLachlan, see David Frank and John Manley, "The Sad March to the Right: J.B. McLachlan's Resignation from the Communist Party of Canada, 1936," *Labour/Le Travail* 30 (Fall 1992): 132-34; David Frank, *J.B. McLachlan: A Biography* (Toronto: James Lorimer, 1999), 445-47; John Manley, "Preaching the Red Stuff: J.B. McLachlan, Communism, and the Cape Breton Miners, 1922-1935," *Labour/Le Travail* 30 (1992): 99-100; "Communism and the Canadian Working Class during the Great Depression," 195-207; and Doug Nesbitt, "J.B. McLachlan, the Communist Party of Canada and the United Front," Social History Project, http://www.socialisthistory.ca/Docs/History/Mclachlan.htm.

49 For the CPC's July 1930 analysis of new party members in District 6, see LAC, CI, Reel 11 [K-279], 495, 98, 101, 153. See also LAC, CPC, Reel M-7376, 1A 0454, A.H.S. to the Editor of the Worker, August 1930.

50 LAC, CPC, vol. 51, File 51-66, "Minutes Seventh Annual Convention of the Lumber Workers Industrial Union of Canada," c. 7 April 1930, 2-3.

51 Ibid. For coverage of the convention, see *Worker*, 12 and 19 April 1930.

52 For an overview of Finnish sport at the Lakehead during this period, see Charles Nathan Hatton, "Headlocks at the Lakehead: Wrestling in Fort William and Port Arthur, 1913-1933" (MA thesis, Lakehead University, 2007).

53 *Worker*, 12 April 1930.

54 LAC, CPC, Reel M-7382, 10C 2005 and 10C 2006, "General Report on the Situation in the Lumber and Agricultural Workers Industrial Union of Canada and Plan for Future Action," c. May 1931, 2-3. For a report on the resolution to affiliate, see *Worker,* 3 May 1930. The change of name was officially reported in the *Worker,* 26 July 1930.

55 *Young Worker,* May 1930, 4.

56 For coverage of the demonstrations, see *Worker,* 3 May 1930; *Fort William Daily Times-Journal* (hereafter *FWDTJ*) and *PANC,* 2 and 3 May 1930; and Betcherman, *The Little Band,* 119-23.

57 LAC, J.L. Cohen fonds (hereafter JL), MG30-A94, vol. 1, "Rex vs. Bruce, et al.," May to June 1930; and *Canadian Labour Defender,* June 1930, 7 and 11. See also Betcherman, *The Little Band,* 121. For more on the life and work of J.L. Cohen, see Laurel Sefton MacDowell, *Renegade Lawyer: The Life of J.L. Cohen* (Toronto: University of Toronto Press, 2001).

58 See *Worker,* 24 and 31 May and 7 June 1930; and *Canadian Labour Defender,* July/August 1930, 9; and February 1932, 8.

59 *Worker,* 5 and 19 July 1930; and A.W. Rasporich, "Faction and Class in Modern Lakehead Politics," *Lakehead University Review* 7, 1 (Summer 1974): 40.

60 LAC, CI, Reel 11 [K-279], 495, 98, 98, 30, "Minutes of the PolCom Meeting," 22 May 1930.

61 Nationally, the CPC's ten candidates polled about 7,000, the highest being 2,200 and the lowest 95. See ibid., 495, 98, 101, 124, "Report of the Situation of the Work of the CPC during the Years of July 1929 – July 1930," 18 August 1930, 8.

62 LAC, CPC, Reel M-7376, 1A 0451, Alf Hautamäki to Mr. T. Ewen, 25 April 1930.

63 *Worker,* 9 August 1930.

64 Betcherman, *The Little Band,* 125-26.

65 LAC, CPC, Reel M-7376, 1A 0496, Unknown LAWIU to J.E. Moe, 3 June 1930.

66 LAC, CI, Reel 11 [K-279], 495, 98, 98, 71, "Minutes of the PolCom Meeting," 2 and 9 August 1930; and *Worker,* 2 August 1930.

67 *Young Worker,* 15 September 1930, 1. Delegates to the conference included: Aleksi Rintala (lumber worker) and Frank Huhtala (lumber worker); from Kaministiqua, Walter Hendricson (lumber and farm worker), Elmer Heikkila (lumber worker), and Armand Erickson (farm worker); from Kivikoski, Ansu Hoxel (lumber and farm worker), Aate Pitkänen (farm worker), Mauri Hoxel (farm worker), Tauno Peterson (lumber worker), and Peterson Pekka (farm worker); from Intola, E. Korhonen (farm worker) and Eino Hostikka (lumber worker).See also *Young Worker,* 6 October 1930, 1.

68 *Canadian Labour Defender,* October-November 1930, n.p. This seizure explains the lack of material from the district offices found locally or in LAC.

69 The CLDL commented that a "savage attack now being made upon the worker is shown to be a cunning, deliberate, far-reaching, vicious policy that must be stoutly withstood by organized and determined effort on the part of the working class of Canada." See LAC, CPC, Reel M-7383, 11C 2871, "Resolution on the Defence of Foreign Born Workers," c. 11-12 July 1930, 1.

70 See Barbara Roberts, *Whence They Came: Deportation from Canada, 1900-1935* (Ottawa: University of Ottawa Press, 1988), 125-58.

71 Ibid., 125.

72 *Canadian Labour Defender,* May 1931, 8; LAC, CPC, Reel M-7377, 3A 1579, Tom Ewen to Alf Hautamäki, 20 March 1931; and Betcherman, *The Little Band,* 127 and 146.

73 LAC, CPC, Reel M-7376, 1A 0462, Unknown to Tim Buck, 20 November 1930. Membership in the region fluctuated between 700 and 800, but much of it came from the LAWIU and remained ethnically Finnish. For similar sentiments, see ibid., 1A 0459, National Executive Committee, LAWIU of C, to G. Lamont, 6 September 1930.

74 LAC, Canadian Security Intelligence Service fonds (hereafter CSIS), RG146, 1025-9-9019, vol. 2, 30-33, Alf Hautamäki to Tim Buck, 31 December 1930.

75 LAC, CPC, Reel M-7376, 1A 0460, National Executive Committee, LAWIU of C, to G. Lamont, 6 September 1930.

76 Ibid., 1A 0470-71, Alf Hautamäki to G. Lamont, 27 November 1930.

77 Ibid., 1A 0460, National Executive Committee, LAWIU of C, to G. Lamont, 6 September 1930.

78 *PANC,* 22 and 24 October 1930.

79 *Worker,* 25 October 1930; and *PANC,* 21 October 1930.

80 *PANC,* 27, 29, and 30 October 1930; *Worker,* 1 November 1930.

81 LAC, CPC, Reel M-7376, 1A 0471, Alf Hautamäki [?] to G. Lamont, 27 November 1930.

82 Ibid., Reel M-7376, Reel M-7380, 8C 0093 and reverse of 8C 0093, "Minutes of District 6 Conference," 23 November 1930, 2; and *Worker,* 11 October 1930.

83 In 1930, the district consisted of seventeen groups within Port Arthur and Fort William. With the exception of Group 1, each had one representative. Additional rural units with a representative were located in the communities of Lappi, Tarmola, Comnee, Finland, Nipigon, Kaministiqua, Alppila, Intola, Kivikoski, Murillo, and Finmark. Department representatives included those from the Organization Department, Co-op. Agit Prop, Trade Union, Women's Department, and Canadian Labour Defence League Buro. LAC, ibid.

84 Ibid.

85 Although this organization is referred to as the Port Arthur Unemployed Association, Port Arthur Unemployed Council of Port Arthur, and Unemployed Organization of Port Arthur, I have gone with the name that appears on the masthead of its "bulletin."

86 LAC, CPC, Reel M-7376, 1A 0474, *Unemployed Bulletin* 4 c., 1930).

87 Ibid., 1A 0465, National Secretary, WUL, to Mary Gilbert, Secretary, Port Arthur Unemployed Association, 25 November 1930; and 1A 0472, Tom Ewen to Mary Gilbert, 4 December 1930.

88 Ibid., 1A 0465, National Secretary, WUL, to Mary Gilbert, Secretary, Port Arthur Unemployed Association, 25 November 1930.

89 Ibid.

90 Ibid., 1A 0476, Tom Ewan to Mary Gilbert, 5 December 1930.

91 Ibid., 1A 0469, National Secretary, WUL, to Alf Hautamäki, 3 December 1930.

92 Ibid., Reel M-7380, "A. Hotomaki [sic] on the IWW and Communism in Port Arthur, Political Committee Minutes," February 1930, cited in A.W. Rasporich, "Ethnicity in Lakehead Politics, 1900-1930," *Polyphony* 9, 2 (1987): 63.

93 LAC, ibid., Reel M-7376, 1A 0470, Alf Hautamäki [?] to G. Lamont, 27 November 1930.

94 Ibid.

95 Rasporich, "Ethnicity in Lakehead Politics," 63.

96 LAC, CPC, Reel M-7376, 1A 0470, Alf Hautamäki [?] to G. Lamont, 27 November 1930.

97 LAC, CI, Reel 1 [K-269], 495, 72, 176, 55, "Anglo-American Secretariat Meeting, 2 July 1932, Report on Canadian Question," 23.

98 Radforth, *Bushworkers and Bosses,* 126; and *Worker,* 21 February 1931.

99 Rasporich, "Faction and Class in Modern Lakehead Politics," 41. For local coverage, consult *PANC,* 12, 13, 16, and 29 December 1930.

100 Gibson was also a worker-poet, writing two known books during his lifetime. These works focused on the plight of the working class at the Lakehead and on his experiences. See *Songs of the Road, and Other Poems* (Port Arthur, 1933), and *Grist for the Mill, and Other Poems* (n.p., 1959).

101 Rasporich, "Faction and Class in Modern Lakehead Politics," 41. For the results in Port Arthur, see *PANC,* 6 and 7 January 1931.

102 LAC, CPC, Reel M-7377, 3A 1541, National Executive Secretary, WUL, to Mary Gilbert, 21 January 1931.

103 LAC, CI, Reel 13 [K-281], 495, 98, 117, 32, "Minutes of the Political Buro of the Communist Party of Canada," 13 February 1931.

104 LAC, CPC, Reel M-7376, 2A 1103, Organizing Secretary of the CPC to Finnish National Fraction Buro, 20 February 1931.

105 Ibid.; and 2A 1104, Organizing Secretary of the CPC to Finnish National Fraction Buro, 20 February 1931.

106 Ibid., Reel M-7378, 4A 2614, "Resolution on the Party Plenum, and the Tasks of the Party in District #6," c. 1931, 2.

107 See, for example, *PANC*, 25-17 February and 10 March 1931.

108 LAC, CPC, Reel M-7377, 3A 1536, Alf Hautamäki to Tom Ewen, 14 January 1931.

109 Karelia has long fascinated historians of Finnish North American socialism. The literature on the subject is extensive. For the most important works on the subject, see Reino Kero, "Emigration of Finns from North America to Soviet Karelia in the Early 1930s," in *The Finnish Experience in the Western Great Lakes Region: New Perspectives,* ed. Michael G. Karni, Matti E. Kaups, and Douglas J. Ollila Jr. (Turku, Finland: Institute for Migration Studies, 1975), 212-21; Kero, "The Canadian Finns in Soviet Karelia in the 1930s," in *Finnish Diaspora I: Canada, South America, Africa, Australia and Sweden,* ed. Michael G. Karni (Toronto: Multicultural History Society of Ontario, 1981), 204-5; Varpu Lindström and K. Börje Vähämäki, "Ethnicity Twice Removed: North-American Finns in Soviet Karelia," in *The Best of Finnish Americana,* ed. Michael Karni (Iowa City: Penfield Press, 1994), 141-47; Alexis Pogorelskin, "New Perspectives on Karelian Fever: The Recruitment of North American Finns to Karelia in the Early 1930s," *Journal of Finnish Studies* 1, 3 (December 1997): 167-78; Ronald Harpelle, Varpu Lindström, and Alexis Pogorelskin, eds., *Karelian Exodus: Finnish Communities in North America and Soviet Karelia during the Depression Era* (Beaverton, ON: Aspasia Books, 2004). The story of "Soviet Finns" in areas other than Karelia can be found, for example, in Jukka Rislakki and Eila Lahti-Argutina, *No Home for Us Here: The Mass Annihilation of the Finnish Border-Hoppers in the Urals in 1938,* trans. Richard Impola (St. Cloud, MN: North Star Press, 2002).

110 Pilli, *The Finnish-Language Press in Canada,* 135-36.

111 LAC, CPC, Reel M-7376, 1A 0126, Tim Buck to Alf Hautamäki, 2 December 1929; and Radforth, *Bushworkers and Bosses,* 125. It has been estimated that 10,000 Finnish men and women from Canada and the United States went to Karelia between 1931 and 1933. See Peter Kivisto, *Immigrant Socialists in the United States: The Case of Finns and the Left* (Rutherford, NJ: Fairleigh Dickinson University Press; Cranbury, NJ: Associated University Presses, 1984), 174; and Harpelle et al., *Karelian Exodus.*

112 LAC, CPC, vol. 17, File 13, A. Kari to Executive Committee, FOC, 28 August 1931; and vol. 17, File 16. For more on Hautamäki's involvement, see also Kero, "Canadian Finns in Soviet Karelia," 205.

113 Radforth, *Bushworkers and Bosses,* 125. Alf Hautamäki and other Finnish Communists at the Lakehead had in fact played a large role in establishing the *Karjalan työkuunta* (Karelian Work Unit) in 1930.

114 See, for example, Tim Buck's correspondence with Niilo Virtanen, a well-known party member in the Sudbury region who had written on the situation. LAC, CPC, Reel M-7377, 2A 1484 and 2A 1485, Buck to Newman, 10 April 1931.

115 Ibid., Reel M-7378, 4A 2613, "Resolution on the Party Plenum, and the Tasks of the Party in District #6," c. 1931, 3.

116 Ibid., Reel M-7377, 3A 1601, Jim Barker to the Workers' Unity League, 31 March 1931.

117 Ibid., Reel M-7378, 4A 2613, "Resolution on the Party Plenum, and the Tasks of the Party in District #6," c.1931, 1.

118 The letter sent to Gilbert from Biniowsky appears to have been lost. In her letter to McEwen, Gilbert comments that the only copies are being sent with her letter and asks that they be returned. It appears that this never happened. See ibid., Reel M-7377, 3A 1545, Alf Hautamäki to T.A. Ewan, 29 January 1931.

119 Barker also attributed the mobilization of the Women's Labour League branches, the Unemployed Council, the YCL, and LAWIU to the two men. Significantly, in all of these organizations, most of the members were Finnish and Ukrainian. While the Port Arthur gathering was attended by over 2,000, the Fort William one, led by Barker and Biniowsky, was much smaller. See Reel M-7377, 3A 1565, Jim Barker, District Organizer, to Tom Ewen, Industrial Department, CPC, 27 February 1931, 1; and *Worker,* 28 February 1931. For local coverage, see *PANC,* 25-17 February and 10 March 1931.

120 Radforth, *Bushworkers and Bosses,* 126.

121 LAC, CPC, Reel M-7377, 3A 1571, P. Saari, E. Smolander, E. Haara (for the local union fraction), Antti Pitkänen and Adolf Savolainen (members of the NEC, L and AWIU of Canada) to Tim Buck, 16 March 1931.

122 Quoted in Radforth, *Bushworkers and Bosses,* 126. The McEwen statement can be found in LAC, ibid., Reel M-7382, 10C 2001 to 10C 2004, "General Report on L and AWIUC Convention," May 1931; and Reel M-7380, 8C 0476 to 8C 0480, "Minutes of the Party Plenum," 1931.

123 LAC, CI, Reel 13 [K-281], 495, 98, 117, 59, "Minutes of the Pol Bureau CPC," 17 April 1931; and LAC, CPC, Reel M-7377, 3A 1617, Org. Sect'y, Political Buro, to Jim Barker, 18 April 1931.

124 LAC, CI, ibid., 495, 98, 117, 79, "Workers' Unity League of Canada. Minutes of 8th Convention Lumber and Agricultural Workers Industrial Union of Canada," 2-5 May 1931, 2.

125 LAC, CPC, Reel M-7377, 3A 1572, Jim Barker to Organization Committee, 17 March 1931; 3A 1571, Alf Hautamäki to Tom Ewen, 17 March 1931; and 3A 1581, Tom Ewen to Jim Barker, 23 March 1931.

126 Ibid., 3A 1585 and 3A 1586, National Executive Secretary, WUL, to the Port Arthur District Conference, L and AWIU of C, 24 March 1931, 1-2.

127 Ibid., Reel M-7378, 4A 2614, "Resolution on the Party Plenum, and the Tasks of the Party in District #6," c. 1931, 2.

128 Ibid., Reel M-7377, 3A 1569, Jim Barker to Central Organization Department, 14 March 1931.

129 Ibid., 3A 1588 and 3A 1588a, Jim Barker to Central Org Dept., 20 March 1931.

130 Ibid., 3A 1589 to 3A 1591, "Minutes of District Six Bureau," 16 March 1931.

131 Ibid., 3A 1563, Telegram, J. Barker to The Worker, 25 February 1931; 3A 1566, Jim Barker to Tom Ewen, 27 February 1931, 2.; and Reel M-7378, 4A 2614, "Resolution on the Party Plenum, and the Tasks of the Party in District #6," c. 1931, 2.

132 LAC, CI, M10-K3, Reel 14 [K-282], 495, 98, 122, 25, Central Organizing Department to All District Organizers, RE: The May Recruiting Drive, 8 April 1931, 2.

133 Ibid., Reel 13 [K-281], 495, 98, 116, 16, Stewart Smith (Anglo-American Secretariat) to Tim Buck, 23 April 1931, 2

134 Ibid., 6.

135 LAC, CPC, Reel M-7377, 3A 1602, National Secretary, Workers' Unity League, to Jim Barker, 3 April 1931.

136 Ibid.

137 LAC, CI, Reel 13 [K-281], 495, 98, 117, 41, "Minutes of Pol Bureau CPC," 13 February 1931.

138 Ibid., 495, 98, 116, 14, Tim Buck to Stewart Smith (Anglo-American Secretariat), 15 April 1931, 2; and 495, 98, 117, 58, "Minutes of Pol Bureau CPC," 17 April 1931, 4.

139 Ibid., 495, 98, 117, 41, "Minutes of Pol Bureau CPC," 13 February 1931.

140 *Worker,* 25 April 1931.

141 Ibid., 6 and 16 May 1931; *FWDTJ,* 1, 2, 6, 9, and 11 May 1931; *PANC,* 1, 2, and 9 May 1931.

142 LAC, CPC, Reel M-7377, 3A 1638, Unknown to Ailiane Hautamäki, 8 June 1931; 3A 1650, H. Myntti, Secretary Treasurer, Food Workers' Union of Canada, to National Executive Secretary, WUL, 19 June 1931; and 3A 1651, National Executive Secretary, WUL, to H. Myntti, Secretary Treasurer, Food Workers' Union of Canada local #1, 22 June 1931.

143 Avakumovic, *The Communist Party in Canada,* 75

144 LAC, CPC, Reel M-7378, 4A 2614 and 4A 2615, "Resolution on the Party Plenum, and the Tasks of the Party in District #6," c. 1931, 2-3.

145 Manley, "Communism and the Canadian Working Class during the Depression," 541-54.

146 *Worker*, 25 July 1931; and *FWDTJ*, 27 June and 2 July 1931. Over the course of the next few months, local Communists would take aim at Moore, Alex Cruikshanks, secretary of the local American Federation of Labor (AFL), and Independent Labour Party (ILP) member Jack MacDonald. See, for example, *Worker*, 25 July and 3 October 1931. He would also later be blamed as the ILPer responsible for the lack of Communist success in the 1932 civic elections in Fort William. See *Worker*, 30 January 1932.

147 LAC, CPC, Reel M-7378, 4A 2614, "Resolution on the Party Plenum, and the Tasks of the Party in District #6," c. 1931, 2.

148 Ibid., Reel M-7380, 8C 0096, Tom Ewen, "Report on District 6," 7 July 1931, 2.

149 Ibid., 8C 0095 to 8C 0096, Tom Ewen, "Report on District 6," 7 July 1931, 1-2.

150 Ibid., 8C 0096, Tom Ewen, "Report on District 6," 7 July 1931, 2.

151 Ibid., 11C 2931, "Canadian Woman's Labour League. Affiliated to the Workers' Unity League of Canada," n.d.

152 Ibid., Reel M-7378, 4A 2615, "Resolution on the Party Plenum, and the Tasks of the Party in District #6," c. 1931, 3.

153 LUA, JMLHC, Tape 5, Harry Bryan Reminiscences, 1972.

154 *PANC*, 20 April 1932. This included in West Fort William sixty-five members of the YCL. The source of this information was reputed to be located in records obtained by the Port Arthur chief of police during a raid on 30 September 1930.

155 See LAC, CPC, Reel M-7377, 3A 1548, Tom Ewen to Mary Gilbert, 4 February 1931; and Reel M-7380, 8C 0096 to 8C 0097, Tom Ewen, "Report on District 6," 7 July 1931, 2-3. Harry Bryan had originally organized the dairy workers along with various dairy farmers in the district of Thunder Bay in 1929. See LUA, Thunder Bay Finnish-Canadian Historical Society fonds (hereafter TBFCHS), MG8, B, 7, 30, Item 2, Interview with Einar Nordstrom, 15 and 19 March, 2 May, and 7 May 1979. According to Nordstrom, the dairy outperformed its commercial counterparts during the Depression. Some mistakes and the eventual lack of need for it led to its going out of business.

156 Betcherman, *The Little Band*, 175. See also *Worker*, 7 November 1931. For general overviews on the arrests of the CPC leaders, see Avakumovic, *The Communist Party in Canada*, 87; Ben Swankey and John Evans Shields, *Work and Wages: A Documentary Account of the Life and Times of Arthur H. (Slim) Evans, 1890-1944* (Vancouver: Trade Union Research Bureau, 1977), 33; F.R. Scott, "The Trial of the Toronto Communists," *Queen's Quarterly* 39 (August 1932): 512-27; and Ahti Tolvanen, *Finntown: A Perspective on Urban Integration. Port Arthur Finns in the Inter-war Period: 1918-1939* (Helsinki: University of Helsinki, 1985), 101.

157 LAC, CPC, Reel M-7382, 10C 2008, "General Report on the Situation in the Lumber and Agricultural Workers Industrial Union of Canada and Plan for Future Action," c. May 1931, 5; and *Worker*, 13 June 1931.

158 LAC, CI, Reel 14 [K-282], 495, 98, 128, 32, John Wein [?] Secretary, National Partifraction Burom UMO [?], 24 October 1931, 2. For Jim Barker's report on the general difficulties in trade union work related to District 6, see *Worker*, 17 October 1931.

159 LAC, ibid.

160 Ibid., 495, 98, 128, 33, John Wein [?] Secretary, National Partifraction Burom UMO [?], 24 October 1931, 3.

161 While groups of the WUL were reputedly active among the Freight Handlers and the Pulp and Paper Industry, this amounted to nine individuals who operated in isolation. See LAC, CPC, Reel M-7378, 4A 2616, "Resolution on the Party Plenum and the Tasks of the Party in District #6," c. 1931, 4.

162 *PANC,* 20 April 1932.

163 LAC, CI, Reel 1 [K-269], 495, 72, 176, 56-57, "Anglo-American Secretariat Meeting, 2 July 1932, Report on Canadian Question," 24-25.

164 Anthony W. Rasporich, "Twin City Ethnopolitics: Urban Rivalry, Ethnic Radicalism and Assimilation in the Lakehead, 1900-70," *Urban History Review/Revue d'histoire urbaine* 18, 3 (February 1990): 215.

165 LAC, CPC, Reel M-7382, 9C 1454 to 9C 1569, "Resolution of the Political Secretariat of the ECCI [Executive Committee of the Communist International] on the Situation and Tasks of the Communist Party of Canada," c. 1930; and Avery, *"Dangerous Foreigners,"* 129.

166 *Worker,* 16 May 1931.

167 In his autobiography, Tom McEwen insisted that the resolution for the 1929 Lumber Workers Industrial Union of Canada strike in the Port Arthur area resulted from the WUL's first experience with mediation. This is unlikely, however, as the WUL was not formed until after the strike had ended. See McEwen, *The Forge Glows Red,* 158.

168 LAC, CPC, Reel M-7376, 1A 0470, Alf Hautamäki to G. Lamont, 27 November 1930. Golden had been active in the region, according to Hautamäki, for three weeks.

CHAPTER 8: WOBBLY RELATIONS

1 John Manley, "Communism and the Canadian Working Class during the Great Depression" (PhD dissertation, Dalhousie University, 1984), 251.

2 *Labour Gazette* 34 (February 1934); and "Report of the Department of Labour," in *Ontario Sessional Papers,* No.67 (1934).

3 *Labour Gazette* 33 (1933): 1180.

4 Manley, "Communism and the Canadian Working Class during the Great Depression," 260.

5 Library and Archives Canada (hereafter LAC), Communist International fonds (hereafter CI), MG10-K3, Reel 2 [K-270], 495, 72, 206, 3, "Meeting Bureau, Anglo-American Secretariat, Report on Canada," 4 May 1932, 3.

6 Lakehead University Archives (hereafter LUA), *Canadan Teollisuusunionistinen Kannatus Liitto* fonds (hereafter CTKL), MG10, E, 10, 12, Herbert Mahler to Eino Markkanen, 10 August 1931.

7 *Canadian Labour Defender,* January 1932, 3.

8 Employment of lumber workers fell 30 percent, from 16,262 in 1931 to 11,646 in 1932. For more on deportations during 1932, see *Labour Gazette* 32 (1932) and 33 (1933): 286-87; Mary Veltri, "Labour Radicalism among Finnish Bushworkers at the Lakehead, 1916-1936" (Honours thesis, Lakehead University, 1981), 87.

9 Lorne and Caroline Brown, *An Unauthorized History of the RCMP* (Toronto: James Lorimer, 1973), 54.

10 *Worker,* 19 March 1932. According to lists published in the *Worker* on its tenth anniversary, the Finnish Organization of Canada (FOC), International Co-operative, Ukrainian Labour-Farmer Temple Association (ULFTA), Women's Section of the ULFTA, Youth Section of the ULFTA, Workers' Benevolent Association, and *Todowyernazu* were operating in Fort William and Port Arthur. Additional organizations could also be found in Kivikoski, Tamola, and other outlying rural areas. See ibid., 26 March 1932.

11 *Young Worker,* 29 January, 5; and 17 February 1932, 5.

12 Ibid., 17 February 1932, 8; and 30 September 1932, 1.

13 Ahti Tolvanen, *Finntown: A Perspective on Urban Integration. Port Arthur Finns in the Inter-war Period: 1918-1939* (Helsinki: University of Helsinki, 1985), 102. In total, forty-eight candidates were nominated in Port Arthur. For local coverage of the elections, see *Port Arthur News-Chronicle* (hereafter *PANC*), 28 December 1931. For "ethnic" solidarity, see LAC, CI, Reel 2 [K-270], 495, 72, 206, 7-8, "Meeting Bureau, Anglo-American Secretariat, Report on Canada," 4 May 1932, 7-8. In

the case of May Day demonstrations in 1932, they occurred and were well attended despite the fact that the "May day united front committees" application to hold a parade was refused by the city councils in both cities at the behest of Port Arthur chief of police George Taylor and Fort William chief of police C.E. Watkins. See *Fort William Daily Times-Journal* (hereafter *FWDTJ*), 29 April 1932. For a report on the "peaceful" gatherings, see *FWDTJ*, 2 May 1932.

14 LAC, CI, ibid. In April, Fort William chief of police C.E. Watkins attacked Communism before the Missionary Society of St. Andrew's Presbyterian Church. He outlined the recent activities and promised that firm action would be taken in the future. See *PANC*, 20 April 1932.

15 *Worker*, 2 July 1932.

16 Ibid., 30 July 1932.

17 LAC, Canadian Security Intelligence Service fonds (hereafter CSIS), RG146, vol. 6, File 1025-9-9103, pt. 1, 0521, "Report of the Plenum on the Canadian Labor Defense League," 7-8 August 1932, 1.

18 Ibid., 0502, "RCMP Western Ontario District Report," 10 August 1932.

19 Ibid., 0481, "Situation and Tasks of the Defense Movement in Canada," August 1932, 5.

20 Ibid., 0496, "Statement on Organization CLDL National Plenum August 1932," 1; *Worker*, 4 June 1932.

21 LAC, ibid., 0458-459, "What are the Patronati?"

22 *Lumber Worker*, September 1932, 1.

23 Ibid., 12.

24 LAC, CI, Reel 1 [K-269], 495, 72, 176, 47, "Anglo-American Secretariat Meeting; Report on Canadian Question," 2 July 1932.

25 *Organizer*, August 1932, 1.

26 Ibid., September 1932, 1.

27 Ibid., August 1932, 2.

28 Ibid., 1.

29 Ibid., 2.

30 Ibid., October 1932, 2. See also LUA, CTKL, E, 10, 6, "Minutes of the First Conference of Canadian IWW Held in Port Arthur, Ontario," 12 September 1932.

31 *Organizer*, August 1932, 4.

32 The decision to change the name of the union back from the Lumber and Agricultural Workers Industrial Union of Canada (LAWIU) to the Lumber Workers Industrial Union of Canada (LWIUC) was made so that the union could grow on that basis and to reflect the reality that no agricultural branches currently existed. See *Lumber Worker*, September 1932, 5-6.

33 *Organizer*, October 1932, 1

34 Ibid., September 1932, 2.

35 Ibid., October 1932, 1.

36 Ibid.

37 Ibid., 3.

38 LUA, Jean Morrison Labour History Collection (hereafter JMLHC), GS186a, Tape 25, Interview with Einar Nordstrom, 1972. This event occurred after Communists attempted to hold demonstrations in early September, only to be blocked by police each time. See, for example, *FWDTJ*, 6 September 1932.

39 *FWDTJ*, 31 October and 1 November 1932; *PANC*, 28 October 1932; *Young Worker*, 11 November 1932, 1; *Worker*, 5 November 1932; LUA, JMLHC, ibid.; *Canadian Labour Defender*, December 1932, 7; and Oscar Ryan, *The Sedition of A.E. Smith* (Toronto: Canadian Labour Defence League, 1934), 7.

40 *Worker*, 15 and 22 October 1932; *FWDTJ* and *PANC*, 19 October 1932; Joseph M. Mauro, *A History of Thunder Bay* (Thunder Bay: City of Thunder Bay, 1981), 317-20; Tolvanen, *Finntown*, 64-66; and Satu Repo (interviewing Ivar Nordström), "Lakehead in the Thirties, a Labour Militant Remembers," *This Magazine* 13, 3 (July/August 1979): 42.

41 *PANC*, 28 and 29 October 1932 ; *Canadian Labour Defender*, December 1932, 7.
42 *PANC*, 31 October 1932; Mauro, *A History of Thunder Bay*, 320; and Tolvanen, *Finntown*, 66.
43 *Worker*, 19 and 26 November 1932.
44 Ibid., 26 November 1932; Tolvanen, *Finntown*, 68; Nils Inkilä, "Finnish National Society 50 Years Old," *Northern Mosaic* (November-December 1976): 10; and Veltri, "Labour Radicalism among Finnish Bushworkers at the Lakehead," 97-98.
45 *Young Worker*, 11 November 1932, 3.
46 The charges were thrown out even though Waywood admitted to making fake coins for "experimental purposes."
47 *Young Worker*, 23 December 1932, 3. For more on the raids, see *FWDTJ*, 9, 21, and 29 November 1932.
48 *Lumber Worker*, December 1932, 13.
49 LUA, CTKL, E, 10, 14, "Canadian Administration Secretary-Treasurer and CEB to the Delegates of Annual Convention assembled," 1 November 1932, 1.
50 Ibid., 2.
51 *Organizer*, November 1932, 3. The activities of both the IWW and CPC did not go unnoticed. The *Toronto Labour Leader*, for example, viewed the Workers' Unity League and the IWW in particular as intolerable. It alleged that attacks were being made by the two organizations on workers unwilling to side with them in labour disputes. As increasingly became the case, it described both the WUL and IWW as "Communistic organizations" that thrived on strikes and violence. It further believed that these two organizations represented the biggest threat to the organized labour movement and asked that both the province of Ontario and the Dominion of Canada take action. See LAC, Department of Labour fonds (hereafter DL), RG27, vol. 365, Strike 228, *Toronto Labor Leader*, 9 November 1934.
52 LUA, CTKL, E, 10, 14, "Canadian Administration Secretary-Treasurer and CEB to the Delegates of Annual Convention assembled," 1 November 1932, 3.
53 Ibid.
54 Ibid., 1.
55 *Young Worker*, 23 December 1932, 4; *Worker*, 3 and 31 December 1932; and *FWDTJ*, 23 December 1932.
56 *Worker*, 14 January 1933. Complete Port Arthur results can be found in *PANC*, 3 January 1933.
57 *Worker*, ibid. For a complete list of candidates in Port Arthur, see *PANC*, 28 December 1932.
58 *Worker*, 25 February 1933; and *FWDTJ* and *PANC*, 18 February 1933.
59 *Worker*, 18 March 1933.
60 Ibid., 15 April 1933.
61 Ibid., 6 May 1933.
62 Ibid., 24 June and 1 July 1933; *FWDTJ*, 7-16 June 1933; *PANC*, 13, 15, and 21 June 1933; and Ian Radforth, *Bushworkers and Bosses: Logging in Northern Ontario, 1900-1980* (Toronto: University of Toronto Press, 1987), 127-28.
63 *Worker*, 1 July 1933; *FWDTJ*, 17 1933.
64 See LAC, Communist Party of Canada fonds (hereafter CPC), MG28-IV4, vol. 16, File 33, M.J. Fenwick, Mass Meeting Secretary, to National Executive, Finnish Organization, 15 November 1933.
65 For a description of the crowds, see Manley, "Communism and the Canadian Working Class during the Great Depression," 265-66.
66 *Worker*, 1 July 1933. This event was not isolated. In the next two months, two similar incidents occurred. For these incidents, see *Worker*, 24 July 1933; *Labour Gazette* 33 (September 1933); *Organizer*, July 1933, 4, and August 1933, 1; and Veltri, "Labour Radicalism among Finnish Bushworkers at the Lakehead," 103.
67 See *Worker*, 29 July 1933; and *PANC*, 26 September 1933.

68 Veltri, "Labour Radicalism among Finnish Bushworkers at the Lakehead," 101.
69 Ibid., 103.
70 Tolvanen, *Finntown,* 82-83.
71 Ibid., 83.
72 LUA, CTKL, E, 10, 17, George MacAdam to CEB, 1 July 1933, 1.
73 Ibid. MacAdam may also have insisted on the establishment of the Canadian Defence Organization for personal reasons. Although he voted against its establishment at the First Annual Convention, he and four other prominent Wobblies – H. Snider, B. Taylor, T. Spenuk, and M. Fedrokpow – had been arrested for their part in the action against the relief camp located in Sioux Lookout, Ontario. MacAdam and Snider were charged as the ringleaders.
74 Ibid.
75 Ibid., 11 September 1933, 1.
76 Ibid., E, 10, 12, Herbert Mahler to H.J. Lindholm, 8 July 1932. The lack of information also characterized the official literature of the IWW during the next two decades. Fred Thompson, a Secretary-Treasurer of the GEB during the late 1930s and, interestingly, a Canadian himself, not only gets the date of the Canadian Administration's establishment wrong but also ignores the entire 1930s except for George MacAdam's imprisonment. Clearly, although Canadian IWW members had a long history of being knowledgeable about events in the United States and supporting striking workers in that country, there is little evidence of commitment on the part of the GEB to the IWW in Canada. See Fred Thompson, *The IWW: Its First Fifty Years (1905-1955): The History of an Effort to Organize the Working Class* (Chicago: Industrial Workers of the World, 1955), 177-78.
77 LUA, CTKL, E, 10, 12, Joseph Wagner to H. Lindholm, 18 January 1933.
78 Ibid., E, 10, 18, Dave Dubé to George MacAdam, 7 July 1933.
79 Ibid., E, 10, 16, H.J. Lindholm to All Members, 12 January 1933.
80 Ibid.
81 Ibid., E, 10, 12, Joseph Wagner to H. Lindholm, 30 January 1933.
82 For more on the Technocractic movement, see William E. Akin, *Technocracy and the American Dream: The Technocratic Movement, 1900-1941* (Berkeley: University of California Press, 1977).
83 LUA, CTKL, E, 10, 17, George MacAdam to CEB, 1 July 1933, 1. At the June convention, George MacAdam went on record as opposing the establishment of a Canadian Wobbly press.
84 Ibid., E, 10, 16, August Torttila to George MacAdam, 12 July 1933, 1.
85 Ibid. See also Peter Campbell's similar arguments in his "The Cult of Spontaneity: Finnish-Canadian Bushworkers and the Industrial Workers of the World in Northern Ontario, 1919-1934," *Labour/Le Travail* 41 (Spring 1998).
86 LUA, CTKL, E, 10, 17, George MacAdam to CEB, 11 September 1933, 2.
87 Ibid., George MacAdam to CEB, 1 July 1933, 1.
88 For a discussion of the Canadian Bushmen's Union, see Radforth, *Bushworkers and Bosses,* 130. For the Communist view of the CBU, see, for example, *Worker,* 20 January 1934.
89 Tolvanen, *Finntown,* 84.
90 LUA, CTKL, F, 15, 10, G. Salverson to Strike Committee, United Front, 7 June 1933. See this file and F, 15, 11 for a series of strike bulletins issued by the committee. Established in 1932, the Co-operative Commonwealth Federation had little presence at the Lakehead during the strike and did not become a force in the region until late 1934.
91 *PANC,* 7 December 1933.
92 Ibid., 20 November 1933.
93 Tolvanen, *Finntown,* 85. For daily coverage of the strike, including the establishment of a commission to investigate why a settlement had not been reached and the almost daily reports of strikers being arrested, see *PANC,* 2 December to 13 December 1933.

94 *PANC,* 11 and 12 December 1933; and Tolvanen, *Finntown,* 84-86. Tolvanen's sources for the eyewitness accounts are from interviews with Yrjö Korpi (January 1973) and Mrs. Elvi Beck (August 1978).

95 *PANC,* 14, 15, 16, and 18 December 1933; and Tolvanen, ibid., 87-89.

96 *Young Worker,* 1 November 1933, 7.

97 *Junior Recruit,* November 1933. Not surprisingly, the YCL disagreed with the Wobbly perspective. See *Young Worker,* 15 November 1933, 6.

98 *Worker,* 17 October 1934; "Speech to First Congress against Fascism," in *Look on Canada, Now, and See History Anew: An Epoch Past and a Life Fashioning under Your Hands Communism, to Which All Roads Lead, Selected Writings of Leslie Morris, 1923-1964* (Toronto: Progress Books, 1970), 16.

99 *Worker,* 19 September 1934.

100 *PANC,* 10 September 1934.

101 "Introduction: The Ukrainian Experience in Canada," in *A Delicate and Difficult Question: Documents in the History of Ukrainians in Canada, 1899-1962,* ed. Bohdan S. Kordan and Lubomyr Y. Luciuk (Kingston: Limestone Press, 1986), 7. The Communist International material in Library and Archives Canada contains a discussion of this situation.

102 *Farmerske Zhyttia,* 25 April 1934, quoted in *Prophets and Proletarians: Documents on the History of the Rise and Decline of Ukrainian Communism in Canada,* ed. John Kolasky (Edmonton: Canadian Institute of Ukrainian Studies Press and University of Alberta Press, 1990), 223-24. Due to Ukrainian Communists' involvement in a number of demonstrations throughout the early 1930s, a series of raids were conducted on the offices of the CLDL in Port Arthur beginning in May 1933, and police in Fort William raided and confiscated all the material in the Ukrainian Labour Temple in that city. As a result, the activities of Ukrainian Communists have been difficult to piece together.

103 *Worker,* 27 January 1934. The UWPA drew attention in January 1934 for paying the mayor of Port Arthur, Charlie Cox, a "social call" and filling his office with as many unemployed workers as would fit. See *Young Worker,* 3 February 1934.

104 The first district conference of the Relief Camp Workers' Union was held during the first week in February. See *Worker,* 24 February 1934.

105 See, for example, *Young Worker,* 5 March and 2 April 1934.

106 Between 900 and 1,000 reportedly took part in the May Day activities in both cities. See *FWDTJ* and *PANC,* 2 May 1934.

107 *Young Worker,* 16 April 1934.

108 Ibid., 14 May 1934.

109 Ibid., 28 May 1934.

110 *Worker,* 16 June 1934.

111 Ibid., 30 June 1934.

112 *Worker,* 29 August 1934.

113 LUA, CTKL, E, 10, 6, "Minutes of the Second Annual Convention of the Canadian Administration of the Industrial Workers of the World," 18 June 1934, 1.

114 Ibid., 2.

115 Ibid., 3.

116 YCL districts reported to be active were Nova Scotia, Montreal, Toronto, Timmins, Sudbury, Port Arthur, Winnipeg, Calgary, Vancouver, and Saskatchewan. See *Young Worker,* 3 September 1934.

117 Tolvanen, *Finntown,* 93.

118 Beverly Rasporich, "Anna of Intola: A Finnish-Canadian Woman with *Sisu,*" in *Great Dames,* ed. Elspeth Cameron and Janice Dickin (Toronto: University of Toronto Press, 1997), 196. Anna claims to have been a lifelong Conservative until that election, demonstrating once again that socialism was not synonymous with Finnish at the Lakehead.

119 A.W. Rasporich, "'Call Me Charlie,' Charlie W. Cox: Port Arthur's Populist Politician," Thunder Bay Historical Museum Society *Papers and Records* 19 (1991): 8.
120 Ibid.; and Royal Canadian Mounted Police, "Weekly Summary Report on Revolutionary Organizations and Agitators in Canada, No. 712, 27 June 1934," in *RCMP Security Bulletins: The Depression Years, Part I, 1933-1934*, ed. Gregory S. Kealey and Reg Whitaker (St. John's: Canadian Committee on Labour History, 1993), 94.
121 See *Young Worker,* 6 October 1934.
122 Radforth, *Bushworkers and Bosses,* 131; and *Ontario Timberworker,* August 1949.
123 Royal Canadian Mounted Police, "Weekly Summary, Report on Revolutionary Organizations and Agitators in Canada, Appendix No. II: Report by Provinces, IV Ontario, 12. Strike of Lumber Workers Continues, No. 728, 17 October 1934," in *RCMP Security Bulletins: The Depression Years,* 341. The CPC had anticipated that a strike would occur since September. See *Worker,* 19 and 22 September 1934.
124 Royal Canadian Mounted Police, "Weekly Summary, Report on Revolutionary Organizations and Agitators in Canada, Appendix No. II: Report by Provinces, IV Ontario, 14. Lumber Workers' Strike Spreading, No. 727, 10 October 1934," in *RCMP Security Bulletins: The Depression Years,* 325. This was not Heenan's first interference in district strikes. See, for example, *Worker,* 15 September 1934.
125 *Worker,* 3 October 1934.
126 Radforth, *Bushworkers and Bosses,* 131; and *Ontario Timberworker,* August 1949.
127 See *Worker,* 24 October and 24 November 1934, for these sentiments.
128 Tolvanen, *Finntown,* 93.
129 John Manley, "'Starve, Be Damned!' Communists and Canada's Urban Unemployed, 1929-1939," *Canadian Historical Review* 79, 3 (September 1998): 489.
130 Campbell, "The Cult of Spontaneity," 144.

EPILOGUE: 1935

1 Until the party was banned during the Second World War, local Communist efforts appear to have gone into the Lumber and Sawmill Workers Union and the League against War and Fascism.
2 The Committee for Industrial Organization did not have a presence at the Lakehead until the early 1950s. In large part, this resulted from the Lumber Workers Industrial Union's decision to rename itself and join the American Federation of Labor's Carpenters' Union. See Jean Morrison, "The Organization of Labour at Thunder Bay," in *Thunder Bay: From Rivalry to Unity,* ed. Thorold J. Tronrud and A. Ernest Epp (Thunder Bay: Thunder Bay Historical Museum Society, 1995), 135.
3 David Frank, *J.B. McLachlan: A Biography* (Toronto: James Lorimer, 1999), 501.
4 See Geoff Eley, *Forging Democracy: The History of the Left in Europe, 1850-2000* (New York: Oxford University Press, 2000), 240-41; and Ian McKay, "For a New Kind of History: A Reconnaissance of 100 Years of Canadian Socialism," *Labour/Le Travail* 46 (Fall 2000): 95-109; and *Rebels, Reds, Radicals: Rethinking Canada's Left History* (Toronto: Between the Lines Press, 2005), 169-83. For more on the Co-operative Commonwealth Federation (CCF) and the Communist perspective, see Library and Archives Canada (hereafter LAC), Communist International fonds (hereafter CI), MG10-K3, Reel 20 [K-288].
5 LAC, Tim Buck Collection, MG32-G3, vol. 1, Series 63, "Tim Buck Reminiscence, Session 15," 1965-66, 597.
6 A.T. Hill, "Highlights of Labour History – Lakehead and Canada" (unpublished manuscript, c. 1973), 5. This anti-fascism was of particular concern for many workers at the Lakehead due to the right-wing extremism favoured in some quarters of the two cities. In January 1935, for example, the *Worker* reported the organization of the "Italian Blackshirts." Modelled directly after Mussolini's

Blackshirts, they began a campaign to organize all Italian workers, a segment of the local population that had not been heavily involved in either the Trades and Labour Councils, the Communist Party of Canada, or the Industrial Workers of the World in the region. See *Worker,* 19 January 1935.

7 Royal Canadian Mounted Police, "Weekly Summary Report on Revolutionary Organizations and Agitators in Canada, No. 740, 16 January 1935," and "No. 741, 23 January 1935," in *RCMP Security Bulletins: The Depression Years, Part II, 1935,* ed. Gregory S. Kealey and Reg Whitaker (St. John's: Canadian Committee on Labour History, 1995), 44 and 60.

8 John Manley, "'Starve, Be Damned!': Communists and Canada's Urban Unemployed, 1929-1939," *Canadian Historical Review* 79, 3 (September 1998): 487.

9 Irving Martin Abella, *Nationalism, Communism, and Canadian Labour: The CIO, the Communist Party, and the Canadian Congress of Labour 1935-1956* (Toronto: University of Toronto Press, 1973), 3. For more on the Communist Party of Canada's presentation of delegates, proposals, and resolutions for the Seventh Comintern Congress, see LAC, CI, Reel 21 [K-289], 495, 98, 172 and 495, 98, 176.

10 See Royal Canadian Mounted Police, "Weekly Summary, Report on Revolutionary Organizations and Agitators in Canada, Appendix No. II: Report by Provinces, V Ontario, No. 767, 27 August 1935," in *RCMP Security Bulletins: The Depression Years, Part II, 1935,* 437-38. For more on the Trek at the Lakehead, see Steve R. Hewitt, "'You Are Making History, You Are Making History': The On to Ottawa Trek in Northern Ontario," Lakehead University Centre for Northern Studies, Research Report No. 38, 1995. For general overviews, see Ronald Liversedge, *Recollections of the On to Ottawa Trek,* ed. Victor Hoar (Toronto: McClelland and Stewart, 1973); Victor Howard, *"We Were the Salt of the Earth!" The On-to-Ottawa Trek and the Regina Riot* (Regina: Canadian Plains Research Centre, 1985); Doug Smith, "On to Ottawa," *Horizon Canada* 9, 99 (1987): 2353-59; and Bill Waiser, *All Hell Can't Stop Us: The On-to-Ottawa Trek and Regina Riot* (Calgary: Fifth House, 2003).

11 *Fort William Daily Times-Journal,* 25 June 1935.

12 *Young Worker,* 26 January 1935.

13 Douglas Thur, "Beat around the Bush: The Lumber and Sawmill Workers Union and the New Political Economy of Labour in Northern Ontario, 1936-1988" (MA thesis, Lakehead University, 1990), 51.

14 LAC, Communist Party of Canada fonds (hereafter CPC), MG28-IV4, vol. 51, File 65, quoted in ibid.

15 Mark Chochla, "Tulio Mior: Bushworker and Labour Leader," Thunder Bay Historical Museum Society *Papers and Records* 28 (2000): 31. For a good overview of the sources available on Canadian Communist involvement in the Spanish Civil War, see George Bolotenko, "The National Archives and Left-Wing Sources from Russia: Records of the Mackenzie-Papineau Battalion, the Communist Party of Canada and Left-Wing Internationals," *Labour/Le Travail* 37 (Spring 1996): 179-203. For the Finnish involvement, see Varpu Lindström, *From Heroes to Enemies: Finns in Canada, 1937-1947* (Beaverton, ON: Aspasia Books, 2000), 13-20. General studies include William C. Beeching, *Canadian Volunteers: Spain 1936-1939* (Regina: Canadian Plains Research Centre, 1989); Victor Hoar, *The Mackenzie-Papineau Battalion* (Toronto: Copp Clark, 1969); and Mark Zuehlke, *The Gallant Cause: Canadians in the Spanish Civil War, 1936-1939* (Vancouver and Toronto: Whitecap Books, 1996).

16 Oiva W. Saarinen, *Between a Rock and a Hard Place: A Historical Geography of the Finns in the Sudbury Area* (Waterloo, ON: Wilfrid Laurier University Press, 1999), 146; and Mayme Sevander, *Of Soviet Bondage: Sequel to "Red Exodus"* (Duluth, MN: OSCAT, 1996), 122-57.

17 *Vapaus,* 27 June 1935, 8, quoted in Saarinen, ibid., 146.

18 LAC, Finnish Organization of Canada fonds (hereafter FOC), MG28-V46, vol. 6, File 15, "Various Minutes of the Enlarged Executive Committee," 1936; Ivan Avakumovic, *The Communist Party in Canada: A History* (Toronto: McClelland and Stewart, 1975), 96-98; and Arja Pilli, *The Finnish-Language Press in Canada, 1901-1939: A Study in the History of Ethnic Journalism* (Turku, Finland: Institute for Migration Studies, 1982), 141.

19 LAC, FOC, vol. 13, File 28, "Report of the Executive Committee of the FOC to the FOC Convention, 1933"; vol. 6, File 7, "Minutes of the FOC Convention, 1937"; vol. 6, File 10, "Minutes of the FOC Convention, 1939"; Donald Avery, *"Dangerous Foreigners": European Immigrant Workers and Labour Radicalism in Canada, 1896-1932* (Toronto: McClelland and Stewart, 1979), 120; Tim Buck, *Thirty Years, 1922-1952: The Story of the Communist Party of Canada* (Toronto: Progress Books, 1952), 26-28; and Pilli, *The Finnish-Language Press in Canada*, 142.

20 Magnuson, quoted in Donald MacKay, *The Lumberjacks* (Toronto: McGraw-Hill Ryerson, 1978), 256.

21 Ian Radforth, *Bushworkers and Bosses: Logging in Northern Ontario, 1900-1980* (Toronto: University of Toronto Press, 1987), 132. For information on the July 1935 strike, see Royal Canadian Mounted Police, "Weekly Summary, Report on Revolutionary Organizations and Agitators in Canada, Appendix No. I: General, 3. The Fort William Area, No. 762, 3 July 1935," in *RCMP Security Bulletins: The Depression Years, Part II, 1935*, 380; and "Weekly Summary, Report on Revolutionary Organizations and Agitators in Canada, Appendix No. I: General, No. 764, 17 July 1935," in *RCMP Security Bulletins*, ibid., 404.

22 For Bruce Magnuson's recollection of these events, see Lakehead University Archives (hereafter LUA), Jean Morrison Labour History Collection (hereafter JMLHC), GS186a, Tape 22, Interview with Bruce Magnuson, 1972.

23 Radforth, *Bushworkers and Bosses*, 132.

24 Alex Gibson argued that the Communists inserted the passages to ensure that the Trades and Labour Council would not agree to joint candidates. See *Worker*, 15 December 1934 and 5 January 1935.

25 Royal Canadian Mounted Police, "Weekly Summary, Report on Revolutionary Organizations and Agitators in Canada, Appendix No. II: Report by Provinces, V. Ontario, 8. 'Voice of Labor' Cease Publication, No. 737, 20 December 1934," in *RCMP Security Bulletins: The Depression Years, Part II, 1935*, 461.

26 *Worker*, 12 January 1935.

27 See *Port Arthur News-Chronicle*, 15 October 1935; and Ahti Tolvanen, *Finntown: A Perspective on Urban Integration. Port Arthur Finns in the Inter-war Period: 1918-1939* (Helsinki: University of Helsinki, 1985), 105.

28 Morrison, "The Organisation of Labour at Thunder Bay," 134-35. The CPC, though, did initially have a period where members questioned what the CCF could offer. For examples of this discussion, see *Young Worker*, 30 June 1934, 4. For the CCF's early years, see Gerald Caplan, *The Dilemma of Canadian Socialism: The CCF in Ontario* (Toronto: McClelland and Stewart, 1973); and D. McHenry, *The Third Force in Canada: The Cooperative Commonwealth Federation 1932-1948* (Berkeley: University of California Press, 1950).

29 Joan Sangster, "The Communist Party and the Woman Question, 1922-1929," *Labour/Le Travail*, 15 (Spring 1985): 25-56.

30 *Young Worker*, 1 November 1933, 5.

31 Allen Mills, *Fool for Christ: The Political Thought of J.S. Woodsworth* (Toronto: University of Toronto Press, 1991), 103.

32 For Communist coverage of Smith's campaign, see *Worker*, 7, 14, and 17 September and 1, 5, and 10 October 1935.

33 Ibid., 19 September and 1 October 1935. Buck's presence at the Lakehead was not without controversy. Consider that shortly after being defeated in the election, Robert Manion in a Fort William speech let loose a diatribe against the CPC and told those present that Tim Buck would be back in prison before long. See *Worker,* 19 October 1935.

34 LAC, Canadian Security Intelligence Service (hereafter CSIS), RG146, vol. 21, File [1025-9-9019] 92-A-00099, partie 2, 001, "Fort William Detachment Report Re: Communist Party of Canada – Mass Meeting – Port Arthur, Ontario, 26 September 1935; 'Tim Buck,'" 960; Royal Canadian Mounted Police, "Weekly Summary Report on Revolutionary Organizations and Agitators in Canada, No. 776, 9 October 1935," in *RCMP Security Bulletins: The Depression Years, Part II, 1935,* 522-23; and *Worker,* 5 October 1935.

35 "Federal Election Results in Fort William and Port Arthur, 1917-1940," in Roy Piovesana, *Robert J. Manion: Member of Parliament for Fort William, 1917-1935* (Thunder Bay: Thunder Bay Historical Museum Society, 1990), 33-34. For the *Worker*'s coverage of Smith's involvement in the election, see every issue between 7 and 19 September, 1 and 10 October, and 19 October 1935. Local coverage of Smith's candidacy can be found in the Fort William and Port Arthur newspapers.

36 As in past campaigns, Smith appears to have relocated to Northwestern Ontario in late August. He led a number of high-profile parades and gave speeches throughout the region that, judging from reports, were well attended. The RCMP reported, for example, that his 12 October parade in Port Arthur consisted of approximately 2,000 people and another in Fort Frances drew 300. Despite these numbers, his election meeting was poorly attended. See Royal Canadian Mounted Police, "Weekly Summary, Report on Revolutionary Organizations and Agitators in Canada, Appendix No. II: Report by Provinces, V Ontario, No. 767, 27 August 1935," 436; "Weekly Summary, Report on Revolutionary Organizations and Agitators in Canada, Appendix No. II: Report by Provinces, IV Ontario, 10. A.E. Smith's Election Meeting Poorly Attended, No. 769, 21 August 1935," 453; and "Weekly Summary, Report on Revolutionary Organizations and Agitators in Canada, Appendix No. II: Report by Provinces, IV Ontario, No. 778, 23 October 1935," 550, in *RCMP Security Bulletins: The Depression Years, Part II, 1935.*

37 The FWFF's full impact is unknown and awaits its first major historical study. For more, see Pilli, *The Finnish-Language Press in Canada,* 143-44. Pilli comments, however, that most of the fifteen locals that were reported to exist in 1935 existed in name only.

38 Piovesana, *Robert J. Manion,* 65, and, for a thorough discussion, Roy Piovesana, "Playing the Party Game: R.J. Manion and the 1935 Election in Fort William," Thunder Bay Historical Museum Society *Papers and Records* 16 (1988): 3-15. For more on the breakdown of urban and rural polls, see Tolvanen, *Finntown,* 106.

39 For the most recent and thorough treatment on the subject of Canadians in the Spanish Civil War, see Michael Petrou, *Renegades: Canadians in the Spanish Civil War* (Vancouver: UBC Press, 2008). In particular, see his appendix listing all those who went to Spain, between 190 and 241.

Bibliography

PRIMARY SOURCES

Archives

Archives of Ontario (AO)
Manuscript Division
F1274: Fred E. Moore fonds (FEM)
Government Archives Division
RG4-32: Attorney General of Ontario Files (AGO)
RG23: Ontario Provincial Police (OPP)

City of Thunder Bay Archives (TBA)
Fort William fonds (FWF)
Series 2: Index to Council Minutes, 1901-68
Series 3: Bylaws, 1892-1969
Series 4: Fort William City Clerk's Files (FWCCF)
Series 16: City of Fort William Annual Reports (FWAR)
Port Arthur fonds (PAF)
Series 72: Licence, Police, and Relief Committee Minutes (LPRC)

Lakehead University Archives (LUA)
General Series
GS186a: Jean Morrison Labour History Collection (JMLHC)
Manuscript Series
MG3: Finlandia Club Collection, 1903-60 (FCC)
MG8: Thunder Bay Finnish-Canadian Historical Society Collection (TBFCHS)
MG10: *Canadan Teollisuusunionistinen Kannatus Liitto* fonds (CTKL)

Library and Archives Canada (LAC)
Manuscript Division
MG10-K3: Communist International fonds (CI)
MG26-H: Robert L. Borden fonds (RBF)
MG28-IV4: Communist Party of Canada fonds (CPC)
MG28-V137: Finnish Association *(Suomalainen Osasto)* of Port Arthur fonds (SOP)
MG28-V46: Finnish Organization of Canada fonds (FOC)
MG30-A94: J.L. Cohen fonds (JL)
MG32-G3: Tim Buck Collection
Government Archives Division
RG2: Records of the Privy Office
RG24: Department of National Defence (DND)
RG25: Department of External Affairs (DEA)
RG27: Department of Labour (DL)
RG76: Department of Citizenship and Immigration (DCI)
RG146: Canadian Security Intelligence Service (CSIS)

Provincial Archives of Manitoba
Manuscript Division
MG10, A3: One Big Union fonds (Reel M308) (OBU)
MG10, A14-2: Robert Boyd Russell Collection (Reels M363-M366) (RBR)

Thunder Bay Historical Museum Society (TBHMS)
Personal Papers
A17: A.T. Hill fonds
Records of Government and the Judiciary
G3: City of Fort William fonds (CFW)

Serials and Newspapers
Appeal to Reason
British Columbia Federationist
Canadan Uutiset
Canadian Forward
Canadian Labour Defender
Citizen and Country
Cotton's Weekly
Edmonton Forum
Edmonton Journal
Farmerske Zhyttia
Fort William Daily Times-Journal
Fort William Morning Herald
Industrial Banner
Industrial Pioneer
Industrial Solidarity
Industrial Unionist
Industrial Worker
Industrialisti
Junior Recruit (Port Arthur)
Labour Gazette
Le Travailleur
Lumber Worker
Metsätyöläinen
One Big Union Bulletin
One Big Union Monthly (Chicago)
Ontario Timberworker
Organizer (Port Arthur)
Port Arthur Daily News
Port Arthur News-Chronicle
Sudbury Star
Thunder Bay Chronicle-Journal
Toronto Labour Leader
Toronto Star
Trades and Labour Congress of Canada Report of Proceedings
Työkansa

Ukrainski Robitnychi Visti
Vapaus
Voice (Winnipeg)
Wage-Earner (Fort William)
Western Clarion
Worker (Toronto)
Young Worker

SECONDARY SOURCES

Books and Articles

Abella, Irving. *Nationalism, Communism, and Canadian Labour: The CIO, the Communist Party, and the Canadian Congress of Labour, 1935-56.* Toronto: University of Toronto Press, 1973.

Adams, Dave. "1919 in Canada: The Birth of a New Left." *Socialist Worker* (December-January 1991). n.p.

Aitchison, J.H., ed. *The Political Process in Canada.* Toronto: University of Toronto Press, 1963.

Akin, William E. *Technocracy and the American Dream: The Technocratic Movement, 1900-1941.* Berkeley: University of California Press, 1977.

Anderson, A.B. "'The Invisible Minority' in Canada: In Search of the Anglo-Canadian Ethnic Group." *Canadian Ethnic Studies Association Bulletin* 9, 3 (1982): 17-18.

Angus, Ian. *Canadian Bolsheviks: The Early Years of the Communist Party of Canada.* Montreal: Vanguard, 1981.

–. *Canadian Bolsheviks: The Early Years of the Communist Party of Canada,* 2nd ed. Vancouver: Trafford Publishing, 2004.

–. "A Party of a New Type, the Socialist Party of Canada and the Birth of Canadian Communism." *Marxism: A Socialist Annual* 4 (2006): 66-74.

Avakumovic, Ivan. *The Communist Party in Canada: A History.* Toronto: McClelland and Stewart, 1975.

Avery, Donald. *"Dangerous Foreigners": European Immigrant Workers and Labour Radicalism in Canada, 1896-1932.* Toronto: McClelland and Stewart, 1979.

–. "Ethnic Loyalties and the Proletarian Revolution: A Case Study of Communist Political Activity in Winnipeg, 1923-1936." In *Ethnicity, Power and Politics in Canada,* ed. Jorgen Dahlie and Tissa Fernando. Toronto: Methuen, 1981.

–. *Reluctant Host: Canada's Response to Immigrant Workers, 1896-1994.* Toronto: McClelland and Stewart, 1995.

Babcock, Robert H. *Gompers in Canada: A Study in American Continentialism before the First World War.* Toronto: University of Toronto Press, 1974.

Barr, Elinor. "Swedes at the Lakehead 1900-1930." Thunder Bay Historical Museum Society *Papers and Records* 20 (1992): 50-62.

Beasley, Thomas F. "The 1909 Freight Handlers' Strike: Col. Sam Steele Searches Strikers for Guns." Thunder Bay Historical Museum Society *Papers and Records* 17 (1989): 18-20.

Beaulieu, Michel S., ed. *Essays in Northwestern Ontario Working Class History: Thunder Bay and Its Environs.* Thunder Bay: Lakehead University Centre for Northern Studies, 2008.

–. "Reacting to the Workers' Revolt: The Lakehead and the Winnipeg General Strike." *Left History* 14, 2 (2009): 18-32.

Beaulieu, Michel S., and Chris Southcott. *North of Superior: An Illustrated History of Northwestern Ontario.* Toronto: James Lorimer, 2010.

Bercuson, D.J. *Confrontation at Winnipeg: Labour, Industrial Relations and the General Strike.* Montreal and Kingston: McGill-Queen's University Press, 1974; revised edition, 1990.

Bercuson, David J. *Confrontation at Winnipeg,* rev. ed. Montreal and Kingston: McGill-Queen's University Press, 1990.

–. *Fools and Wise Men: The Rise and Fall of the One Big Union*. Toronto: McGraw-Hill Ryerson, 1978.

Betcherman, Lita-Rose. "Lèse Majesté: The Trial of Aaro Vaara." *Beaver* 78, 5 (October/November 1998): 12-18.

–. *The Little Band: The Clashes between the Communists and the Political and Legal Establishment in Canada, 1928-1932*. Ottawa: Deneau Publishers, 1982.

Black, J.L. *Canada in the Soviet Mirror: Ideology and Perception in Soviet Foreign Affairs*. Ottawa: Carleton University Press, 1998.

Bolotenko, George. "The National Archives and Left-Wing Sources from Russia: Records of the Mackenzie-Papineau Battalion, the Communist Party of Canada, and Left-Wing Internationals." *Labour/Le Travail* 37 (Spring 1996): 179-203.

Borkenau, F. *World Communism: A History of the Communist International*. Ann Arbor: University of Michigan Press, 1962.

Boudreau, Joseph A. "1914-1919: Interning Canada's 'Enemy Aliens.'" *Canada: An Historical Magazine* 2, 1 (September 1974): 15-27.

Bradwin, Edmund W. *The Bunkhouse Man*. Toronto: University of Toronto Press, 1972.

Brody, David. *Steelworkers in America: The Nonunion Era*. Cambridge, MA: Harvard University Press, 1960.

Brown, Lorne A., and Caroline Brown. *An Unauthorized History of the RCMP*. Toronto: James Lorimer, 1973.

Brown, Robert Craig, and Ramsay Cook. *Canada 1896-1921: A Nation Transformed*. Toronto: McClelland and Stewart, 1974.

Buck, Tim. *Thirty Years: 1922-1952: The Story of the Communist Movement in Canada*. Toronto: Progress Books, 1952.

Bumsted, J.M. *The Winnipeg General Strike of 1919: An Illustrated History*. Winnipeg: Watson Dwyer Publishing, 1994.

Cameron, Elspeth, and Janice Dickin, eds. *Great Dames*. Toronto: University of Toronto Press, 1997.

–. "In Defence of the Labour Theory of Value: The Socialist Party of Canada and the Evolution of Marxist Thought." *Journal of History and Politics* 10 (1992): 61-86.

–. "The Cult of Spontaneity: Finnish-Canadian Bushworkers and the Industrial Workers of the World in Northern Ontario, 1919-1934." *Labour/Le Travail* 41 (Spring 1998): 117-46.

–. *Canadian Marxists and the Search for a Third Way*. Montreal and Kingston: McGill-Queen's University Press, 1999.

Canada Suomalainen Sosialistijärjeston Ensimmäisen Edustajakokouksen Pöytäkirja, Port Arthuissa, Ont. Port Arthur: Työkansa Publishing, 1914.

Canada's Party of Socialism: History of the Communist Party of Canada, 1921-1976. Toronto: Progress Books, 1982.

Canadan Suomalainen Järjestö 24 Vuotta. Sudbury: Vapaus Publishing, 1936.

Carr, E.H. *Socialism in One Country. Vol. 3: 1924-1926*. London: Macmillan, 1964.

–. *The Russian Revolution from Lenin to Stalin, 1917-1929*, with a new introduction by R.W. Davies. New York: Palgrave Macmillan, 2004.

Chochla, Mark. "Sabbatarians and Sunday Street Cars." Thunder Bay Historical Museum Society *Papers and Records* 17 (1989): 25-36.

–, ed. "Tulio Mior, Bushworker and Labour Leader." Thunder Bay Historical Museum Society *Papers and Records* 28 (2000): 23-50.

Coates, Ken, and Bill Morrison, eds. *The Historiography of the Provincial Norths*. Thunder Bay: Lakehead University Centre for Northern Studies, 1996.

Conley, James R. "Frontier Labourers, Crafts in Crisis, and the Western Labour Revolt: The Case of Vancouver, 1900-1919." *Labour/Le Travail* 23 (1989): 9-37.

Dahlie, Jorgen, and Tissa Fernando, eds. *Ethnicity, Power and Politics in Canada.* Toronto: Methuen, 1981.

Drachkovitch, Milorad M., ed. *The Revolutionary Internationals, 1864-1943.* Palo Alto, CA: Stanford University Press, 1966.

Draper, Theodore. *American Communism and Soviet Russia: The Formative Period.* New York: Viking Press, 1960.

Dubofsky, Melvyn. *We Shall Be All: A History of the Industrial Workers of the World.* Chicago: Quadrangle Books, 1969.

Ducin, Livio. "Unrest in Algoma Lumber Camps: The Bushworkers' Strikes of 1933-1934." In *50 Years of Labour in Algoma,* ed. by Livio Ducin et al. Sault Ste. Marie: Algoma University College, 1978.

Ducin, Livio, et al., eds. *50 Years of Labour in Algoma.* Sault Ste. Marie: Algoma University College, 1978.

Dunk, Thomas W. *It's A Working Man's Town: Male Working-Class Culture.* Montreal and Kingston: McGill-Queen's University Press, 1991; reprinted 1994.

Dupuis, Michael. "Winnipeg's Red Scare." *Beaver* (August-September 2007): 38-43.

Eklund, William. *Builders of Canada: History of the Finnish Organization of Canada, 1911-1971.* Translated by Vappu Tyyskä. Toronto: Finnish Organization of Canada, 1987.

–. "The Formative Years of the Finnish Organization of Canada." In *Finnish Diaspora I: Canada, South America, Africa, Australia and Sweden,* ed. by Michael G. Karni. Toronto: Multicultural History Society of Ontario, 1981.

Eley, Geoff. *Forging Democracy: The History of the Left in Europe, 1850-2000.* New York: Oxford University Press, 2000.

Esposito, Anthony V. *The Ideology of the Socialist Party of America, 1901-1917.* New York: Garland, 1997.

Flynn, Elizabeth Gurley. *Memories of the Industrial Workers of the World.* New York: American Institute for Marxist Studies, 1977.

Foner, Philip S. *History of the Labor Movement in the United States. Vol. 4: The Industrial Workers of the World, 1905-1917.* New York: International Publishers, 1965.

Forsey, Eugene A. *The Canadian Labour Movement 1812-1901.* Ottawa: Canadian Historical Association, 1974.

Frank, David. *J.B. McLachlan: A Biography.* Toronto: James Lorimer, 1999.

Frank, David, and John Manley. "The Sad March to the Right: J.B. McLachlan's Resignation from the Communist Party of Canada, 1936." *Labour/Le Travail* 30 (Fall 1992): 132-34.

Friesen, Gerald. "'Yours in Revolt': The Socialist Party of Canada and the Western Labour Movement." *Labour/Le Travail* 1 (1976): 139-57.

Furet, François. *The Passing of an Illusion: The Idea of Communism in the Twentieth Century,* translated by Deborah Furet. Chicago: University of Chicago Press, 1999.

Gaillie, Duncan. *Social Inequality and Class Radicalism in France and Britain.* Cambridge: Cambridge University Press, 1983.

Gambone, Larry. *The Impossibilists: Selections from the Press of the Socialist Party of Canada and the One Big Union, 1906-1938.* Montreal: Red Lion Press, 2002.

Ganz, A. Harding. "The German Expedition to Finland, 1918." *Military Affairs* 44, 2 (April 1980): 84-91.

Geary, Dick. *Karl Kautsky.* Manchester: Manchester University Press, 1987.

Glotzer, Albert. *Trotsky: Memoir and Critique.* Buffalo: Prometheus Books, 1989.

Gompers, Samuel. *American Labor and the War.* New York: George H. Doran, 1919.

Goode, Patrick, ed. *Karl Kautsky: Selected Political Writings.* London: Macmillan, 1983.

Goodrich, Austin. *Study in SISU: Finland's Fight for Independence.* New York: Ballantine Books, 1960.

Granatstein, J.L., and R.D. Cuff, eds. *War and Society in North America.* Toronto: Thomas Nelson and Sons, 1971.

Gregorovich, J.B., ed. *Ukrainian Canadians in Canada's Wars: Materials for Ukrainian Canadian History.* Toronto: Ukrainian Canadian Research Foundation, 1983.

Gutkin, Harry, and Mildred Gutkin. *Profiles in Dissent: The Shaping of Radical Thought in the Canadian West.* Edmonton: NeWest Press, 1997.

Gutman, Amy, et al. *Multiculturalism and "The Politics of Recognition": An Essay by Charles Taylor.* Princeton, NJ: Princeton University Press, 1992.

Hak, Gordon. "British Columbia Loggers and the LWIU, 1919-1922." *Labour/Le Travail* 23 (Spring 1989): 67-90.

–. "The Communists and the Unemployed in the Prince George District, 1930-1935." *BC Studies* 68 (Winter 1985-86): 45-61.

Hampden, Jackson J. "German Intervention in Finland, 1918." *Slavonic and East European Review* 18 (July 1939): 93-101.

Harney, Robert. ed. *Gathering Place: People and Neighbourhoods in Toronto.* Toronto: Multicultural History Society of Ontario, 1985.

Harney, Robert, and J. Vincenza. Scarpaci, eds. *Little Italies of North America.* Toronto: Multicultural History Society of Ontario, 1981.

Harpelle, Ronald, Varpu Lindström, and Alexis Pogorelskin, eds. *Karelian Exodus: Finnish Communities in North America and Soviet Karelia during the Depression Era.* Beaverton, ON: Aspasia Books, 2004.

Harzig, Christiane, ed. *The Press of Labour Migrants in Europe and North America, 1880s to 1930s.* Bremen, Germany: Publications of the Labor Newspaper Preservation Project, 1985.

Heron, Craig. *The Canadian Labour Movement: A Short History.* Toronto: James Lorimer, 1989.

–, ed. *The Workers' Revolt in Canada, 1917-1925.* Toronto: University of Toronto Press, 1998.

Hewitt, Steve R. "'You Are Making History, You Are Making History': The On to Ottawa Trek in Northern Ontario." Lakehead University Centre for Northern Studies, Research Report No. 38, 1995.

Hobbs, Margaret, and Joan Sangster, eds. *The Woman Worker, 1926-1929.* St. John's: Canadian Committee on Labour History, 1999.

Hodgson, John. *Communism in Finland.* Princeton, NJ: Princeton University Press, 1967.

Hovi, Kalervo. "The Winning of Finnish Independence as an Issue in International Relations." *Scandinavian Journal of History* 3 (1978): 47-73.

Howard, Victor. *"We Were the Salt of the Earth!" The On-To-Ottawa Trek and the Regina Riot.* Regina: Canadian Plains Research Centre, 1985.

Iacovetta, Franca, with Paula Draper and Robert Ventresca, eds. *A Nation of Immigrants: Women, Workers, and Communities in Canadian History, 1840s-1960s.* Toronto: University of Toronto Press, 1998.

Index to the Thunder Bay Historical Museum Society Papers and Records, Volumes I-XXI, 1973-1993. Thunder Bay: Thunder Bay Historical Museum Society, 1994.

Jackson, Robert. *At War with the Bolsheviks.* London: Tandem, 1974.

Jamieson, Stuart. *Industrial Relations in Canada,* 2nd ed. New York: St. Martin's Press, 1974.

Jennings, Jeremy. *Syndicalism in France: A Study of Ideas.* New York: Palgrave Macmillan, 1990.

Jewell, Gary. *The History of the IWW in Canada.* Chicago: Industrial Workers of the World, 1975.

–. "The History of the IWW in Canada." *Our Generation* 11, 3 (1976): 35-45.

Johanningsmeier, Edward P. *Forging American Communism: The Life of William Z. Foster.* Princeton, NJ: Princeton University Press, 1994; reprint with new preface, 1998.

Jussila, Osmo. *Maakunnasta valtioksi: Sumomen valtion synty.* Helsinki: WSOY, 1978.

–. "Die russische Reichsgesetzgeburng in Finnland in den Jahren 1809-1898." *Jahrbücher für Geshichte Osteuropas* 33 (1985): 345-65.

–, Seppo Hentilä, and Jukka Nevakivi. *Suomen poliittinen historia.* Helsinki: WSOY, 2000.

Kalbfleish, Herbert Karl. *The History of the Pioneer German Language Press of Ontario, 1835-1918.* Toronto: University of Toronto Press, 1968.

Karni, Michael G., ed. *The Best of Finnish Americana*. Iowa City: Penfield Press, 1994.

–. *Finnish Diaspora I: Canada, South America, Africa, Australia, and Sweden*. Toronto: Multicultural History Society of Ontario, 1981.

–. *Finnish Diaspora II: United States*. Toronto: Multicultural History Society of Ontario, 1981.

Karni, Michael G., Matti E. Kraups, and Douglas J. Ollila Jr., eds. *The Finnish Experience in the Western Great Lakes Region: New Perspectives*. Turku, Finland: Institute for Migration Studies, 1975.

Kealey, Gregory S. "1919: The Canadian Labour Revolt." *Labour/Le Travail* 13 (1984): 11-44.

–. "State Repression of Labour and the Left in Canada, 1914-1920: The Impact of the First World War." *Canadian Historical Review* 7, 3 (September 1993): 281-314.

–. *Workers and Canadian History*. Montreal and Kingston: McGill-Queen's University Press, 1995.

Kealey, Gregory S., and Bryan Palmer. *Dreaming of What Might Be: The Knights of Labor in Ontario, 1880-1900*. New York: Cambridge University Press, 1982.

Kealey, Gregory S., and Peter Warrian, eds. *Essays in Canadian Working Class History*. Toronto: McClelland and Stewart, 1976.

Kealey, Gregory S., and Reg Whitaker, eds., *The RCMP Security Bulletins: The Depression Years, Part I, 1933-34*. St. John's: Canadian Committee on Labour History, 1993.

–, eds. *The RCMP Security Bulletins: The Depression Years, Part II, 1935*. St. John's: Canadian Committee on Labour History, 1995.

–, eds. *The RCMP Security Bulletins: The Early Years, 1919-29*. St. John's: Canadian Committee on Labour History, 1994.

Kelley, Ninette, and Michael Trebilcock. *The Making of the Mosaic: A History of Canadian Immigration Policy*. Toronto: University of Toronto Press, 1998.

–. *Migration from Finland to North America in the Years Between the United States Civil War and the First World War*. Turku: Institute for Migration Studies, 1974.

Kerr, George D. "Canadian Press Censorship in WW I." *Journalism Quarterly* 59, 2 (1982): 235-39.

Keshen, Jeffrey. "All the News That Was Fit to Print: Ernest J. Chambers and Information Control in Canada, 1914-1919." *Canadian Historical Review* 73, 3 (September 1992): 315-43.

–. *Propaganda and Censorship during Canada's Great War*. Edmonton: University of Alberta Press, 1996.

Kirkconnell, Watson. "Kapuskasing – An Historical Sketch." *Queen's Quarterly* 28 (1921): 264-78.

Kivisto, Peter. *Immigrant Socialists in the United States: The Case of Finns and the Left*. Rutherford, NJ: Fairleigh Dickinson University Press; London; Cranbury, NJ: Associated University Presses, 1984.

Klehr, Harvey, and John Earl Haynes. *The American Communist Movement: Storming Heaven Itself*. New York: Twayne Publishers, 1992.

Kolasky, John. *Prophets and Proletarians: Documents on the History of the Rise and Decline of Ukrainian Communism in Canada*. Edmonton: Canadian Institute of Ukrainian Studies Press and University of Alberta Press, 1990.

–. *The Shattered Illusion: The History of Pro-Communist Organizations in Canada*. Toronto: PMA Books, 1979.

Kostiainen, Auvo. *The Forging of Finnish-American Communism, 1917-1924: A Study in Ethnic Radicalism*. Turku, Finland: Turun Yliopisto, 1978.

Kordan, Bohdan S., and Lubomyr Y. Luciuk, eds. *A Delicate and Difficult Question: Documents in the History of Ukrainians in Canada, 1899-1962*. Kingston: Limestone Press, 1986.

Kouhi, Christine. "Labour and Finnish Immigration to Thunder Bay: 1876-1914." *Lakehead University Review* 9, 1 (Spring 1976): 41-55.

Leier, Mark. "Responses to Professors Palmer, Strong-Boag, and McDonald." *BC Studies* 3 (Autumn 1996): 93-98.

–. *Where the Fraser River Flows: The Industrial Workers of the World in British Columbia*. Vancouver: New Star Books, 1990.

–. "W[h]ither Labour History: Regionalism, Class, and the Writing of BC History." *BC Studies* 3 (Autumn 1996): 61-75.
Lenin, V.I. *Collected Works*. Moscow: Foreign Languages Publishing House, 1960-70.
–. *Left-Wing Communism: An Infantile Disorder*. Moscow: Foreign Languages Publishing House, 1952.
Lindström, Varpu. *Defiant Sisters: A Social History of Finnish Immigrant Women in Canada*, 2nd ed. Beaverton, ON: Aspasia Books, 2003.
–. *The Finns in Canada*. Ottawa: Canadian Historical Association, 1985.
Lipton, Charles. *The Trade Union Movement of Canada, 1827-1959*. Montreal: Canadian Social Publications, 1966.
Liversedge, Ronald. *Recollections of the On to Ottawa Trek*, ed. Victor Hoar. Toronto: McClelland and Stewart, 1973.
Logan, Harold. *Trade Unions in Canada*. Toronto: Macmillan, 1948.
Look on Canada, Now, and See History Anew: An Epoch Past and a Life Fashioning under Your Hands Communism, to Which All Roads Lead, Selected Writings of Leslie Morris, 1923-1964. Toronto: Progress Books, 1970.
Luciuk, Lubomyr. *A Time for Atonement: Canada's First National Internment Operations and the Ukrainian Canadians, 1914-1920*. Kingston: Limestone Press, 1988.
MacDowell, Laurel Sefton. *Renegade Lawyer: The Life of J.L. Cohen*. Toronto: University of Toronto Press, 2001.
–. "The Mysterious Deaths at Onion Lake." *Beaver* (April/May 1995): 32-34.
MacDowell, Laurel Sefton, and Ian Radforth, eds. *Canadian Working Class History: Selected Readings*, 2nd ed. Toronto: Canadian Scholar's Press, 2000.
Macgillivray, George B. *A History of Fort William and Port Arthur Newspapers from 1875*. Toronto: Bryant Press, 1968.
MacLaren, Roy. *Canadians in Russia, 1918-1919*. Toronto: Macmillan of Canada, 1976.
MacPherson, Ian. *Each for All: A History of the Co-operative Movement in English Canada, 1900-1945*. Toronto: Macmillan, 1979.
Manley, John. "Canadian Communists, Revolutionary Unionism and the 'Third Period': The Workers' Unity League, 1929-1935." *Journal of the Canadian Historical Association*, New Series 5 (1994): 167-94.
–. "Does the International Labour Movement Need Salvaging? Communism, Labourism and the Canadian Trade Unions, 1921-1928." *Labour/Le Travail* 41 (Spring 1998): 147-180.
–. "Moscow Rules? 'Red' Unionism and 'Class against Class' in Britain, Canada, and the United States, 1928-1935." *Labour/Le Travail* 56 (Fall 2005): 9-50.
–. "Preaching the Red Stuff: J.B. McLachlan, Communism, and the Cape Breton Coal Miners, 1922-1935." *Labour/Le Travail* 30 (1992): 65-114.
–. "'Starve, Be Damned!' Communists and Canada's Urban Unemployed, 1929-1939." *Canadian Historical Review* 79, 3 (September 1998): 466-91.
Maroney, Paul. "'The Great Adventure': The Context and Ideology of Recruiting in Ontario, 1914-1917." *Canadian Historical Review* 77, 1 (March 1996): 62-98.
Martynowych, Orest T. *Ukrainians in Canada: The Formative Period, 1891-1924*. Edmonton: Canadian Institute of Ukrainians Studies Press, 1991.
–. "The Ukrainian Socialist Movement in Canada, 1900-1918." *Journal of Ukrainian Graduate Studies* 1 (1976): 27-44.
Marunchak, Michael H. *The Ukrainian Canadians: A History*. Winnipeg and Ottawa: Ukrainian Free Academy of Science, 1970.
Masters, D.C. *The Winnipeg General Strike*. Toronto: University of Toronto Press, 1950.
Mauro, Joseph M. *A History of Thunder Bay*. Thunder Bay: City of Thunder Bay, 1981.

McCallum, Todd. "Not A Sex Question? The One Big Union and the Politics of Radical Manhood." *Labour/Le Travail* 42 (1998): 15-54.

–. "The Strange Tale of Tom Cassidy and Catherine Ross, or Free Love, Heterosexuality, and the One Big Union." *Journal of the Canadian Historical Association* 9 (1998): 125-54.

McCormack, A. Ross. *Reformers, Rebels, and Revolutionaries: The Western Canadian Radical Movement, 1899-1919*. Toronto: University of Toronto Press, 1977.

McDonald, Robert. "'The West Is a Messy Place.'" *BC Studies* 3 (Autumn 1996): 88-92.

McEwen, Tom. *The Forge Glows Red: From Blacksmith to Revolutionary*. Toronto: Progress Books, 1974.

McIlroy, John, and Alan Campbell. "'Nina Ponomareva's Hats': The New Revisionism, the Communist International, and the Communist Party of Great Britain, 1920-1930." *Labour/Le Travail* 49 (Spring 2002): 147-88.

McKay, Ian. "For a New Kind of History: A Reconnaissance of 100 Years of Canadian Socialism." *Labour/Le Travail* 46 (Fall 2000): 69-125.

–. *Reasoning Otherwise: Leftists and the People's Enlightenment in Canada, 1890-1920*. Toronto: Between the Lines Press, 2008.

–. *Rebels, Reds, Radicals: Rethinking Canada's Left History*. Toronto: Between the Lines Press, 2005.

–. "The Liberal Order Framework: A Prospectus for a Reconnaissance of Canadian History." *Canadian Historical Review* 81, 3 (September 2000): 617-45.

McNaught, Kenneth, and David J. Bercuson. *The Winnipeg Strike: 1919*. Don Mills, ON: Longman Canada, 1974.

Metsaranta, Marc. *Project Bay Street: Activities of Finnish-Canadians in Thunder Bay before 1915*. Thunder Bay: Finnish Canadian Historical Society, 1989.

Mills, Allen. *Fools for Christ: The Political Thought of J.S. Woodsworth*. Toronto: University of Toronto Press, 1991.

Mishler, Paul C. *Raising Reds: The Young Pioneers, Radical Summer Camps, and Communist Political Culture in the United States*. New York: Columbia University Press, 1999.

Moritz, Theresa, and Albert Moritz. *The World's Most Dangerous Woman: A New Biography of Emma Goldman*. Vancouver and Toronto: Subway Books, 2001.

Morris, Leslie. *The Story of Tim Buck's Party, 1922-1939*. Toronto: New Era Publishers, 1939.

Morrison, Jean. "Cobalt Agitators Played a Part in Lakehead Labour Battles." *Highgrader Magazine* (Christmas 2005): 22-23.

–. "Colbalt Agitators Stir Up Lakehead Union Interest." *Highgrader Magazine* (Fall 2005): 24-26.

–. "Ethnicity and Class Consciousness: British, Finnish, and South European Workers at the Canadian Lakehead before World War 1." *Lakehead University Review* 9, 1 (1976): 55-65.

–. "Frederick Urry, Architect: The Wage-Earner's Advocate." Thunder Bay Historical Museum Society *Papers and Records* 14 (1986): 8-22.

–. "Labour in Fort William and Port Arthur, 1903-1913." Thunder Bay Historical Museum Society *Papers and Records* 1 (1973): 23-30.

–. *Labour Pains: Thunder Bay's Working Class in Canada's Wheat Boom Era*. Thunder Bay: Thunder Bay Historical Museum Society, 2009.

–, ed. *Lake Superior to Rainy Lake, Three Centuries of Fur Trade History: A Collection of Writings*. Thunder Bay: Thunder Bay Historical Museum Society, 2003.

–. *Superior Rendezvous-Place: Fort William in the Canadian Fur Trade*. Toronto: Natural Heritage Books, 2001.

Morton, Desmond. "Some Millennial Reflections on the State of Canadian Labour History." *Labour/Le Travail* 46 (Fall 2000): 11-36.

–, with Terry Copp. *Working People: An Illustrated History of Canadian Labour*. Ottawa: Deneau and Greenburg Publishers, 1980.

Morton, D., and G. Wright. *Winning the Second Battle: Canadian Veterans and the Return to Civilian Life, 1915-1930*. Toronto: University of Toronto Press, 1987.

Muirhead, B.W. "A Short History of Thunder Bay." *Polyphony* 9, 2 (1987): 5-9.

Muirhead, Bruce. "Harry Bryan – A Man of Fanatical Conviction." Thunder Bay Historical Museum Society *Papers and Records* 17 (1989): 37-43.

Niitemaa, V., et al., eds. *Old Friends – Strong Ties*. Vaasa, Finland: Institute of Migration, 1976.

Otter, W.D. *Internment Operations, 1914-1920*. Ottawa: n.p., 1921.

Paivo, Aku. *Canadan Suomalainen Sosialisti jarjeston Ensimmainen Edustaja-Kokouksen Poytakirja*. Port Arthur: Työkansan Kirjapaino, 1914.

Palmer, Bryan. "Class and the Writing of History: Beyond BC." *BC Studies* 3 (Autumn 1996): 76-84.

–. "Maurice Spector, James P. Cannon, and the Origins of Canadian Trotskyism." *Labour/Le Travail* 56 (Fall 2005): 91-148.

–. *Working-Class Experience: The Rise and Reconstitution of Canadian Labour, 1800-1980*. Toronto: Butterworth, 1983.

Palmer, Howard. *Immigration and the Rise of Multiculturalism*. Toronto: Copp Clark, 1975.

Patrias, Carmela. *Relief Strike: Immigrant Workers and the Great Depression in Crowland, Ontario, 1930-1935*. Toronto: New Hogtown Press, 1990.

Penner, Norman. *Canadian Communism: The Stalin Years and Beyond*. Toronto: Methuen, 1988.

–. *The Canadian Left: A Critical Analysis*. Scarborough ON: Prentice Hall Canada, 1977.

–, ed. *Winnipeg 1919: The Strikers' Own History of the Winnipeg General Strike*, 2nd ed. Toronto: James Lorimer, 1975.

–. "The One Big Union in International Perspective: Revolutionary Industrial Unionism 1900-1925." *Labour/Le Travail* 7 (Spring 1981): 41-66.

Petrone, Penny. *Breaking the Mould*. Toronto: Guernica, 2001.

Petryshyn, J. "Class Conflict and Civil Liberties: The Origins and Activities of the Canadian Labour Defence League, 1925-1940." *Labour/Le Travail* 10 (Autumn 1982): 39-64.

–. "R.B. Bennett and the Communists, 1930-1935." *Journal of Canadian Studies* 9, 4 (1974): 43-55.

Phillips, Paul A. *No Power Greater: A Century of Labour in British Columbia*. Vancouver: BC Federation of Labour; Boag Foundation, 1967.

Pilli, Arja. *The Finnish-Language Press in Canada, 1901-1939: A Study in the History of Ethnic Journalism*. Turku, Finland: Institute for Migration Studies, 1982.

Piovesana, Roy. "Playing the Party Game: R.J. Manion and the 1935 Election in Fort William." Thunder Bay Historical Museum Society *Papers and Records* 16 (1988): 3-15.

–. *Robert J. Manion: Member of Parliament for Fort William, 1917-1935*. Thunder Bay: Thunder Bay Historical Museum Society, 1990.

Pogorelskin, Alexis. "New Perspectives on Karelian Fever: The Recruitment of North American Finns to Karelia in the Early 1930s." *Journal of Finnish Studies* 1, 3 (December 1997): 165-78.

Polvinen, Tuomo. *Valtakunta ja rajamaa: N. I. Bobrikov Sumomen kenraalikuvernöö 1898-1904*. Helsinki: WSOY, 1984.

Porter, John. *The Vertical Mosaic: An Analysis of Social Class and Power in Canada*. Toronto: University of Toronto Press, 1965.

Potestio, John. *The Italians of Thunder Bay*. Thunder Bay: Lakehead University, Chair of Italian Studies, 2005.

Potestio, John, and Antonio Pucci, ed. *The Italian Immigrant Experience*. Thunder Bay: Canadian Italian Historical Association, 1988.

Potrebenko, Helen. *No Streets of Gold: A Social History of the Ukrainians in Alberta*. Vancouver: New Star Books, 1977.

Puntila, LA. *The Political History of Finland, 1809-1966*, translated by David Miller. Helsinki: Otava Publishing, 1974.

Radforth, Ian. *Bushworkers and Bosses: Logging in Northern Ontario, 1900-1980.* Toronto: University of Toronto Press, 1987.

Raffo, Peter. "Oral Witness versus Documentary Evidence: The Case of Rosvall and Voutilainen." Thunder Bay Historical Museum Society *Papers and Records* 29 (2001): 3-34.

Rasporich, A.W. "'Call Me Charlie,' Charlie W. Cox: Port Arthur's Populist Politician." Thunder Bay Historical Museum Society *Papers and Records* 19 (1991): 2-20.

–. "Ethnicity in Lakehead Politics, 1900-1930." *Polyphony* 9, 2 (1987): 61-66.

–. "Faction and Class in Modern Lakehead Politics." *Lakehead University Review* 7, 1 (Summer 1974): 31-65.

–. "Twin City Ethnopolitics: Urban Rivalry, Ethnic Radicalism and Assimilation in the Lakehead, 1900-1970." *Urban History Review/Revue d'histoire urbaine* 18, 3 (February 1990): 210-30.

Ratz, David Karl. "Aid to Civil Power: The 96th 'Lakehead Superior Regiment' 1909 and 1912." Thunder Bay Historical Museum Society *Papers and Records* 19 (1991): 51-64.

Rees, Tim and Andrew Thorpe, eds. *International Communism and the Communist International, 1919-43.* Manchester, UK: Manchester University Press, 1998.

Repo, Satu. "Lakehead in the Thirties, a Labour Militant Remembers." *This Magazine* 13, 3 (July/August 1979): 42-43.

–. "Rosvall and Voutilainen: Two Union Men Who Never Died." *Labour/Le Travail* 8/9 (Autumn/Spring 1981/82): 79-102.

Ridley, F.F. *Revolutionary Syndicalism in France: The Direct Action of Its Time.* Cambridge: Cambridge University Press, 1970.

Rislakki, Jukka, and Eila Lahti-Argutina, *No Home for Us Here: The Mass Annihilation of the Finnish Border-Hoppers in the Urals in 1938,* translated by Richard Impola. St. Cloud, MN: North Star Press, 2002.

Roberts, Barbara. *Whence They Came: Deportation from Canada, 1900-1935.* Ottawa: University of Ottawa Press, 1988.

Robin, Martin. *Radical Politics and Canadian Labour, 1880-1930.* Kingston: Queen's University Industrial Relations Centre, 1968.

Rodney, William. *Soldiers of the International: A History of the Communist Party of Canada, 1919-1929.* Toronto: University of Toronto Press, 1968.

Ross, Gerald. "Fort William's Enemy Alien 'Problem' during the First World War." Thunder Bay Historical Museum Society *Papers and Records* 22 (1994): 1-22.

Rutherdale, Robert. *Hometown Horizons: Local Responses to Canada's Great War.* Vancouver: UBC Press, 2004.

Ryan, Oscar. *The Sedition of A.E. Smith.* Toronto: Canadian Labour Defence League, 1934.

Saarinen, Oiva W. *Between a Rock and a Hard Place: A Historical Geography of the Finns in the Sudbury Area.* Waterloo, ON: Wilfrid Laurier University Press, 1993.

Safarian, A.E. *The Canadian Economy in the Great Depression.* Toronto: McClelland and Stewart, 1970.

Salvadori, Massimo. *Karl Kautsky and the Socialist Revolution, 1880-1938.* London: New Left Books, 1979.

Sangster, Joan. "The Communist Party and the Woman Question, 1922-1929." *Labour/Le Travail* 15 (Spring 1985): 25-56.

–. *Dreams of Equality: Women on the Canadian Left, 1920-1950.* Toronto: McClelland and Stewart, 1989.

–. "Finnish Women in Ontario, 1890-1930." *Polyphony* 3 (1981): 46-54.

Saywell, John. "Labour and Socialism in British Columbia: A Historical Survey of Historical Developments before 1903." *British Columbia Quarterly* 15 (July-October 1951): 129-50.

Schulze, David. "The Industrial Workers of the World and the Unemployed in Edmonton and Calgary in the Depression of 1913-1915." *Labour/Le Travail* 25 (Spring 1990): 46-75.

Scollie, F.B. "The Creation of the Port Arthur Street Railway 1890-95: Canada's First Municipally-Owned Street Railway." Thunder Bay Historical Museum Society *Papers and Records* 18 (1990): 40-58.

–. "Louis Lawrence Peltier (1853-1939): Railway Labour Leader, Mayor of Fort William 1909-10." Thunder Bay Historical Museum Society *Papers and Records* 32 (2004): 10-30.
Scott, F.R. "The Trial of the Toronto Communists." *Queen's Quarterly* 39 (August 1932): 512-27.
Scott, Jack. *Plunderbund and Proletariat.* Vancouver: New Star Books, 1975.
Service, Robert. *Comrades! A History of World Communism.* Cambridge, MA: Harvard University Press, 2007.
Sevander, Mayme. *Of Soviet Bondage: Sequel to "Red Exodus."* Duluth, MN: OSCAT, 1996.
Sharpe, D.A. "Enlistment in the Canadian Expeditionary Force 1914-1918: A Regional Analysis." *Journal of Canadian Studies* 18, 4 (Winter 1983-84): 15-29.
Simon, Roger. *Gramsci's Political Thought: An Introduction,* rev. ed. London: Lawrence and Wishart, 1991.
Smith, A.E. *All My Life: An Autobiography.* Toronto: Progress Books, 1977.
Smith, Jay. "Russia and the Origins of the Finnish Civil War of 1918." *American Slavic and East European Review* 14, 4 (December 1955): 481-502.
Southcott, Chris. "Ethnicity and Community in Thunder Bay." *Polyphony* 9, 2 (1987): 10-20.
–, ed. *Provincial Hinterland: Social Inequality in Northwestern Ontario.* Halifax: Fernwood Publishing, 1993.
Stearns, P. *Revolutionary Syndcalism and French Labor: A Cause without Rebels.* New Brunswick, NJ: Rutgers University Press, 1971.
Stewart, Bryce M., comp. *Report of a Preliminary and General Social Survey of Fort William,* directed by the Department of Temperance and Moral Reform of the Methodist Church and the Board of Social Service and Evangelism of the Presbyterian Church. n.p., 1913.
–, comp. *Report of a Preliminary and General Social Survey of Port Arthur,* directed by the Department of Temperance and Moral Reform of the Methodist Church and the Board of Social Service and Evangelism of the Presbyterian Church. n.p., 1913.
Strong-Boag, Veronica. "Moving Beyond Tired 'Truths': Or, Let's Not Fight Old Battles." *BC Studies* 3 (Autumn 1996): 84-87.
Swankey, Ben, and John Evans Shields. *Work and Wages: A Documentary Account of the Life and Times of Arthur H. (Slim) Evans, 1890-1944.* Vancouver: Trade Union Research Bureau, 1977.
Swettenham, John. *Allied Intervention in Russia 1918-1919, and the Part Played by Canada.* Toronto: Ryerson Press, 1967.
Swyripa, Frances, and John Herd Thompson, eds. *Loyalties in Conflict: Ukrainians in Canada during the Great War.* Edmonton: Canadian Institute of Ukrainian Studies, University of Alberta, 1985.
Thompson, Fred. *The IWW: Its First Fifty Years (1905-1955): The History of an Effort to Organize the Working Class.* Chicago: Industrial Workers of the World, 1955.
Tolvanen, Ahti. *Finntown: A Perspective on Urban Integration. Port Arthur Finns in the Inter-war Period: 1918-1939.* Helsinki: University of Helsinki, 1985.
–. "Population Development of Finns in Port Arthur." *Polyphony* 9, 2 (1987): 43-45.
Tommila, Päiviö. *Suuri adressi.* Helsinki: WSOY, 1999.
Tronrud, Thorold J. *Guardians of Progress: Boosters and Boosterism in Thunder Bay, 1870-1914.* Thunder Bay: Thunder Bay Historical Museum Society, 1993.
Tronrud, Thorold J., and A. Ernest Epp, eds. *Thunder Bay: From Rivalry to Unity.* Thunder Bay: Thunder Bay Historical Museum Society, 1995.
Tucker, Robert C. "The Emergence of Stalin's Foreign Policy." *Slavic Review* 36, 4 (December 1977): 563-89.
Upton, Anthony F. *The Finnish Revolution, 1917-1918.* Minneapolis: University of Minnesota Press, 1980.
Van der Linden, Marcel, and Lex Heerma van Voss, eds. *Class and Other Identities: Gender, Religion and Ethnicity in the Writing of European Labor History.* New York and Oxford: Berghahn Books, 2002.

Virtanen, Keijo. *Settlement or Return? Finnish Emigrants (1860-1920).* Helsinki: Migration Institute, 1979.
Waiser, W.A. *Park Prisoners. The Untold Story of Western Canada's National Parks, 1915-1946.* Calgary: Fifth House, 1995.
Wallace, C.M., and Ashley Thomson, eds. *Sudbury: Rail Town to Regional Capital.* Toronto: Dundurn Press, 1993.
Weisbord, Merrily. *The Strangest Dream: Canadian Communists, the Spy Trials, and the Cold War.* Montreal: Véhicule Press, 1983; reprint, 1994.
Wilson, J. Donald. "The Finnish Organization of Canada, the 'Language Barrier,' and the Assimilation Process." *Canadian Ethnic Studies* 9, 2 (1977): 107-16.
–. "Matti Kurikka and A.B. Mäkelä: Socialist Thought among Finns in Canada, 1900-1932." *Canadian Ethnic Studies* 10, 2 (1978): 9-21.
Wilson, J. Donald, and Jorgen Dahlie. "Introduction." *Canadian Ethnic Studies* 10, 2 (1978): 1-8.
Workers' Benevolent Association of Canada. *Friends in Need: The WBA Story, a Canadian Epic in Fraternalism.* Winnipeg: Workers' Benevolent Association of Canada, 1972.
Worley, Matthew. *Class against Class: The Communist Party in Britain between the Wars.* London: I.B. Tauris, 2002.
Wuorinen, John H. "Finland's War of Independence, 1918." *American Scandinavian Review* 51 (1963): 389-95.
Young, W.R. "Conscription, Rural Depopulation, and the Farmers of Ontario." *Canadian Historical Review* 53, 3 (September 1972): 289-320.
Yrjö, Ravio. *Kanadan Suomalaisten Historia,* vol. 1. Sudbury: n.p., 1979.
Yuzyk, Paul. *Ukrainians in Manitoba: A Social History.* Toronto: University of Toronto Press, 1953.
Zaslow, Morris. *Opening of the Canadian North, 1870-1914.* Toronto: McClelland and Stewart, 1971.
Zettergerh, Seppo, ed. *Suomen historian pikkujättiläinen.* Porvoo, Finland: WSOY, 1978.

Electronic Resources

Gambone, Larry. *The Impossibilists: Selections from the Press of the Socialist Party of Canada and the One Big Union, 1906-1938.* Montreal: Red Lion Press, 2002. Online excerpt: Socialist History Project, http://socialisthistory.ca/Docs/Imposs/Impossibilists1.htm.
"J.B. McLachlan Resigns from the Communist Party (1936), a Letter to Tim Buck, 13 June 1936." Socialist History Project, http://www.socialisthistory.ca.
Nesbitt, Doug. "J.B. McLachlan, the Communist Party of Canada and the United Front." Socialist History Project, http://www.socialisthistory.ca.
Parliament of Canada. "History of Federal Ridings since 1867." http://www.parl.gc.ca.

Film

Letters from Karelia. Directed by Kelly Saxberg. Montreal: National Film Board of Canada, 2004.

Unpublished Works and Theses

Allen, Martha Isobel Gerard, "A Survey of Finnish Cultural, Economic, and Political Development in the Sudbury District of Ontario." MA thesis, University of Western Ontario, 1954.
Babcock, Robert Harper. "The AFL in Canada, 1896-1908: A Study in American Labor Imperialism." PhD dissertation, Duke University, 1970.
Baxter, Theresa. "Selected Aspects of Canadian Public Opinion on the Russian Revolution and on Its Impact on Canada, 1917-1919." MA thesis, University of Western Ontario, 1973.
Beaulieu, Michel S. "A Proletarian Prometheus: Socialism, Ethnicity, and Revolution at the Lakehead, 1900-1935." PhD dissertation, Queen's University, 2007.
Cahan, Jacqueline F. "A Survey of the Political Activities of the Ontario Labour Movement, 1850-1935." MA thesis, University of Toronto, 1945.

Dupuis, Michael. "The Response of the Toronto Daily Press to the Winnipeg General Strike." MA thesis, University of Ottawa, 1973.

Hatton, Nathan. "Headlocks at the Lakehead: Wrestling in Fort William and Port Arthur, 1912-1913." MA thesis, Lakehead University, 2007.

High, Steven C. "'A Municipal Ownership Town': The Organization and Regulation of Urban Services in Port Arthur, 1875-1914." MA thesis, Lakehead University, 1994.

Hill, A.T. "Highlights of Labor History – Lakehead and Canada." Thunder Bay, c. 1973.

–. "Highlights of Labor History – Lakehead, Canada and World." Thunder Bay, c. 1973.

Homel, Gene Howard. "James Simpson and the Origins of Canadian Social Democracy (Socialism in Toronto, 1890-1914)." PhD dissertation, University of Toronto, 1978.

Jalava, Mauri Amiko. "'Radicalism or a "New Deal"?' The Unfolding World View of the Finnish Immigrants in Sudbury, 1883-1932." MA thesis, Laurentian University, 1983.

Johnson, Ross Alfred. "No Compromise – No Political Trading: The Marxian Socialist Tradition in British Columbia." PhD dissertation, University of British Columbia, 1976.

Kaipio, Taisto Matti. "German War Aims in Finland, 1918." PhD dissertation, University of Toronto, 1976.

Karni, Michael G. "Yhteishyvä – or, for the Common Good: Finnish Radicalism in the Western Great Lakes Region 1900-1940." PhD dissertation, University of Minnesota, 1975.

Kouhi, Christine. "Finnish Immigrants in Thunder Bay 1876-1914." Honours thesis, Lakehead University, 1975.

Kratz, Peter V. "'Sudburyn Suomalaiset': Finnish Immigrant Activities in the Sudbury Area, 1882-1939." MA thesis, University of Western Ontario, 1980.

MacDonald, Marvin. "An Examination of Protestant Reaction towards the Non-English Speaking Immigrant in Port Arthur and Fort William, 1903-1914." MA thesis, Lakehead University, 1976.

Manley, John. "Communism and the Canadian Working Class during the Great Depression: The Workers' Unity League, 1903-1936." PhD dissertation, Dalhousie University, 1984.

Morrison, Jean. "Community and Conflict: A Study of the Working Class and Its Relationship at the Canadian Lakehead, 1903-1913." MA thesis, Lakehead University, 1974.

Pelt, Melvin Leonard. "The Communist Party of Canada, 1929-1942." MA thesis, University of Toronto, 1964.

Penner, Norman. "The Socialist Idea in Canadian Political Thought." PhD dissertation, University of Toronto, 1975.

Samuels, Elliot. "The Red Scare in Ontario: The Reactions of the Ontario Press to the Internal and External Threat of Bolshevism, 1917-1919." MA thesis, Queen's University, 1972.

Sillanpää, Lennard Paul Charles. "A Political and Social History of Canadians of Finnish Descent in the District of Sudbury." MA thesis, University of Helsinki, 1973.

Thur, Douglas. "Beat around the Bush: The Lumber and Sawmill Workers Union and the New Political Economy of Labour in Northern Ontario, 1936-1988." MA thesis, Lakehead University, 1990.

Troop, George R. "Socialism in Canada." MA thesis, McGill University, 1922.

Veltri, Mary. "Labour Radicalism among Finnish Bushworkers at the Lakehead, 1916-1936." Honours thesis, Lakehead University, 1981.

Warrian, Peter. "The Challenge of the One Big Union Movement in Canada, 1919-1921." MA thesis, University of Waterloo, 1971.

Index

Note: "(f)" after a page number indicates an illustration

Aalto, Arthur, 140

ACCL. *See* All-Canadian Congress of Labour (ACCL)

AFL. *See* American Federation of Labor (AFL)

Agricultural Industrial Unit (AIU), 135

Agricultural Workers Industrial Union card, 192(f)

Ahlqvist, John W.: appointed to CPC executive, 108; concern over OBU control, 82; on divisions within SPC, 33; expelled by CPC leadership, 145, 146-47; fights wartime ban against FSOC, 60; first chairman of FSOC, 34; refusal to comply with Politburo, 144; work with CPC, 237*n*33

Aho, David, 123

All-Canadian Congress of Labour (ACCL), 132, 195

Allen, F.B., 26-27

Amalgamated Mine Workers of Nova Scotia, 183-84, 189

Amalgamated Postal Workers of Canada (Port Arthur), 230*n*22

Amalgamated Section of Carpenters (Port Arthur), 230*n*22

American Federation of Labor (AFL): battles with OBU, 72, 82; Brotherhood of Carpenters and Joiners, 20; Bryan's activities with, 16-17, 19; Carpenters' Union, 267*n*2; comes to Lakehead, 16-17; CPC's attempts to infiltrate, 116; and Depression-era unemployment, 156; favours industrial harmony over revolution, 204; focus on Anglo workers, 20; lack of support to industrial workers, 49; Lakehead affiliates join OBU, 75; LWIUC affiliates with, 205; membership fees, 50

Amerikan Suomalainen Työväenliito Imatra (Imatra) , 21-24, 215*n*43, 216*n*60. *See also Osasto*

Anderson, Fred, 188

Anderson, Garfield, 207

Anglo-American Secretariat. *See* Comintern (Communist International), Anglo-American Secretariat

Anglo-Canadian workers: and continuance of SPC locals, 34-35; CPC's failure to reach, 183; CPC's gains, 102, 182; lack of interest in CPC, 115-16, 125, 132; lack of interest in IWW, 51; power in labour movement, 6, 8, 27, 32; priority for CPC, 132, 136, 160-61, 168-69, 172, 183; wariness toward WPC, 100

Arnberg, William, 92, 123, 231*n*34, 241*n*99

Austrian workers, 46, 47, 60, 223*n*38

Barker, Herbert, 37, 40, 56, 222*n*25, 227*n*107

Barker, Jim: in 1931 demonstrations, 260*n*119; *aka* Sam Langley?, 180, 256*n*47; deportation, 180; dissatisfied with Hautamäki, 170; as organizer for CPC, 161, 168, 173; organizes demonstrations, 174; reports on membership losses, 176

Bartenders' Union, 19, 221*n*15

Batters, Alfred, 207

Beck, Adam, 234*n*117

Beck, Arnold, 97

Bell, George, 222*n*25

Bell Telephone, 17-18

Bennett, R.B., 185

Benouski, M., 248*n*8

Berg, Carl, 234*n*100

Biniowsky, Michael, 126, 146, 170, 260*n*119

Boiko (on executive of first Lakehead WPC branch), 97

Bolotynuk, Peter, 162

Bolshevik (October) Revolution, Russia, 42, 61, 77-78, 81

Bolshevism, 54, 59-60, 70, 72, 77-79

Bolshevization: of CPC, 110-11, 116-17, 124, 130-31, 168; failure with LAWIU Finns, 171; precedes Stalin, 242*n*4; reorganizes party structure along factory/industrial lines, 110-11; unpopularity in Lakehead, 142

Booker, James, 40, 222*n*25
Boom, Doug, 97
Borden, Robert, 57
Borg, Holmer, 55, 106, 114, 121
Boulter, Garfield, 205
Boyce, William, 248*n*8
Boychuk, Michael, 107
Bricklayers and Masons (Port Arthur), 230*n*22
Brooker, James, 27
Brotherhood of Boiler Makers and Iron Shipbuilders, 230*n*22
Brotherhood of Carpenters, 71
Brotherhood of Pulp, Sulphite, and Paper Mill Workers, 230*n*22
Brotherhood of Railway Carmen, 230*n*22
Brown, J., 56
Brown, William, 234*n*117
Bruce, Frank, 162, 164, 165
Bruce, Malcolm, 112, 115, 230*n*19
Bryan, Harry: at 1910 TLC meeting, 218*n*105; and 1913 street railway workers strike, 40; 1914 provincial election campaign, 44; 1923 provincial election campaign, 102; and 1926 lumber strikes, 117, 123, 245*n*58; anti-conscription activities, 52, 56, 227*n*107; attempts to bridge OBU-LWIU divide, 67; blacklisted, 17-18; establishes IWW branch, 50, 224*n*65; establishes LWIUC, 96-97; establishes SDPC branches, 49, 58, 234*n*63; establishes SPC branch, 24; and establishment of SDPC, 34, 219*n*118; on executive of CLC, 231*n*34; at Fort William memorial for Lenin, 104; heads Farmers' Unity League, 207; initially opposes Buck, 146; leaves Lakehead, 220*n*162; on LWIUC executive, 125; organizational background, 16-17; as organizer for AFL, 16-17, 20; as organizer for CPC, 112-13, 120, 125-26; as organizer for ILP, 19; as organizer for OBU, 82, 84-85, 86-87, 96, 234*n*117, 234*n*123, 235; as organizer for OSP, 22; as organizer for WPC, 97-98, 101; as organizer for WUL, 175-76, 261*n*155; at Russian Revolution anniversary, 121; shift to communism, 92; support of Zura, 80
Buck, Tim: becomes head of CPC, 150; and CPC's growing factionalism, 145; on CPC's involvement in AFL and TLC, 116; on Finns and Ukrainians in CPC, 160; initial opposition to Bolshevization, 111; internal CPC fight with S. Smith, 130; organizer for District 3 of WPC, 98; release from prison, 207, 270*n*33; reports to Comintern, 124, 132; rise through CPC ranks, 168; union experience, 237*n*25
Buhay, Beckie, 82, 112, 120, 125
Bukharin, Nikolai, 130
Buller, Annie, 113

Cahan, C.H., 59, 60, 227*n*129
Canadan Teollisuusunionistinen Kannatus Liitto (CTKL), 105, 181, 188, 192-93
Canadian Brotherhood of Railway Employees, 230*n*22
Canadian Bushmen's Union, 195-96, 197, 204
Canadian Defence Organization (CDO), 191-93, 265*n*73
Canadian Executive Branch (CEB), 183-84, 185, 191
Canadian Labour Defence League (CLDL): and 1930 May Day arrests, 162; and 1932 arrests of CPC members, 181-82; branches across Canada, 124; CDO attempts to compete with, 191-92; English branch, 128; establishes *Patronati*, 182; fights against discriminatory deportation, 164; and murder of Rosvall and Voutilainen, 255*n*24; police targeting of, 164, 166, 180, 190, 266*n*102; support for UATC, 255*n*35
Canadian Labour Party, 102, 114, 117, 119-20
Canadian Legion auxiliary police force, 162, 164, 165
Canadian Northern Coal and Ore Dock Company, 37
Canadian Northern Railway. 3, 16, 25, 37-38. *See also* railways
Canadian Pacific Railway, 1909 freight handlers strike, 29, 31; 1913 strike, 40; 1920 staff cuts, 234*n*106; ethnicities of freight handlers, 25; labour organization branch in Lakehead, 16; railyards as socialist focal point in Fort William, 3-4; workers targeted by officials, 47, 223*n*42. *See also* railways
Canadian Socialist Federation (CSF), 33, 34
Canadian Socialist League (CSL), 18, 23
Carey, John, 132-33, 142-43, 146, 248*n*8
Carrick, J.J., 26, 36, 217*n*78, 244*n*32
Carter, W.J., 37

CCF. *See* Co-operative Commonwealth Federation (CCF)
CDO. *See* Canadian Defence Organization (CDO)
CEB. *See* Canadian Executive Branch (CEB)
Central Labour Council (CLC), Fort William: decline, 105; established, 71, 231*n*34; General Workers' Unit, 71, 72, 73, 75-76; Moore's involvement, 244*n*23; and OBU fractioning, 84-87, 234*n*102; supporters, 73-74
Central Labour Union (CLU), 17, 19
Cerutti, M., 231*n*34
Checkley, William, 70, 92, 104, 106, 109, 230*n*19
Chepusiak, J., 248*n*8
Christie, R., 231*n*34
CIO. *See* Congress of Industrial Organizations (CIO)
Citizens' and Ratepayers' Unemployed Association, Fort William, 159, 189, 255*n*33
Citizens' Unemployed Association, 174
Clarke, Don, 200
CLC. *See* Central Labour Council (CLC)
CLDL. *See* Canadian Labour Defence League (CLDL)
CLU. *See* Central Labour Union (CLU)
Cohen, J.L., 162-63
Comintern (Communist International): 1935 alliance with social democrats, 11; appeal for Canadian social activists, 93, 98; class-against-class policy, 131, 154; conditions for entry, 236*n*18; established, 90; FOC incorporates policies of, 74-75; Popular Front policy, 203; as propaganda machine, under Stalin, 110; Third Period political theory entered, 129; United Front policy, 90, 197, 243*n*6
Comintern (Communist International), Anglo-American Secretariat: accepts CPC membership, 93; criticizes CPC, 131-32, 135-36, 143, 149-50, 160; lack of understanding of CPC challenges, 135; low interest in early CPC, 94; pushes to create separate Communist unions, 154
Committee for Industrial Organization, 202, 267*n*2
communism: appeal for Canadian socialists, 90-91, 236*n*13; early Canadian attempts to form party, 236*n*12; enemy of syndicalism, 91; government fears of, 133; growing popularity in 1920s, 102; principles of United Front, 90; rivalry with fascism, 129; Second International, 32, 33, 34; Third Period, 129-30, 153, 154. *See also* Comintern (Communist International)
Communist Party of Canada (CPC): 1925 federal election, 114, 124; 1929 lumber strike, 147-49; 1930 municipal and provincial elections, 158-59, 163, 257*n*61; 1931 arrest of leaders, 176; 1932 lumber strike, 181; 1933 municipal elections, 189; 1935 municipal and federal elections, 11, 205-6; 1935 paradigm shift, 202-4, 207-8; antagonism and rivalry with IWW, 101-2, 105, 118-19, 121-22, 126-28, 137, 139-40, 143, 156, 161-62, 181, 184-85, 187, 241*n*98, 254*n*19; appeal for Finns and Ukrainians, 91; Bolshevization of, 110-11, 116-17, 124, 130-31, 168; class-against-class policy, 130-31; cooperation with IWW, 190-91, 201; criticized by Comintern, 131-32, 135-36, 143, 149-50, 160; demoralization under repression and Bolshevization, 181; differences from IWW, 106-7; early attempts to form, 236*n*12; early years, 94-95, 98; efforts to move from language basis to trade/industry basis, 131-32, 136-37, 142-43; efforts toward English- and French-speaking workers, 132, 134, 136, 158, 160-61, 172-73; established, 89, 91-93, 235*n*134; ethnic and regional tensions, 99-100, 111-12, 131-33, 135-37, 158, 159-60, 237*n*25, 243*n*8, 251*n*73; fight for legality, 197; fight against unemployment, 156-57; Finnish member transfer requests to USSR, 169; growth and reorganization, 104-5, 107-8; headquarters in Port Arthur, 89; influence of Lenin's writings, 90, 93; internal contradictions and fractioning, 99-100, 108, 132-33, 135-37, 139-40, 144-46, 150, 154, 156, 176-77, 182-83; language/ethnic agitprops, 124, 126, 128, 135, 247*n*110; membership, 115, 124-26, 179, 248*n*120; and murder of Rosvall and Voutilainen, 157-58; organization of separate Communist unions, 154; organizer inconstancy, 197-98; political action policy, 93; political districts in Lakehead, 98, 107, 238*n*51, 242*n*107; Popular Front policy, 11,

182, 203-4, 208; reliance on non-Anglo workers, 169-70; "Stalinization" of, 131, 136-37; successes (1930s), 191, 196; United Front efforts, 90-91, 107, 189, 197, 200, 201; waning influence (early 1930s) among youth, women, and agricultural workers, 175-76. *See also* Workers' Party of Canada
Communist Party of Russia, 110
Communist Red International of Labour Unions, 92
Congress of Industrial Organizations (CIO), 11
conscription, First World War: and 1917 federal election, 57-58; worker sentiments/activities against, 51-52, 55-56
Conservative Party of Canada: 1908 provincial election, 27; 1911 provincial election, 36; 1917 federal election, 57; 1926 federal election, 120
Co-operative Commonwealth Federation (CCF): 1934 provincial election, 199; 1935 municipal and federal elections, 11, 205-7; changes socialist landscape in Canada, 206-8; established, 195, 206, 265*n*90; presence in Lakehead, 206-7, 265*n*90
Cosmishin, Mike, 99, 146, 158, 162
Cowan, Donald, 52
Cox, Charlie, 200, 266*n*103
CPC. *See* Communist Party of Canada (CPC)
Cruikshanks, Alex, 261*n*146
CSF. *See* Canadian Socialist Federation (CSF)
CSL. *See* Canadian Socialist League (CSL)
CTKL. *See Canadan Teollisuusunionistinen Kannatus Liitto* (CTKL)

Danalinski, Elsie, 162-63
Darrell (mayor of Port Arthur), 159
De Leon, Daniel, 97
Debs, Eugene, 16, 19, 51, 225*n*68
demonstrations: 1912, in support of dock workers, 37; 1912 or 1914, Port Arthur, 30(f); 1916, internment camp uprising, 228*n*146; 1918, various, 59-60; 1924, May Day, 108; 1929, protesting police harassment, 146; 1930, various, 159, 162-63, 164; 1931, various, 170, 174, 176, 260*n*119; 1932, various, 186, 255*n*24, 262*n*13, 263*n*38; 1933, various, 190, 196; 1934, various, 198, 200, 266*n*106
Dennis, Albert Hugh, 39, 57-58, 72, 75, 208, 227*n*125
deportations: of Barker (1932), 177, 180, 256*n*47; demonstrations against, 255*n*24; of Holm (1930), 164; of Panttaja (1930), 164; of Sandberg (1932), 186; of suspected Wobblies, as strike-breaking measure, 80; threat of, during Depression, 164, 169, 180; threat of, during First World War, 44, 48, 222*n*30
Dixon, James, 105, 245*n*58
Dominion Police, 55
Draper, P.M., 31
Dunbar, James Asher, 57-58, 222*n*25, 227*n*125

Eames, H.M., 231*n*34
elections: 1902 municipal, 17-18; 1904 federal, 18-19; 1908 provincial, 27-29; 1911 municipal and provincial, 36-37; 1913 municipal, 38-39; 1914 provincial, 44-45, 221*n*20, 222*n*22; 1915 municipal, 45, 222*n*25; 1917 federal, 57-58; 1923 provincial, 102; 1925 federal, 114-15, 124, 244*n*31, 244*n*32, 245*n*35; 1926 federal, 117, 119-20; 1930 municipal and provincial, 158-59, 163, 168, 257*n*61; 1932 municipal, 181, 262*n*13; 1933 municipal, 189; 1934 provincial, 198-99, 200; 1935 municipal and federal, 10-11, 200, 205-6, 269*n*24, 270*n*36
Electrical Workers (Port Arthur), 230*n*22
enemy aliens, wartime: dismissed from jobs, 46; fears of, 45-46, 51, 58-60; internment of, 46, 61; lack of union support, 48; registration of, 46, 223*n*38
English, Leo T., 24, 26-27, 32, 35, 216*n*56, 217*n*78
Erickson, Armand, 257*n*67
ethnicity: and divisiveness of CPC Bolshevization, 111-12; and enemy alien suspicions in wartime, 45-48, 51, 55, 58-59, 223*n*38; of membership in SPC, 24-25; and postwar socialism, 43; shaping Lakehead socialism, 3, 6-8, 16, 89; and societal prejudices, 42-44, 59, 156; of striking workers, 56-57. *See also specific ethnic groups*

Farmers' Unity League, 175, 207
fascism, 11, 129, 197-98, 202-4, 208, 267*n*6
Fedrokpow, M., 265*n*73
Finland: civil war, 23, 54; effect of Russian Revolution, 53-54; independence from Russia, 23, 54; social democratic movements, 20, 81; syndicalism, 81; universal suffrage, 23

Finlayson Street Labour Hall, Fort William, 234*n*107
Finnish agitprop, 128
Finnish-American Workers' League (*Amerikan Suomalainen Työväenliito Imatra*), 21-24, 215*n*43, 216*n*60. *See also Osasto*
Finnish Association, 95
Finnish Building Company, 61, 81, 97, 105, 231*n*32
Finnish Federation, SDPC, 60
Finnish Labour Temple, Port Arthur: 1910 TLC annual meeting, 31; 1911 municipal election and proposed tax exemption for Temple, 36; 1914 first convention of FSOC, 47; 1918 closure, 61, 231*n*32; anti-conscription meetings, 52, 56; not CLC headquarters, 85; CLC meetings, 234*n*107; constructed, 20; debt assumed by FOC/OBU, 71, 74, 81; Finnish socialist focal point, 72, 74, 89; held by SDPC, 52; IWW takes over, 105; police targeting of, 180
Finnish National Party Fraction Bureau, 168
Finnish Organization of Canada (earlier, FSOC): 1923 reorganization, 103; 1933 labour strike, 190; affiliation with OBU, 68-69, 70, 75, 81; affiliation with TUEL, 87; affiliation with WPC/CPC, 93, 94, 95, 96, 102, 170, 204-5, 237*n*33; break with OBU, 84, 88; continues Depression-era work despite repression, 262*n*10; CPC's attempts to censure and control, 144-47, 160; cultural, social, and economic centre for Finnish workers, 143-44; factional disputes with ULFTA, 170; instructed to bring in new recruits, 168-69; IWW inroads in late 1920s, 140; membership, 205; policies and programs, 74-75; power in left-wing politics, 133; turns Finnish Labour Temple over to OBU, 81
Finnish Organization of Fort William, 255*n*35
Finnish Organization of Port Arthur, 255*n*35
Finnish Social Democratic Party, 140
Finnish Socialist Organization of Canada (later, FOC): 1911 elections, 36; backbone of wartime IWW, 50; established, 34, 47; growth, 219*n*124; and "hall socialism," 23; and lumber industry, 50; and mining industry, 224*n*66; renamed FOC, 229*n*14; wartime suspicions of, 59-60, 229*n*14
Finnish Socialist Party of Canada, 81
Finnish Socialist Section, WPC, 94, 103
Finnish Support Circle, 95
Finnish Women's Federation, 126, 247*n*107
Finnish workers: 1926 lumber strike, 246*n*63; 1935 municipal and federal elections, 206; 1935 shift to moderation, 207-8; appeal of communism's United Front, 91; building of Lenin's statue, 1, 8; centrality in LAWIU lessened, 174; Communists, join forces with other ethnicities, 181; in CPC, and Bolshevization, 112, 116, 243*n*8; divergent views of syndicalism, 81; emigration to Karelia, 1, 8, 169; employment at railways, 25; "hall socialism," 23; Labour Day gathering, 21(f); negative effects of Stalin's intolerance of Finns, 204; not hired, to stem growth of CPC and IWW, 187; participation in labour unrest and union organizations, 20, 21-25, 27-28, 31, 32-33; population in Lakehead, 6, 20; postwar surveillance and repression, 72, 79-80; "Reds" from Finland, 54, 226*n*93; role in 1908 provincial election, 27; role in 1911 elections, 36-37; in Russia's October Revolution, 1; socialist presence in Lakehead, 6-8, 16, 22-23, 62; support of IWW, 50, 76; support of OBU, 70, 71, 75, 76-77, 81-82; support of OBU declines, 83, 85-86, 88, 89; support of Russian Revolution, 53-54; support of SDPC, 39; support of WPC/CPC, 98, 100, 101, 108, 115, 126, 133, 136, 239*n*52, 240*n*81, 245*n*35; support of YCL, 133; wartime suspicions of, 44, 47-48, 55, 59-60; "Whites," 147, 158, 182, 184, 187, 196, 228*n*133
Finnish Workers' and Farmers' Federation, 207, 270*n*37
Finnish Workers' Sports Club, 181
Finnish Workingmen's Association of Fort William, 24
Finnish Workingmen's Association of Port Arthur, 20, 21. *See also Imatra*
First World War: conscription issue, 51-52, 55-56, 57-58; enemy alien suspicions, 45-48, 51, 55, 58-59, 223*n*38; ethnic and political prejudices, 42-44; police surveillance and repression of socialists, 45, 55, 59-60; promotes more radical social/political protest, 42-43, 60-62; and Russian Revolution, 53-54
Food Workers' Union, 174, 176

Fort William, enemy alien designations in, 46; Finnish population, 20, 22; immigration to, 3, 6, 211*n*21; labour and socialist organizations before early 1900s, 16; locations of socialist activity, 3, 5; metropole of resource-rich hinterland, 3, 5; population drop during First World War, 43; population growth in early 1900s, 6, 15-16, 211*n*23; shipping hub, 5; Ukrainian workforce, 47, 163; unemployment in Great Depression, 156; unions at start of Depression, 255*n*29. *See also* Lakehead; Port Arthur
Fort William East End Provista Society, 103
Fort William Paper Company, 133
Fort William Ratepayers' Association, 189
Fort William Socialist Local: wartime growth, 48
Fort William Temperance Society (*Pohjankukka*), 21, 22
Foster, William Z., 92
Freight Shed Workers' Union, 255*n*35
French-Canadian workers: and 1934 strikes, 200; CPC's failure to recruit, 183; priority for CPC and IWW, 134, 136, 139, 160, 168-69, 172, 174, 183, 199
Friberg, L., 106
FSOC. *See* Finnish Socialist Organization of Canada

Galician workers, 46
Galt, Annie, 146
General Recruiting Union (GRU), 135, 184, 188, 199, 254*n*19
General Workers' Unit, CLC, Fort William, 71, 72, 73, 75-76
German workers, 46, 47, 60
Germany: syndicalism, 81
Gibson, Alex: 1930 municipal election, 168; 1933 municipal election, 189; 1935 municipal and federal elections, 205, 269*n*24; establishes WPC local in Port Arthur, 102; leading figure in WUL, 168, 176; leads League for Municipal Progress, 189; poet, 258*n*100; on Port Arthur Trades and Labour Council, 142, 248*n*8; supports Smith in 1925 federal election, 114; work with CPC, 120, 248*n*8
Gilbert, Mary: in 1931 demonstrations, 170; initiates soup kitchens, 166; leading figure in WUL, 168, 176; negative perceptions of, 172; rapid rise through CPC ranks, 164; targeted by police, 165-66; tensions with Hautamäki, 166-67
Gillbanks, Jack, 198-99, 200
Golden, J.D., 134, 147-48, 178, 199-200
Goldman, Emma, 28, 217*n*88
Gompers, Samuel, 16
Grain Elevator Workers' Union, 57
Great War Veterans' Association, 60
Greek workers, 20, 25
Gröndahl, K.E., 39

Haidiuk, Nykola, 223*n*42
Hakala, Waino, 162
Hall, Moses, 218*n*105
Harris, J.P., 70, 230*n*19
Hautamäki, Ailiane, 126, 170
Hautamäki, Alf: and 1926 lumber strikes, 117, 119, 245*n*58; and 1929 lumber strike, 147-49; in 1931 demonstrations, 170; concerns about ULFTA's disaffection with CPC, 163; criticisms of CPC strategies, 141-43, 147, 157, 160, 161; criticisms of WUL, 165, 167, 170, 177; dissatisfaction with, 138-40, 170-71, 175; fears police arrest, 166; initially opposed Buck, 146; on LAWIU executive, 164; leaves Lakehead, 207; on LWIUC executive, 125; and LWIUC reorganization, 113; organizational background, 95; as organizer for CPC, 93, 101, 248*n*8; re-election despite party and union opposition to, 138-40; at Russian Revolution anniversary, 121; on strength of LAWIU, 165; suspended, 171; tensions with Gilbert, 166-67
Haywood, William, 49
Heenan, Peter, 114, 200, 267*n*124
Heikkila, Elmer, 257*n*67
Heikkinen, Andrew, 158-59
Hendrickson, Martin, 55
Hendricson, Walter, 257*n*67
Hicks, William Madison, 37-40, 49
Hill, Amos Tobias (A.T.): accused of plot to undermine CPC, 145; arrested for demonstrations, 146; continues IWW despite wartime ban, 60; with CPC executive, 108; disagrees with open association with Comintern, 107; dismissed from IWW, 55; on FOC's affiliation with OBU, 70; initial opposition to Bolshevization, 111; on IWW,

49; on IWW view of Russian Revolution, 54; leads CPC unemployed association, 159; misunderstands Lakehead divisions, 173; organizational background, 50, 225*n*68; as organizer for CPC, 94-95, 96, 101, 237*n*33; as organizer for IWW, 50, 51, 224*n*65, 237*n*25; on RCMP harassment of Finns, 47; reports on Bolshevization, 116; shift to communism, 87, 92; smoothes over FOC-CPC rift, 145, 146, 252*n*84
Hitler, Adolf, 203
Hoito Restaurant, Port Arthur, 105, 246*n*63
Holder, William, 67
Holm, Eric, 86, 164
Hostikka, Eino, 257*n*67
Howard, W., 106
Howe, C.D., 206
Hoxel, Ansu, 257*n*67
Hoxel, Mauri, 257*n*67
Huhtala, Frank, 257*n*67
Hyman, Karl, 231*n*37

Ibbetson, Percy Victor, 186
ILP. *See* Independent Labour Party (ILP)
Imatra, 21-24, 215*n*43, 216*n*60. *See also Osasto*
immigration: and communist versus social democratic beliefs, 111; importance to CPC, 107; to Lakehead, 3, 5, 15, 17, 43, 211*n*21; link with socialism, 41; political opposition in mid-1920s, 114; and success of IWW, 106
Independent Labour Party (ILP): 1904 federal election, 18-19; 1908 provincial election, 27; 1911 municipal and provincial elections, 36; 1913 growth, 40; 1913 municipal elections, 39; 1914 provincial election, 44, 222*n*22; 1917 federal election, 57-58; 1926 federal election, 120; Anglo orientation, 20; animosity with SDPC, 35-36; anti-communist position, 159; Batters as representative, 207; Bryan's support for, 19; dissolution, 25; efforts to block CPC, 174; and potential unification of working class, 41
Independent Labour Party of New Ontario, 35, 37
Industrial Workers of the World (IWW): 1926 lumber strike, 117-18, 120, 121-22, 123, 127; 1929 lumber strike, 147-49; 1932 lumber strike, 181; 1933 labour strike, 190; antagonism and rivalry with CPC, 101-2, 105, 118-19, 121-22, 126-28, 137, 139-40, 143, 156, 161-62, 181, 184-85, 241*n*98, 254*n*19; appeal for immigrants, 55; branch established in Lakehead, 49-50; Canadian Administration activities, 188-89, 199-200; Canadian Administration formed, 181, 183, 184, 265*n*76; and CDO, 191-93; cooperation with CPC, 190-91, 201; Depression-era recruitment efforts, 156, 161; efforts toward Canadian administration, 134; interest in "technocracy," 194; and internal strife in OBU, 87; labour mistrust of, 264*n*51; lack of Anglo worker support, 51; lack of conventions in late 1920s-early 1930s, 185; member opportunities/benefits, 50-51, 55; membership, 188; and murder of Rosvall and Voutilainen, 157-58; need for organizers, 193, 195; pamphlet advertisement, 155(f); philosophy and principles, 51, 55, 75-79, 81; police surveillance and investigations, 76, 79-80, 232*n*59; principles adopted by OBU, 70; reliance on immigrants, 106; reorganization, 183; revitalization between the wars, 76, 79, 101, 108-9, 112, 114, 118, 123, 126-27, 131, 139-40; rivalry with OBU, 75-76; support for Russian Revolution, 53-54; takes over Finnish Temple, 105; US administration of, 134, 135, 188, 193, 265*n*76; wartime suspicions of and ban against, 59-60, 68
International Carpenters and Joiners of America, 205
International Co-operative, 104-5, 262*n*10
International Women's Day demonstrations, 174
Iron Workers union, 19
Italian workers: 1913 municipal elections, 39; Blackshirts' efforts to organize, 267*n*6; employment at railways, 25; interest in WPC/CPC, 102, 240*n*79; participation in labour unrest and union organizations, 20, 31; postwar movement away from labour action, 61; socialist presence in Lakehead, 7; support for WPC/CPC, 115; wartime suspicions of, 47
IWW. *See* Industrial Workers of the World (IWW)

Jaakkola, J., 234*n*117
Jaaska, K., 186

Janatuinen, S., 231*n*34
Jordan, E.C., 18-19, 22, 24
Jouppi, E.M., 246*n*85
Junior Wobblies, 193, 196, 198, 200

Kallio-Kannasto, Sanna, 55. *See also* Kannasto, Sanna
Kannasto, Sanna, 47, 126, 247*n*107. *See also* Kallio-Kannasto, Sanna
Karelia Autonomous Soviet Republic: created, 169; Finnish Canadian statue of Lenin in, 1; Finnish Canadians' migration to, 1, 8, 169, 204-5, 208, 259*n*111, 259*n*113
Katainen, Peter, 222*n*25
Keefer, Francis Harry, 2, 58, 227*n*125
Kettridge, A.E., 56, 222*n*25, 227*n*107
King, William Lyon Mackenzie, 11, 206
Kiovisto, Allie, 231*n*37
Kivikoski, Ontario, 34
Knight, Joe, 86
Knights of Labor, 16
Koivu, Anna, 200, 266*n*118
Koivu, William, 231*n*37
Koivukoski (CBU executive member), 195
Koivukoski, Kosti, 187
Korhonen, E., 257*n*67
Kukkel, C., 219*n*118
Kuusela, Ed, 97
Kyro, A., 227*n*124

Labour Day, 7, 17, 21(f), 35, 116
labourism: divide with socialism, 15-16, 27, 31, 44-45; entry into direct politics in Lakehead, 19; ethnic divisions in Lakehead, 6-7, 15-16; potential unification with socialism, 40-41
Lakehead: as battleground between OBU and LWIU, 66-67; as "breeding place of revolution," 2, 79-80; definition, 210*n*3; economic activity based on resource extraction, 2, 3, 5, 17, 74, 140; economic depression before First World War, 43; encourages alliance between communists and syndicalists, 91; ethnic populations, 6, 20, 46-47, 211*n*21, 222*n*23; Great Depression, 153; immigration to, 3, 5, 15, 17, 43, 211*n*21; linkages to United States, 5-6; map, 4(f); socialism transformed by First World War, 43; as transportation hub, 3, 5; wartime labour shortages, 46, 51-52. *See also* Fort William; Port Arthur
Langley, Sam, 180, 256*n*47
Laurier, Sir Wilfrid, 19
Law, N., 248*n*8
League Against War and Fascism, 267*n*1
League for Municipal Progress, 189
Lenin, Vladimir Il'ich: death, 104, 110; influence on Canadian communists and socialists, 90, 93; statue of, built by Finnish Canadians, 1-2, 8, 210*n*1; Western criticisms of, 53
Liberal Party: 1908 provincial election, 27; 1911 provincial election, 36; 1926 federal election, 120; 1935 federal election, 10-11, 206; labour participants (Lib-Lab), 15, 33, 67, 120
Lindholm, H.J., 183, 184, 193-94
Lockhead (Loughead), Richard, 37, 86, 92, 234*n*117
Long (WPC organizer), 102
Lumber and Agricultural Workers Industrial Union of Canada (LAWIU, also known as LWIUC): 1930s' strikes and demonstrations, 179, 260*n*119; 1932 convention, 182; affiliation with WUL, 162; Bolshevization not taken up, 171; continued activity and success despite WUL, 175; difficulty of inclusion of farmers, 175; efforts to make less Lakehead-centred, 173-74; emigration of leaders to Karelia, 169; financial problems during Depression, 165, 172; name changed back to LWIUC, 263*n*32; recruitment efforts during Depression, 164-65; rivalry with LWIU, 181; tensions with WUL, 167, 171-72; youth section, 162
lumber/pulp and paper industry: 1926 strikes, 117-18, 120, 121-23; Finnish workers and CPC, 136; in Lakehead economy, 17; shipments through Lakehead, 5; strikes, 55, 117-18, 120, 121-23, 146-49, 179, 181, 191, 196, 199, 200, 205, 246*n*63; workers, challenges for socialist organizers, 51, 225*n*72; workers, IWW success with, 50-51, 55, 59, 114; workers, OBU failure with, 82-85, 87-88, 233*n*87; workers, OBU success with, 71, 73, 74-75
Lumber and Sawmill Workers Union, 11, 74-75, 208, 267*n*1
Lumber Workers Industrial Union (LWIU): 1926 lumber strike, 246*n*63; 1929 lumber strike, 146-48; affiliation with OBU, 71, 82;

break with OBU, 84-85, 87-88; decline and fall, 11, 197, 204; disputes about OBU, 82-84, 233*n*87; growth, 50-51, 76; interest in merger with LWIUC, 134; internal divisiveness, 134-35; joins AFL's Carpenters' Union, 267*n*2; and members who also harvested or organized, 134-35; rivalry with LAWIU, 181; rivalry with LWIUC, 121-23, 126-27, 137; some members affiliate with WPC, 101
Lumber Workers Industrial Union of Canada (Communist) (LWIUC): 1926 lumber strikes, 117-18, 119, 246*n*63; 1929 lumber strike, 146-48; 1933 labour strike, 190; 1934 convention, 199; changes name to LAWIU, 162; cooperation with IWW, 118, 190-91; decline and fall, 197, 204; enters Prairies, 146; established, 87, 97; Hautamäki's leadership questioned, 138-39; Hill and Hautamäki organize for, 101; membership growth, 115, 125, 142, 190-91; and murder of Rosvall and Voutilainen, 157-58; name changed back from LAWIU, 263*n*32; reorganizations, 113, 139; replaced by Lumber and Sawmill Workers Union, 11, 205; rivalry with LWIU, 121-23, 126-27, 137; and unemployment in late 1920s, 140-41
LWIU. *See* Lumber Workers Industrial Union (LWIU)
LWIUC. *See* Lumber Workers Industrial Union of Canada (Communist) (LWIUC)
Lyones, J., 231*n*34

MacAdam, George, 188, 191-95, 265*n*73, 265*n*76, 265*n*83
MacBrayne, E.M., 242*n*115
MacDonald, J.A. (with IWW), 122
MacDonald, John (Jack): appointed to CPC executive, 108; and CPC's slow progress in "Stalinization," 131; instructions on non-English members, 99; involvement with ILP, 237*n*25; on loss of CPC members to US, 107; supported by *Vapaus*, 144; targeted by CPC, 261*n*146
Machinists (Port Arthur), 230*n*22
Magnuson, Bruce, 205, 207, 208
Maguire, Trevor, 107
Mahler, Herbert, 193
Maki, Evert, 81-82
Maki, L., 195
Manaryk, Steve, 248*n*8
Manion, Robert J., 58, 120, 203, 208, 227*n*125, 270*n*33
Manitoba Social Democratic Party, 34
Mann, Ernest, 222*n*25
Manthus, W., 49
Marine and Transport Union, 127
Marino, E., 47
Marxism: debates over interpretation, 16, 55; and SPC members, 18; under Stalin, 110
May Day: 1911 or 1912 parade, 32(f); 1922 celebrations, 100; 1924 celebrations, 108; 1925 celebrations, 115; 1930 demonstrations, 162-63; 1931 demonstrations, 174; 1932 demonstrations, 262*n*13; 1933 demonstrations, 196; 1934 demonstrations, 198, 266*n*106
McEwen, Tom: concerns about Gilbert's ideology, 167; criticizes Barker for insufficient recruitment, 173; dissatisfaction with Hautamäki, 171; on Gibson, 168; lack of national leadership, 174; leads WUL, 154, 163; and PAUA food kitchens, 166; questions inclusion of farmers in LAWIU, 175
McGuire, James P., 37, 40-41
McKiernan, John, 24
McLachlan, J.B., 161, 170
McLeod, Angus, 97, 248*n*8
McLeod, Finley, 97
McMurray, E.J., 80
McNeil, Michael, 183
Mekela, George, 219*n*118
Midgley, Victor, 82, 88, 234*n*127
Mills, Harry, 73
mining industry: contributes to Lakehead boom, 3; and FSOC in Sudbury, 224*n*66; Ukrainian workers and CPC, 136; Ukrainian workforce, 95; in US, 50
Minnesota: IWW activities, 50, 54; IWW stronghold, 79; Lakehead linkages, 5, 50; police surveillance of suspected agitators, 79-80
Mior, Tulio, 204
Moore (Mrs. Fred), 113
Moore, Fred E.: 1930 municipal election, 158-59; 1933 municipal election win, 189; efforts to block CPC, 174; establishes English branch of CLDL, 128, 248*n*119; establishes League for Municipal Progress, 189; establishes

second Fort William branch of SDPC, 49; on Fort William Trades and Labour Council, 70, 73; founding member in Fort William SDPC, 37; leaves Trades Council, 208; and OBU, 75; ongoing involvement in CLC, 244*n*23; supports working-class initiatives, 113, 243*n*19; suspected of Bolshevism, 230*n*20; targeted by CPC, 261*n*146
Moore, Tom, 68
Mooring, George, 27
Moriarty, William, 99, 100, 107, 116-17, 118, 237*n*25
Morrell, Hugo, 234*n*117
Morris, Leslie, 108, 197
Mortimer, John T., 27
Murphy, Harvey, 158
Murray, S.C., 26
Musicians' Union, 255*n*35
Mustonen, A., 227*n*124
Mutual Elevator Company, Fort William, 53

National Ukrainian Agitprop, 126, 128, 135, 247*n*110
National Unemployed Workers' Association, 174
Nayda (CPC candidate in 1933 municipal election), 189
Naylor, Joe, 85
Neil, S.G., 146
Nelson, John, 231*n*37
newspapers, ethnic, political, or organizational: *Appeal to Reason* (socialist, US), 26, 27-28; *Cotton's Weekly* (SPC), 33; *Industrial Worker* (IWW), 194; *Industrialisti* (IWW, US), 23, 59, 121; *OBU Bulletin*, 193; *One Big Union Monthly*, 77, 79; *Organizer* (IWW, Canadian), 183; *Pohjantahi* (*Imatra*), 23; *Tyókansa* (Finnish), 224*n*56; *Työmies* (*Imatra*), 23, 59; *Väkäleuka* (Finnish), 28; *Vapaus* (Finnish), 54, 55, 60, 82, 123, 144; *Wage Earner* (ILP), 35, 38, 48; *Worker* (CPC), 99, 160-61
Nicolaichuk, B., 248*n*8
Nicolas II of Russia, 53-54
Nordstrom, Einar, 97, 186
Nyman, Carl, 231*n*37

OBU. *See* One Big Union (OBU)
October (Bolshevik) Revolution, Russia, 42, 61, 77-78, 81
Oliver, John, 40-41, 48
Ollikkala, Edward, 72, 231*n*36
One Big Union (OBU): 1929 lumber strike, 149; appeal for Wobblies, 70-71, 79; CEB/IWW interest in, 184, 189; decline and fall in Lakehead, 65-67, 85-86, 91, 105-6, 109, 241*n*99; established, 65, 68, 69-70; and establishment of CPC, 93; Finnish members, 70, 71-72, 73-75; internal divisions, 82-85, 87-89; members solicited by Hautamäki, 95; perceived link with Winnipeg General Strike, 69, 70, 79; philosophy and principles, 68, 70, 75-79, 81; police surveillance and investigations, 76, 79-80; potential union with IWW, 134; rapid growth in Lakehead, 70, 71, 72-74; rivalry with IWW, 75-76; TLC worries about, 72; unifying role among workers, 68-69, 71-72
Ontario Labour Party, 57
Ontario Provincial Police (OPP), 76, 79-80, 147, 195
Ontario Socialist League (OSL), 18
Ontario Socialist Party (OSP), 18, 19, 20, 22, 23
OPP. *See* Ontario Provincial Police (OPP)
Osasto, 24, 103, 216*n*60. *See also Imatra*
OSL. *See* Ontario Socialist League (OSL)
OSP. *See* Ontario Socialist Party (OSP)

Pannanen, Andrew, 231*n*37
Panttaja, Akselt, 164
Paris Commune, 126, 185
Parnega, Dan, 164
Parras, Emeli, 92
Patronati (Finnish), Port Arthur, 182
Pattison, J.R., 208
Pekka, Peterson, 257*n*67
Peltier, Louis, 19, 29-30, 39-40, 44-45, 61, 73
Pelto (IWW organizer), 76
Perunuk, W., 248*n*8
Peterson, Tauno, 257*n*67
Petrone, Penny, 61
Pigeon River Lumber/Timber Company, 146, 181, 196, 199
Pitkänen, Aate, 8, 257*n*67
Plumbers and Pipe Fitters (Port Arthur), 230*n*22

Pohjankukka (Fort William Temperance Society), 21, 22
police. 1909 freight handlers' strike, Fort William, 29; 1912 CNR dock workers' strike, 37; 1913 street railway workers' strike, 40; 1929 lumber strike, 147; 1933 strike arrests and violence, 191, 196; and anti-conscription league, 56; Depression-era surveillance and repression of leftists, 162, 164-66, 180-82, 186-87, 190, 195, 257*nn*68-69, 266*n*102; postwar surveillance and harassment of Finns, 72, 74, 76, 79-80, 232*n*59; surveillance and investigations of IWW and OBU, 55, 76, 232*n*59; wartime surveillance and repression of labourers, 46, 55; *See also specific forces.*
Polish workers, 46
Popovich, Matthew, 95, 111, 141-42, 144
Popular Front policy, 11, 182, 203-4, 208
Port Arthur: eastern and western influences, 5-6; enemy alien designations in, 46; Finnish population, 20, 21-22, 163; immigration to, 3, 6, 211*n*21; labour and socialist organizations before early 1900s, 16; locations of socialist activity, 3; metropole of resource-rich hinterland, 3, 5; population growth in early 1900s, 6, 15-16, 211*n*23; sabotage fears, 45, 222*n*30; unions at start of Depression, 255*n*29; wartime anti-conscription activities, 52. *See also* Fort William; Lakehead
Price, William, 176
Profintern. *See* Red International of Labour Unions (RILU, Profintern)
Provista Society, 142, 197
Puro, Henry (John Wiita), 82

Quinn, Jack, 197

railways, 3, 5, 6, 15. *See also* Canadian Northern Railway; Canadian Pacific Railway
Ray, S.W., 37
RCMP: 1909 freight handlers' strike, 29; 1930 raid on LAWIU and CLDL offices, 164; Depression-era quashing of demonstrations, 165-66, 186, 200; Depression-era surveillance and repression of leftists, 181-82, 195; and "good effect" of IWW in Northwestern Ontario, 106; report increase in WUL membership, 204; surveillance and investigations of IWW and OBU, 76, 79-80; wartime harassment of Finns, 47-48. *See also* police; Royal North-West Mounted Police
Red International of Labour Unions (RILU, Profintern), 92, 131
Reid, D.S., 205
Relief Camp Workers' Union, 198, 266*n*104
Revolutionary Socialist Party of British Columbia, 23
RILU. *See* Red International of Labour Unions (RILU, Profintern)
Rintala, Aleksi, 257*n*67
RNWMP *See* Royal North-West Mounted Police (RNWMP)
Rossvall, Viljo, 157-58, 167, 177, 254*n*22
Roukalla, Emil, 189
Royal North-West Mounted Police, 72, 162, 231*n*36, 231*n*37. *See also* police
Russell, R.B., 105, 235*n*134
Russell and Newaygo Timber Company, 55
Russian Revolution: anniversary celebrations, 120; Canadian socialist support for, 52, 53-54, 91; considered failure by CEB, 185; effect on socialist supporters and critics in Canada, 53; sparks enthusiasm for socialism in Lakehead, 43, 53, 61; as symbol of solidarity, 69, 71
Russian workers, 59-60, 220*n*152
Ruthenberg, Charles, 92

Saikula, Victor, 231*n*37
Salo, Kalle, 113
Salo, William, 80
Salverson, George, 195
Sandberg, Emil, 186
Sangster, S.F.H., 44
Scandinavia: syndicalism, 81
Scandinavian workers, 115, 220*n*152
Scandinavian Workers' Society Hall, Port Arthur, 186
Scarlett, Sam, 114
Scott, Howard, 194
SDPC. *See* Social Democratic Party of Canada
Second International (SDPC)
Shaughnessy, Thomas (1st Baron), 19
Shearer, J.G., 26
Sheet Metal Workers (of Port Arthur), 230*n*22
Shevlin Clark Sawmill, Fort Frances, 51

Sifton, Clifford, 19
Sillanpaa (LAWIU member), 171
Simpson, James, 31
Skarra, Arne, 97, 166, 248*n*8
Slup, John, 237*n*33
Smellie, T.S.T., 18
Smith, A.E.: 1925 federal election, 114-15, 213*n*40, 244*n*31, 244*n*32, 245*n*35; 1926 federal election, 117, 119-20, 213*n*40; 1930 provincial election, 163; 1935 election campaign, 213*n*40, 270*n*36; death, 208; directs CLDL, 124; organizer for CLP, 113
Smith, Stewart, 130, 173, 207
Snider, H., 265*n*73
Social Democratic Party of Canada (SDPC): 1913 municipal elections, 39; 1914 provincial elections, 44, 221*n*20, 222*n*22; activism in trade unionism, 37-38; animosity with ILP, 35-36; anti-war position, 45, 221*n*17; disappearance, 96; established, 34; and establishment of CPC, 93; Finnish Federation, 60; fraud charges against Hicks, 39; growth, 39, 40, 58, 220*n*152; Moore's attempts to re-establish, 49; provincial formations, 33; Ukrainian branch, 46-47, 223*n*41; wartime anti-conscription activities, 52, 55-56, 227*n*107; wartime ban against, 59, 68; and wartime depression, 43; and wartime fears of enemy aliens, 48; wartime membership decline, 48; wartime support for Belgium and France, 44; wartime suspicions of, 60
Social Gospel Movement, 16
socialism: 1935 shift to new paradigm, 202-4; divide with labourism/trade unionism, 15-16, 27, 31, 44-45; effects in Canada of Russian Revolution, 53-54; effects of First World War, 60-62; government fears of, 2, 28, 59, 80; link with violence, 40, 41, 42, 51; organizations made illegal under War Measures Act, 59; potential unification with labourism, 40, 41; shaped by Lakehead ethnicities, 3, 6-8; shaped by Lakehead individuals and organizations, 2-3; wartime anti-conscription sentiments/activities, 51-52, 55-56, 57-58; wartime suspicions against, 45, 55, 59-60
Socialist Party of Canada: 1908 provincial election, 27-29; divisions within, 31-35; established, 18, 23-24; expels Finnish Canadian locals, 33, 35; Finnish branches, 24; *Imatra* considers joining, 22; locals across Canada, 24, 220*n*152; shrinks in early 1920s, 96; view of OBU, 68
Sonquist, G., 248*n*8
Southern, James, 120
SPC. *See* Socialist Party of Canada
Spector, Maurice: appointed to CPC executive, 108; involvement with SDPC, 237*n*25; organizes for CLP, 102; pro-Trotsky, 131, 137, 144
Spenuk, T., 265*n*73
Stalin, Joseph: attacks and eventually expels Trotsky, 242*n*4; intolerance toward Finns, 204; and Marxism-Leninism as only acceptable socialist doctrine, 110; pitted against Bukharin and Trotsky, 130
Stanley, Edward, 234*n*117
Steam Operating Engineers (Port Arthur), 230*n*22
Steele, Sam, 29
Stephenson, James, 19
Stewart, Bryce, 41
Stewart, Charles, 203
strikes: 1906, freight handlers, 25; 1909, freight handlers, 29-31, 40, 218*n*100; 1912, CNR dock workers, 37-38, 40, 41; 1913, street railway workers, 40-41; 1914, barkeepers, 221*n*15; 1915, plumbers, 49; 1917, elevator employees, 56-57; 1917, freight handlers, 55; 1917, pulp mill workers, 55; 1918, various, 59, 60; 1926, lumber workers, 117-18, 120, 121-23, 246*n*63; 1929, lumber, region-wide, 146-49; 1929, lumber workers, 147-49; 1932, lumber workers, 181; 1933, various, 179, 190-91, 195, 196, 199; 1934, various, 179, 200; 1935, lumber, 205; and ethnic tensions, 25; first ones in Lakehead, 17; prewar, coal handlers, 71; US lumber workers, 54. *See also* Winnipeg General Strike
Structural Iron Workers (Port Arthur), 230*n*22
suffrage parade, 35(f)
Sundqvist, George, 139, 146
Suomalainen Socialisti Osasto (Osasto), 24, 103, 216*n*60. *See also Imatra*
Superior District Lumber Workers Industrial Union (US), 54
Support League of Canadian Industrial Unionists (CTKL), 105, 181, 188, 192-93

Suski, Edwin, 125
Sweden, 54
Swedish workers, 222*n*22
Sykes, E.E., 231*n*34
Sykes, F.W., 234*n*106
syndicalism: attacked by WPC, 97; in Europe, 81, 91; Finnish Canadian views, 81, 90, 101, 234*n*127; in IWW philosophy, 51, 121, 141; in Lakehead, 91, 101; in LWIU philosophy, 118; in OBU philosophy, 68, 91; organizations made illegal under War Measures Act, 59
Syrjälä, Frans, 55, 218*n*110

Taylor, B., 265*n*73
Taylor, George, 166, 262*n*13
Teamsters union, 19
telephone system: attempts to organize women operators, 85; municipal ownership in Lakehead, 17-18
temperance societies, 20, 21, 22, 23
Third International. *See* Comintern (Communist International)
Third Period communism, 129-30, 153, 154
Thompson, Fred, 193, 265*n*76
Thunder Bay. *See* Fort William; Lakehead; Port Arthur
TLC. *See* Trades and Labour Congress of Canada (TLC)
Todowyernazu, 262*n*10
Torttila, August, 194
Trade Union Educational League (TUEL): 1928 calls for changes, 131; creation and purpose, 234*n*126, 238*n*47; disbanded, 154; Finns affiliate with, 95; FOC organizes for, 87; ignores Canadian members, 143
Trades and Labour Congress of Canada (TLC): 1910 annual meeting, 31; 1918 conference, 68; campaigns against OBU, 72-73; CPC attempts to infiltrate, 116; CPC efforts to win members, 132; and Depression-era unemployment, 156; favours industrial harmony over revolution, 204; focus on Anglo workers, 20, 31; membership fees, 50; postwar fracturing, 44, 68, 69, 72; pro-conscription decision, 52
Trades and Labour Council, Fort William: 1908 support for Urry in federal election, 28; 1913 street railway workers strike, 40; 1930s revitalization, 208; anti-communist position, 159; anti-conscription sentiments, 51; lack of wartime support to non-British workers, 48; and OBU, 70, 72-73, 75, 231*n*41; SDPC attempts to undermine, 38; wartime battles with SDPC, 49; and Winnipeg General Strike, 67
Trades and Labour Council, Port Arthur: 1908 support for Urry in federal election, 28; 1909 freight handlers strike, 30; 1910 annual meeting, 31, 218*n*105; 1913 street railway workers strike, 40; 1915 plumbers strike, 49; 1925 support for Smith in provincial election, 114; 1933 strike, 190; 1935 municipal election, 205; anti-communist position, 159; anti-conscription sentiments, 51; established, 25-26, 217*n*72; lack of wartime support to non-British workers, 48; and OBU, 70, 73, 75, 231*n*40; SDPC attempts to undermine, 38; support for UATC, 255*n*35; Varley's meeting with, 231*n*40; and Winnipeg General Strike, 67
Trans-Canada Highway, 190, 198, 203
Trotsky, Leon, 130
Trotskyism, 137
TUEL. *See* Trade Union Education League (TUEL)

UFTLA. *See* Ukrainian Labour-Farmer Temple Association (UFTLA)
Ukraine, 197
Ukrainian Labour-Farmer Temple Association (UFTLA): continues work despite repression, 180-81, 262*n*10; factional disputes with FOC, 170; history, 95-96; interest in WPC, 95, 96, 98; lack of progress late 1920s, 141-42; member concerns about communism, 103-4; power in left-wing politics, 133; souring relationship with CPC, 136, 163; support for UATC, 255*n*35; value to members, 98; Women's Section, 262*n*10; youth activities, 181, 262*n*10
Ukrainian Labour Temple, Fort William, 141, 162, 180, 190, 197, 266*n*102
Ukrainian League, 80
Ukrainian Social Democratic Party, 33, 95
Ukrainian workers: concerned about role of Communists, 103; employment at railways, 25; factionalism, 197, 241*n*86; not hired,

to stem growth of CPC and IWW, 187; participation in labour unrest and union organizations, 20, 31; repression of, during First World War, 44; socialist presence in Lakehead, 7-8; support for SDPC, 39, 220*n*152; support for WPC/CPC, 96, 98, 101, 115, 116, 126, 135-37, 239*n*52, 243*n*8; wartime population in Lakehead, 46-47; wartime suspicions of, 46, 59-60, 228*n*146
Ulvila, Matt, 217*n*79
Unemployed Association of Port Arthur (UAPA), 142, 166, 206
Unemployed Association of the Twin Cities (UATC), 159, 166, 201, 203, 255*n*35
Unemployed Workers' Protective Association (UWPA), 197-98, 266*n*103
unemployment: early 1920s, 85, 88; Great Depression, 153, 156, 169, 188, 262*n*8; increasing concern between the wars, 112, 113; IWW blames lack of relief on Communists, 183; Lakehead as hub, 163; late 1920s, 140-41; and unorganized workers at Lakehead, 132-33
unions. *See specific unions*
United Brotherhood of Carpenters and Joiners (Port Arthur), 230*n*22
United Brotherhood of Railway Employees, 213*n*5
United Front: and 1933 municipal election, 189; 1934 renewal, 197, 201; and 1935 federal election, 200; abandoned for Third Period, 130; appeal for Canadian Finnish socialists, 90-91; continues despite Bolshevization, 243*n*6; CPC applies, 107
United States: Bolshevik supporters, 78; Communist Party, 184; CPC members move to, 107, 124; divisiveness of Bolshevization of Communist party, 111; Finnish Bureau of Communist Party, 252*n*81; IWW activism, 49, 51, 54
United Workers and Farmers, 198
unorganized workers: CPC efforts to organize, 132; tensions with organized labour, 25, 31; wartime activism, 60-61; and Winnipeg General Strike, 67; WUL efforts to organize, 154
Urry, Frederick: 1908 provincial election, 28-29; and 1909 freight handlers strike, 30; 1911 provincial election, 36; and 1912 dock workers strike, 37-38; and 1913 municipal elections, 38-39; and 1913 street railway workers strike, 40-41; attempts to bridge socialist/labourite divide, 28, 31, 36; and creation of ILP, 35; forms Port Arthur TLC, 25, 26-27; organizational background, 25-26; support for Belgium and France in First War, 44
Ursin, John, 234*n*123
Uusi Yrtys Raittiusseura, 22

Vaara, Arno, 144, 145, 146-47, 160
Varley, William, 72, 73, 231*n*40
Veltri, Mary, 191
Viita, Nick, 121, 246*n*85
Voutilainen, Janne, 157-58, 167, 177, 254*n*22

Wagner, Joseph, 193, 194
War Measures Act, 46, 53, 59, 93, 103
Watkins, C.E., 262*n*13
Watters, James C., 49, 68
Waywood, Walter, 187
WBA. *See* Workers' Benevolent Association (WBA)
Welsh, William, 56, 117, 120, 208, 227*n*107
Western Dry Dock and Shipbuilding Company, Fort William, 51-52
Western Federation of Miners, 49
Western Labour Conference (1919), 68, 69-70
wheat industry: boom ends before First World War, 43; Depression and unemployment, 153; IWW inroads, 75, 114; shipments through Lakehead, 5, 15, 17, 43, 153
White Finns, 147, 158, 184, 187, 195-96, 228*n*133
Wiita, John. *See* Puro, Henry (John Wiita)
Wilen, Emil, 170, 171, 172
Wilson, Sid, 37, 44, 57, 58, 222*n*25
Winch, E.E., 82-83, 85
Winnipeg General Strike: inspirational to socialists, 79; lack of Lakehead support, 67, 229*n*8; perceived link with OBU, 69, 70, 79; post-strike trials, 52; as watershed moment in Canadian socialism, 65
Wirta, John, 144, 145, 146-47
Wisconsin: IWW activities, 54
WLL. *See* Women's Labour League (WLL)
Wobblies. *See* Industrial Workers of the World (IWW)

women: auxiliary to FOC, 113; in CLC, 85; in CPC, 113, 115; gain vote in Finland, 23; in *Imatra*, 22, 215*n*43; suffrage parade, 35(f); unemployment in Depression, 159
Women's Labour League (WLL), 113, 124, 126, 170, 260*n*119
Workers' Benevolent Association (WBA), 96, 103-4, 262*n*10
Workers' Party of Canada (WPC): 1923 provincial election, 102; 1924 May Day, 108; dissolution, 107; engages labour in Lakehead, 94-96; established as public face of CPC, 93; establishes branch in Lakehead, 97; ethnic and regional tensions, 94, 99; Finnish Section, 95, 101, 240*n*81; growth among Finns, decline in English membership, 104; language/ethnic sections, 94, 96, 98, 99, 237*n*32; and Lenin's death, 104; limited success, 117; name changed to CPC, 107, 141*n*96; policy of political action, 93; political fractions, 99-101, 103; recruitment efforts, 95, 97-103, 104-5; structure, 93-94. *See also* Communist Party of Canada (CPC)
Workers' Unity League (WUL): 1931 demonstrations, 174; 1932 lumber strike, 181; 1933 strikes, 190; cooperation with IWW, 201; dissatisfaction with Hautamäki, 171; dissolution, 11, 202, 203; established, 253; exacerbates CPC problems in Lakehead, 176-77; initial failures, 158, 161, 255*n*26; labour mistrust of, 264*n*51; lack of national leadership, 174; lack of understanding of local situation, 173, 177; police targeting of, 180; recruitment attempts through FOC, 168-69; role in unrest of early 1930s, 179; targets unorganized workers, 154, 156; tensions with LAWIU, 167, 171-72; unemployment association, 166; youth activities, 181
working class, in Lakehead: apathy between the wars, 112; depression before First World War, 43; ethnic and political mix, 6-7, 15-16, 43; ethnicity as core issue, 43; participation in socialism, 1-3; participation in union activities, 1-2; socialist/labourite divide, 28, 31-33
Workingmen's Club, Fort William, 39-40
Wright, Sam, 205
WUL. *See* Workers' Unity League (WUL)
Wynn, T.H., 222*n*25

YCL. *See* Young Communist League (YCL)
Young, Rod, 222*n*25
Young, S.C., 37
Young Communist League (YCL): 1931 demonstrations, 260*n*119; 1932 activities, 181; 1932 police raid, 187; 1933 labour strike, 190; blame Ukrainian CPC leadership for lack of progress on Comintern goals, 136; branches established by Bryan, 113; children's clubs, 104; cultural contributions, 108; decreasing activity, 172, 261*n*154; early leaders, 241*n*90; efforts to combine forces with other young workers, 196-97, 198; and Food Workers' Union, 176; growth, 115, 162; importance of Finnish membership, 104; lack of progress in late 1920s, 141; support for UATC, 255*n*35; support for UWPA, 197-98; WLL efforts, 126
Young Pioneers, 126, 133
Young Workers League, 130(f)

Zakar, Peter, 198
Zura, (Mrs.), 233*n*80
Zura, Sava W., 80-81

Printed and bound in Canada by Friesens

Set in Machine, Meta and Minion by Artegraphica Design Co. Ltd.

Copy editor: Francis Chow

Proofreader: Kate Spezowka

Indexer: Heather Ebbs

Cartographer: Eric Leinberger